Christian Martyrdom in Late Antiquity
(300 – 450 AD)

Arbeiten zur Kirchengeschichte

Begründet von
Karl Holl† und Hans Lietzmann†

herausgegeben von
Christian Albrecht und Christoph Markschies

Band 116

De Gruyter

Christian Martyrdom in Late Antiquity (300–450 AD)

History and Discourse, Tradition and Religious Identity

Edited by

Peter Gemeinhardt and Johan Leemans

De Gruyter

ISBN 978-3-11-026351-0
e-ISBN 978-3-11-026352-7
ISSN 1861-5996

Library of Congress Cataloging-in-Publication Data

A CIP catalog record for this book has been applied for at the Library of Congress.

Bibliographic information published by the Deutsche Nationalbibliothek

The Deutsche Nationalbibliothek lists this publication in the Deutsche Nationalbibliografie; detailed bibliographic data are available in the Internet at http://dnb.dnb.de.

Printing: Hubert & Co. GmbH & Co. KG, Göttingen
∞ Printed on acid-free paper

Printed in Germany

www.degruyter.com

Contents

PETER GEMEINHARDT / JOHAN LEEMANS

Christian Martyrdom in Late Antiquity: Some Introductory Perspectives

Martyrdom featured prominently in the lives and discourses of late antique Christian communities of the fourth and fifth centuries. The "Great Persecution" of the early fourth century and, later on, inner-Christian conflicts, brought forth a considerable number of martyrs, martyr cults and martyr texts. The martyr's shrine was an important place for the local community, the martyr a potent intercessor and the yearly *panèguris* or martyr's festival a culmination point in the life of the local community. Within the context of these martyr cults a large number of texts originated: calendars, martyrologies, passions, sermons, legends, miracle stories. Though the martyr cult goes back as early as the middle of the second century AD with the *Martyrdom of Polycarp*, it is fair to say that during the fourth century a proliferation in martyr cults and martyr texts took place. Almost all the case studies collected in this volume deal with texts coming from the years 350–450. Thus, they document the stage of martyr texts which laid the foundation on which much of later Medieval and Byzantine hagiography would flourish. The scholarly interest of this volume obviously rests in the first place in the individual contributions. Taken as a whole, however, these contributions may also be of methodological interest in that they document a variety of approaches to the textual material. This variety surely is linked to the differences of expertise and interest between the individual contributors. It may, we believe, also partially be explained by the specific nature of the text which allows for a diversity of approaches on the one hand and is presenting a host of difficulties on the other.

It is no exaggeration, indeed, to say that the scholarly analysis of martyr texts is fraught with difficulties. The example of the martyr Euphemia of Chalcedon is an interesting case in point. Euphemia was a martyr whose death is traditionally placed under the Diocletian Persecution. During the second half of the fourth century her cult in Chalcedon was well-established, as is demonstrated by its inclusion in the *Martyrologium Hieronymianum* and, highly likely, in its source, the *Martyrologium Syriacum*, which ultimately goes back to ca. 360. Moreover, by that time the shrine with her relics had become a place known well beyond Chalcedon. In 384, the famous Egeria made during her pilgrimage to the Holy Land a stop in Chalcedon to visit the very illustrious martyrium of Euphemia, known to her of old[1]. In 399 the emperor Arcadius and the Gothic leader Gainas met in Chalcedon, in the "martyrium, there where the body of the martyr Euphemia lies"[2]. Half a century later, the sanctuary would become even more famous because of the council of 451 that took place within its walls[3] and again a century later a full description of the sanctuary was included by Evagrius Scholasticus in his *Ecclesiastical History* (2.3)[4].

In the context of this cult, in Chalcedon and beyond, a rich and complex hagiographical dossier originated which spans from the late fourth century to the late Byzantine period[5]. The two earliest texts already suffice to indicate some of the problems one has to grapple with in dealing with hagiographical texts. The first of these is a late fourth century detailed description (ἔκφρασις) of a painting of Euphemia's martyrdom by Asterius of Amaseia[6]. Asterius describes in loving detail

1   Peregrinatio Egeriae 23.7, in: Egérie, *Journal de voyage (Itinéraire)*. Introduction, texte critique, traduction, notes et cartes par Pierre Maraval, SC 296 (Paris: Les éditions du Cerf, 1987, repr. 1997), 230.35–39.

2   Socrates, *Hist. eccl.*, 6.6.12, in Socrates, *Kirchengeschichte*, herausgegeben von Günter Christian Hansen, GCS N.F. 1 (Berlin: Akademie Verlag, 1995), 319.7–9.

3   Alfons Maria Schneider, Sankt Euphemia und das Konzil von Chalkedon, in Alois Grillmeier, Heinrich Bacht (eds.), *Das Konzil von Chalkedon. Geschichte und Gegenwart*, vol. I: *Der Glaube von Chalkedon* (Würzburg: Echter Verlag, 1951), 291–302.

4   Rudolf Naumann, Hans Belting, *Die Euphemia-Kirche am Hippodrom zu Istanbul und ihre Fresken*, Istanbuler Forschungen 25 (Berlin: Mann, 1966).

5   All the texts have been collected and edited by F. Halkin, Euphémie de Chalcédoine. Légendes Byzantines, SHG 41 (Brussels: Société des Bollandistes, 1965).

6   Greek text in Halkin, Euphémie de Chalcédoine, 4–8 and Cornelis Datema, ed., Asterius of Amasea. Homilies I–XIV, Text, Introduction and Notes (Leiden: Brill, 1970), 153–155. English translations with commentary in Cyril Mango, The Art of the Byzantine Empire 312–1453: Sources and Documents (Englewood Cliffs: Prentice Hall, 1972), 37–39; Elizabeth A. Castelli, Asterius of Amasea; Ekphrasis on the Holy Martyr Euphemia, in Richard Valantasis (ed.), Religions of Late Antiquity in Practice (Princeton and Oxford: Princeton University Press, 2000), 462–468 and Johan Leemans, Wendy Mayer, Pauline Allen, Boudewijn Dehandschutter, 'Let us Die That we May Live'. Greek Homilies on Christian Martyrs from Asia Minor, Palestine and Syria (c. 350 AD – c. 450 AD) (London and New York: Routledge, 2003), 174–176. About Asterius and this text, see also Wolfgang Speyer, Asterios von Amaseia, RAC

what is in fact a series of paintings. The first describes the scene in the courtroom: the severe judge on his throne, the guards of the office and many soldiers, secretaries and two soldiers dragging the virgin Euphemia to her judge. The second scene portrays her torture: her executioners are hammering out her teeth. In the third scene Euphemia is in prison, alone: she sits down, stretching her hands to heaven, calling on God, and while she is praying, the sign of the cross appears above her head: a symbol, Asterius opines, of the suffering that awaits her but, one could say, equally a vision communicating divine support and approval. In the final painting, Euphemia is depicted in the middle of flames, with a rejoicing face, looking forward to her heavenly reward. The paintings clearly represent the traditional stages in the account of the martyr's life leading to her death (interview with the judge – tortures – prison – execution) and hint at some of the literary topoi (e.g. the vision received while in prison and the martyr's joy). All in all the images on the paintings nicely fit in what to expect of a hagiographical story as we know them through literary writings.

The earliest *Passio Euphemiae* (BHG 619d) is hard to date: the text may have been written on occasion of the Council hold in her shrine in 451 or later in the fifth or even early sixth century[7]. The surprise is that this text, while following the basic structure of a martyr text and including many of the topoi one can expect from a epic passion, seems to depict the end of a completely different person: in this passion appears no underlining that Euphemia was a virgin, no erasing of her teeth, no miraculous stay in prison with the vision of the cross and no death on the pyre! Instead, the text – as can be expected – starts with a description of a persecution in Chalcedon and how Euphemia and her companions (!) attract attention because of their refusal to sacrifice to Zeus, as had been decreed. This sets in motion the normal storyline. They are tortured during nineteen days and sent back to prison. Euphemia is brought for the proconsul Priscus again and, upon her renewed refusal to sacrifice to Zeus, is tortured in many different ways: beaten up, the hot furnace, the pyre (from which she is miraculously saved). In between there is the sideline of two of her executioners who, impressed by her courage, convert to Christianity and die in the arena. Follow new interrogations, new tortures (some of which she miraculously escapes), new discussions with the proconsul. Ultimately she is thrown for the wild beasts, utters a last prayer and dies.

Supplementum 4 (1986), 626–639 and Id., Die Euphemia-Reden des Asterios von Amaseia. Eine Missionsschrift für gebildete Heiden, JbAC 14 (1971), 39–47.

7   Halkin, *Euphémie de Chalcédoine*, x–xii; Greek text: ibid., 13–33.

The differences with Asterius' text are obviously so strong that they raise fundamental questions regarding the historical value of hagiographical texts. It is clear that historical accuracy is not the primary concern of their authors but, despite the martyr's fame, in Euphemia's case of Delehaye's three coordinates to establish a cult (name, date and place) on the basis of these earliest texts only the last two seem ascertained[8]. This is obviously a quite extreme case but it opens up a cluster of issues regarding the connection, or better, tension between hagiography and history, to hint at the title of a recent book[9]. What is the historical value of hagiographical texts and how to evaluate the information about the martyr they contain? External evidence from other sources is of course a decisive factor but in the absence of this – which is more often than not the case – one is left with very difficult, almost subjective judgments. Does the use of hagiographical topoi argue against historicity or is it possible that they contain a core of historical facts? And what with the data of social, cultural or literary history these texts contain? Is, to give just one example, the information about the instruments and ways of torture to be trusted or not?[10] Is it more plausible that a martyr such as Euphemia was burnt on a pyre than that she was thrown into a pool with carnivorous fish or do we have to discard the second torture as coming from the author's fantasy because it occurs not very often in martyr texts? Or what with historical characters: no problem of course if there is other evidence for them, but what if this is not the case?

Fortunately, Euphemia's epic passion is to such an extent coloured by novel-like characteristics and by historically evidently unreliable information that its value as an historical source is indeed limited – at best – to the coordinates of Delehaye. But, evidently, it is not an histori(ographi)cal work, which immediately raises the question: what, then, is its purpose(s)? Is it 'religiöse Unterhaltungsliteratur', or should we go a step further and assume an edifying purpose of some sort? And, if so, how would that have functioned in a time the persecutions belonged to an already distant past? In many other martyr texts this edifying purpose is certainly present. Many fourth century panegyrics on the martyrs state this *expressis verbis* as one of their purposes. Then, martyr texts of the late fourth century can be read as attempts to pre-

---

8 H. Delehaye, Cinq leçons sur la méthode hagiographique, SHG 21 (Brussels: Société des Bollandistes, 1934).

9 Timothy D. Barnes, *Early Christian Hagiography and Roman History*, Tria Corda 5 (Tübingen, Mohr Siebeck, 2010).

10 Cf. Jean Vergote, Folterwerkzeuge, in *RAC* 8 (1972), 112–140.

sent the martyr as an example worthy of imitation. In these panegyrics, the story of the martyrs who died in a persecution long ago is recontextualised to serve the pastoral purposes of the present day. Thus, many martyr texts aim at contributing to the Christian identity of their readers and hearers[11].

In doing so, these texts move the reader away from the historical truth. The *dramatis personae* are reduced to a bare minimum and the text is structured along the lines of an oppositional framework: Christians are not the victims of a persecution but they are the winning party in a combat with cosmological proportions, a combat between persecutors and persecuted, good and bad, God and his helpers and the Devil and his accomplices. The superiority of Christianity vis-à-vis the pagan religion is a corollary to that. The use of biblical quotations and of rhetoric is adding to this overall picture and is always worth special attention[12]. In this way a discourse of martyrdom is developed in support of the building of the Christian identity of the readers and hearers. Alongside this main topic, the tapestry of the text often also contains other threads: the conversation between the martyr and the judge is in some texts quite extensive and construed along the lines of an initiation in the Christian faith and hence gets apologetic and catechetical overtones. Not seldom theological content is brought into the texts. In Augustine's martyr sermons, anti-Pelagian and anti-Donatist themes are present[13] and in the witty conversation the martyr Theodore the Recruit according to Gregory of Nyssa had with his judge, the theme of divine impassibility is central[14]. This aspect may remind us that, ultimately, hagi-

---

11   As attempts to read martyr texts of the later fourth century along these lines may be mentioned Lucy Grig, *Making Martyrs in Late Antiquity* (London: Duckworth, 2004); Johan Leemans, Grégoire de Nysse et Julien l'Apostat. Polémique antipaïenne et identité chrétienne dans le Panégyrique de Théodore, *REAug* 53 (2007), 15–33.

12   Alison Goddard Elliott, *Roads to Paradise: Reading the Lives of the Early Saints* (Hanover and London: University Press of New England, 1987), 1–15 (ch. I).

13   See e.g. in this volume the contribution by Anthony Dupont.

14   With a stubborn expression on his face and undaunted purposefulness he gave them the following witty answer: "I cannot call them gods, because in truth they are not. In honouring deceiving demons with the name god you are wrong. To me Christ is God, the Only-begotten Son of God. Because of my faith in him and my confession of it, let he who is wounding me cut me; let he who is whipping me lacerate me; let he who is burning me bring the flame close; let he who is taking offence at these words of mine cut out my tongue, for each part of the body owes to its Creator an act of endurance…". While they (sc. "the tyrants") were holding back for a moment indecisively, deliberating on what should be done, one of the soldiers in his unit, who thought to be witty, said, in order to ridicule the martyr's answer: "Theodore, has your God a Son? Does he beget, just like man, with passion?" "With passion", he said, "my God did not beget but I do confess the Son and I call his begetting fitting

ographical texts about martyrs are also theological texts, texts about the divine and how this interacts with our world. The narratives of visions and miracles are not coincidentally part and parcel of hagiography.

A final element requiring attention when studying hagiographical texts is the place of the text in the hagiographical dossier in its entirety. Other texts about the same martyr or saint may have direct or indirect connections of dependence with the text under study or shared stereo-typical elements that may help to understand the text better[15]. This is illustrated, e.g., by the texts surrounding the first hermit, Anthony (who is a case in point for the transformation of the martyrological discourse in Late Antiquity). As is well known, the *Vita Antonii* written by Athanasius of Alexandria immediately after the hermit's death in 356 competes with the tradition of Anthony in the *Sayings of the Desert Fathers* as well as with Anthony's own letters (if they should be ascri-bed to him, as Samuel Rubenson has convincingly argued)[16]. To these earliest texts, other mentions of Anthony, e.g., in the Pachomian litera-ture, in Palladius' *Historia Lausiaca* or in Jerome's monastic novels may be added. Together they represent a hagiographical discourse which testifies to a plurality of images and receptions of the saint who is a figure of history and at the same time of tradition. Therefore, the saint is capable of providing different role models or "Leitbilder" and thus of constituting identities for different Christian communities[17].

The title of the present volume being „Christian Martyrdom in Late Antiquity (300–450 AD): History and Discourse, Tradition and Religi-ous Identity", its aim is to highlight some characteristic features of Christian martyrology after the persecutions by the Roman emperors had ceased. Every martyr text is different in the problems and possibili-

---

for God. You, however, o pitiable man with the intellect of a child, don't you blush or hide due to your confession in a female god and your veneration for her, a mother of twelve children, a kind of very fertile demon who just like a hare or a sow effort-lessly conceives and gives birth!" (Gregory of Nyssa, In Theodorum; translation taken from Leemans/Mayer/Allen/Dehandschutter, 'Let us Die That we May Live', 87).

15 For a relatively intricate example of this, see Johan Leemans, Hagiography and Historical-Critical Analysis: The Earliest Layer of the Dossier of Theodore the Re-cruit (BHG 1760 and 1761), in id., ed., *Martyrdom and Persecution in Late Antique Christianity. Festschrift Boudewijn Dehandschutter* (Leuven: Peeters, 2010), 135–161.

16 See Samuel Rubenson, *The Letters of St. Antony. Monasticism and the Making of a Saint* (Minneapolis: Fortress Press ²1995), 35–42.

17 St Anthony's biography, its sources (his *Letters*, Athanasius's *Life*, and the *Sayings of the Desert Fathers*) and their reception the history of Christianity as well as in modern literature and art are discussed in a forthcoming monograph: Peter Gemeinhardt, *Antonius der Einsiedler: Leben, Lehre, Legende* (München: C.H. Beck, in print 2013).

ties it offers, and the texts discussed in this volume are no exception. Yet, as has become clear from what is being said so far, grosso modo the four concepts in the subtitle demarcate the square within which the study of the martyr texts in this volume will take place. The following brief survey of the contributions in this volume may make this more concrete.

An introductory section tackles general questions at the nexus of history and hagiography. Timothy Barnes (Edinburgh) in his paper on "Early Christian Hagiography and the Roman Historian" points in a concise form to overarching problems that are elaborated in some of the following contributions. Barnes advocates the primacy of historical evidence and a careful contextualization of all sources, which should incorporate a range of aspects as wide as possible (socio-political, cultural, religious etc.). Drawing a schematic history of the ancient hagiographic activity, he dwells on the historical and theological changes which rendered the epoch 350–400 more complex and thus more difficult to study – for the historian as well as for the hagiographer. He mentions the explosion of compositional forms, the emergence of hagiographic fiction or even forgery, the evolution to new theologies of martyrdom, the apparition of paradigmatic texts written by often manipulative authors. With illustrative case-studies and by challenging commonly accepted theories, Barnes decidedly warnes against such a hasty interpretation of textual data.

Theofried Baumeister (Mainz) emphasizes in his paper "Zur Entstehung der Märtyrerlegende" various sources for the patristic theology of martyrdom: first, Hellenistic Judaism as expressed in the Hebrew Scriptural heritage assumed by the Christian hagiographic productions (the Book of Daniel, 2 and 4 Maccabees), next, the pagan philosophical resistance against the tyrant (e.g., in the lives of philosophers). He underlines that Christian texts of the first century do not employ the term martyr, although elements of a theology of martyrdom can already be identified in them. On the other hand, Late Antique hagiography, with its many literary species, should be seen rather as narrative theology than a kind of "Volkslegende" (e.g. the legend of George the Dragon-Fighter). Baumeister adds an excursus on Coptic hagiography, thus revealing a new, secondary dimension inherent to martyr-texts: they present a "Lebensgeschichte".

A first thematic section collects papers on Greek hagiographical texts. In his paper on "Author and Authority: Literary Representations of Moral Authority in Eusebius of Caesarea's The Martyrs of Palestine",

James Corke-Webster (Manchester) examines Eusebius' techniques of constructing a type of authority specific to the martyr – moreover, one developed in contrast with preceding models. His starting point rests in socio-linguistic theories formulated by Doron Mendels and Alan Bell. Eusebius is seen as a composer of narratives aware of his audience and his effect on that audience. Of particular interest are the authoritative figures of the father (involving, e.g., the martyr's renunciation of his/her family, or the correct treatment of dependants) and the martyr's silence – as opposed to the emphasis on speech manifest in previous hagiographic productions. For Eusebius, the paradoxical authority of the martyr is visible in his innocent silent resistance or in his correct behavior as pater familias. Such presentation informs and shapes the audience's view on authority in the direction Eusebius wanted it.

Peter Gemeinhardt (Göttingen) endeavours to read the first hermit's Life as a martyrological text ("Vita Antonii oder Passio Antonii? Biographisches Genre und martyrologische Topik in der ersten Asketenvita"). A careful analysis of Athanasius' Vita Antonii in relation to hagiographic commonplaces and the pagan genre of the lives of holy men lead him to propose a new interpretative dimension, that of a passio. Thus, the Vita Antonii appears to be one of the first "martyr-biographies", moreover, one defining the type of the new martyr (a "martyr in life"), who needed to be invested with an identity after the anti-Christian persecutions had ceased. Anthony, the prototype of all who wish to become new martyrs, is an ascetic, an athlete of God, e-vangelizing the world and fighting demons and heresies – a very convenient way of legitimizing Athanasius' public image of being himself a martyr for orthodoxy. The Vita Antonii constructs thus an ideal way of life; it does however not legitimize a cult of this saint, which was invented only two centuries later.

The last paper of this section, written by Ekkehard Mühlenberg (Göttingen), analyses Greek homilies on martyrs delivered by Cappadocian theologians, namely "Gregor von Nyssa über die Vierzig und den ersten Märtyrer (Stephanus)". As Gregory's two encomia on the Forty Martyrs of Sebaste are posterior to Basil of Caesarea's homily on the same martyrs, Mühlenberg reckons it appropriate to compare how the two authors reflected on their topic, and what the differences suggest about their purposes. In doing so, he is able to reconstruct some features of Christian piety not as expressed in theory, but as Gregory surprised them in practice. In the same time, Mühlenberg observes certain hagiographic exaggerations against which Gregory militated, as well as the tendencies he wanted to eliminate from his community and those he intended to give a firm ground. A short analysis on the encomium on the proto-martyr Stephen confirmes his conclusions and sets Gregory's panegyric activity in his wider anti-heretic struggle.

Complementary to this section, the next three contributions concentrate on Latin texts of the fourth and early fifth century. Peter Kuhlmann (Göttingen) reflects on "Christliche Märtyrer als Träger römischer Identität. Das Peristephanon des Prudentius und sein kultureller Kontext". By employing classical education and poetic skills, Prudentius aims at establishing a memory of the martyrs that meets the expectations of noble and erudite Roman Christians. He thus construes a new form of identity which connects Roman and Christian values. By stressing semantic correlations, e.g., to the writings of Horace as well as continuities to the Roman past on the cultural level and, finally, the importance of the city of Rome as the new centre of Christian martyrology, Kuhlmann situates the 'Peristephanon' within the late antique discourse on Roman tradition and history in the light of its being rapidly christianised. The martyrs become prototypes of the new role-model of a Roman Christian.

In the following paper, "Augustine's Homiletic Definition of Martyrdom. The Centrality of the Martyr's Grace in his Anti-Donatist and Anti-Pelagian Sermones ad Populum", Anthony Dupont (Leuven) reconstructs the way in which Augustine moulded his definition of martyrdom in reaction to two different heresies: whereas in the anti-Donatist homilies Augustine had to face the enthusiasm for martyrdom showed by the opposing party, in the anti-Pelagian homilies the focus shifts to the grace of God. Correspondingly, in the first corpus the topic of martyrdom is used to legitimize orthodoxy and the unity of the Church; in the second, to affirm the primacy of God's grace. Augustine insists that martyrdom, manifest in patientia, graciously afforded by God to the martyr, is not constituted by poena, but by a correct causa, namely iustitia (dying for Christ, that is, professing an orthodox creed and striving for unity in the Church) – a gift of God on its turn. A common thread in both homiletic series is the caution commanded by Augustine, seeking to control popular devotion to the martyrs: as martyrdom is God's grace, it is always God who should be venerated through the martyr.

This section is closed by Hajnalka Tamas (Leuven) whose paper is entitled "'Eloquia divina populis legere': Bible, Apologetics and Asceticism in the Passio Pollionis". She challenges the historical reliability of the Passio Pollionis, proposing as setting for its composition Pannonia, in the last quarter of the 4th century. Accordingly, she points to some specific concerns of that context reflected in this passion: on a general

level, loosened moral standards of the new converts, paralleled by an
incipient asceticism; deficiencies in Christian social interaction. Thus,
the text, interpreted as a manual of orthopraxis, defines the ideal Christian behaviour by employing apologetic argumentation. Faith is defined as adherence to a distinctive Christian social ethos, implying ascetic practices.

The volume is completed by two contributions which transgress the
borders of the Roman Empire. Johan Leemans (Leuven) in his paper on
"The Martyrdom of Sabas the Goth: A Historical and Literary Approach" approaches the Passio Sabae from different perspectives, combi-
ning three methodological approaches. First, following compositional
analysis, he highlights a historical core, as well as a sum of hagiographic topoi, such as Sabbas' panegyric, the cosmic proportions con-
densed in his martyrdom, the tortures and miracles – which he then
interprets through literary and hagiographic lenses. Finally, he applies
an audience-oriented analysis to the text. As the relics of Saint Sabas,
the Passio along with them, were translated to Cappadocia (and thus
crossed the borders of the empire), Leemans identifies two possible
audiences for the text: for the Goth converts, it served as a national
legacy, Sabas being both a Goth and an ideal Christian; for the Cappadocian audience, it outlined a model-Christian, an example to be imitated in times of persecution, like those of the late 4th century.

Finally, Dmitrij Bumazhnov (Göttingen) in his paper on "Der Tod
des Einsiedlers für einen Verbrecher beim heiligen Isaak von Ninive
und im Liber Graduum. Ein neues Zeugnis für die 'Märtyrer der Liebe'?" deals with the seventh-century writer Isaac of Niniveh who deals
with the case that a hermit might be forced to act as judge and thus had
to decide whether a criminal should be sentenced to death. By acquit-
ting the latter, though he is guilty, the hermit-judge risks being killed
himself and thus becoming a martyr, according to Isaac. Bumazhnov
refers to the Syriac 'Book of Steps' in order to explain the scenario: The
hermit as a "martyr of divine love" is ought to act merciful toward a
criminal and is therefore reproached by other Christians who claim that
the death penalty should be uttered and executed if it is justified. The
conflict between mercy and justice which Isaac seems to face in the
seventh century thus can be traced back to Syriac discourses of Late
Antiquity.

The contributions in this volume were given as lectures during a workshop at the Lichtenberg-Kolleg at the University of Göttingen on February 20–22, 2011.[18] As the organisers of this workshop, we should like to give our warmest thanks to the colleagues from Germany and other countries who agreed to present papers and to prepare them for publication or, in the case of Peter Kuhlmann and Dmitrij Bumazhnov, to submit their papers at a later time. The lectures were given in English and German, and we decided to retain the respective language, preserving the characteristics of different languages, scholarly traditions, and discourses. We should also like to extend our thanks to the Lichtenberg-Kolleg and its staff for housing this workshop in its building, the Historical Observatory at Göttingen, and also for the administrative and financial support. In editing the present volume, Antje Marx, Jan-Philipp Behr and Sandra Klinge of Göttingen and Liesbeth Van der Sypt and Hajnalka Tamas of Leuven were involved, and we thank them very much for their collaboration. Finally, we are grateful to the editors of the series "Arbeiten zur Kirchengeschichte", Christoph Markschies and Christian Albrecht, for accepting this volume in their series and to Sabina Dabrowski of de Gruyter publishers for her editorial advice. It is hoped that this collection of case studies, exemplary as they may be, will shed new light on some prominent and also on some hitherto neglected texts and thus further the debate about Christian Martyrdom in Late Antiquity.

---

18   The Lichtenberg-Kolleg is the recently established Institute for Advanced Study at the University of Göttingen. It is a central element of the university's institutional strategy „Göttingen: Tradition – Innovation – Autonomy", financed by the Excellence Initiative of the German Federal and State Governments and the German Research Foundation (DFG).

A. General Questions

TIMOTHY D. BARNES

Early Christian Hagiography and the Roman Historian[1]

For more than forty years I have consciously tried to live up to the sobriquet bestowed on me by a contemporary polymath as a "questioner of widely held beliefs" who breaks with convention as often as he can[2]. I shall therefore begin this essay by summarising what I see as the single most important historical conclusion which I believe that I established in my recent book on hagiography[3] before discussing some texts and topics on which the book touched only in passing and which were addressed during the conference. My reason for doing so is in part because hardly any of the many reviews that were published of my historical and literary study of Tertullian made any mention of what I regarded as my single most important conclusion, to which I had emphatically drawn attention in my introduction, namely, that "Tertullian can be used to disprove Eusebius'" interpretation of early ecclesiastical history and to penetrate beneath his theories to the real situation of Christians in the reign of Septimius Severus[4]. I argued that this was the realities of the social standing and status of Christians in the Carthage in the age of the Severi from the mid-190s to the reign of Septimius Severus' son Caracalla as revealed and documented in the

---

1   I have largely retained the format of my introductory lecture, though I have tried to take account of the papers which were subsequently delivered at the conference when revising my text for publication.

2   Anthony Grafton and Megan Williams, *Christianity and the Transformation of the Book. Origen, Eusebius, and the Library of Caesarea* (Cambridge, MA & London: Belknap Press, 2006), 142.

3   Timothy D. Barnes, *Early Christian Hagiography and Roman History*, Tria Corda. Jena Lectures on Judaism, Antiquity and Christianity 5 (Tübingen: Mohr Siebeck, 2010).

4   Timothy D. Barnes, *Tertullian. A Historical and Literary Study* (Oxford, 1971: Clarendon Press), 2.

voluminous writings of Tertullian. This showed that the interpretative framework of the history of Christianity in the Roman Empire before Constantine which Eusebius of Caesarea set forth in his *Ecclesiastical History* was fundamentally flawed. Since all or almost all modern accounts of the history of the early church still in the 1960s adopted or followed Eusebius' framework, this seemed to me, though not to most of my reviewers[5], to raise important questions about Eusebius and, implicitly, about Constantine and his role in history.

The most important conclusion of my recent study of the relevance of early Christian hagiography to reconstructing and understanding the history of the Roman Empire from the middle of the second century into the fifth is that Christian hagiography powerfully reinforces the evidence of Eusebius that Christianity was legalised in A.D. 260, not in the early fourth century, as is still asserted even in books of otherwise impeccable scholarship.[6] The prime evidence for this proposition is known to all, though it has rarely been both credited and interpreted correctly. In his *Ecclesiastical History* Eusebius quotes a rescript of Gallienus allowing Christian bishops to recover churches confiscated in the persecution of Valerian and summarises another rescript which allowed bishops to recover Christian cemeteries. The rescript which Eusebius quotes, apparently in full, reads as follows:

> Imperator Caesar Publius Licinius Gallienus Pius Felix Augustus to Dionysius, Pinnas, Demetrius and the other bishops.
>
> I have ordered that the benefits conferred by my gift should be spread throughout the whole world, so that they withdraw from the places of worship. Consequently you too can also use the ruling in my rescript so that no-one harasses you. This was granted by me long ago, as far as it is possible to be fulfilled by you, and therefore Aurelius Quirinius, the *magister summae rei*, will observe the ruling given by me.[7]

Gallienus' words reveal the background to his reply to the Egyptian bishops whom he names. He had been given a petition which these bishops had addressed to him after the collapse of the usurping regime

---

5   With the conspicuous exception of Paul Petimengin, who subjected my book to searching scrutiny in his review-article "Tertullianus Redivivus", *REAug* 19 (1973), 177–185, at 185.

6   As an example I adduce a fine book by a papyrologist and Greek scholar whom I have known and respected for fifty years: the timeline in Peter Parsons, *City of the Sharp-Nosed Fish. Greek Lives in Roman Egypt* (London: Weidenfeld & Nicolson, 2007) contains the entry "313 The Emperor Constantine issues his edict of toleration" (xii).

7   Translation taken from Barnes, *Early Christian Hagiography*, 100, which modifies, but only slightly, that by Fergus Millar, *The Emperor in the Roman World 31 BC – AD 337* (London: Duckworth, 1977), 572.

of Macrianus and Quietus, which had seized Egypt after the capture of Valerian by the Persians in 260 and lasted until early 262. When Gallienus states that "this was granted by me long ago", he refers back to what was presumably an edict issued in the second half of 260 in which he had restored confiscated Christian property throughout the Roman Empire. The unspecified "they" who were still occupying Christian churches will have been identified in the bishops' petition, which does not survive: they were people who were in 262 still in possession of church buildings confiscated under Valerian's anti-Christian legislation of 257 and 258. Hence the rescript documents two vitally important facts. First, and most obviously, Gallienus asserts the right of either bishops or Christian communities to own property. Second, and by inference, either bishops or Christian communities as corporate entities had owned the property now restored to them *before* it was confiscated. Since no society where the rule of law prevails allows criminal organizations to enjoy the right of owning property in their own name, it follows, first, that Christianity had been tolerated *de facto* as a permitted religion before the confiscation, and second, that in 260 Christianity attained full recognition under the law. The prevailing idea that this first happened in or during the decade of the "Great Persecution", whether in 313, 311 or 306, is false and has produced a false perspective and false interpretations of Constantine. I have tried to set the record straight in my new study of Constantine.[8] But it was my investigation of early Christian hagiography at a period when modern governments were introducing legislation to prevent criminal organizations like the mafia from controlling property through indirect and apparently legitimate means that led me to realize the true significance of Gallienus' rescripts.

Between the earliest Christian accounts of the trial and execution of martyrs in the 150s and the end of the "Great Persecution" in 313 we possess, by my count, nineteen independent texts which were composed very shortly after the martyrdoms which they describe.[9] By "independent" I mean texts which are transmitted as independent compositions, excluding those documents in standard collections of early *acta martyrum* which survive only because they are quoted *in extenso* by Eusebius of Caesarea. The geographical and chronological distribution of these authentic texts reveals fundamental contrasts between different

---

8   Timothy D. Barnes, *Constantine. Dynasty, Religion and Power in the Later Roman Empire* (Chichester: Wiley-Blackwell, 2011), Chapters 2–4.

9   Barnes, *Early Christian Hagiography*, 355–359.

periods.[10] Before 260, eight of the ten authentic texts come from Africa or the province of Asia; after 260 there is no similar geographical concentration. The chronological distribution is even more significant: four texts come from the period down to the very early third century; from the decade 250-259 there survive six, one from the reign of Decius and five from the persecution under Valerian in 257-259; from the years between 260 and 303 there are none, since the Marcellus whose *Acts of Marcellus* survive must be classified as a conscientious objector rather than a Christian martyr; finally, no fewer than eight survive from the years 303-311 – three from Africa, two from Egypt, and one each from Sicily, Thessalonica, Roman Armenia.[11] This distribution led me to ask myself what happened in 260 – and Eusebius' *Ecclesiastical History* provided a clear and entirely credible answer to my question.

It will have become obvious to any reader that I disagree deeply and fundamentally with Lucy Grig's study of early Latin martyr texts published in 2004. Grig's approach is primarily a literary one, and she ridicules the very possibility of historical criticism of such texts, in effect repudiating the whole science of critical hagiography as developed and practised by the Bollandists since the seventeenth century.[12] Her slighting of ancient evidence comes out most clearly when she asserts that "the purported *acta* format" of texts like the *Acta Scillitanorum* is merely a literary construct, without taking any account of the indubitable fact that Christians could undoubtedly obtain copies of the *acta* of trials of fellow Christians.[13] The proof comes from a Greek text that Grig nowhere mentions, even though Hippolyte Delehaye long ago and Fergus Millar more recently noted its relevance. [14] Dionysius of Alexandria quoted verbatim the documentary record of

---

10   Barnes, *Early Christian Hagiography*, 364–365.

11   Barnes, *Early Christian Hagiography*, 361–365, cf. 106–110.

12   Lucy Grig, *Making Martyrs in Late Antiquity* (London: Duckworth, 2004), 146–151, where Grig uses quotation marks both when she writes about the Bollandists' development of "the 'critical' study of hagiography" in the seventeenth century (151) and in an endnote which criticizes a twentieth century Bollandist because he "still insists upon the 'scientific' nature of hagiography as a branch of scholarship" (184 n. 1).

13   Grig, *Making Martyrs*, 24. On the same page Grig proceeds to deny the authenticity and historicity of both the so-called *Martyrdom of Polycarp* and the *Passion of Pionius* on the grounds that neither is a court record: the premiss is obviously correct since the former is a letter and the latter a literary passion, but both are texts demonstrably written very shortly after the events which they narrate (Barnes, *Early Christian Hagiography*, 59–61, 74–76, 93–94, 358, 367–378).

14   Hippolyte Delehaye, *Les passions des martyrs et les genres littéraires* (Brussels: Société des Bollandistes, 1921), 304–308; Fergus Millar, *JThS.NS* 24 (1973), 240.

his court appearance before L. Mussius Aemilianus, of which he had obtained a copy (Eusebius, *HE* 7.11.11-16). [15] Since Dionysius both quotes the legal proceedings as they were officially recorded (ὡς ὑπεμνηματίσθη) and gives a highly coloured account of them which partly misrepresents the official record that he quotes, this familiar passage from Eusebius' *Ecclesiastical History* could have provided Grig with a starting point for a serious investigation of the contrast between the literary representation of martyrs and historical reality.

It is precisely this task, however, that the historian who uses hagiographical texts and documents must tackle. The superb Bollandist scholar Hippolyte Delehaye provided the classic example of the transformation of historical reality into unrealistic and anachronistic fiction. Procopius, a humble lector and exorcist in the church of Scythopolis, was executed at Caesarea on 7 June 303. Procopius' contemporary Eusebius of Caesarea described his martyrdom in his *Martyrs of Palestine*; but by the eighth century this humble lector and exorcist had become one of the great Byzantine military saints, alongside Theodore of Euchaïta, Saint George and Demetrius, the patron and protector of Thessalonica.[16]

*

The nature of Christian hagiography inevitably changed when there were no more martyrs. Admittedly, hagiography in the old style did not disappear completely. There were Donatist martyrs in Africa under Constantine, there is a specifically Donatist hagiography[17], and in this volume Anthony Dupont discusses Augustine, martyrdom and the Donatists. Persecution of Christians resumed briefly in the East in the early 320s under Licinius, even though he had defeated the persecuting emperor Maximinus in 313 as a champion and liberator of the Christians of Asia Minor. From this period we have a letter written from prison by the Forty Martyrs of Sebaste (*BHG* 1203), about whose commemoration by Gregory of Nyssa Ekkehard Mühlenberg writes below. Half a century after the 'Great Persecution' ended in 313, hagiography on the old model again became possible when a significant number of Christians were executed in the brief reign of Julian as

---

15 Barnes, *Early Christian Hagiography*, 55–57.

16 Hippolyte Delehaye, *Les legendes grecques des saints militaires* (Paris: Librairie Alphonse Picard et fils, 1909), 77–89, 214–233; id., *Les légendes hagiographiques*, SHG 18 (Brussels: Société des Bollandistes, ³1927), 119–139.

17 Barnes, *Early Christian Hagiography*, 152–153.

sole emperor, who are counted as martyrs even though Julian made sure that they were all convicted of and executed for crimes other than their religion.[18] Moreover, there was persecution of Christians for their religious beliefs outside the Roman Empire in the fourth century – in Persia shortly after the death of Constantine[19] and among the Goths in the reign of Valens, of which we have precious testimony in the dossier of Sabas the Goth[20], which includes a passion (*BHG* 1607) whose rhetorical elements Johan Leemans analyses below.

More important for the history of culture in the Roman Empire, however, are two literary developments in the second half of the fourth century. One is the arrival on the scene of deliberate hagiographical fiction; the other is the spread of hagiographical themes and approaches into widely different literary genres in both Greek and Latin.

*

Deliberate hagiographical fiction began, I believe, in the reign of Julian. Admittedly, there is much that appears unreal in the *Life of Antony*, which was composed in the late 350s and assimilates its hero, who was a Copt who knew little or no Greek, to a philosopher in the Platonic tradition and presents his life as an ascetic as a constant battle with demons. The authorship of the *Life of Antony* has been a matter of sharp scholarly disagreement. It is now, however, generally agreed that Athanasius put into circulation as his own an account of Antony as an ascetic which reworked, adapted and expanded a written text composed by someone else, probably Serapion of Thmuis, as his introductory letter acknowledged.[21] This was proved by Martin Tetz in 1982[22], whose case can be significantly strengthened, since the *Life* throughout juxtaposes Athanasian and non-Athanasian vocabulary, Athanasian and non-Athanasian ideas and attitudes. There is still, however, as Peter Ge-

---

18 For Christians martyred under Julian, see Hanns Christof Brennecke, *Studien zur Geschichte der Homöer: Der Osten bis zum Ende des homöischen Reichskirche*, BHTh 73 (Tübingen: Mohr Siebeck, 1988), 114–157.

19 Richard W. Burgess (with Raymond Mercier), The Date of the Martyrdom of Simeon bar Sabba'e and the "Great Persecution", *AnBoll* 117 (1997), 9–66.

20 Hippolyte Delehaye (with A. D. Serruys), Saints de Thrace et de Mésie, *AnBoll* 31 (1912), 160–300, at 216–221, cf. ibid. 288–291; Barnes, *Early Christian Hagiography*, 236.

21 Barnes, *Early Christian Hagiography*, 160–170.

22 Martin Tetz, Athanasius und die Vita Antonii. Literarische und theologische Relationen, *ZNW* 73 (1982), 1–30. Repr. in id., *Athanasiana. Zu Leben und Lehre des Athanasius*, Wilhelm Geerlings/Dietmar Wyrwa, eds., BZNW 78 (Berlin/New York: Walter de Gruyter, 1995), 155–184.

meinhardt's paper below makes clear, room for continuing disagreement over exactly how much of the *Life* comes from Athanasius' own hand and how much he has reproduced with little or no change from his exemplar.

However that may be and whatever fictions the *Life of Antony* may contain, it is certain that Antony himself was a real person and that the account of his activities in the *Life of Antony* contains a large amount of genuine fact.[23] Athanasius sent the *Life of Antony* from Egypt to his ecclesiastical supporters in the West in the late 350s, and within a few years someone in central Asia Minor composed the earliest largely fictitious passion. Theodotus of Ancyra suffered martyrdom when Maximinus ruled Asia Minor, that is, between May/June 311 and May 313. The extant *Passion of Theodotus* (*BHG* 1782)[24] was written fifty or more years later, probably shortly after the death of the emperor Julian (26 June 363). Its author, who claims to have been a young boy in the reign of Maximinus, wrote an account of his trial, tortures and death which combines authentic details from 312 with a vast array of hagiographical clichés to such an extent that Delehaye classified it as an "epic passion".[25] On the other hand, Stephen Mitchell claimed the passion as an authentic historical record.[26] Both views are half right and half wrong.[27] For the passion both preserves precious details such as the fact that Theodotus owned a wine shop where he gave refuge to endangered Christians and contains passages such as the following:

> None of the tools of punishment was left unused, not fire, not iron, not hooks. Surrounding him completely and tearing off his clothing, they fixed him to the wood, stood back and lacerated his ribs, everyone as strongly as he could. But they could not sustain the toil. The martyr smiled with pleasure at those who were striking him; he received the trial of each of the tortures in silence, neither changing the expression on his face nor giving in

---

23 Hermann Dörries, Die *Vita Antonii* als Geschichtsquelle, *NAWG.PH* (1949), 357–410, reprinted in his *Wort und Stunde* 1 (Göttingen: Vandenhoeck & Ruprecht, 1966), 145–224; Derwas James Chitty, *The Desert a City. An Introduction to the Study of Egyptian and Palestininian Monasticism under the Christian Empire* (Oxford: Basil Blackwell, 1966; London/Oxford: Mowbrays, ²1977), 2–19, 27–26; Peter Brown, *The Making of Late Antiquity* (Cambridge, MA/London: Harvard University Press, 1978), 81–90. For a somewhat more skeptical approach to the *Life*, note David Brakke, *Athanasius and the Politics of Asceticism* (Oxford: Oxford University Press, 1995), 201–265.

24 Ed. by Pio Franchi de' Cavalieri, *I martirii di s. Teodoto e di s. Ariadne, con un'appendice sul testo originale del Martirio di s. Eleutherio*, StT 6 (Rome, 1901), 9–87. (References are to the chapters, pages and lines in this edition.)

25 Hippolyte Delehaye, La passion de. S. Théodote d'Ancyre, *AnBoll* 22 (1903), 320–328.

26 Stephen Mitchell, The Life of Saint Theodotus of Ancyra, *AnSt* 31 (1982), 93–113.

27 Barnes, *Early Christian Hagiography*, 155–159.

to the savagery of the tyrant (for he had our Lord Jesus Christ as his helper) until those who were striking him tired. When they were exhausted, others approached and took over from the first crew. The gloriously triumphant combatant surrendered his body as if it were not his own to the executioners to be wounded and torn apart and he kept his belief in the Lord of all unbending. Theotecnus ordered his ribs to be drenched in strong vinegar and torches to be applied to him. As the holy man smarted from the vinegar and his ribs were on fire, smoke arose. As a result, when he noticed the smoke from his roasting flesh, he showed displeasure by wrinkling his nose. When he saw this, Theotecnus hastily leapt from his official chair and said: "Where is the nobility of your words now, Theodotus? For I see that you are giving in to the tortures quite quickly."… The martyr said: "Do not be surprised, *consularis*, that I wrinkled my nose when I noticed the smoke. Rather instruct your bodyguard to carry out all your orders in full, as I see that they have become exhausted. Please devise tortures and attempt every device, so that you may learn the endurance of an athlete and discover that my Lord Jesus is helping me." (27, pp. 77.23-78.17).[28]

It is hard to believe that the *Martyrdom of Theodotus* is, as it claims in one passage, a first-hand account by one "Nilus" who was in prison with the martyr and has told nothing but the truth (36, p. 84.20-22). Nevertheless, both Theotecnus, the governor who executed Theodotus, and the martyr himself were real persons. Theotecnus is known from Eusebius as a *curator* of the city of Antioch whom the emperor Maximinus rewarded for his anti-Christian activities in that city by making him the governor of a province (Eusebius, *HE* 9.2-3, 9.11.5-6): it is the *Passion of Theodotus* alone which identifies the province as Galatia.[29] And Theodotus himself is a genuine martyr with a cult in a specific place, namely the modern Turkish village of Kalecik, forty miles north north east of Ankara.[30]

The earliest saint who never existed is Paul of Thebes, whom Jerome brazenly invented as an alleged predecessor of Antony. A Latin translation of the *Life of Antony* was an immediate literary sensation when it appeared in the 360s. Jerome's *Life of Paul* (*BHL* 6596) is a literary *tour de force*, designed to outdo the *Life of Antony* and to display the author's literary skills. It is also complete fiction from beginning to end, as Jerome's more critical contemporaries realized. Some years later, therefore, Jerome composed a *Life of Hilarion of Gaza* (*BHL* 3879) in which he not only shows off his talent for fine writing and reveals a sense of humour, but makes use throughout of a letter in which

28   Translation taken from Barnes, *Early Christian Hagiography*, 158–159.
29   Barnes, *Early Christian Hagiography*, 157–158.
30   Mitchell, Life of Saint Theodotus, 95–101.

Epiphanius, the bishop of Salamis in Cyprus, where Hilarion died, announced his death to the world and described his life briefly.[31] The historian of the later fourth century confronts another hagiographical text which is both more important and more problematical.[32] It is Sulpicius Severus' *Life of Martin of Tours*, which is a *Fälschung* in the technical sense defined by Ernst Bernheim (1850-1942) in his handbook of historical method, which was widely used in German universities during the Wilhelmine era, going through several editions between 1889 and 1914[33], though it fell out of favour in the Weimar Republic, when its author's positivism went out of fashion and his Jewish ancestry made his work highly suspect to patriotic Germans.[34] Bernheim defined a *Fälschung* quite simply as a work which is not what it claims to be, either whole or in part,[35] and that is the sense in which Hermann Dessau, Theodor Mommsen and Otto Seeck all used the word when they declared that the *Historia Augusta* was a *Fälschung* around 1890.[36] Bernheim's definition of *Fälschung* remains important, indeed in my opinion it is a concept which any critical historian must

---

31 On these two lives, see Barnes, *Early Christian Hagiography*, 176–192.

32 Barnes, *Early Christian Hagiography*, 199–234.

33 Ernst Bernheim, *Lehrbuch der historischen Methode. Mit Nachweis der wichtigsten Quellen und Hülfsmittel zum Studium der Geschichte* (Leipzig: Duncker & Humblot, 1889; a second edition was published in 1894, the third and fourth together in 1903, the fifth and sixth together in 1908, with a reprint in 1914). The success of Bernheim's manual can perhaps be gauged from the fact that its size expanded from 530 pages in 1889 to 842 pages in 1914.

34 On Bernheim, see briefly Gottfried Opitz, *Neue Deutsche Biographie* 2 (Berlin: Duncker & Humblot, 1955), 125. After 1914 his *Lehrbuch der historischen Methode* was not reprinted for more than forty years until it appeared as the Burt Franklin Bibliographical and Reference Series no. 21 (New York: B. Franklin, 1960), although an abbreviated Spanish version comprising 324 pages was published under the Republican regime during the Spanish civil war as Ernesto Bernheim, *Introducción al Estudio de la Historia*, trad. P. Galindo Romeo (Barcelona: Editor Labor, 1937).

35 Bernheim explained what he meant by *Fälschung* quite clearly: "Wenn eine Quelle ganz oder zu einem Teile sich für etwas anders ausgibt, als sie tatsächlich ist, sei sie nun überhaupt garnicht historisches Material oder sei sie es in anderer als der vorgeblichen Weise, so haben wir mit Fälschung, bez(iehungs)w(eise) partieller Fälschung oder Verunechtung zu tun; die Quelle ist verfälscht bez(iehungs)w(eise) verunechtet" (*Lehrbuch*[2], 242 = *Lehrbuch*[5,6], 330).

36 Timothy D. Barnes, Was heisst Fälschung?, *AKuG* 79 (1997), 259–267, cf. Hartwin Brandt, Hermann Dessau, Otto Hirschfeld, Otto Seeck, Theodor Mommsen und die *Historia Augusta*, in: Lavinia Galli Milić/Nicole Hecquet-Noti, eds., *Historiae Augustae Colloquium Genevense in honorem F. Paschoud septuagenarii. Les traditions historiographiques de l'Antiquité tardive: Idéologie, propagande, fiction, réalité*. Historiae Augustae Colloquia, Nova Series 11: Colloquium Genevense MMVIII (Bari: Edipuglia, 2010), 93–103.

constantly employ in the analysis of both literary and documentary sources.[37] For to call a written source a *Fälschung* is to declare that it is not what it purports to be without making any imputation about the date of or the motive for its composition. Why is that important? Because it is constantly argued by defenders of suspect texts that unless a motive can be detected, then the work cannot be a *Fälschung* or forgery. That was the line taken by Arnaldo Momigliano in his classic, crafty, dishonest and disastrously influential paper "The *Historia Augusta*: An Unsolved Problem of Historical Forgery".[38] But the inference that a literary text cannot be the *Fälschung* or forgery because we cannot explain who wrote it or when and why it was written is fallacious, no matter how often it is deployed in defence of suspect texts such the purported letter of Clement of Alexandria about a secret gospel of Saint Mark which Morton Smith forged and published.[39]

---

37   Timothy D. Barnes, *Fälschung* and "Forgery", *Hist.* 44 (1995), 497–500.

38   Arnaldo Momigliano, *JWCI* 17 (1954), 22–46, reprinted with additions in his *Secondo contributo alla storia degli studi classici* (Rome: Edizioni di storia e letteratura, 1960), 105–143, and again in his *Studies in Historiography* (London, Weidenfeld & Nicolson, 1966), 143–180. Momigliano's dishonesty lies in his sleight of hand in posing the issue under discussion. He declares that "I shall assume that you believe the *Historia Augusta* to be a forgery or a *Fälschung*, if you believe that the *Historia Augusta* was written after Constantine... But I shall assume that you do not believe the *Historia Augusta* to be a forgery if you believe that it was written under Constantine by one or more people who concealed their identity and the true date of composition" (*Studies* 148–149). On any normal definition of the two words except Momigliano's dishonest one, the *Historia Augusta* would be both a forgery and a *Fälschung* if it was composed by fewer than six authors with different names from those of "Aelius Spartianus" and company at the various times when they claim to be writing, whether or not the work was composed before the death of Constantine on 22 May 337: see, for example, Timothy D. Barnes, *The Sources of the Historia Augusta*, Collection Latomus 155 (Brussels: Latomus, Revue d'études latines, 1978), 13–18.

39   Morton Smith, *Clement of Alexandria and a Secret Gospel of Mark* (Cambridge, MA: Harvard University Press, 1973), cf. Scott G. Brown, The Question of Motive in the Case against Morton Smith, *JBL* 125 (2006), 351–383. For myself, I have believed the alleged letter of Clement to be inauthentic ever since Smith published it (see *Constantine and Eusebius* [Cambridge, MA and London: Harvard University Press, 1981], 352–353 n. 113) and I am sympathetic to recent (and very heterogeneous) arguments that point to Smith himself as the author of the letter which he claimed to have "discovered": Steven C. Carlson, *The Gospel Hoax: Morton Smith's Invention of Secret Mark* (Waco: Baylor University Press, 2005); Peter Jeffery, *The Secret Gospel of Mark Unveiled: Imagined Rituals of Sex, Death and Madness in a Biblical Forgery* (New Haven/London: Yale University Press, 2007); Francis Watson, Beyond Suspicion: on the Authorship of the Mar Saba Letter and the Secret Gospel of Mark, *JThS.NS* 61 (2010), 128–170. It may be relevant that according to his instructions all of Smith's papers were destroyed after his death.

Sulpicius' *Life of Martin* is a *Fälschung* because, whereas Martin was born in 317, as Sulpicius well knew, it presents him as born in 337 and attributes to him a military career in the Roman army as a teenager – a career that lasted for five years and can be dated precisely to the period autumn 352 to c. October 357.[40] As with Jerome's *Life of Paul*, some of those who read the *Life of Martin* detected that Sulpicius was not the honest and truthful biographer that he claimed to be. Sulpicius' answer to his detractors was more effective than Jerome's: he supplemented the *Life* proper first with three letters, then with a dialogue which observed the norms of that genre in Greek and Latin and set out to show that Martin was superior to all the holy men of Egypt. Sulpicius' success can be gauged from the fact that not only was his veracity accepted without exception by modern scholars until Ernst Babut challenged it in 1910–1912[41], but it was stoutly defended against Babut's well-founded scepticism by Hippolyte Delehaye, Jacques Fontaine and a large array of other scholars and historians until the end of the twentieth century.[42]

---

40 Timothy D. Barnes, The Military Career of Martin of Tours, *AnBoll* 114 (1996), 25–32. My arguments were dismissed as unconvincing and my conclusion as excessively sceptical by Meinolf Vielberg, *Der Mönchsbischof von Tours im "Martinellus". Zur Form des hagiographischen Dossiers und seines spätantiken Leitbilds*, UALG 79 (Berlin/New York: Walter de Gruyter, 2006), 26 n. 83.

41 Ernst-Charles Babut, *Saint Martin de Tours* (Paris: Librairie Ancienne H. Champion, n. d., publ. 1912), first published as a series of articles in the *Revue d'histoire et de littérature religieuses*, N. S. 1 (1910), 466–487; 513–541; 2 (1911), 44–78; 160–182; 255–272; 431–463; 513–543; 3 (1912), 120–159; 240–278; 289–329.

42 See Hippolyte Delehaye, Saint Martin et Sulpice Sévère, *AnBoll* 38 (1920), 5–136; Jacques Fontaine, Vérité et fiction dans la chronologie de la "Vita Martini", *Saint Martin et son temps*, StAns 46 (Rome: Herder, 1961), 189–236; id., Sulpice Sévère a-t-il travesti saint Martin de Tours en martyr militaire?, *AnBoll* 81 (1963), 31–58; id., *Sulpice Sévère: Vie de Saint Martin*, vol. 1, SC 133 (Paris: Éditions du Cerf, 1967), 171–210; vol. 2, SC 134 (1968), 439–440, 517, 524. The more cautious and nuanced defence of Sulpicius' veracity by Clare Stancliffe, *St. Martin and his Hagiographer. History and Miracle in Sulpicius Severus* (Oxford: Clarendon Press, 1983), 111–202, betrays its apologetic nature in several passages (for example, 137: "by pushing Hilary's departure as late as is plausible, … it is possible to accept Sulpicius' story of Martin and Hilary meeting – albeit briefly – in 356"). For unguarded use of the *Life of Martin* by good scholars and historians writing in English, note Philip Rousseau, *Ascetics, Authority and the Church in the Age of Jerome and Cassian* (Oxford: Oxford University Press, 1978), 143–165; Raymond van Dam, *Leadership and Community in Late Antique Gaul* (Berkeley: University of California Press, 1985), 119–140; Richard M. Price, The Holy Man and Christianization from the Apocryphal Apostles to St. Stephen of Perm, in: James Howard-Johnston / Paul Anthony Hayward, eds., *The Cult of Saints in Late Antiquity and the Middle Ages* (Oxford: Oxford University Press, 1999), 215–238, at 219, 224 n. 21.

*

In my recent book I deliberately avoided any systematic discussion of hagiographical texts from the fifth century and later, contenting myself with an examination of certain texts and problems which interested me – for example, the lives of the monk Isaac, who opposed John Chrysostom in Constantinople (*BHG* 955, 956), the life of Saint Germanus of Auxerre by Constantius of Lyon (*BHL* 3453), and the thoroughly fraudulent *Life of Porphyry, Bishop of Gaza* (*BHG* 1570), which claims to have been written by his companion Mark the Deacon, and which most historians of the period have been unable to resist using for its vivid narrative of events in Gaza and Constantinople around 400, even though it is demonstrably a confection from the age of Justinian.[43] There are clearly many other hagiographical texts from the fifth and later centuries which are of importance to the historian; indeed, in the early Byzantine period the lives of saints take over the role which inscriptions had played for the Greco-Roman world as the only systematic source available for writing social history.[44]

James Corke-Webster focuses in his paper in the present volume on the literary and rhetorical aspects of Eusebius' *Martyrs of Palestine*, which my book discussed primarily as a contemporary source for the Diocletianic persecution in the East between 303 and 311.[45] There is no reason, therefore, for me to say anything here about that work. Nor do I wish to discuss the *Passio Pollionis* (*BHL* 6869), which Hajnalka Tamas analyses below, since my book deliberately avoided any discussion of Pannonian martyrs under Galerius because of their problematical documentation, even though the passion of Irenaeus, who was bishop of Sirmium (*BHL* 4466), is in-cluded in standard modern collections of authentic early hagiogra-phical documents.[46] Nor shall I expatiate on

---

43 Barnes, *Early Christian Hagiography*, 242–246, 252–256, 260–283.

44 Barnes, *Early Christian Hagiography*, 235–236.

45 Barnes, *Early Christian Hagiography*, 119–125.

46 Barnes, *Early Christian Hagiography*, 346, 349, 355. Jerome, *Chronicle* 229[e] Helm, registers the martyrdom by drowning of Quirinus, the bishop of Siscia, in an entry which shows knowledge of a passion of Quirinus: this was perhaps an earlier version of the surviving *Passio Quirini* (*BHL* 7035–7038), which is held to be ancient, though not contemporaneous, by Agostino Amore, *Bibliotheca Sanctorum* (Rome: Città Nuova Editrice, 1968), 1333. Jerome, who has added this entry to Eusebius' *Chronicle* (though Helm does not mark it as an addition), had no evidence for the precise year of Quirinus' death: although it is the third and last item under year 2 of Constantine = year 4 of the "Great Persecution", which corresponds to the Julian year 308 in Jerome's chronological system, the entry is sandwiched between those for the deaths of Maximian in 310 and Galerius in 311 (229[d,f] Helm).

the spread of hagiogra-phical literary forms, techniques and approaches into a wide variety of literary genres from the late fourth century onwards. That is a vast theme and would require extensive discussion. I shall merely note that hagiography had already become central to Christian literature in both Greek and Latin by the end of the fourth century. [47] The Spanish poet Prudentius provides what is perhaps the clearest illustration of the importance of hagiography for Latin literature and Latin literati. Prudentius consciously set himself up as a Christian Virgil and Chris-tian Horace combined and composed a series poems on martyrs, which in 404/405 he included in a collected edition of his works under the title *Peristephanon*, that is, "On the Crowns <of the Martyrs>".[48] Prudentius also set out his literary creed in a separate long poem of more than a thousand lines, which has the literary form of a passion and which modern editors have mistakenly printed as if it belonged to this cycle of martyr poems (*Peristephanon* 10).[49] It is significant that Prudentius chose to expound this theme dear to his heart through an imaginary speech by a Diocletianic martyr, namely Romanus of Antioch, whom pious devotion had already endowed with the miraculous power of speaking volubly even after his tongue had been cut out.[50]

I do wish, however, to say something about two Greek texts which illustrate the early stages of the process. They are the so-called *Life of*

---

47 Barnes, *Early Christian Hagiography*, 235.

48 On this cycle of poems (which includes one on Quirinus of Siscia), see Martha A. Malamud, *A Poetics of Transformation. Prudentius and Classical Mythology* (Ithaca/ London: Cornell University Press, 1989); Anne-Marie Palmer, *Prudentius on the Martyrs* (Oxford: Clarendon Press, 1989), esp. 98–179 (on Prudentius' literary emul- ation of the Augustan poets, including Ovid); Michael Roberts, *Poetry and the Cult of the Martyrs. The Liber Peristephanon of Prudentius* (Ann Arbor: University of Michigan Press, 1993).

49 On the special place of this poem in Prudentius' œuvre, see Klaus Thraede, *Studien zur Sprache und Stil des Prudentius*, Hyp. 13 (Göttingen: Vandenhoeck & Ruprecht, 1965), 68–70, 122–137; Rainer Henke, *Studien zum Romanushymnus des Prudentius* (Frankfurt/New York: Peter Lang, 1983). The poet's immediate source appears to be a lost prose passion of Romanus in Greek: Hippolyte Delehaye, S. Romain martyr d'Antioche, *AnBoll* 50 (1932), 241–283; Rainer Henke, Der Romanushymnus des Prudentius und die griechische Prosapassio, *JbAC* 29 (1986), 59–65.

50 See Barnes, *Early Christian Hagiography*, 240, 390 n.6: the clause "nor was the tongue of his understanding silenced from preaching" (*Mart. Pal.* 2.2 [L]) is omitted in one of the surviving versions of the passage in the Syriac translation of the long recension (p. 338 Lawlor & Oulton) and was probably not in Eusebius' original text of 311.

Macrina (*BHG* 1012)[51] and the *Funerary Speech* for John Chrysostom of which the first full and critical edition was published by Martin Wallraff in 2007 (*BHG* 871)[52]: both of these texts contain hagiographical elements and a hagiographical approach although neither is primarily either a biography in the normal sense of that term or the account of a martyrdom as that word is normally understood.

*

Modern scholars have, with very few exceptions, persistently insisted that what Gregory wrote in commemoration of his deceased sister Macrina is a biography. For one scholar the text is important because it is not merely "a saint's life", but "the earliest surviving biography of a Christian woman".[53] And a comparison of Gregory's memoir with the lives of Plotinus by Porphyry and of Pythagoras by Iamblichus begins by asserting that all three texts "purport to convey edifying information within the framework of a biography"[54]. In fact, the three texts differ from one another in form, conception and purpose, and none is a normal biography. The title of Iamblichus' *De Vita Pythagorica* does not mean "On the Life of Pythagoras" at all, but, as Gillian Clark correctly renders it, "On the Pythagorean Life", that is, on the proper way of life according to Pythagoras: Iamblichus concentrates on Pythagoras' philosophy and he composed the work as "the introduction of a ten-volume sequence on Pythagorean philosophy".[55] Similarly, Porphyry did not compose his *Life of Plotinus* as a self-contained literary work to be read as an independent text. He composed it as an introduction or preface to the collected edition of Plotinus' treatises which he prepared

---

51   Best edited, with a helpful French translation, by Pierre Maraval, *Vie de Sainte Macrine*, SC 178 (Paris: Éditions du Cerf, 1971), 136–267.

52   Ed. by Martin Wallraff, *Oratio funebris in laudem Sancti Iohannis Chrysostomi. Epitaffio attribuito a Martirio di Antiochia (BHG 871, CPG 6517)* (Spoleto, 2007). George Bevan and I have prepared an annotated English translation for the series Translated Texts for Historians (Liverpool: Liverpool University Press, forthcoming).

53   Derek Krueger, Writing and the Liturgy of Memory in Gregory of Nyssa's Life of Macrina, *JECS* 8 (2000), 483–510, at 485–486.

54   Anthony Meredith, A Comparison between the Vita S. Macrinae of Gregory of Nyssa, the Vita Plotini of Porphyry and the De Vita Pythagorica of Iamblichus, in: Andreas Spira, ed., *The Biographical Works of Gregory of Nyssa. Proceedings of the Fifth International Colloquium on Gregory of Nyssa (Mainz, 6-10 September 1982)*, PatMS 12 (Philadelphia: Philadelphia Patristic Foundation, 1984), 181–196, at 181.

55   Gillian Clark, *Iamblichus: On the Pythagorean Life*, Translated Texts for Historians 8 (Liverpool, 1989), ix.

for publication thirty years after Plotinus' death. While Porphyry natu-
rally depicted the older philosopher, who died in 270, as a holy man,
his main purpose was to convince readers of the *Enneads* that Plotinus
composed all his best work with Porphyry at his side and assisting him.
Porphyry devotes a great deal of space to the chronology of Plotinus'
individual treatises, which number fifty four in his edition: he divides
them into three categories:

> According to the time of writing – early manhood, vigorous prime, worn-
> out constitution – so the tractates vary in power. The first twenty-one
> pieces manifest a slighter capacity, the talent being not yet matured to the
> fullness of nervous strength. The twenty-four produced in the mid-period
> display the utmost reach of the powers and, except for the short treatises
> among them, attain the highest perfection. The last nine were written when
> the mental strength was already waning, and of these the last four show
> less vigour even than the five preceding (6.26-37, trans. S. MacKenna).

The three groups into which Porphyry divides Plotinus' treatises are (1)
those written before Porphyry arrived in Rome in 263, (2) those written
in the five years when Porphyry was in Rome and constantly
conversing with Plotinus (263–268), and (3) those written after Porphyry left Rome in 268 and went to Sicily. Since Plotinus was born in
204/205 and died in 270, Porphyry's biographical schema is bizarre and
grotesque. He has taken the normal sequence of youth, maturity and
old age and distorted it: according to him, Plotinus was immature until
he was almost sixty, in his "vigorous prime" for a mere five years
between his late fifties and mid-sixties, when he suddenly became
senile with a "worn-out constitution". The motive for the distortion is
all too easy to detect: Porphyry presents himself as the inspirer of all his
master's best work.[56]

In contrast to Porphyry's *Life of Plotinus*, Gregory's so-called *Life of
Macrina* is an independent literary work, but it neither is nor claims to
be a biography in any sense of the word. In formal terms, it is a letter,
as its opening sentence explicitly states, admittedly an unusually long
letter, but a letter nevertheless:

> The literary form of this work, so far as the style of its heading goes, may
> appear to be a letter, but its length exceeds the bounds of a letter and

---

56   Timothy D. Barnes, *CIR.NS* 36 (1985), 197–198, in criticism of Patricia Cox, *Biography
     in Late Antiquity: A Quest for the Holy Man*, The Transformation of the Classical
     Heritage 6 (Berkeley: University of California Press, 1983), who proceeds as if both
     the *Life of Plotinus* and Eusebius' discontinuous account of the life, career, writings
     and pupils of Origen in Book Six of his *Ecclesiastical History* (6.1–3, 8, 14.8–19.19, 23–
     26, 30, 32–33, 36–38, 39.4, with Origen's death noted in *HE* 7.1) were paradigmatic
     biographies of 'holy men'.

extends into a rather lengthy quasi-historical monograph (εἰς συγγραφικὴν μακρηγορίαν[57] παρατεινόμενον). My excuse is that the subject on which you commanded me to write is too great for the tidy confines of a letter. You will surely not have forgotten our meeting. I came across you in Antioch[58] when I was on my way to visit Jerusalem in accordance with a vow in order to see the evidence of our Lord's sojourn in the flesh in that region. We talked of all sorts of things ... and, as often happens in these circumstances, the flow of our conversation turned to the life of an esteemed person. A woman was the starting-point of our narration – if indeed she was a woman, for I do not know if it is proper to use that natural designation for one who rose above nature. ... Since you expressed the view that a history of her good deeds would be profitable, so that such a life should not disappear in the course of time..., I have decided that it is good to obey you and, so far as it lies in my power, to give a brief account of her attainments in an artless and simple narrative. (1, lines 1–10, 12–17, 24–26, 29–31 Maraval: my translation)[59]

Who is the person whom Gregory addresses in the second person singular and whom he had met in Antioch not long before? Unfortunately, the original title of the work, if Gregory gave it one, is lost. The manuscripts all agree that the work is about Macrina or about the life of Macrina, while one manuscript describes the work as a "letter written to Euprepius", another as a "letter to Hierius", and a third as addressed to Olympius the ascetic. But there is no good reason to believe that these are anything more than descriptions of the text and later guesses about the name of the addressee, which had already been lost.

What is the work if it is not a *Life of Macrina* in the normal sense? Several recent writers in English have begun to approach the truth, even though they still follow convention in calling the text about which they write "Gregory of Nyssa's *Life of Macrina*" in their titles. Nearly thirty years ago Georg Luck rightly observed that "Gregory's *Letter*

---

57 Before Gregory the word μακρηγορία appears to be used only by Philo, *On Dreams* 2.128.1, and Philostratus, *Life of Apollonius* 7.35.11. The Atticist Pollux recommended using the synonym μακρολογία in preference to it (2.121).

58 A later passage fixes the date of this encounter to the autumn of 379, when Gregory attended a council of bishops in Antioch "nine months or a little more" after the death of Basil of Caesarea (15, lines 1–3 Maraval). Basil's decease is firmly dated to 1 January 379: Timothy D. Barnes, The Collapse of the Homoeans in the East, *StPatr* 29 (1997), 3–16, at 6–13.

59 My version differs somewhat from the translation by Virginia Woods Callahan, *Saint Gregory of Nyssa: Ascetical Works*, FaCh 58 (Washington, 1967), 163: in particular she renders δι' ὀλίγων, ὡς ἂν οἷός τε ὦ, τὰ κατ' αὐτὴν ἱστορῆσαι as "to write her life story as briefly as I could" – which illicitly puts the words "life story" into Gregory's mouth.

Concerning the Life of Macrina – this is the title which the work has in the manuscript tradition – seems a rather unusual biography from various points of view"[60]. More recently Georgia Frank has noted the multifaceted presentation of Macrina: "in the course of the *Life*, we come to know Macrina as sister, daughter, confessor, near-bride, near-angel, relief-worker, martyr, monastic leader, and philosopher"[61]. Similarly, Francine Cardman recognises the complexity of Gregory's "portrait of a woman who is sister and saint as well as teacher, guide, examplar, and miraculous healer", and praises the virtues of his work "as social history", as "witness to liturgical practice" and "as an instance of the evolving genre of hagiography", as well as a biography which "reflects the rhetorical standards of the period"[62]. Moreover, by asking whose life Gregory has written and by posing the question "where is Macrina in Gregory's narrative?", Cardman brings out the fact that the bulk of this so-called biography has more to say about the author and the family to which both author and subject belong than about Macrina herself. Hence James Warren Smith was quite right to describe Gregory's work as a "hagiographical tribute to his sister" and to observe that his "biography of Macrina could as easily have been entitled *De Morte Macrinae*"[63].

The best analysis of what Gregory's letter really is has been given by Wendy Helleman, who drops the misleading word "life" from the title of her article.[64] Helleman emphasises the hagiographical aspects of the work and its constant reference to martyrs. She correctly divides the so-called *Vita* into three nearly equal parts, in each of which death is the predominant theme. The first section describes Macrina's ancestry and upbringing, then records the successive deaths of her betrothed, who is not named, of her brother Naucratius, of her father and her mother

---

60 Georg Luck, Notes on the Vita Macrinae by Gregory of Nyssa, in: Spira, ed., *Biographical Works of Gregory of Nyssa*, 21–32, at 21. After this promising opening to his essay, however, Luck lapsed into the conventional mistake of treating Gregory's letter as a biography in the same sense as the *Life of Antony*, Possidius' *Life of Augustine* and other similar lives are biographies.

61 Georgia Frank, Macrina's Scar: Homeric Allusion and Heroic Identity in Gregory of Nyssa's Life of Macrina, *JECS* 8 (2000), 511–530, at 528.

62 Francine Cardman, Whose Life Is It? The Life of Macrina by Gregory of Nyssa, *StPatr* 37 (2001), 33–50, who also observes that Gregory "portrays Macrina as a model of Christian perfection, an outstanding example of ascetic achievement who has transcended the limits of the body."

63 James Warren Smith, A Just and Reasonable Grief: The Death and Function of a Holy Woman in Gregory of Nyssa's Life of Macrina, *JECS* 12 (2004), 57–84, at 58, 59.

64 Wendy E. Helleman, Cappadocian Macrina as Lady Wisdom, *StPatr* 37 (2001), 76–102.

Emmelia and of Basil of Caesarea. The central section gives an account of the last two days of Macrina's life, while the third and final section narrates her burial and a miracle which she performed during her lifetime. The very structure of the work focuses the reader's attention on the death of Macrina, which is framed by the deaths of close relatives and the consequences of her own death – a focus which it shares with both the gospels and accounts of martyrs.[65] Moreover, Gregory implicitly portrays his sister as a martyr belonging to a family of martyrs.

As he approached Macrina's convent Gregory dreamt three times that he was carrying in his hands the relics of martyrs which emitted a bright light (15.15-16: ἐδόκουν γὰρ λείψανα μαρτύρων διὰ χειρὸς φέρειν). After Gregory reached the convent and conversed with his mortally ill sister, he realised the meaning of his dream: it portended the death of Macrina. For what he had just seen was truly "the relic of a holy martyr, who had been dead to sin (Romans 6.11; 8.10-11), but shone forth by the grace of the <Holy> Spirit dwelling in her" (19.13–15: ἦν γὰρ ὡς ἀληθῶς τὸ προκείμενον θέαμα μάρτυρος ἁγίου λείψανον, ὃ τῇ μὲν ἁμαρτίᾳ νενέκρωτο, τῇ δὲ ἐνοικούσῃ τοῦ πνεύματος χάριτι κατελάμπετο). After Macrina died, an "all-night vigil was performed over her with the singing of hymns as in a festival for martyrs (33.6–8: τῆς οὖν παννυχίδος περὶ αὐτὴν ἐν ὑμνῳδίαις καθάπερ ἐπὶ μαρτύρων πανηγύρεως τελεσθείσης). And finally, Macrina's body was taken in slow and solemn procession from her convent to "the House of the Holy Martyrs, where the bodies of our parents had been laid to rest" (34.16-17: ἐπὶ τὸν τῶν ἁγίων μαρτύρων οἶκον, ἐν ᾧ καὶ τὰ τῶν γονέων ἀπέκειτο σώματα). In brief, it seems to me that the hagiographical elements in Gregory's letter or treatise are far more important than the biographical elements.

*

The *Funerary Speech* for John Chrysostom was delivered by a disciple of John in a city near Constantinople very shortly after news or rumours arrived of John's death in or near distant Comana: since John died on 14 September 407, the *Speech* was almost certainly delivered during October 407. What we have is of course a rewritten, expanded and elaborated version of the speech actually delivered, but this final version must have been completed before the spring of 408. It is

---

65   Helleman, Cappadocian Macrina, 87–88.

therefore our earliest source to give an account of the deposition, exiles and death of John.[66] The orator makes it clear that from the formal point of view the speech is an ἐπιτάφιος λόγος, a speech which ought to have been delivered as the body of John was laid to rest in the earth. But the *Leitmotif* of the whole speech is that, so far from being an exiled bishop who has died in disgrace (which was the official story put out by the emperor and the imperial administration), John is a martyr who is now in paradise interceding with God on behalf of his persecuted and disconsolate followers on earth. Let me give some typical quotations from the speech:

> The company of the martyrs has received one who fought with them and with them won the crown. In short, all <the holy ones> have one of their own.

> That saint asked constantly that a single recompense be made for him – to lose his life as a martyr.

> The time summons us to the martyrdom of our father, a martyrdom that crowns our father through the nature of the deed and proclaims God's complete wisdom, his fine planning and his ability to discover ways of access in inaccessible places.[67]

> If he is still alive, my brothers, we shall see him at some time sitting on the throne like Joseph and distributing spiritual sustenance to all (Gen 41.56, 42–45); but if he has really migrated to the true life and has returned to the longed-for Christ, we have a martyr to serve as an intercessor for us.

> Wondrous father, "press on, have a good journey and rule" (Ps 44:5): set foot in the royal halls of Christ, lightening our bereavement with your memory, pray constantly and entreat your and our lord Christ, who has invested you with the desired crown of martyrdom, that we may walk in the footsteps of your virtue and be deemed worthy of the same <heavenly> portion as you in Christ Jesus our Lord, to whom be glory and power now and forever to all eternity. Amen.

As it was in the beginning with the gathering of the relics of Polycarp, who was burned to death in Smyrna on 23 February 157, was then in 407, when the followers of John Chrysostom lamented his death, and still is now, Christian hagiography and the cult of the saints are indissolubly linked to each other.

---

66 On the date and historical importance of the speech, see my preliminary study, The Funerary Speech for John Chrysostom (*BHG* [3] 871 = *CPG* 6517), *StPatr* 37 (2001), 328–345.

67 Reproducing the word-play in the Greek between πόρους (= "ways of access") and ἀπόροις (= "inaccessible places").

THEOFRIED BAUMEISTER

Zur Entstehung der Märtyrerlegende

Das erste erhaltene frühchristliche Schriftstück, in dem die Martyriumsterminologie enthalten ist, der die Zukunft gehören sollte, ist bekanntlich das Martyrium Polycarpi, ursprünglich ein Brief der Gemeinde von
Smyrna kurz nach dem Tod ihres Bischofs Polykarp um 160 nach
Christus.[1] Das griechische Wort μάρτυς = Zeuge bezeichnet hier eindeutig den Blutzeugen, das heißt den seines Glaubens wegen hingerichteten Christen, dessen Tod aus christlicher Perspektive so positiv
als Zeugnis interpretiert wird.[2] Da der Wortgebrauch nicht erklärt
wird, setzt ihn das Schreiben offensichtlich bei den Adressaten als bekannt voraus. Auf dem Weg über das Lehnwort *martyr* in der lateinischen Kirche hat die entsprechende Terminologie die modernen Sprachen erreicht und schließlich die Grenzen des christlichen Bekenntnis-
ses überschritten. Manche Forscher halten den Zusammenhang des
christlichen *terminus technicus* und der auf diese Weise bezeichneten
Sache nun für so eng, dass sie mit dem Aufkommen der typisch christlichen Terminologie auch die Genese des Martyriums verbinden, das
heißt das Märtyrertum sei wie die entsprechende christliche Terminologie rein christlichen Ursprungs oder Martyrium als Sache und eindeutiger Begriff müsse von den gesellschaftlichen Bedingungen des
Römischen Reiches im 2. Jahrhundert nach Christus her verstanden
werden.[3] Solche Vorgehensweisen rechnen nicht genügend mit der
Ungleichzeitigkeit der Geschichte von Sachen und Wörtern. Eine Sache

---

1   Zum aktuellen Forschungsstand vgl. Johan Leemans, ed., Boudewijn Dehandschut-
    ter, *Polycarpiana: Studies on Martyrdom and Persecution in Early Christianity. Collected
    Essays*, BEThL 205 (Leuven et al.: Peeters, 2007).

2   Theofried Baumeister, *Martyrium, Hagiographie und Heiligenverehrung im christlichen
    Altertum*, RQ.S 61 (Rom et al.: Herder, 2009), 9–137, besonders 12–17, 39f. u.ö.; ders.,
    Genese und Entfaltung der altkirchlichen Theologie des Martyriums, TC 8 (Bern et al.: Pe-
    ter Lang, 1991), XI–XXVI, besonders XX–XXIII, 61, Anm. 8 u.ö.

3   Vgl. etwa Hans Freiherr von Campenhausen, *Die Idee des Martyriums in der alten
    Kirche* (Göttingen: Vandenhoeck & Ruprecht, [2]1964); Glen W. Bowersock, *Martyrdom
    and Rome* (Cambridge: University Press, 1995, reprinted 1998).

kann alt sein, doch erst im Verlauf ihrer Geschichte entsteht das Bedürfnis knapper und eindeutiger Benennungen. Im Christentum gab es Versuche, das Martyrium als „Bekenntnis" oder „Leiden" mit Angabe des Grundes zu bezeichnen, die zugunsten der genannten Terminologie aufgegeben wurden.[4] Das Ringen um die adäquate Terminologie gehört also mit zu einer älteren umfassenden Geschichte der Sache, die zunächst einmal zumindest bis in die Anfänge des Christentums zurückverfolgt werden kann. Im Sinn einer undogmatischen Religionsgeschichte kann man den Tod Jesu als Martyrium verstehen, das schon früh durch die ersten Christen im Zusammenhang der Christologie und Soteriologie von den Martyrien der Jünger Jesu abgehoben wurde. Darüber hinaus ist es für alle, die die Ursprungsbedingungen des Christentums kennen, völlig klar, dass das Phänomen des urchristlichen Martyriums in der Tradition des vorchristlichen Judentums steht. Die christliche Theologie des Martyriums kann begriffen werden als Fortführung und Modifikation einer breiten jüdischen Bemühung um Sinngebung des gewaltsamen Todes glaubensstarker Juden und allgemein der Verfolgung jüdischer Frommer. Als Beginn einer durchgehenden und modifizierten jüdisch-christlichen Traditionslinie können gut Ereignisse zur Zeit des syrischen Herrschers Antiochus IV. Epiphanes (*regnavit* 175-164 vor Christus) bestimmt werden, die Anlass für theologische Reflexionen und literarische Gestaltungen wurden.[5]

Dem antichristlichen neuplatonischen Philosophen Porphyrius, der die heiligen Schriften des Judentums und Christentums gut kannte, war bereits aufgefallen, dass das Buch Daniel nicht von demjenigen verfasst worden sein könne, nach dem es benannt sei, sondern dass es von einem anonymen Autor stammen müsse, der es zur Zeit des Antiochus Epiphanes in Judäa geschaffen habe, und dass nicht Daniel die Zukunft weissage, sondern der tatsächliche Verfasser Vergangenes erzähle; was er bis auf Antiochus Epiphanes berichte, enthalte wahre Geschichte, erst danach weiche er von den Geschehnissen ab, da er sie

---

4   Vgl. die Terminologie des Martyriums bei Justin dem Märtyrer und im „Hirt des Hermas".

5   Zu den historischen Hintergründen vgl. etwa Klaus Bringmann, *Hellenistische Reform und Religionsverfolgung in Judäa. Eine Untersuchung zur jüdisch-hellenistischen Geschichte* (175-163 vor Christus), AAWG.PH III, 132 (Göttingen: Vandenhoeck & Ruprecht, 1983). – Insgesamt zur Fragestellung vgl. Jan Willem van Henten, ed., *Die Entstehung der jüdischen Martyrologie*, StPB 38 (Leiden et al.: Brill, 1989); Marie-Françoise Baslez, The Origin of the Martyrdom Images: From the Book of Maccabees to the first Christians, in: Géza G. Xeravits/József Zsengellér, eds., *The Books of the Maccabees: History, Theology, Ideology*, JSJ Suppl. 118 (Leiden/Boston: Brill, 2007) 113–130.

noch nicht gekannt habe.[6] Die moderne Exegese sieht denn auch in den Weissagungen Daniels ein *uaticinium ex euentu* und interpretiert dementsprechend die einzelnen Teile des Buches.

In Dan 11 wird gut die Schnittstelle zwischen den Bezügen zur bekannten Geschichte in Form der Weissagung und der zur Zeit der Redaktion des Buches tatsächlich noch erwarteten Zukunft ab 11,40 deutlich.[7] Im Jahr 168 vor Christus hatte Antiochus IV. Epiphanes einen zweiten Feldzug gegen Ägypten unternommen, den er auf römischen Druck hin abbrach. Mit dem Rückzug ging eine Steigerung der antijüdischen Religionspolitik unter anderem durch Unterstützung der hellenistischen Kreise in Jerusalem einher, deren Kehrseite eine blutige Unterdrückung der standhaften Opposition war, zu der auch die Redaktoren von Dan gehörten. In dieser Gruppe der sogenannten Verständigen oder Weisen kam es zu gewaltsamen Todesfällen, die in Dan 11,35 als Reinigung und Läuterung unter ihnen interpretiert wird. Gemeint sein dürfte, dass die moralische Qualität der Gruppe im Sinn ihrer Lehre vom unbedingten Vertrauen auf Gottes Eingreifen zunahm und entsprechende Unvollkommenheiten überwunden wurden. Für die Getöteten selbst könnte der Tod als Gelegenheit der Läuterung verstanden worden sein. Die Verfasser dürften ihre Redaktionstätigkeit in der Zeit zunehmender Unterdrückung ab 167 vor Christus bis etwa kurz vor dem Tod des Antiochus IV. 164 vor Christus, den sie noch nicht kannten, vorgenommen haben. Für die Zeit danach rechneten sie

---

6   Vgl. Hieronymus, In Dan., prologus (CCL 75A, 771,1–8 Glorie): „Contra prophetam Danielem duodecimum librum scribit Porphyrius, nolens eum ab ipso cuius inscriptus est nomine esse compositum sed a quodam qui temporibus Antiochi, qui appellatus est Epiphanes, fuerit in Iudaea, et non tam Danielem uentura dixisse quam illum narrasse praeterita; denique quidquid usque ad Antiochum dixerit, ueram historiam continere, siquid autem ultra opinatus sit, quae futura nescierit esse mentitum ..." Hieronymus schrieb den Kommentar zu Daniel im Jahr 407; siehe Silvano Cola, *San Girolamo: Commento a Daniele. Traduzione, introduzione e note*, Commenti patristici all'Antico Testamento (Rom: Città Nuova, 1966), 11; vgl. auch die englische Übersetzung: Gleason L. Archer, Jr., *Jerome's Commentary on Daniel* (Grand Rapids, MI: Baker Book House, 1958 = 1977), 15. Speziell zu Porphyrius und Daniel vgl. Pier Franco Beatrice, Pagans and Christians on the Book of Daniel, *StPatr* 25 (1993), 27–45, 36–40; Timothy D. Barnes, Porphyry against the Christians: Date and the Attribution of Fragments, *JThS.NS* 24 (1973), 424–442; Adolf von Harnack, ed., *Porphyrius „Gegen die Christen", 15 Bücher. Zeugnisse, Fragmente und Referate*, APAW.PH 1 (Berlin: Verlag der königl. Akademie der Wissenschaften, Georg Reimer, 1916), 67–73.

7   Übersetzung und Kommentierung von Dan 11,29–36.40–12,4 durch Günter Mayer bei Baumeister, *Genese*, 2–7. Vgl. auch Theofried Baumeister, *Die Anfänge der Theologie des Martyriums*, MBTh 45 (Münster: Aschendorff, 1980), 13–23. Ein neuer Kommentar: Dieter Bauer, *Das Buch Daniel*, NSK.AT 22 (Stuttgart: Katholisches Bibelwerk, 1996).

entsprechend 12,1–4 mit dem Eingreifen Michaels, des himmlischen Schutzpatrons, und mit einem Erwachen der Toten zur Belohnung oder Bestrafung sowie einer besonderen Auszeichnung ihrer Gruppe.

Der ermittelte Zeitrahmen der Redaktion des Buches Daniel inmitten der religiösen Bedrängnis unter Antiochus IV. ist nun auch wichtig für die Interpretation der beiden Legenden über die drei Jünglinge im Feuerofen nach Dan 3 und des Daniel in der Löwengrube nach Dan 6. Beide Erzählungen waren wohl ursprünglich selbstständige Geschichten über göttliche Rettung in höchster, auswegloser Not. Durch die Einfügung in das Buch Daniel erhalten sie auch die Bedeutung des Trostzuspruches in der lebensgefährlichen Situation der Religionsverfolgung. Im Kontext dieser Redaktion gelten die drei jungen Männer als solche, die eher den Tod auf sich nehmen, als dass sie den geforderten paganen Kultakt leisten. Dan 3,17f. formuliert dementsprechend als Bekenntnis der Drei an die Adresse des Königs: „Wenn überhaupt jemand, so kann nur unser Gott, den wir verehren, uns erretten; auch aus dem glühenden Feuerofen und aus deiner Hand, König, kann er uns retten. Tut er es aber nicht, so sollst du, König, wissen: Auch dann verehren wir deine Götter nicht und beten das goldene Standbild nicht an, das du errichtet hast." Seit dem 2. Jahrhundert nach Christus hat man solche Personen Märtyrer oder Bekenner genannt. In den griechischen Übersetzungen der hebräisch-aramäischen Schrift (Dan 1 und 8–12 hebräisch, Dan 2–7 aramäisch) wurde die Geschichte vom Feuerofen durch Gebetszusätze weiter ausgestaltet, während zur Löwengrube von Dan 6 eine Parallelerzählung mit der wunderbaren Speisung Daniels inmitten der Löwen durch den Propheten Habakuk dem Buch angeschlossen wurde.[8] Die Christen sahen in den drei jungen Männern und in Daniel Märtyrer;[9] deren Rettungen hat man auf den theologisch gedeuteten Tod von Märtyrern bezogen oder zu einem retardierenden Motiv der christlichen Märtyrerlegende umgestaltet.

Die griechischen Makkabäerbücher lassen ebenfalls erkennen, dass die Religionsverfolgung unter Antiochus IV. blutige Opfer der Stand-

---

8   Otto Plöger, *Zusätze zu Daniel*, JSHRZ I,1 (Gütersloh: Gerd Mohn, 1973), 63–87.

9   Vgl. Ernst Dassmann, *Sündenvergebung durch Taufe, Buße und Martyrerfürbitte in den Zeugnissen frühchristlicher Frömmigkeit und Kunst*, MBTh 36 (Münster: Aschendorff, 1973), 258–370 u.ö.; Hans Reinhard Seeliger, Πάλαι μάρτυρες. Die Drei Jünglinge im Feuerofen als Typos in der spätantiken Kunst, Liturgie und patristischen Literatur, in: Hansjakob Becker/Reiner Kaczynski, eds., *Liturgie und Dichtung*, vol. 2, PiLi 2 (St. Ottilien: Eos Verlag, 1983), 257–334; Juliane Ohm, *Daniel und die Löwen. Analyse und Deutung nordafrikanischer Mosaiken in geschichtlichem und theologischem Kontext*, PThSt 49 (Paderborn: Schöningh, 2008), 163–177 u.ö.; Jutta Dresken-Weiland, *Bild, Grab und Wort. Untersuchungen zu Jenseitsvorstellungen von Christen des 3. und 4. Jahrhunderts* (Regensburg: Schnell und Steiner, 2010), 233–247, 302–311.

haften forderte (vgl. 1Makk 1,41–64),[10] über die vor allem 2Makk 6,12 – 7,42 und 4Makk theologisch reflektieren und legendarisch erzählen. Der Verfasser von 2Makk, der in 2,23 angibt, eine Zusammenfassung nach dem größeren Werk des Jason von Kyrene vorzulegen, unterbricht seine Darstellung in 6,12–17, um dem Leser eine theologische Verstehenshilfe im Gedanken der göttlichen Erziehung für die folgenden zwei Geschichten über Eleasar (6,18–31) und die sieben Brüder mit ihrer Mutter (7,1–42) an die Hand zu geben.[11] Die beiden in sich geschlossenen Erzählungen, die sich in zentralen Punkten unterscheiden, dürften wohl ursprünglich selbstständig überliefert worden sein; der Redaktor von 2Makk hat sie nur geringfügig verändert und seiner Leidenstheologie von 6,12–17 angepasst. Im Mittelpunkt der Geschichte des bejahrten Schriftgelehrten Eleasar steht das Thema der Vorbildlichkeit des Martyriums vor allem für die Jugend, das bekanntlich Christen seit Ende des 2. Jahrhunderts in den Termini der Zeugnisbegrifflichkeit ausgedrückt haben. Das Motiv, das Leben des Märtyrers retten zu wollen, begegnet später sowohl in historisch zuverlässigen christlichen Martyriumstexten wie auch in zahlreichen Legenden. Anders als bei Eleasar ist in der folgenden Legende der sieben Brüder mit ihrer Mutter der Auferweckungsglaube zentral. Der König selbst ist gegenwärtig; die Märtyrer drohen ihm und beschimpfen ihn; die Leiden und der Heroismus der Märtyrer übersteigen jedes Maß. Doch ist deutlich, dass nicht literarische Fabulierlust die Geschichte gestaltet, sondern theologische Überzeugung der von Gottes Macht abgeleiteten moralischen Überlegenheit, die anschaulich vermittelt wird. Über diese theologische Grundaussage hinaus verknüpft der Redaktor die Legende mit seiner zuvor präsentierten Auffassung göttlicher Erziehung und des stellvertretenen Ertragens der Sündenstrafe des Volkes durch die selbst schuldlosen Märtyrer.

Das ursprünglich wohl hebräisch oder aramäisch verfasste, jedoch nur griechisch erhaltene erste Makkabäerbuch dürfte um 100 vor Christus in Jerusalem entstanden sein. Zu etwa gleicher Zeit, vielleicht etwas

---

10 Alfred Rahlfs/Robert Hanhart, eds., *Septuaginta*, vol. 1 (Stuttgart: Deutsche Bibelgesellschaft, ²2006), 1042f.; Wolfgang Kraus/Martin Karrer, eds., *Septuaginta Deutsch* (Stuttgart: Deutsche Bibelgesellschaft, 2009), 666; Klaus-Dietrich Schunck, *1. Makkabäerbuch*, JSHRZ I,4 (Gütersloh: Gerd Mohn, 1980), 302f.; Stephanie von Dobbeler, *Die Bücher 1/2 Makkabäer*, NSK.AT 11 (Stuttgart: Katholisches Bibelwerk, 1997), 18–21.

11 Rahlfs/Hanhart, *LXX*, I, 1103, 1113–1118; Kraus/Karrer, *LXX Deutsch*, 697, 702–705; Baumeister, *Genese*, 2–13; Christian Habicht, *2. Makkabäerbuch*, JSHRZ I,3 (Gütersloh: Gerd Mohn, 1976); Jan Willem van Henten, *The Maccabean Martyrs as Saviours of the Jewish People. A Study of 2 and 4 Maccabees*, JSJ Suppl. 57 (Leiden et al.: Brill, 1997).

früher oder später, jedenfalls unabhängig davon schrieben Jason von
Kyrene und der auf dessen Werk fußende Verfasser von 2Makk, der
wiederum mit den Märtyrergeschichten das Thema für 4Makk liefer-
te.[12] Die Datierung dieser Schrift ist strittig; meist denkt man an das 1.
Jahrhundert nach Christus, genauer an die erste Hälfte oder verstärkt
an das Ende; einige Forscher vertreten einen Ansatz bis ins 2. Jahrhundert nach Christus. Mit dieser Spätdatierung geht eine Neubewertung
des Charakters der Schrift einher. Man rechnet heute nicht nur damit,
dass bei der Überlieferung christliche Interpolationen in den Text gelangt sind, sondern dass jüdische Gegenpositionen zu christlichen The-
ologumena wie etwa dem Thema des Sühnetodes markiert worden
seien, statt jüdische Einflüsse auf frühchristliche Schriften anzunehmen,
was wiederum eine Frühdatierung von 4Makk voraussetzt.[13] Meines
Erachtens muss erklärt werden, dass 4Makk in die Septuaginta gelangt
ist und früh christlich rezipiert worden ist mit beträchtlichen Auswir-
kungen auf die christliche Martyriumsliteratur. Dies aber lässt sich
besser durch nicht zu späte Abfassungszeit und einen unpolemischen
jüdischen Charakter von 4Makk verstehen. Die Schrift beginnt philoso-
phisch und belegt sodann die These der Herrschaft der gottesfürchti-
gen Vernunft über die Affekte durch die Märtyrergeschichten nach
2Makk 6 und 7, in denen die Sicht des heroischen Todes entsprechend
griechischem Verständnis und stets bestimmende jüdische Theologie
eine Symbiose eingehen. Der moralische Sieg der Märtyrer, ihre Stand-
haftigkeit, Überredungsversuche des Königs und Steigerung der Foltern, Verachtung der Schmerzen und Unempfindlichkeit, Rhetorik und
erzählende, anschauliche Theologie – all das prägt die legendarische
Darstellung und enthält das Potential für spätere christliche Entfaltun-
gen.
      Dass diese Entwicklung schon im frühen 4. Jahrhundert feststellbar
ist, zeigt ein Abschnitt in der Oratio ad sanctorum coetum, deren Herkunft von Konstantin dem Großen I. in letzter Zeit wieder verstärkt
vertreten wird.[14] In panegyrischer Art schildert der Redner in c. 22

---

12   Rahlfs/Hanhart, *LXX*, I, 1157–1184; Kraus/Karrer, *LXX Deutsch*, 730–746; Hans-Josef
     Klauck, *4. Makkabäerbuch*, JSHRZ III,6 (Gütersloh: Gerd Mohn, 1989); Baumeister,
     Genese, 15–19; ders., *Anfänge*, 45–51.
13   Vgl. Hans-Josef Klauck, Rezension G. Scarpat, Quarto libro dei Maccabei, Brescia,
     2006, und D. A. DeSilva, 4 Maccabees, Leiden/Boston, 2006, Biblica 89 (2008), 284–
     288. – Zur späteren christlichen Rezeption vgl. Raphaëlle Ziadé, *Les martyrs Macca-
     bées: de l'histoire juive au culte chrétien. Les homélies de Grégoire de Nazianze et de Jean
     Chrysostome*, SVigChr 80 (Leiden/Boston: Brill, 2007).
14   Vgl. Theofried Baumeister, Konstantin der Große und die Märtyrer, in: ders., *Marty-
     rium*, 113–137, 121–123.

Christenverfolgung und Martyrium seiner jüngsten Vergangenheit. Dabei wird die „θεοσέβεια" (Gottesfurcht) personifiziert und angeredet, sie sei herangetreten und habe sich selbst ausgeliefert, doch die Grausamkeit gottloser Menschen, die mit dem Einwirken von Feuer verglichen wird, habe ihr Ruhm eingebracht.[15] Staunen habe alle erfasst, die sie sahen, die Henker und Folterer, die sich müde arbeiteten und aufs schlimmste vergeblich abmühten, während sich die Fesseln lösten, die Folterwerkzeuge versagten und das Feuer ausging; die Diener Gottes jedoch seien unerschütterlich fest geblieben angesichts der Leiden, auch nicht für einen Augenblick wankten sie in ihrer „παρρησία" (freie Sprache, freimütiges Bekenntnis).

Die Stelle steht offensichtlich in der Tradition des Bildes vom mutigen Philosophen als unerschütterlichem Freund der Wahrheit und dem Tyrannen, der im letzten trotz Einsatz all seiner zerstörerischen Mittel moralisch besiegt wird.[16] Da diese Motive auch in das jüdische vierte Makkabäerbuch, das ja unter Christen tradiert wurde, Eingang gefunden hat, ist nicht verwunderlich, dass es weiterhin Berührungspunkte gerade mit der Martyriumsvorstellung dieser Schrift gibt. Im Unterschied dazu ist jedoch die Wunderthematik bereits weiter entwickelt. Während 4Makk bei der Geringschätzung der Schmerzen, der Vergeblichkeit der Anstrengungen der Folterknechte und bei der Andeutung des Wunderbaren stehen bleibt,[17] geht die Rhetorik des kleinen Abschnitts der Oratio ad coetum sanctorum einen Schritt weiter, indem wiederholtes Durchkreuzen der Folterbemühungen behauptet wird.

Der zu Anfang des 4. Jahrhunderts noch kleine Bach wuchs im Verlauf der Jahrzehnte der Tolerierung und Förderung des Christentums, in denen man mit wachsender Bewunderung auf die heroischen Zeiten der Verfolgungen zurückblickte, an zu einem riesigen Strom, so dass um 400 nach Christus bereits Märtyrerromane wie die Georgslegende entstanden, deren ursprüngliche Fassung das sogenannte Volksbuch

---

15 Oratio ad sanctorum coetum 22,2f. (GCS Euseb. 1, 188 Heikel); Ivar A. Heikel, *Kritische Beiträge zu den Constantin-Schriften des Eusebius (Eusebius Werke Band 1)*, TU 36,4 (Leipzig: Hinrichs`sche Buchhandlung, 1911), 81; Friedhelm Winkelmann, Annotationes zu einer neuen Edition der Tricennatsreden Eusebs und der Oratio ad sanctum coetum in GCS (CPG 3498.3497), in: *ANTIΔΩPON. Festschrift Maurits Geerard*, vol. 1 (Wetteren: Cultura, 1984), 1–7, hier 7; BKV² Euseb. 1, 264 Pfättisch; Mark Edwards, *Constantine and Christendom: The Oration to the Saints. The greek and latin Accounts of the Discovery of the Cross. The Edict of Constantine to Pope Silvester*, Translated Texts for Historians 39 (Liverpool: University Press, 2003), 54f.

16 Vgl. Andreas Alföldi, Der Philosoph als Zeuge der Wahrheit und sein Gegenspieler der Tyrann, *Scientiis artibusque. Collectanea Academiae Catholicae Hungaricae* 1, 1955-57, (Rom: Herder, 1958), 7–19.

17 Baumeister, *Anfänge*, 47f.

ist, das man sodann purgierend und historisierend überarbeiten musste, um es dem Durchschnittsgeschmack anzupassen.[18] Die aus apoka-
lyptischen Versatzstücken gebildeten Szenen der Auferweckung des
Märtyrers vor seinem endgültigen Tod zeigen, dass weiterhin theologische Anliegen in der Gestaltung von Legenden wirksam waren, allerdings auf einem insgesamt einfachen Niveau. Der Gedanke des Sieges
der Märtyrer über ihre Verfolger fand Ausdruck in herausfordernder
Rhetorik und vielfach variierten Wundern der Bewahrung vor wilden
Tieren und dem Feuer, die im letzten auf die bekannten Szenen im
Buch Daniel zurückgeführt werden können. Es ist auffällig, dass ausgerechnet die ursprüngliche Georgslegende, die in Ägypten zunächst eine
Variante in einem vielfältigen Bild der Märtyrerhagiographie war, dort
seit dem 5. Jahrhundert verstärkt stilbildend wurde, so dass sich ein
vorherrschender Typus von Märtyrerlegenden herausbildete, den man
als koptischen Konsens bezeichnen kann.[19] Je mehr das Repertoire der
eigentlichen Martyrien einander angeglichen wurde, umso mehr vari-
ierte man die Geschichten vor dem Martyrium, die auch dazu dienten,
Verwandtschaftsverhältnisse zu kreieren, die der Kultgeographie be-
nachbarter Verehrungsstätten und ihrer Wallfahrtsfeste Rechnung tru-
gen.[20] Die einzelnen Märtyrerlegenden im koptischen Ägypten entwickelten sich zu Kultätiologien, die einem Ort Erlösung in einem umfassenden Sinn bis in die Bedürfnisse des alltäglichen Lebens hinein zu-
sprachen. Im Blick auf den vor seinem endgültigen Tod durch himmli-
sches Eingreifen stets wiederhergestellten Leib des Märtyrers, den die
Gegner unbedingt zerstören wollen, kann vermutet werden, dass ein
anschauliches Bild von Erlösung attraktiv war, das den alten Vorstellungen von Heil als Sicherung der Integrität des Körpers entsprach.

---

18 Vgl. die Überblicksdarstellungen: Wolfgang Haubrichs, Georg, Heiliger, *TRE* 12
    (1984), 380–385; ders., Georg, hl. I, *LThK*[3] 4 (1995), 476–478, jeweils mit Literatur.
    Siehe auch Timothy D. Barnes, *Early christian Hagiography and roman History*, Tria
    Corda. Jenaer Vorlesungen zu Judentum, Antike und Christentum 5 (Tübingen:
    Mohr Siebeck, 2010), 318–321.
19 Baumeister, *Martyrium*, 141–195; ders., *Martyr invictus. Der Martyrer als Sinnbild der
    Erlösung in der Legende und im Kult der frühen koptischen Kirche*, FVK 46 (Münster: Re-
    gensberg, 1972).
20 Insgesamt zum jährlichen Märtyrerfest vgl. Johan Leemans/Wendy Mayer/Pauline
    Allen/Boudewijn Dehandschutter, *„Let us die that we may live." Greek Homilies on
    Christian Martyrs from Asia Minor, Palestine and Syria* (c. AD 350 – AD 450) (Lon-
    don/New York: Routledge, 2003).

Anhang: Moderne Märtyrerlegenden?

Um die Frage nach der Existenz neuzeitlicher Märtyrerlegenden zu beantworten, müsste zunächst geklärt werden, ob und wie der Gattungsbegriff Legende überhaupt nach der Epoche der Aufklärung auf moderne Texte anwendbar sei.[21] In einem weiteren Schritt müsste geklärt werden, wie heute auf Grund innerchristlicher, religionsgeschichtlicher und humanistischer Diskussionen die Begriffe Märtyrer und Martyrium definiert werden. So hat es etwa im Zusammenhang mit der lateinamerikanischen Theologie der Befreiung Bemühungen gegeben, den klassischen Martyriumsbegriff so zu erweitern, dass auch das Eintreten für Gerechtigkeit, selbst ohne explizit christliche Bezüge terminologisch integriert wird.[22] Zu beachten ist weiterhin, dass die Auseinandersetzung mit dem islamistisch begründeten Phänomen der Selbstmordattentäter dazu zwingt, eine Debatte über die Begriffe zu führen. Im Blick auf diese und ähnliche Diskussionen könnte man also Texte auswählen, die man als neue Märtyrerlegenden bezeichnen kann und die man paradigmatisch untersuchen würde.[23] So könnte man, um ein Beispiel zu nennen, fragen, ob implizite und explizite Bezüge zur heiligen Schrift des Christentums in historischen Kontexten dazu berechtigen, von christlichen Märtyrerlegenden zu sprechen.[24] Hier dagegen soll von einem umgangssprachlichen Gebrauch des Wortes Legende ausgegangen werden.[25] Das Wort wird gern benutzt, um eine Überhö-

---

21 Ein Beispiel: Hans-Peter Ecker, *Die Legende. Kulturanthropologische Annäherung an eine literarische Gattung*, Germanistische Abhandlungen 76 (Stuttgart/Weimar: J. B. Metzler, 1993).

22 Vgl. etwa die beiden Themenhefte: Concilium 19 (1983), Heft 3 („Martyrium heute") und Concilium 39 (2003), Heft 1 („Martyrium in neuem Licht"); siehe auch Ludger Weckel, *Um des Lebens willen. Zu einer Theologie des Martyriums aus befreiungstheologischer Sicht* (Mainz: Matthias-Grünewald, 1998).

23 Material bieten etwa Hannes Gertner, ed., *Geschichte der Märtyrer. Verfolgt für den Glauben* (Aschaffenburg: Pattloch, 1984); Helmut Moll, ed., *Zeugen für Christus. Das deutsche Martyrologium des 20. Jahrhunderts*, vol.1/2 (Paderborn et al.: Schöningh, ⁴2006); Karl-Josef Hummel/Christoph Strohm, eds., *Zeugen einer besseren Welt. Christliche Märtyrer des 20. Jahrhunderts* (Leipzig/Kevelaer: Evangelische Verlagsanstalt, Butzon & Bercker, 2000); Friederike Pannewick, ed., *Martyrdom in Literature: Visions of Death and Meaningful Suffering in Europe and the Middle East from Antiquity to Modernity*, Literaturen im Kontext. Arabisch – persisch – türkisch 17 (Wiesbaden: Reichert, 2004); Sigrid Weigel, ed., *Märtyrer-Porträts. Von Opfertod, Blutzeugen und heiligen Kriegern* (München: Wilhelm Fink, 2007).

24 Vgl. etwa Engelhard Kutzner, Pater Kilian (Joseph) Kirchhoff, in: Moll, *Zeugen*, vol. 2, 749–753, 751f.

25 Vgl. Gerhard Wahrig, ed., *dtv-Wörterbuch der deutschen Sprache* (München: Deutscher Taschenbuch Verlag, 1978), 499.

hung auszusagen, die einer hagiographischen Stilisierung in den alten Legenden entspricht. Bestimmte Ereignisse und Personen werden zur Legende, weil die allgemeine Erinnerung sie verklärt, sie sind legendär, weil sie das normale Maß übersteigen. Das Wort Legende kann jedoch auch benutzt werden, um einen Abstand zur Wirklichkeit auszusagen. Auch in diesem Fall gewinnt man den Maßstab an den alten Legenden, weil man weiß, dass Wunder, wenn überhaupt, nur selten vorkommen und Heiligengeschichten oft nicht deckungsgleich mit alltäglicher Erfahrung und tatsächlicher Geschichte sind. In diesem Sinn spricht man etwa von der Dolchstoßlegende mit Bezug auf die Erklärung der deutschen Niederlage beim Ersten Weltkrieg im Militär oder von der *leyenda negra*, mit der als antispanisch empfundene Züge der Geschichtsschreibung charakterisiert werden.[26] Seit Luthers Verdikt über die Legende als „Lügend"[27] und entsprechenden Einschätzungen der Aufklärung bedeutet legendär auch so viel wie „unglaubhaft", „unwahrscheinlich" und Legende „unglaubwürdige Geschichte" oder einen „verzerrt dargestellten historischen Vorgang". Umgangssprachlich macht man in einem solchen Zusammenhang oft keinen Unterschied zu Märchen, Mythos, Sage oder Fabel.

Es scheint nun, dass bei der modernen Erforschung der Historie der christlichen Märtyrer des Altertums Geschichtslegenden entstanden sind, die von Christel Butterweck als „fable convenue", also als verabredete Fabel, auf die man sich verständigt hat, bezeichnet wurden.[28] Da der Eindruck entstehen kann, dass ihr Buch von manchen bewusst oder unbewusst übersehen wird, es also unverdientermaßen nicht rezipiert wird, soll hier gewissermaßen als Gegengewicht der Inhalt in Grundzügen referiert werden. Insgesamt wird deutlich, dass Historiker des Altertums gut daran tun, Ergebnisse der Klassischen Philologie und Patristik zu berücksichtigen, da es ja nicht nur darauf ankommt, antike Quellen zu übersetzen, sondern man muss sie auch literarisch einordnen und dementsprechend in ihrem historischen Wert beurteilen. Ein großer literarischer Zusammenhang, den die Autorin zunächst behandelt, ist die Apologie, wobei sie wegen der Bedeutung, die der Person des Sokrates sowohl in der paganen, wie auch der jüdischen und christlichen Literatur zukommt, genetisch vorgeht und dessen Verteidigung nach Platon an den Anfang stellt. Für die gesamte spätere Topik wich-

---

26   Vgl. *Brockhaus. Studienausgabe* 13 (Leipzig/Mannheim: Brockhaus, 2001), 356.

27   Ecker, *Legende*, 238–243.

28   Christel Butterweck, ‚*Martyriumssucht' in der Alten Kirche?*, BHTh 87 (Tübingen: Mohr Siebeck, 1995), 218–244 u.ö.; *Duden. Das Fremdwörterbuch*, Duden 5 (Mannheim et al.: Dudenverlag, 2007), 309: „Fable convenue (‚verabredete Fabel'): etwas Erfundenes, das man als wahr gelten lässt."

tig wurde die Aussageabsicht Platons, die in folgender Weise zusammengefasst wird: „Obwohl Sokrates mit einem Todesurteil rechnen mußte und Grund gehabt hätte, sich zu verbergen, begab er sich freiwillig vor Gericht, um eine Sache zu verteidigen, derentwegen er ungerechterweise hingerichtet, später jedoch rehabilitiert wurde" (S. 12). Die Rezeption des Topos wird bei Josephus Flavius, in 4Makk, bei verfolgten Philosophen der römischen Kaiserzeit, in der Vita des Apollonius von Tyrana von Philostrat und in zahlreichen christlichen Schriften nachgewiesen. Den Römerbrief des Ignatius von Antiochien, den die Verfasserin hier einordnet, interpretiert sie vom zentralen Konzept des Einklangs mit dem göttlichen Willen her, für das sie auf Parallelen bei Epiktet hinweisen kann. Ignatius hat also schon zuvor erkannt, dass sein gewaltsamer Tod dem Willen Gottes entspricht, und deshalb solle er auch nicht von den Römern verhindert werden. Völlig eindeutig ist der Bezug auf Sokrates und die Topik des freiwilligen Sterbens als apologetisches Argument bei Justin dem Märtyrer. Weitere Schwerpunkte sind sodann sachgerecht Tertullian, Origenes und Athanasius, abgeschlossen durch eine Zusammenfassung, aus der folgendes Urteil zitiert werden soll (S. 88):

> „In der apologetischen Argumentation wird die Todesbereitschaft als christliche Grundhaltung beschrieben, so daß auch historisierende Berichte über spektakuläre Einzelfälle nur zur Illustration dienen. Indem das Erzwungene dort als freiwillig geleistet dargestellt wurde, konnte die Harmlosigkeit der Verfolgten betont und der Vorwurf gegen die Verfolger verstärkt werden. Da aber mit diesen Beispielen argumentiert werden sollte, darf man aus der Aussageabsicht weder historische Tatbestände rekonstruieren noch auf die Martyriumstheologie des jeweiligen Autors rückschließen. Die Beispiele dienten gleichsam als ‚Wegweiser' zu den theologischen Aussagen, auf die es den Apologeten ankam; denn die Martyriumsbereitschaft sollte beim Gegner die Frage nach den Gründen wachrufen, damit die Apologeten diese Frage missionarisch beantworten konnten."

Im zweiten großen Teil behandelt die Autorin den Vorwurf „der Todessucht im polemischen Kontext" (S. 90), zunächst von Seiten der Nichtchristen, die das Martyrium ablehnten und als schlecht begründeten sowie sinnlosen Selbstmord darstellten, dann auch von Seiten der Großkirche, die die Haltung christlicher Dissidenten, im einzelnen von Montanisten, Donatisten und Melitianern zu diskreditieren versuchte, indem man ihren Märtyrern falsche Motive und unvernünftige, dämonische Besessenheit zuschrieb. Je nach Kontext konnte also Bekenntnisbereitschaft aus christlicher Sicht positiv-apologetisch oder negativ-polemisch qualifiziert werden. Insgesamt vertrat man in der Kirche meist eine mittlere Linie, indem man einerseits vor Fanatismus warnte und zur Flucht vor lokalen Verfolgungen riet. Zum anderen entwickelte man die Gattung der *exhortatio ad martyrium*, um Festgenommene und andere Gefährdete immun zu machen angesichts der Möglichkeit des Glaubensabfalls. In der Bekenntnissituation sollten Christen bereit sein zum Martyrium, statt durch Formen der Glaubensverleugnung ihr Leben zu retten. Unter dem Titel: „Die Aufforderung zum Martyrium in Seelsorge und Lehre" (S. 148) werden im dritten Kapitel sowohl Fragen der Gattung wie die einzelnen Schriften der Autoren Tertullian, Origenes und Cyprian untersucht. Der vierte Hauptteil bespricht sodann das Motiv der Leidensbereitschaft in den sogenannten Acta martyrum, in den historischen Schriften des Eusebius von Caesarea (Palästina), in einer ausgewählten panegyrischen Predigt des Basilius von Caesarea (Kappadokien) und im Eulalia-Hymnus des Prudentius. In einer Reihe von Texten sind bereits die Kräfte am Werk, welche die antike Märtyrerlegende geschaffen haben und von denen schon die Rede war. Die Verfasserin behandelt zum Beispiel die Themen des Freimuts (παρρησία) der Märtyrer und des im Martyrium gesehenen moralischen Sieges, der manchmal durch Züge von Provokation ausgestaltet wird. Andere plausible Nachrichten berichten, dass bei Prozessen anwesende Christen sich im Protest gegen Ungerechtigkeit selbst in Gefahr bringen oder anderweitig auffallen. Ihre Primärintention ist nicht das Provozieren des Martyriums, das dann jedoch die Folge ihres Verhaltens ist. Ansätze zur Legendenbildung lassen sich besonders in der Schrift des Eusebius über die Märtyrer in Palästina ausmachen. Im Übrigen muss natürlich jeder Text in Bezug auf den historischen Gehalt in der literarischen Gestaltung einzeln untersucht werden.

Für unseren Zusammenhang ist der letzte Teil der Arbeit mit der Überschrift: „Martyriumssucht als fable convenue" (S. 218) besonders wichtig. Die Verfasserin stellt sich die Aufgabe, an ausgewählten Beispielen zeigen zu wollen, „warum die Vorstellung einer Martyriumssucht in der Alten Kirche vielen heute so selbstverständlich ist, daß sie davon sprechen können, ohne ihre Redeweise begründen zu müssen" (S. 218). Beda Venerabilis steht mit seiner Kirchengeschichte des englischen Volkes in der Tradition der historischen Schriften des Eusebius; mit seiner Fassung der Albanslegende prägte er das Bild, das man sich bei den Angelsachsen seit dem frühen Mittelalter vom Märtyrer machte. Über Alban erzählte er, dass sich dieser in den Kleidern eines verfolgten Klerikers selbst den Soldaten gestellt habe. Die Märtyrer von Cordoba der Jahre 850-859 wurden in den frühen Texten so dargestellt, dass sie unter muslimischer Herrschaft das Martyrium provoziert hatten. Die Ketzerpolemik des Hochmittelalters folgte offensichtlich den entsprechenden altkirchlichen Mustern. Luther griff auf altkirchliche

Motive zurück, um Martyrien der Reformation theologisch zu interpretieren und im Sinn der Freiwilligkeit zu stilisieren. Der englische Lyriker John Donne (1572-1631) berief sich für seine Rechtfertigung des Selbstmordes auf die „freiwilligen" Martyrien, die Baronius ermittelt hatte „und die in fast unveränderter Zusammenstellung noch heute üblicherweise zum Beleg für die altkirchliche ‚Martyriumssucht' herangezogen werden" (S. 232). Im Pietismus begegnet das Argument im Zusammenhang mit dem zentralen Anliegen der geistlichen Erneuerung der Kirche und der Idealisierung früherer Zustände, an denen man Maß nimmt (vor allem in Differenziertheit Philipp Jacob Spener und Gottfried Arnold). Einflussreich war sodann die Aufklärung mit ihrem Einwirken auf die Wissenschaftskultur des 19. Jahrhunderts und bis heute. Für Lessing (1729-1781) waren die Märtyrer Schwärmer, und die Christen hatten nach ihm die Verfolgungen selbst herausgefordert. In der „Encyclopédie", auf die man sich gern stützte, verallgemeinerte man Tillemont, der vorsichtig vermutet hatte, Montanisten hätten Verfolgung provozieren wollen. Gibbons „History of the Decline and Fall of the Roman Empire" machte den Christen, in den Belegen gestützt auf Baronius und Tillemont, einen intoleranten Fanatismus zum Vorwurf. „Während Gibbon die Darstellung der ersten Kirchenhistoriker – nicht zu Unrecht – sehr kritisch beurteilte, rechnet er, wo er auf die bekannten Quellen zum Thema ‚Martyriumsverlangen' zu sprechen kommt, keineswegs mit einer zweckgebundenen Argumentation der antiken Verfasser. Von einer ‚Martyriumssucht' zu sprechen, hält er für plausibel, weil diese seinem Bild vom untoleranten Fanatismus der frühen Christen entspricht" (S. 243f.). Unter ganz anderen Vorzeichen rezipierte die Romantik das Thema in apologetischer Zielsetzung, während historische Darstellungen gerne bis in die Gegenwart mehr oder weniger Gibbon folgen.

In der Einleitung ihres Buches bezieht sich Butterweck auf den vielbeachteten Aufsatz von Geoffrey E. M. de Ste. Croix: „Why were the Early Christians persecuted"[29] und dessen Wirkungsgeschichte in der angelsächsischen Welt. Nach de Ste. Croix kam das sogenannte freiwillige Martyrium auch in der Großkirche weitaus häufiger vor als gemeinhin angenommen und konnte sowohl zum Ausbruch wie auch zur Intensivierung von Christenverfolgungen führen. Im Schlusswort[30]

---

29 In: *PaP* no. 26 (1963), 6–38, jetzt auch in: Geoffrey E. M. de Ste. Croix, *Christian Persecution, Martyrdom, and Orthodoxy*, Michael Whitby/Joseph Streeter, eds. (Oxford: Oxford University Press, 2006, reprinted 2008), 105–152; Butterweck, *Martyriumssucht*, 1–7, besonders 2f.

30 Ebd., 245f.

kehrt Butterweck nach einem knappen Resümee ihrer Ergebnisse zum Ausgangspunkt zurück und endet mit folgendem Urteil (S. 246):

> „Baronius hat die noch heute gängigen Belege für das angenommene historische Phänomen zusammengestellt, und die Aufklärung gab sie – in diesem Fall kritiklos, da nur vermeintlich kritisch – an die folgenden Generationen weiter. Wir stehen daher mit aller Wahrscheinlichkeit vor dem Problem, daß hinsichtlich der Martyriumssucht ‚Wahrheit (hier Martyrium) und Dichtung (seine Deutungen und Darstellungen) vermischt und zur fable convenue verfestigt' (Heinz Liebing) worden sind. Für die These Ste. Croix's, von der wir ausgegangen sind, bedeutet dies mindestens, daß die angegebenen Textstellen, deren apologetisch-polemische Intention überall nachgewiesen werden konnte, zur Begründung nicht ausreichen. Die Frage nach den Ursachen der Christenverfolgungen ist durch die Wiederaufnahme des Topos von der ‚Martyriumssucht' in keinem Fall beantwortet."

Die Studie Butterwecks von 1995 wird, wenn ich recht gesehen habe, im Aufsatz von Anthony R. Birley aus dem Jahr 2000: „Die ‚freiwilligen' Märtyrer. Zum Problem der Selbst-Auslieferer"[31] nicht erwähnt. Glen W. Bowersock, Martyrdom and Rome (Cambridge, 1995), konnte sie aus zeitlichen Gründen nicht kennen. Diese letzte Arbeit zeigt, dass an modernen Geschichtslegenden zum altkirchlichen Martyrium zum Teil fleißig weitergestrickt wird. Doch in großer Mehrheit haben auch die alten Christen gerne gelebt[32] – ein solches Urteil legen sowohl kritischer Umgang mit den Quellen wie auch der gesunde Menschenverstand nahe. Alte Legenden steigerten den Mut jüdischer und christlicher Märtyrer, um ihn zu bewundern, während moderne Vorurteile oft eine mehr oder weniger generelle Provokation voraussetzen, um die alten Verfolgungen historisch zu begründen. Natürlich gab es einzelne Fälle eines provozierenden Hindrängens zum Martyrium, allerdings sollte man sie nicht in der Art der alten Märtyrerlegende und unter ihrem Einfluss verallgemeinern.

---

31 In: Raban von Haehling, ed., *Rom und das himmlische Jerusalem. Die frühen Christen zwischen Anpassung und Ablehnung* (Darmstadt: Wissenschaftliche Buchgesellschaft, 2000), 97–123.

32 Vgl. Dorothea Wendebourg, Das Martyrium in der Alten Kirche als ethisches Problem, *ZKG* 98 (1987), 295–320, besonders 306, 312. Siehe auch Bernhard Kötting, Martyrium und Provokation, in: ders., *Ecclesia peregrinans*, vol. 1 (Münster: Aschendorff, 1988), 231–238; ders., Darf ein Bischof in der Verfolgung die Flucht ergreifen?, in: ebd. 536–548; Johan Leemans, The Idea of „Flight for Persecution" in the Alexandrian Tradition from Clement to Athanasius, in: L. Perrone et al., eds., *Origeniana octava: Origen and the Alexandrian Tradition*, vol. 2, BEThL 164 (Leuven: Peeters, 2003), 901–910; Theofried Baumeister, Die montanistischen Martyriumssprüche bei Tertullian, in: ders., *Martyrium*, 91–106.

B. Greek Hagiography

JAMES CORKE-WEBSTER

Author and Authority

Literary Representations of Moral Authority in Eusebius of Caesarea's *The Martyrs of Palestine*[*]

Characters in stories can have a powerful impact in the real world. This was true in antiquity as it is now. As Aaron Johnson concisely states, 'Literary portraits of holy men (and sometimes women) possessed the capacity to shape the world and lives of late antique readers.'[1] In this article I will examine the literary portraits of state officials, and the martyrs they condemn to death, in *The Martyrs of Palestine*, a largely unappreciated text penned by the 4th century church historian Eusebius of Caesarea. My aim is to show that Eusebius employs a rhetoric of temperance and intemperance, based upon Roman conceptions of ideal paternal authority, to construct his characters far more carefully than has previously been acknowledged. State officials in Eusebius are figures of unprecedented irrationality and violence; the martyrs they abuse are by contrast calm and self-controlled, despite their vulnerability. I suggest that these literary portraits are designed to recast these authority figures to be more appropriate to the politically changing environment of the early 4th century.

1. Literary History in the Early 4th Century

The first quarter of the 4th century AD saw a key shift in the power balance of the late Roman Empire. Christians, who at the start of the

* I must express warm thanks to the Manchester Late Antiquity group, David deVore, Roberta Mazza, Alison Sharrock, and Veronica Wood who all read versions of this paper, and above all to Kate Cooper, without whom it would simply not have been possible.
1 Aaron Johnson, Ancestors as Icons: The Lives of Hebrew Saints in Eusebius' Praeparatio Evangelica, *GRBS* 44 (2004), 245.

century had found themselves the objects of a new persecution, by 325 stood securely behind a sympathetic emperor in an increasingly Christian empire. Our main witness to this extraordinary period is Eusebius of Caesarea, a historian with a front-row seat to this unfolding drama. This Palestinian scholar-turned-bishop was the first to tell the story of the first three hundred years of the church, and in so doing defined the parameters within which that period has been viewed ever since. The medium for this was his *Ecclesiastical History*, a narrative work without precedent, which has nevertheless been studied less for its literary characteristics than its documentary ones.[2] Eusebius though was not the unimaginative writer he has sometimes been labelled.[3] Close analysis of his writing reveals significant literary sophistication.

Recent Eusebian scholarship has become increasingly aware of this. In noting the lack of literary quality in historical writing of the 4th century Averil Cameron cites Eusebius as the innovative exception.[4] Doron Mendels, in his 1999 study *The Media Revolution of Christianity* highlighted the narrative complexity of the *Ecclesiastical History* by suggesting it be read as "media history".[5] In suggesting that Eusebius acted like a modern news editor, selecting and manipulating his sources to tailor stories to his readers, Mendels emphasises Eusebius'

---

2   Eusebius' unprecedented techniques of collecting and quoting primary sources continue to be the subject of scholarly attention; see e.g. Andrew James Carriker, *The Library of Eusebius of Caesarea*, SVigChr 67 (Leiden/Boston: Brill, 2003); Anthony Grafton/Megan Williams, eds., *Christianity and the Transformation of the Book: Origen, Eusebius and the Library of Caesarea* (Cambridge MA/London: Harvard University Press, 2006).

3   See for example the dismissal of Eusebius' style in Andrew Louth's introduction to Geoffrey Arthur Williamson's popular translation of the *Ecclesiastical History*: 'Such writing is enormously valuable to have, though tedious to read', *The History of the Church: From Christ to Constantine* (London: Penguin Books, 1965 [repr. 1989]), xiii. This goes back to Photius' dismissal of Eusebius in the 9th century 'his style is neither agreeable nor brilliant, but he was a man of great learning': *Bibliotheca* 13, trans. René Henry, Photius Bibliothèque (Paris: Société d'Édition les Belles Lettres, 1959), 11.

4   'It is perhaps surprising that Christian history – history written from the Christian point of view, that is, not the more specialised history of the church – is conspicuously absent from the fourth-century list of Christianized literary forms', Averil Cameron, *Christianity and the Rhetoric of Empire: The Development of Christian Discourse* (Berkeley/Los Angeles/Oxford: University of California Press, 1991), 140.

5   Doron Mendels, *The Media Revolution of Early Christianity: An Essay on Eusebius's Ecclesiastical History* (Grand Rapids MI/Cambridge, UK: Eerdmans, 1999). Mendels own view is that Eusebius manipulates his material in the pursuit of greater publicity and interest for a sympathetic pagan audience. There are numerous reasons for questioning this suggestion, but these are not pertinent to the present discussion.

care in narrative construction and his remarkable awareness of his audience.[6] More recently Erica Carotenuto has suggested that Eusebius was capable even of fabrication.[7] She demonstrates convincingly that Eusebius generates a story about five Egyptians in chapter 11 of *The Martyrs of Palestine* using recycled material from elsewhere in that text and from Origen's *On the Principles* 4.3.6–8.[8] This article goes further than most previous scholarship in recognising that Eusebius' narrative writings are as much literary as historical enterprises.

Carotenuto's article is particularly welcome because of the attention given to Eusebius' treatise *The Martyrs of Palestine*, traditionally rather neglected by scholarship.[9] This text is Eusebius' narrative of the fate of certain Christians in Palestine during the Diocletianic persecution (303-311). Eusebius himself was Palestinian, and elected bishop of Caesarea in 314/315. The text has been transmitted in two recensions. The shorter is preserved in the original Greek, and contains largely the same stories as the longer, but in less detail.[10] The longer is preserved in Greek only

---

6   Allan Bell coined the term "audience design" for the way a speaker changes his style depending on the audience. See Allan Bell, Language Style as Audience Design, *Language in Society* 13 (1984), 145–204.

7   Erica Carotenuto, Five Egyptians Coming from Jerusalem: Some Remarks on Eusebius, "De martyribus palestinae" 11.6–13, *CQ* 52 (2002), 500–506.

8   For example the story, identical in many respects, of the five Egyptians in *MP* 8.1 LR.

9   Apart from the studies on its dating and transmission below, and an early discussion of chronology by Hugh Lawlor, The Chronology of Eusebius' Martyrs of Palestine, in: id., *Eusebiana: Essays on The Ecclesiastical History of Eusebius Pamphili I, ca. 264-349AD Bishop of Caesarea* (Oxford: Philo Press, 1912 [repr. 1973]), *The Martyrs of Palestine* is sadly neglected. Lawlor and Oulton's commentary on the text is very brief and deals mainly with questions of dating and historical accuracy (Hugh Lawlor and John Oulton, *Eusebius: The Ecclesiastical History and the Martyrs of Palestine*, vol. 2 (New York/Toronto: The MacMillan Co., 1927)). When it is used, it is normally as supplementary evidence after book 8 of the *Ecclesiastical History* for the Great Persecution; William Frend, *Martyrdom and Persecution in the Early Church. A Study of Conflict from the Maccabees to Donatus* (Oxford: Blackwells, 1965), 477–535 is typical. There have been a number of studies that have focused on *The Martyrs of Palestine* as means to a completely different end; see e.g. Saul Lieberman, The Martyrs of Caesarea, *AIPh* 7 (1939-44), 395–446; Joseph Patrich, The Martyrs of Caesarea: The Urban Context, *SBFLA* 52 (2002), 321–346. The survey article of Joseph Verheyden, Pain and Glory: Some Introductory Comments on the Rhetorical Qualities and Potential of the Martyrs of Palestine by Eusebius of Caesarea, in: Johan Leemans, ed., *Martyrdom and Persecution in Late Ancient Christianity: Festschrift Boudewijn Dehandschutter*, BEThL 241 (Leuven: Peeters, 2010) represents a welcome change from this trend, although I do not agree with all the conclusions therein.

10   The short recension is included in most, but not all, of the extant manuscripts of the *Ecclesiastical History*. In some it is found at the close of book 10, in one in the middle of book 8 starting at chapter 13, and in the majority between books 8 and 9.

in a series of fragments, and then in some fragments of a later Latin translation and in a complete Syriac translation.[11] The Syriac translator appears to have taken some liberties with Eusebius' original, extending certain stories and adding speeches or miracles.[12] Numerous textual issues indicate that the short recension was an abridgement of the long, so the Greek fragments of the long recension are most likely to preserve Eusebius' original intentions for this text.

The dating and interrelationship of the two recensions is bound into the complex discussion surrounding the dating, editions and revisions of the *Ecclesiastical History*. Though debate continues, a consensus position has begun to emerge. I follow with the majority of current scholars the conclusions of Richard Burgess in his seminal 1997 article.[13] In brief, this states that the long recension was completed almost immediately after the persecution in Palestine ceased (temporarily) in April 311 following the Edict of Toleration. Subsequently, Eusebius abbreviated it to produce our short recension, which formed part of the first edition of the *Ecclesiastical History*, produced in 313/314. When Eusebius issued a second edition of the *Ecclesiastical History* in 315/316 he replaced the short recension with the current book 8, encompassing a greater geographical span.[14] At this point the long recension

---

    However, it is not included either in the Syriac or Rufinus' translations of the *Ecclesiastical History*.

11 For details see Lawlor and Oulton, *Eusebius,* vol. 2, 46–50. The Greek fragments were discovered and published in Hippolyte Delehaye, Eusebii Caesariensis De Martyribus Palaestinae Longioris Libelli Fragmenta, *AnBoll* 16 (1897), 113–139; the Syriac version, partially available in Stephen Assemani, *Acta Sanctorum martyrum orientalium et occidentalium* (Rome: Città del Vaticano, 1748), was published in full in William Cureton, *History of the Martyrs in Palestine, by Eusebius, Bishop of Caesarea, Discovered in a Very Antient* (sic) *Syriac Manuscript* (London/Edinburgh: Williams & Norgate, 1861).

12 See e.g. Erica Carotenuto, Eusebius of Caesarea on Romanus of Antioch: A Note on Eusebius, De Martyribus Palestinae (Syriac translation) 7,7–9,9, *CJ* 98 (2003), 389–396.

13 Richard Burgess, The Dates and Editions of Eusebius' Chronici Canones and Historia Ecclesiastica, *JTS* 48 (1997), 471–504. The literature on this topic is extensive; other key contributions include: Lawlor/Oulton, *Eusebius,* vol. 2, 1–11; Timothy Barnes, The Editions of Eusebius' Ecclesiastical History, *GRBS* 21 (1980), 191–201; id., *Constantine and Eusebius* (Cambridge MA/London: Harvard University Press, 1981), 148–50, 154–8; id., Some Inconsistencies in Eusebius, *JThS.NS* 35 (1984), 470–475; Andrew Louth, The Date of Eusebius' Historia Ecclesiastica, *JThS.NS* 41 (1990), 111–123. For a timeline that takes into account Burgess' suggestions, see Carriker, *The Library of Eusebius,* 37-41.

14 That the short recension was once where book 8 stands now was the brilliant suggestion of Timothy Barnes; see Barnes, Some Inconsistencies, 470–471; building on Joseph Lightfoot, Eusebius of Caesarea, in: William Smith/Henry Wace, eds., *A*

was lightly edited and issued in a second edition.[15] There is a further complication, however. A passing phrase in the 315/316 second edition of the *Ecclesiastical History* indicates that Eusebius intends to produce his account of the martyrs from Caesarea in the future.[16] Burgess solves this by suggesting that Eusebius failed to publish the initial long recension before the persecution in Palestine began again in November 311, and when persecution finally ceased in summer 313 (following the Edict of Milan), had already decided to incorporate a shorter version into the *Ecclesiastical History*. The long recension was thus only needed again after the short recension had been replaced by the current book 8 in 315/316, hence its eventual publication at this point.

This theory gives a prominence to *The Martyrs of Palestine* which has not been fully appreciated. The Greek fragments of the long recension become our record of a text written in 311, before the first edition of the *Ecclesiastical History* had been published, but edited and issued in 315/316 after it had been. In 311 Eusebius' major literary projects had been his *Defence of Origen*, *Life of Pamphilus* and *Chronicle*.[17] *The Martyrs of Palestine* can thus be read as the stepping stone from these biographical and chronological endeavours to the vast new project of narrative history that combined the two. *The Martyrs of Palestine* is usually treated by scholars only as an addendum to studies of the *Ecclesiastical History* because of a perceived later date and the assumption that it is just a personal memorial. Both are questionable judgements.[18] *The Martyrs of Palestine* takes on considerable significance however if seen as Eusebius' first attempt to engage with the genre of narrative history and the immediate precursor to his magnum opus. It provides

---

Dictionary of Christian Biography, vol. 2 (London: Murray, 1880), 319–321, and Lawlor and Oulton, *Eusebius*, vol. 2, 7–9.

15 Burgess hypothesises that Eusebius spent little time on revisions, The Dates and Editions, 503.

16 EH 8.13.7, 'Yet I shall make known to posterity in another work those with whom I was personally conversant' (τούτους καὶ τοῖς μεθ' ἡμᾶς γνωρίμους δι' ἑτέρας ποιήσομαι γραφῆς). It is also odd that Eusebius would reissue a shorter form of something he had only recently published.

17 See e.g. Carriker, *The Library of Eusebius*, 37–38.

18 *The Martyrs of Palestine* is usually treated as Eusebius' personal eye-witness account of the suffering of friends and colleagues. However, while some figures were clearly known to Eusebius, this is also the case in the *Ecclesiastical History*, and since many of the martyrs in *The Martyrs of Palestine* died outside Palestine, as Eusebius freely admits, it is very unlikely that all the stories it includes are eyewitness accounts (see e.g. *MP* 5.3 LR; Aedesius dies in Alexandria). The frequent miracle stories might also point in this direction. *The Martyrs of Palestine* should be read on the same level as the *Ecclesiastical History*.

an opportunity to see Eusebius tentatively exploring themes and
literary styles which he will develop more systematically in his
Ecclesiastical History and throughout his literary career.[19] It is as a
prolegomenon to a wider study of Eusebius' literary characterisations
of authority then that I hope this article can stand.

2. Literary Portraits of Authority Figures in *The Martyrs of Palestine*

Hayden White has suggested that a concern for authority lies at the
heart of every narrative: 'narrative in general, from the folktale to the
novel, from the annals to the fully realised "history", has to do with the
topics of law, legality, legitimacy, or, more generally, *authority*.'[20] It is
Eusebius' literary treatment of authority figures, in particular representatives of the Roman state, that I will address here. I suggest that in the
repeated portraits of state officials in *The Martyrs of Palestine* we can
observe Eusebius wrestling with how to characterise these figures at
this limenal moment in history. By his novel characterisations in these
highly charged and violent narratives I suggest Eusebius begins to
construct a rhetoric of legitimate and illegitimate authority by which
his readers are encouraged to judge these figures.

The Martyrs of Palestine recounts the suffering and death of
Eusebius' countrymen in a decade mercifully past. But in the perse-
cution-free window of summer 311 when the long recension was first
composed and in 315/316 when it was finally published, the Christians
could believe that official edicts of toleration and the rise of a
sympathetic emperor hinted at a brighter future. It is impossible to
know the extent of Eusebius' editing of the long recension in 315/316.
But it remains a key witness to Eusebius' initial literary engagement
with these seismic cultural shifts. He stood at a crossroads between a
past where the Christian church often viewed itself as standing in
opposition to the Roman state, and a future where it seemed they
would be increasingly aligned. It is in an attempt to trace and guide
that union that Eusebius wrote the *Ecclesiastical History*. But the long
recension of *The Martyrs of Palestine* can shed light on his first steps in

---

19   Literary questions surrounding the genre and style of *The Life of Constantine* written
     at the end of Eusebius' life have produced a scholarly industry of their own.
20   Hayden White, The Value of Narrativity in the Representation of Reality, *Critical
     Inquiry* 7.1 (1980), 17.

this direction, experimenting with a literary medium to memorialise but also re-appropriate the past.

Four stories are preserved in the Greek fragments of the long recension; the martyrdoms of Apphianus (4.1–15), his brother Aedesius (5.2-3, really just a brief addendum to Apphianus' tale), Theodosia (7.1–2) and Pamphilus and his companions (11.1–28). It is unlikely to be coincidence that it are these sections which are preserved, since from what we can deduce from the Syriac translation and the Greek short recension, Apphianus' and Pamphilus' stories in particular are the two most significant sections, while Theodosia's combines elements from both. It is on these three passages that I will focus my attentions, since they demonstrate most clearly the dynamics between state officials and martyrs characteristic of this text.

In the first of these stories the detailed portrayals of the Palestinian martyr Apphianus and Urban, the Roman governor of Palestine at this point (306), introduces us to a dynamic that will become increasingly familiar as we read more of Eusebius' martyr stories. Apphianus, one of the most memorable characters in the whole work, represents our most detailed picture of the vulnerable yet self-controlled Eusebian martyr. Urban on the other hand, the official before whom he is dragged, is presented as a caricature of uncontrollable rage. Before we meet either, though, we are alerted to Eusebius overt presence as conduit of the story. Almost immediately we read, 'In these circumstances what word of ours could suffice to describe worthily the divine love of the martyr Apphianus?' (τίς ἂν ἐπαρκέσειεν ἡμῖν λόγος εἰς ἐπαξίαν διήγησιν τοῦ θείου ἔρωτος τοῦ μάρτυρος Ἀπφιανοῦ; *MP* 4.2 LR).[21] The story continues to be littered with reminders of Eusebius' literary presence ('germane to the present work' and 'if we must place on record' follow closely in this first paragraph, for example).[22] The reader remains aware of Eusebius as writer throughout the narrative.

---

21 Translations taken from Lawlor and Oulton, *Eusebius*, vol. 1; Greek text: Gustave Bardy, ed., *Eusèbe de Césarée. Histoire ecclésiastique*, 3 vols., SC 31/41/55 (Paris: Les Éditions du Cerf), 1:1952; 2:1955; 3:1958); http://stephanus.tlg.uci.edu/inst/browser.

22 The short recension displays this tendency too: 'I mean Apphianus' (Ἀπφιανόν φημι, *MP* SR 4.2); 'this too with good reason we shall do' (εὐλόγως δὴ καὶ τοῦτο ποιήσομεν, *MP* 4.4 SR); 'The agonies the blessed one endured from this, I believe no words can express' (ἐφ' οἷς ὁποίας ἤνεγκεν ὁ μακάριος ἀλγηδόνας, πάντα λόγον ὑπεραίρειν μοι δοκῶ, *MP* 4.12 SR); and 'although we know not this fact perfectly, we are not convinced that we ought not in every case to hand down the truth in an historical narrative' (ἡμᾶς δ' οὖν, καίπερ τοῦτ' ἀκριβῶς εἰδότας, οὐχ αἱρεῖ λόγος μὴ οὐχὶ ἐκ παντὸς τἀληθὲς παραδοῦναι τῷ λόγῳ τῆς ἱστορίας, *MP* 4.14 SR).

Apphianus, introduced in 4.2–4, is described in a way reminiscent of many other martyr figures in Eusebius's writings.[23] Not yet twenty (εἰκοστὸν οὔπω τῆς τοῦ σώματος ἡλικίας ἔτος εἰσεληλυθὼς ἦν) and from an elite pagan background (τὸ δὲ γένος τῶν ἀπὸ τῆς Λυκίας διαφανῶν καὶ τὰ πρῶτα φερομένων ἐν πλούτῳ καὶ τοῖς ἄλλοις ἀξιώμασιν), he has received an excellent education (δι' ὃ δὴ σπουδῇ τῶν γονέων ἐπὶ τὰ κατὰ τὴν Βηρυτὸν παιδευτήρια λόγων ἕνεκα ἐστέλλετο καὶ ποικίλων μαθημάτων συνείλεκτο παρασκευήν). Particularly interesting are those character traits which mark him as characteristically Eusebian. Though young, he does not act his age, but behaves instead with the decorum of a respected elder (τῆς μὲν τῶν νέων συνουσίας καὶ συνδιατριβῆς κρείττων ἐγίνετο, ἤθει δὲ πρεσβυτικῷ καὶ σεμνοῦ βίου καὶ τρόπου καταστάσει ἑαυτὸν ἐκόσμει). He is defined above all by his 'self-control' (τὴν ἐγκράτειαν) and his 'absolute chastity and sobriety' (ἁγνείαν τὴν παντελῆ καὶ σωφροσύνην).

Dissatisfied with his pagan education and the household that provided it, Apphianus slips away from his family one night and travels to Caesarea. There he is educated as a Christian under Pamphilus, Eusebius' own mentor.[24] However, he slips away from his new Christian family too in order to be martyred. Eusebius again eulogises about Apphianus' positive qualities in 4.7. Here the standard martyr traits of 'courage' (τὸ θάρσος) and 'boldness' (τὴν παρρησίαν) are interspersed with the slightly less predictable 'constancy' (τὴν ἔνστασιν), 'self-control' (τὴν ἐγκράτειαν) and 'prudence' (τὴν φρόνησιν). Again, it is his overall temperance that is brought out most strongly. Apphianus approaches the governor Urban as the latter is sacrificing and stays his arm, attempting to correct his idolatrous error. This is not presented as a challenge; instead Eusebius implies that this is kindly correction, not aggressive prevention.[25]

---

23 See e.g. the selection of martyrs in *EH* 4.15.5–6; 8.7.4; 8.12.3–5.

24 The lack of attention paid to this moment of departure from home is of particular interest. In contrast with earlier martyr texts where family conflict (particularly between parents and children) and renunciation are focus points (e.g. *The Martyrdom of Saints Perpetua and Felicitas*), Eusebius seems to make as little as possible of this here. I hope to treat this in more detail elsewhere.

25 This is not to say that *The Martyrs of Palestine* provides no evidence of confrontation between martyr and governor. The Greek fragment of the long recension preserving the story of Apphianus' brother Aedesius (5.2–3) is a case in point, since Aedesius does confront Urban and berates him verbally and physically. However, a number of caveats are worth mentioning. His action is motivated by Urban's grave mistreatment of another Christian, and as we shall see such care for the welfare of others is characteristic of Eusebian martyrs. Furthermore, though Aedesius is the better educated of the two brothers, it is Apphianus, who acts far less aggressively,

At this point we encounter Urban and the other state representatives that accompany him. In 4.10–11 he is first referenced indirectly but ominously when these attendees are called 'the demon's servants' (οἱ δὲ δαιμόνων ὑπηρέται). When Apphianus gently tries to dissuade Urban from sacrificing, the response of Urban's entourage is disproportionately aggressive: 'as if a branding iron had touched their senses, [they] rent him, struck him on the face, trampled him with their feet as he lay on the ground, and pounded his mouth and lips until they tore them' (πληγέντες ὥσπερ ὑπό τινος καυτῆρος τὰς φρένας... σπαράττουσι παίοντες κατὰ πρόσωπον καὶ χαμαὶ κείμενον τοῖς ποσὶ καταπατοῦντες πιεσμοῖς τε τὸ στόμα καὶ τὰ χείλη διασπῶντες). Urban himself then demonstrates 'his native cruelty, as if it were some good thing' (ὥσπερ τινὸς ἀγαθοῦ τῆς οἰκείας ὠμότητος) by punishing Apphianus personally. He and his circle are defined by their senselessness and personal cruelty, demonstrated by their excessive violence. This is characteristic of state officials in Eusebius' narratives.[26]

Urban's title, 'that noble governor of the province' (ὁ γενναῖος τοῦ ἔθνους ἡγούμενος) not only contains a hint of irony, but also reminds the reader that his role involves governing the people of a country. His actions against Apphianus here though are motivated not by his duty as governor but by personal cruelty. In 4.12, after a spell in the stocks, Apphianus is whipped and torn. Urban then speaks with him and, frustrated by his refusal to answer properly,[27] orders further torture: 'The judge now became infuriated; and, exasperated by the invincible utterances of the martyr, he gave orders that they should swathe his feet in linen cloths soaked in oil and set them on fire' (ὃ δὲ εἰς μανίαν ἤδη χωρῶν καὶ κινούμενος ἐπὶ τῇ τοῦ μάρτυρος ἀνικήτῳ φωνῇ λίνοις ἐλαίῳ δευθεῖσιν τοὺς πόδας περιπλέξαντας αὐτοῦ πῦρ

---

who is afforded more attention. The contrast between these two brothers could also be the result of the long recension's unusual editing process. Given that Eusebius spent time with this text in 311 immediately after some of the deaths described, and then in 315/316 after several years of reflection, we might well expect some variance. I suggest that the evident Eusebian preference for Apphianus is evidence of an increasing focus on such non-combative martyr figures.

26 See e.g. EH 5.1.9; 6.39.5; 8.14.1-16.

27 'In answer to the judge's many questions he made no further confession than that he was a Christian; and when he next asked who he was, whence he came, and where he was staying, he confessed nothing, except that he was a slave of Christ.' (πολλὰ τοῦ δικαστοῦ πυνθανομένου οὐδὲν πλεῖον ἢ Χριστιανὸν ἑαυτὸν ὡμολόγει εἶναι, εἶτα ἐρωτώμενος ὅστις εἴη καὶ πόθεν, ποῖ τε εἴη μένων, οὐδὲν ἕτερον ἢ Χριστοῦ δοῦλον ἑαυτὸν ὡμολόγει, MP 4.12 LR).

ὑφάψαι προστάττει). Urban's excessive violence contrasts strongly with Apphianus' calm endurance of it.

As their interaction intensifies, it becomes clear that these characters are polar opposites. Where Apphianus lives up to his introduction as a youth of remarkable self-control, Urban's increasing frustration (εἰς μανίαν ἤδη χωρῶν) and lack of rationality (κινούμενος) motivates this unusual and exquisitely painful form of torture. This reaches its climax when Apphianus withstands even this with equal calm and dignity. His continuing calm triggers yet more rage in his torturers: 'the oppressors of the martyr were raging like demons; they were pained to the heart, as if they, and not he, were bearing the terrible sufferings; they gnashed their teeth; their minds were at fever heat' (οἱ μὲν γὰρ ἐλύττων οἷα δαίμονες, καὶ τὰς ψυχὰς ὀδυνώμενοι, ὡς ἂν αὐτοὶ τὰ δεινὰ πάσχοντες, πρίοντες τοὺς ὀδόντας καὶ τοὺς λογισμοὺς καόμενοι). This language of gnashing teeth and burning minds is more characteristic of rabid animals than court officials.

The martyr's self-control is further indicated by his ability to withstand torture. Of the three day interaction between Apphianus and Urban, most of Eusebius' discussion concerns the detail of the torture inflicted by the latter and the former's endurance of it. The description of the martyr's burning feet is particularly graphic.[28] Throughout his writing on martyrdom, Eusebius shows an almost disturbing interest in the details of the martyrs' suffering, and particularly in novel methods of torture.[29] This graphic detail is, I suggest, more than just a sensationalist hook to keep an audience's attention, though no doubt it served that purpose too.[30] The gravity of the horror experienced by the martyr further accentuates his/her capacity for self-controlled endurance.

Closer inspection reveals that Apphianus' quiet endurance is the quality Eusebius draws out most often throughout this story. When first beaten after intercepting Urban, we are told simply that 'he had

---

28 'And when the torturers carried out the order and the martyr was suspended on high, it was a fearful sight to see: his sides so rent, his whole body so swollen, and the fashion of his face altered; and the fierce fire had burnt his feet for so long that the flesh was melted and flowed like wax, and the flames penetrated to the bones as if they were dry reeds' (ἀνήρτητο δὲ ὑψηλῶς ὁ μάρτυς, φοβερὸν [δὲ] θέαμα τοῖς ὁρῶσιν ἦν, οὕτω μὲν τὰς πλευρὰς διερρωγώς, οὕτω δὲ διωγκηκὼς καὶ τοῦ προσώπου τὴν μορφὴν ἠλλοιωμένος, πολλῷ τε τῷ πυρὶ τοὺς πόδας ἐπὶ μακρὸν καιόμενος χρόνον, ὡς διαρρεῖν μὲν τηκομένας κηροῦ δίκην τὰς σάρκας, τῶν δὲ ὀστέων καθάπερ ξηρῶν καλάμων εἴσω δικνεῖσθαι τὸ πῦρ, MP 4.12 LR)

29 E.g. EH 8.9.1; 8.12.6.

30 See e.g. Mendels, The Media Revolution, 88; also Janet Davis, Teaching Violence in the Schools of Rhetoric, in: Hal Drake, ed., Violence in Late Antiquity: Perceptions and Practices (Hampshire/Burlington: Ashgate, 2006), 197–204.

undergone all this with the utmost bravery' (ἃ δὴ πάντα ἀνδρειότατα ὑποστάς, *MP* 4.10 LR). Having then been scourged, his only reaction is a lack thereof: 'The veritable martyr of God, indeed, remained like adamant...' (ὁ μὲν δῆτα θεοῦ μάρτυς, οἷά τις ἀδάμας, *MP* 4.12 LR). After his second bout of torture we read simply that: 'the sufferer cared for none of these things' (ἀλλ' οὐδὲν τούτων ἔμελεν τῷ πάσχοντι, *MP* 4.13 LR).[31] Endurance is the physical manifestation of the calm self-control and constancy that characterise Apphianus and most other Eusebian martyrs, just as violent rage is the hallmark of Urban and other state officials' lack of self-control.[32]

Eusebius' careful telling of this detailed story introduces us to a mode of martyr narrative characteristic of his literary writings. The dynamic between martyr and state official is controlled by the careful deployment of a rhetoric of moral authority. Eusebius' depiction of the governor Urban centres around the latter's lack of self-control, and the anger and violence that result from this. This is further highlighted because the martyr, despite his apparent youth and vulnerability, is marked by precisely that calm self-control, manifested in his extra-ordinarily self-possessed tolerance for torture. These two figures display the opposing sides of the same behavioural ideal.

31　This language is even more pronounced in the short recension: 'having endured with the utmost bravery countless blows over his whole body' (μυρίας καθ' ὅλου τοῦ σώματος πληγὰς ἀνδρειότατα ὑπομείνας, *MP* 4.10 SR); 'he displayed every kind of endurance in the face of suffering and terrible agonies' (πᾶσαν ἐνδείκνυται πρὸς πόνους καὶ φρικτὰς ἀλγηδόνας καρτερίαν, *MP* 4.11 SR); 'he did not yield even before torments such as these' (μηδὲ πρὸς τὰ τοσαῦτα ἐνδιδόντος, *MP* 4.12 SR); 'The agonies the blessed one endured from this, I believe no words can express' (ἐφ' οἷς ὁποίας ἤνεγκεν ὁ μακάριος ἀλγηδόνας, πάντα λόγον ὑπεραίρειν μοι δοκῶ, *MP* 4.12 SR) and 'But since he did not yield even before this treatment, and his adversaries were now worsted and all but despairing when confronted with his superhuman endurance...' (ἀλλὰ γὰρ οὐδὲ ταῦτα ἐνδούς, ἡττημένων ἤδη καὶ μόνον οὐκ ἀπειρηκότων πρὸς τὴν ὑπὲρ ἄνθρωπον καρτερίαν αὐτοῦ τῶν ἀντιπάλων... *MP* 4.13 SR).

32　The eventual method of death merits mention. Apphianus is drowned, a capital punishment repeated on numerous occasions in *The Martyrs of Palestine* but rarely in martyr narratives outside it. Drowning by being tied in a sack together with a dog, a rooster, a monkey and a snake was the classic punishment for parricide (but written out of the law in 55BC, see Max Radin, The Lex Pompeia and the Poena Cullei, *JRS* 10 (1920), 119–130) and indeed the short recension in 5.1 tells the story, immediately after Apphianus, of the young-man Ulpian killed in precisely this manner (sans rooster and monkey). Since such a punishment is completely unmerited, it may be that we have here another subtle reference to the father-son dynamic between governor and martyr that I suggest Eusebius is trying to elicit (see below). It is also possible that drowning is simply a particularly non-agonistic method of death, at least when compared with *condemnatio ad bestias*.

*   *   *

The story of Theodosia in 7.1–2 employs this same rhetoric by focusing on different aspects of this character's interaction with Urban. Theodosia is an even more vulnerable character than Apphianus, on account of both her age and her gender. She is 'a certain maid from Tyre, consecrated and all-holy, who led a virgin life in the service of God, not yet full eighteen years of age' (τις ἱερὰ καὶ παναγία κόρη τῶν ἀπὸ Τύρου τῷ τοῦ θεοῦ παιδὶ παρθενευομένη, οὐδὲ ὅλων ἐτῶν ὀκτωκαίδεκα). As with Apphianus, her temperance is highlighted by her unexpected possession of it; a mere youth, and female no less. She is one of many female martyrs in Eusebius' narrative writings.[33] This phenomenon can be explained, I suggest, by Eusebius' preference for vulnerable martyrs. When Theodosia is taken to Urban, he is inexplicably personally offended and grows angry, as he did with Apphianus. We are told that 'some feeling, I know not what, came over him, and he was filled immediately with rage and fury' (ἀλλ' οὗτος οὐκ οἶδ' ὅ τι παθών ... παραχρῆμα θυμοῦ καὶ λύττης ἐμπίμπλαται). As with Apphianus, this is linked to an inability to remain objective; he reacts 'as if the maid had done him the greatest injury' (ὥσπερ τὰ μέγιστα πρὸς τῆς κόρης ἠδικημένος). Again martyr and state official behave in opposing fashion.

Linguistically the contrast between state official and martyr is particularly clear here.[34] When Theodosia refuses to sacrifice, Urban is characterised as 'like a wild beast' (ὁ θηριωδέστατος). This bestial language is repeated elsewhere of Urban and other Eusebian state officials; Apphianus' torturers 'gnashed their teeth' (πρίοντες τοὺς ὀδόντας) in frustration, for example. George Lakoff and Mark Johnson, in their seminal 1980 book *Metaphors We Live By*, have suggested that linguistic expressions combine in narratives to form conceptual metaphors, which determine the way we subconsciously approach a

---

33 For more on this see Elizabeth Clark, Eusebius on Women in Early Church History, in: Harold Attridge/Gohei Hata, eds., *Eusebius, Christianity and Judaism* (Leiden/New York: Brill, 1992), 256–269.

34 This metaphorical language is especially clear in the account of Apphianus in the short recension. There Apphianus is introduced as 'that blessed martyr, that truly guileless lamb' (τοῦ μακαρίου καὶ ὡς ἀληθῶς ἀμνοῦ ἀκάκου μάρτυρος, MP 4.2 SR), while Urban and his minions are subsequently described 'as if they were wild beasts' (θηρῶν δίκην ἀγρίων, MP 4.10 SR). It is odd that this metaphor exists in the short but not the long recension; most likely Eusebius added it into the short recension and simply neglected to incorporate it into the long recension when he reissued that text in 315/316.

topic.[35] Use of one metaphor, for example, encourages readers to ignore other potential systems of meaning which might have been pertinent.[36] Personification metaphors are especially good at determining reader response.[37] The repeated animalistic language emphasises these state officials' lack of basic human rationality. The reader is encouraged to internalise subsequent interactions between state official in these terms; as wild beast against vulnerable innocent. The behaviour of the judge prevents this being read as a normal trial or interrogation scene.[38]

As with Apphianus, the prevailing dynamic is of endurance: 'the pitiless one drove into the very bones and entrails; so perseveringly did he punish the girl, who received his tortures in silence' (ὀστέων τε αὐτῶν εἴσω δὴ καὶ σπλάγχνων ὁ ἀνηλεὴς ἐχώρει, ἐπιμόνως τὴν παῖδα τιμωρούμενος σιγῇ τὰς βασάνους δεχομένην). Eusebius emphasises her youthful beauty: 'she gave him a keen, earnest look with her eyes, and with a gentle smile upon her face (she was then in the full bloom of her beauty)' (τοῖς ὀφθαλμοῖς ὀξὺ καὶ ἀτενὲς μβλέψασα, ὑπομειδιῶντι προσώπῳ ἐπήνθει δὲ αὐτῇ καὶ τὸ τῆς ἀκμῆς κάλλος). Like Apphianus, Theodosia is drowned after Urban perceives that torture would not break her, since 'he was become a laughing-stock to the girl' (ἑαυτὸν γέλωτα τῆς κόρης ἐνόμενον). Theodosia is characterised by unbelievable endurance despite her supposed vulnerability.

In this story though, we see another key Eusebian criterion for judging legitimate authority emerging; concern for others. Theodosia comes to the attention of the authorities because she approaches certain other Christian prisoners to request they remember her in their martyrdom. Urban's casual treatment of the Christians arraigned before him is contrasted by Theodosia's acute awareness of them. When she breaks her silence,[39] it is to express enthusiasm that she will soon be united with her fellow martyrs: 'I fare now in accordance with my prayers, since I have been judged worthy to join the company of the martyrs of God' (με πράττειν νῦν ὅτε τῶν τοῦ θεοῦ μαρτύρων κοινωνίας τυχεῖν ἠξιώθην). In Eusebius' account Theodosia's suffer-

---

35 George Lakoff and Mark Johnson, *Metaphors We Live By* (Chicago IL/London: University of Chicago Press, 1980 [rep. 2003]), 5–6.

36 Lakoff/Johnson, *Metaphors*, 10; see also 67.

37 Lakoff/Johnson, *Metaphors*, 33.

38 I am grateful to a conversation with Lesley Dossey for this idea. Cf. also Apphianus' label of the representatives of the state as 'drunkards' (οἷα μεθύοντας, *MP* 4.13, LR).

39 The oddity of this speech coming after Eusebius has declared that Theodosia suffered in silence may be another relic of the delay between this text's production and publication, and any editing it underwent before the latter.

ings prove of merit for other Christians. By her death she prevents the
executions of those other confessors she had originally approached. It is
particularly noteworthy that Eusebius links her salvific actions with her
endurance.

> 'For she who as the champion of them all had taken upon herself their
> sufferings; by her firmness and strength of soul she had unnerved the
> savage judge, and thus had turned him into a coward to face those who
> came after her.'

> 'ἡ γὰρ πρόμαχος ἁπάντων τοὺς αὐτῶν ἀναδεξαμένη πόνους καὶ τὸν
> ὠμὸν δικαστὴν καὶ ῥώμῃ ψυχῆς παραλύσασα, δειλὸν καὶ εἰς τοὺς μετὰ
> ταῦτα κατεστήσατο.'

> (Eusebius, *The Martyrs of Palestine* Long Recension 7.2)

It is precisely by her 'firmness' (εὐτονίᾳ) and 'strength of soul' (ῥώμῃ
ψυχῆς) that Theodosia ends this interaction (παραλύσασα) with an
official described only as 'savage' (ὠμὸν). It is her calm endurance in
the face of a bestial adversary which saves the lives of her fellow
confessors. Self-control and an ability to care for others are combined
here, and as evident in Theodosia as they are absent in Urban.

*   *   *

The story of the martyrdom of Pamphilus and his companions in
chapter 11 is the other episode of great length in *The Martyrs of
Palestine*. By 310, when these events supposedly occurred, Urban had
been replaced by Firmilian, but there is no noticeable difference in their
characters or behaviour.[40] Both conform to the same Eusebian literary
typos of illegitimate authority. Firmilian is first described in this story
as follows: '...the judge was convulsed with anger and downright rage,
and, being at his wit's end, contrived devices of various kinds against
them, that he might not be worsted' (ὁ δικαστὴς ἀγανακτικῶς καὶ
μάλα ὀργίλως σφαδάζων καὶ τὸν λογισμὸν ἀπορούμενος, ποικίλας,
ὡς ἂν μὴ ἡττηθείη, τὰς κατ' αὐτῶν ἐπενόει μηχανάς, *MP* 11.1n, LR).
His rage is emphasised by strong language: he physically spasms
(σφαδάζων) through irritation (ἀγανακτικῶς) and rage (ὀργίλως).
Like Urban, Firmilian is characterised by his inability to control his
emotions, and his treatment of those arraigned before him is also

---

40 When Firmilian first appears at the start of chapter 8 Eusebius introduces him as
    'Firmilian, who at that time had succeeded to the province of Urban. Now he was a
    man far from peaceable. Indeed in ferocity he surpassed his predecessor, for he had
    been a soldier in the wars, and he was experienced in war and bloodshed' (*MP* 8.1
    LR, extant only in the Syriac translation).

motivated by his rage and personal affront. As with Urban, the contrasting qualities of the martyrs before him serve to highlight Firmilian's own moral failings. In this story though the role of concern for others in Eusebius' rhetoric of legitimate and illegitimate authority (touched upon in his picture of Theodosia) is drawn out further.

Pamphilus was Eusebius' own mentor, and we know from the *Ecclesiastical History* that they had written the majority of a *Defence of Origen* together after Pamphilus was imprisoned, which Eusebius finished alone.[41] In many ways the story of Pamphilus' martyrdom is the pinnacle of this text, but it is noteworthy that Pamphilus dies as part of a group, and his fellow confessors are afforded equal attention.[42] Their combined ability to endure novel and diverse sufferings is marked from the start (again Eusebius own presence as narrator is made explicit).

> 'the conflict which we beheld, whose story we are now to tell, was without parallel in our experience, comprising as it did, all in one, every bodily age and mental development, with differences of life and conduct, and is adorned with manifold forms of tortures and the varied crowns of perfect martyrdom.'
>
> 'τὸν περὶ ὧν ὁ λόγος ἀγῶνα σπανιώτατον ὧν ἡμεῖς ἔγνωμεν, ἱστορήσαμεν, ἀθρόως ἐν αὐτῷ πᾶν εἶδος ἡλικιῶν τε σώματος καὶ ψυχῶν ἀγωγῆς βίου τε καὶ ἀναστροφῆς διαφόρου περιειληφότα βασάνων τε ποικίλοις εἴδεσι καὶ τοῖς κατὰ τὸ τέλειον μαρτύριον ἐνηλλαγμένοις στεφάνοις κεκοσμημένον' (*MP* 11.1a–b LR).

The characteristics of the group contribute to an overall picture of Eusebius' preferred conception of martyrdom, all in contrast to the figure of the state official opposing them. The lengthiest description of Pamphilus indicates his key characteristics for Eusebius. A well-brought up pagan, once educated in Berytus he progressed to the study of Scripture (exactly the same upbringing as Apphianus). The core of his character though is his concern for those around him. As we are being told of Firmilian's mistreatment of others, we are being introduced to our main protagonist who always acts altruistically (as, Eusebius notes, the etymology of his name Πάμ-φιλος suggests). His identity is literally bound into his regard for others: 'In fact he gave

---

41 *EH* 6.33.4. The first book alone of the *Defence* survives in the Latin translation of Rufinus.

42 Commenting on a large group of martyrs in brief individual detail is also a favourite Eusebian technique, and is repeated elsewhere in his writing. See e.g. *EH* 6.4.1–6.5.1; 6.39.1–42.1; 7.12.1; 8.6.1–6. Also interesting in this regard is the supposedly 2nd century AD letter of the churches in Lyons and Vienne to the church in Smyrna, extant only in book 5 of the *Ecclesiastical History* (5.1.1–3.3).

away what came to him from his fathers, and distributed it all among
the naked, the maimed and the poor, while he himself lived in poverty'
(ἀποδόμενος γέ τοι τὰ εἰς αὐτὸν ἐκ προγόνων ἥκοντα γυμνοῖς,
πηροῖς καὶ πένησιν τὰ πάντα διένειμεν, αὐτὸς δὲ ἐν ἀκτήμονι διῆγε
βίῳ', *MP* 11.2–3). [43] Pamphilus' selfless treatment of others only
highlights further Firmilian's brutality.

The stress upon the kindness Pamphilus displayed ('dear and
friendly to all', πάντων... φίλος τε καὶ προσήγορος) and his treatment
of the naked, maimed and poor is noteworthy, and found repeated in
various forms for each of his companions. Martyrs' treatment of the
weak in the community is a characterisation found repeatedly in
Eusebius but far less frequently before him. After Pamphilus we are
introduced to Valens, an old man well-versed in the Scriptures and a
deacon of the church of Aelia (*MP* 11.4 LR), and then to Paul of Jamnia,
a man described as 'hasty in action and fervent in spirit'
(θερμουργότατος καὶ τῷ πνεύματι ζέων ἀνήρ, *MP* 11.5 LR), and
about whom we are subsequently told least.[44] Next of the twelve to be
described are five Egyptians arrested at the gates of Caesarea and
brought before Firmilian together with Pamphilus and the others. As
with Apphianus and Theodosia, their brief responses to the judge's
questions (*MP* 11.8–12) produce the same reaction of frustration and
anger in Firmilian as in Urban: 'The judge, on the other hand, was
puzzled and shook with impatience...' (ὁ δὲ δικαστὴς ἀπορούμενος
ἐσφάδαζεν, *MP* 11.12 LR). [45] Firmilian's impatience is highlighted
against the calm responses of the martyrs.

The next martyr marks the start of a series of stories carefully
constructed by Eusebius to highlight Firmilian's failure to elicit willing
obedience from his subordinates. His failing is deliberately contrasted
with Pamphilus' success. As Firmilian sentences Pamphilus and the
others to decapitation, Porphyry, a young servant from Pamphilus'
own household, shouts out from the crowd and demands the bodies for
burial. Porphyry is mentioned briefly at the start of the chapter as one
who 'outwardly was a servant of Pamphilus, but in affection differed

---

43   In fact, Pamphilus' actual death is paid very little attention, a fact well noted in
     Verheyden, *Pain and Glory*. I intend to treat this more fully in a future publication,
     but I suggest that for Eusebius Pamphilus' martyrdom is less significant than this
     other achievements. This same is true of Eusebius' treatment of Origen, for example.

44   Cf. the relative lack of attention paid to Aedesius, Apphianus' hot-headed brother.

45   The judge is said not to understand the martyrs' reference to Jerusalem. The oddity
     of a Roman governor not knowing the local name of such a prominent city should
     encourage us further in reading these stories as literary constructions as much as
     historical reminiscences.

nothing from a brother, or rather a veritable son, and never failed to imitate his master in everything' (τὸ μὲν δοκεῖν τοῦ Παμφίλου γεγονὼς οἰκέτης, διαθέσει γε μὴν ἀδελφοῦ καὶ μᾶλλον γνησίου παιδὸς διενηνοχὼς οὐδὲν ἢ ἐλλείπων τῆς πρὸς τὸν δεσπότην κατὰ πάντα μιμήσεως, *MP* 11.1f LR). At the moment of his fateful interruption in 11.15, he is described again in similar terms. As with Apphianus and Theodosia, his youth is emphasised (οὐδ' ὅλων ὀκτωκαίδεκα ἐτῶν) and that 'for sobriety and manners [he] was beyond all praise' (σωφροσύνης δὲ ἕνεκα καὶ τρόπων πάντα καλύπτων ἐγκώμια). His relationship to Pamphilus is again likened to that between a son and a father ('a true nursling of Pamphilus', Παμφίλου γνησίου παιδός). Like Apphianus, it seems he too had been Pamphilus' pupil, since he was 'skilled in the art of penmanship…as we might expect from one trained under such a man (καλλιγραφικῆς ἐπιστήμης ἔμπειρος…ὡς οἷα ὑπὸ τηλικῷδε ἀνδρὶ συνησκημένος, *MP* 11.16 LR). Though technically Pamphilus' servant, Eusebius' description makes him as much a student and a son.

Pamphilus' positive relationship with Porphyry is contrasted with Firmilian's reaction to the boy. After Porphyry speaks, we read in 11.16 that 'the judge, who was not a human being, but a wild beast or more savage than any wild beast, neither admitted the reasonableness of the request nor made allowance for the young man's age' (ὁ δὲ οὐκ ἄνθρωπος, ἀλλὰ θὴρ καὶ θηρίου παντὸς ἀγριώτερος, μήτε τῆς αἰτήσεως τὸ εὔλογον ἀποδεξάμενος μήτε τῷ τῆς ἡλικίας ἀπονείμας νέῳ συγγνώμην; *MP* 11.18 LR).' It is Porphyry, the youngest martyr, who suffers the most gruesome torture, and for whom Firmilian's 'mercilessness and inhumanity knew no respite' (παράμονον δὲ τὸ ἀνηλεὲς καὶ ἀπάνθρωπον κεκτημένος). What is more, we are told explicitly that Firmilian's actions are bestial (θὴρ καὶ θηρίου παντὸς ἀγριώτερος) precisely because he did not take into account the age of the boy (τῷ τῆς ἡλικίας… νέῳ; *MP* 11.16 LR) and act appropriately. This dynamic highlights this aspect of Eusebius' rhetoric of legitimate and illegitimate authority.

A subsequent martyr completes the image of Firmilian's moral failing. Theodolus, another of the twelve, is a servant in Firmilian's own household. His treatment by his own master encourages direct comparison with the shining example of Pamphilus and his servant Porphyry. Furthermore it is Theodolus who angers Firmilian most. Spotted greeting another Christian with a kiss in 11.24, 'he was brought before his master, whom he infuriated to anger more than did the others, and received the same martyrdom as the Saviour in His Passion; for he was delivered to the cross' (προσάγεται τῷ δεσπότῃ, μᾶλλόν τε αὐτὸν τῶν ἄλλων ἐπ' ὀργὴν ὀξύνας, ταὐτὸν τοῦ σωτηρίου μαρτύριον πάθους σταυρῷ παραδοθεὶς ἀνεδέξατο). These stories all play with these interwoven hierarchical relationships, and their relative treatment of dependents condemns Firmilian in the reader's eyes at the same time as it elevates Pamphilus. They are judged by the same criteria of moral authority – their capacity for self-control and its effect on their interactions with their dependents.

One final character makes clear the direction of Eusebius' thought. Seleucus is a Cappadocian ex-soldier known for his physical excellence: 'For in stature and bodily strength, and size and vigour, he far excelled his fellow-soldiers, so that his appearance was a matter of common talk, and his whole form was admired on account of its size and symmetrical proportions' (καὶ αὐτῇ ἡλικίᾳ καὶ ῥώμῃ σώματος μεγέθει τε καὶ ἰσχύος ἀρετῇ πλεῖστον ὅσον τοὺς λοιποὺς ἐπλεονέκτει, καὶ τὴν πρόσοψιν δὲ αὐτὴν περίβλεπτος ἦν τοῖς πᾶσι τό τε πᾶν εἶδος ἀξιάγαστος μεγέθους ἕνεκα καὶ εὐμορφίας, MP 11.21 LR). However, Eusebius makes it clear that though Seleucus was a perfect specimen of physical masculinity, it was not his strength, size or vigour that qualified him for martyrdom.

> '...as if he were their father and guardian he showed himself a bishop and patron of destitute orphans and defenceless widows and of those who were distressed with penury or sickness. It is likely that on this account he was deemed worthy of an extraordinary call to martyrdom by God, who rejoices in such things more than in the smoke and blood of sacrifices.'

> '...ὀρφανῶν ἐρήμων καὶ χηρῶν ἀπεριστάτων τῶν τε ἐν πενίαις καὶ ἀσθενείαις ἀπερριμμένων ἐπίσκοπος ὥσπερ καὶ ἐπίκουρος πατρὸς καὶ κηδεμόνος δίκην ἀναπέφανται· ὅθεν δὴ εἰκότων πρὸς τοῦ τοῖς τοιοῖσδε μᾶλλον τῶν διὰ καπνοῦ καὶ αἵματος θυσιῶν χαίροντος θεοῦ τῆς κατὰ τὸ μαρτύριον παραδόξου κλήσεως ἠξιώθη' (MP 11.22 LR).

It is his pastoral care for the vulnerable in the Christian community (orphans, widows, the poor and sick) that marks him as a likely martyr, not his suitability for conflict, as we might expect. Seleucus provides perhaps the best example of this aspect of Eusebius' reshaping of the figure of the martyr. He is the latest example of a pattern we have found repeated throughout *The Martyrs of Palestine*. But to understand why Eusebius employs this particular rhetoric in his characterisations we must first understand those conceptions of authority which would have been more familiar to him and his audience.

3. Traditional Conceptions of Authority Figures

We have observed a repeated tendency in Eusebius' martyr stories in *The Martyrs of Palestine* to characterise state officials by their lack of self-control, and their failure to engage correctly or successfully with subordinates because of it. By contrast, the martyrs whom they treat so badly are marked by their remarkable demonstrations of precisely those characteristics. To fully understand the reasons behind this deliberate rhetorical strategy we must understand the classic conceptions of the authority of the state official and the role of the martyr against which Eusebius is reacting.

By the time Eusebius picked up his pen martyr narratives were already a feature of the early Christian literary corpus. Though earlier martyr stories were written at a diversity of time and locale that warns against over-generalisation, nevertheless recent scholarship has increasingly read martyr acts thought to date from the 2nd and 3rd centuries as the documents of a Christianity which conceived of itself as resistance movement.[46] These accounts of the trials and deaths of Christians sought to appropriate the cultural dynamics of the Roman arena. Since Foucault's theories of authority and humility appeared in 1977 a series of publications has outlined how the punishment of criminals in such a public setting was supposed to both humiliate the criminal and further establish the authority of the punishing state.[47] As Maureen Tilley argued in a seminal article, the Christian martyr's ability to endure torture and subsequent embrace of death removed this element of humiliation and so implicitly challenged the authority of the state.[48] Kate Cooper has pinpointed how this challenge worked. Since the martyr's declaration of the superiority of Christianity was

---

46 Judith Perkins has suggested that this literature was produced at the same time as, and as an alternative to, a competing corpus of Greek elite literature seeking different solutions to the perceived similar problems of living under the Roman hegemony. See e.g. Judith Perkins, *The Suffering Self: Pain and Narrative Representation in the Early Christian Era* (London/New York: Routledge, 1995). See also id., *Roman Imperial Identities in the Early Christian Era* (London/New York: Routledge, 2009).

47 Michel Foucault, *Discipline and Punish: The Birth of the Prison*, trans. Alan Sheridan (New York: Pantheon, 1977). See also e.g. David Potter, Martyrdom as spectacle, in: Ruth Scodel, ed., *Theater and Society in the Classical World* (Ann Arbor: University of Michigan Press, 1993), 53–88; Carlin Barton, The Scandal of the Arena, *Representations* 27 (1989), 1–36; Katherine Coleman, Fatal charades: Roman executions staged as mythological enactments, *JRS* 80 (1990), 44–73; Brent Shaw, Body/Power/Identity: Passions of the Martyrs, *JECS* 4 (1996), 269–312.

48 Maureen Tilley, The ascetic body and the (un)making of the world of the martyr, *JAAR* 59 (1991), 467–479;

vindicated by the persistence of his/her claim to truth under torture (the Roman method of testing truth claims), the competing claim of the official, of the superiority of the Roman hegemony, came under scrutiny instead.[49] These martyr narratives were designed to question the legitimacy of the whole Roman enterprise, and ultimately invalidate it.

For this reason in numerous 2nd and 3rd century martyr acts the focus is upon the agonistic contest between martyr and governor, where martyrs are conceived as powerful and charismatic competitors in a violent contest, and the state officials are remarkably neutral figures, serving simply as mouthpieces for the Roman establishment.[50] The defeat of the latter is thus the defeat of the ideal of the Roman Empire as a whole. It is this central dynamic that Eusebius reshapes in his own 4th century martyr narratives, where the martyr becomes an increasingly vulnerable figure in contrast to the indeterminate rage of the Roman judge.

Eusebius' literary characterisations also adopt and adapt basic conceptions of Roman official authority. I turn now to consider the scholarship of the last century which has changed our understanding of how the Romans envisaged the Roman official. I will discuss here the ideal qualities both of the Roman judge and the Roman political leader, since Christians in martyr narratives are most commonly tried under the so-called *cognitio ex ordine* process, and so are judged by Roman proconsuls.[51] These individuals play twin roles, since they act as legal judges for this particular case, but as governors are also local representatives of the emperor, and so embody his authority as a Roman leader.

The authority of the ideal *iudex* for the Romans was primarily marked by self-control and rationality. Jill Harries notes that the ideal judge acts fairly and must avoid cruel or threatening behaviour.[52] The exercise of authority can include ordering violent action if the situation demands, but it must be done without emotion, and the judge himself should remain remote. Harries notes that in late antique legal codes, if it could be demonstrated that he had acted in anger a judge could be

---

49 Kate Cooper, The Voice of the Victim: Gender, Representation and Early Christian Martyrdom, *The Bulletin of the John Rylands Library of Manchester* 80.3 (1998), 147–157.

50 Jill Harries, Constructing the Judge: Judicial accountability and the culture of criticism in late antiquity, in: Richard Miles, ed., *Constructing Identity in Late Antiquity* (London/New York: Routledge, 1999), 225, notes the remarkably neutral treatment of Roman officials in 2nd and 3rd century Christian martyr literature.

51 See e.g. Gary Bisbee, *Pre-Decian Acts of Martyrs and Commentarii*, HDR 22 (Philadelphia: Fortress Press, 1988).

52 Harries, Constructing the Judge, 219.

held liable for acting unjustly.[53] William Harris too in his 2002 survey of anger in the ancient world notes that control of temper was integral to the cumulative picture of positive official authority figures gleaned from imperial sources.[54] Though matters become more complicated in late antiquity, self-control remained the prime marker of authority for a judge, and in the eastern half of the empire at least the major component of "manliness".[55] This is intimately tied to the image of the Emperor propagated by Augustus: 'From Augustus' time onwards, the positive or negative character of a Roman ruler – and of a potential ruler – could be signalled by his control over his anger, or the lack of it.'[56] Most recently, Leanne Bablitz has drawn attention to the passivity of the Roman judge: his role is primarily as listener. If a contest occurs, it is between the defendants or between advocates – the judge is not supposed to be part of the courtroom "struggle".[57]

When we turn to the ideal image of the Roman leader, however, a further element becomes important. We can only understand the moral authority of the ideal Roman leader if we appreciate the close connections between this figure and the Roman *pater*. The classic statement of this link is Weinstock's 1971 *Divus Julius*. Weinstock traced the link between parenthood and political authority back to the award of the title *parens patriae* to Cicero. This title was later taken by Augustus, who also subsequently received the title *pater patriae* (which became standard for many successive emperors). Weinstock argued that the title was an expression of the emperor's unlimited political power, since he had complete authority over his subjects, much as the Roman father did over his son.[58] Recent scholarship has explored how

---

53 Harries, Constructing the Judge, 222.

54 William Harris, *Restraining Rage: The ideology of anger control in classical antiquity* (Cambridge MA./London: Harvard University Press, 2001).

55 For further discussion see e.g. Lin Foxhall/John Salmon, eds., *Thinking Men: Masculinity and its Self-Representation in the Classical Tradition* (London/New York: Routledge, 1998); id., eds., *When Men Were Men: Masculinity, Power and Identity in Classical Antiquity*, Leicester-Nottingham Studies in Ancient Society 8 (London/New York: Routledge, 1998); Joseph Roisman, *The Rhetoric of Manhood: Masculinity in the Attic Orators* (Berkeley: University of California Press, 2005); Lesley Dossey, *Wife Beating and Manliness in Late Antiquity*, PaP 199 (2008), 33.

56 Harris, *Restraining Rage*, 248; see also 111–116; 220–221, 241 and 261.

57 Leanne Bablitz, *Actors and Audience in the Roman Courtroom* (London/New York: Routledge, 2007), 89–90. Entry to the *album iudicum*, the list of judges, was in part dependent on a character examination, but the details of this have unfortunately not survived (ibid. 92-3).

58 Stefan Weinstock, *Divus Julius* (Oxford: Clarendon Press, 1971), 200–205. Weinstock does note in passing the importance of the affectionate side to the father in the

Augustus' reforms and self-stylising encouraged a familial model of government.[59] Beth Severy, for example, notes that as Augustus' rule progressed there developed 'a new way of conceiving of Augustus' role in the state – as the father of a Roman family.'[60] Leader and father were intertwined in the Roman imagination.

However, this recent scholarship has had to take into account a sea change in our understanding of the Roman father itself. Weinstock believed the core ideology of the Roman *pater* to be his absolute authority over his household and the obedience due to him. The work of Richard Saller in particular however has revealed that the authority of the *pater familias* was based as much on his positive treatment of his wife, children and other dependents as his ability to force them to obey.[61] Ideal paternal authority was thus based around the ability to elicit obedience in reciprocal, affectionate relationships. In particular, the Roman father should have no need of recourse to violence against any member of his household except small children.[62] Saller's suggestions have been largely accepted by subsequent scholarship on the

---

emperor's love for his people, but concentrates on the authoritarian implications and the unsymmetrical nature of the relationship now implied. See also Andreas Alföldi, *Der Vater des Vaterlandes im Römischen Denken* (Darmstadt: Wissenschaftliche Buchgesellschaft, 1971), 48–49 – for the assertion that clemency was one of the virtues of the parens but not the most important one.

59   Beth Severy, *Augustus and the Family at the Birth of the Roman Empire* (London/New York: Routledge, 2003), 158–186.

60   Severy, *Augustus and the Family*, 61.

61   For this classic view see e.g. Lewis Henry Morgan, *Ancient Society* (London: MacMullen & Co., 1877), London; more recently Paul Veyne, *A History of Private Life. From Pagan Rome to Byzantium* (Cambridge, MA: Belknap Press of Harvard University Press, 1987). Saller's critique built on the earlier questioning of John Crook, Patria Potestas, *CQ* n.s. 17 (1967), 113–122. His own publications here are extensive; see e.g. Richard Saller and Brent Shaw, Tombstones and Roman Family Relations in the Principate. Civilians, Soldiers and Slaves, *JRS* 74 (1984), 124–156; Richard Saller, Familia, Domus, and the Roman Conception of the Family, *Phoenix* 38 (1984), 336–355; id., Patria potestas and the Stereotype of the Roman Family, *Continuity and Change* 1 (1986), 7–22; id., Slavery and the Roman Family, *Slavery and Abolition* 8 (1987), 65–87; id., Pietas, Obligation, and Authority in the Roman Family, in: Peter Kneissl/Volker Losemann, eds., *Alte Geschichte und Wissenschaftsgeschichte: Festschrift für Karl Christ zum 65. Geburtstag* (Darmstadt: Wissenschaftliche Buchgesellschaft, 1988), 392–410; id., Roman Kinship: Structure and Sentiment, in: Beryl Rawson/Paul Weaver, eds., *The Roman Family in Italy: Status, sentiment, space* (Oxford: Clarendon Press, 1999), 7–34.

62   See especially Richard Saller, Corporal Punishment, Authority and Obedience in the Roman Household, in: Beryl Rawson, ed., *Marriage, Divorce and Children in Ancient Rome* (Oxford: Clarendon Press, 1991 [repr. 2004]), 157–164.

Roman family[63], and though the nature of Saller's evidence means his own conclusions only hold until the end of the 2nd century, scholars extending his investigations into late antiquity have found that in the Greek East at least his conclusions remain valid.[64]

This fundamental shift in our conception of the Roman father's authority has impacted upon our understanding of the use of paternal imagery in describing Roman leaders. [65] Eva Marie Lassen in an excellent article on metaphorical use of Roman family imagery notes that in Cicero or Pliny's treatments of the father-leader synergy it is specifically the father's temperance that is associated with the ideal official.[66] Of the paternal characteristics attributed to Augustus, the most common was paternal *clementia*, and this virtue featured prominently in early imperial "propaganda". It is precisely this ability of the Roman father to elicit obedience based on mutual affection rather than violent discipline, fore-grounded by Saller, that we find most commonly utilised in contemporary discussions of recommended behaviour for Roman officials. This attitude towards one's dependents is bound up

---

63 See e.g. Suzanne Dixon, *The Roman Family* (Baltimore/London: Johns Hopkins University Press, 1992).

64 Antti Arjava has confirmed that legally at least 'There can be no doubt that patria potestas continued to be the cornerstone of Roman family law, and also an essential element of the law of property and inheritance', Antti Arjava, *Paternal Power in Late Antiquity*, JRS 88 (1998), 164. Emiel Eyben, Fathers and Sons, in: Beryl Rawson, ed., *Marriage, Divorce and Children in Ancient Rome* (Oxford: Clarendon Press, 1991 [repr. 2004]), 114–143, and Peter Garnsey, Sons, Slaves – and Christians, in: Beryl Rawson/Paul Weaver, *The Roman Family in Italy*, 101–121 agree in essence that concrete attitudes towards the distinction between sons and slaves did not change, although Garnsey maintains that metaphorical use of the language related to them did. For an evolution in attitudes towards violence in particular in the West see e.g. Theodore De Bruyn, Flogging a Son: The Emergence of the pater flagellans in Latin Christian Discourse, JECS 7 (1999), 249–290.

65 'By integrating the family metaphors – the metaphors of father and son in particular – into the political and administrative system, some of the attitudes and ideals connected with the family were transferred to the attitudes and ideals connected with certain public offices' (Eva Marie Lassen, The Roman Family: Ideal and Metaphor, in: Halvor Moxnes, ed., *Constructing Early Christian Families: Family as Social Reality and Metaphor* (London/New York: Routledge, 1997), 111).

66 When Cicero gained the title parens patriae, it was specifically for his salvific actions in saving Rome from Catiline's conspiracy, and various military commanders were also called pater in recognition of their acts on behalf of the people. When Octavian gained the title in 45/44 BC, the official reason was because he had saved the country from civil war. The same is true of the eventual awarding of the title pater patriae; though he was not given the title officially until 2 BC, there are extant coins from 20 BC where he was proclaimed *conservator* and *parens*: "SPQR PARENTI... CONS(ervatori) SUO"; see Lassen, *The Roman Family*, 113.

with the good leader's self-control. [67] Harris observes that the good ruler should restrain his anger towards his subjects just as the good father curbs his anger towards wife and children.[68] It is a self-control that engenders such calm, reciprocal dealings with one's dependents that marks the ideal Roman father and, by extension, Roman leader.

This connection between Roman leader and Roman father has great significance in literary assessments of authoritative figures in the antique world. If the qualities of the good leader are those of the good father, it follows that a leader can be judged by his ability to demonstrate the characteristics of the good Roman *pater*. In her 1992 article, Kate Cooper, building on Helen North's concept of a "rhetoric of *sophrosune*" and Jack Winkler's use of that motif, explains the need for modern scholars to appreciate literary manipulations of a rhetoric of (in)temperance in antique descriptions of a man's domestic affairs as a way of assessing his suitability for public office.[69] In a society characterised by "zero-sum competition" for positions of authority, casting aspersions on the domestic capabilities of others, and defending and advertising your own abilities in that sphere was crucial.[70]

In a more recent article Cooper considers the rhetorical implications of Saller's picture of a reciprocal relationship between parent and child.[71] In explaining how public authority of Roman officials was dependent on their cultivation and performance of private power, she emphasises that a man's claim to legitimate authority was grounded in the public demonstration of his ability to elicit loyal obedience from

---

67 I note myself for example Juvenal, commenting: "When you finally enter your long-awaited province as its Governor, bridle and limit your anger and your greed, too, have some sympathy for the impoverished provincials" ('Expectata diu tandem provincia cum te rectorem accipiet, pone irae frena modumque pone et avaritiae, miserere inopum sociorum...', *Satires* 8.87–89); transl. by Susanna Morton Braund, *Juvenal and Persius*, LCL 91 (Cambridge, MA: Harvard University Press, 2004).

68 Harris, *Restraining Rage*, 316.

69 Kate Cooper, Insinuations of Womanly Influence: An Aspect of the Christianization of the Roman Aristocracy, *JRS* 82 (1992), 150–164; citing Helen North, *Sophrosyne. Self-Knowledge and Restraint in Classical Antiquity* (Ithaca: Cornell University Press, 1966) and Jack Winkler, *The Constraints of Desire: The Anthropology of Sex and Gender in Ancient Greece* (London/New York: Routledge, 1990).

70 Cooper, Insinuations, 152. See also id., *The Virgin and the Bride* (Cambridge, MA./London: Harvard University Press, 1996) for a discussion of how in ancient literature sexual temperance emerges as an index by which to measure the claims to power of male protagonists (12-13), which in turn can provide the means by which a group can claim the allegiance of new members by indicating the moral superiority of its leadership over and against the leadership of other groups (17).

71 Kate Cooper, Closely Watched Households: Visibility, Exposure, and Private Power in the Roman domus, *PaP* 197 (2007), 7.

dependents in his own household. Cooper hypothesises that a desire to publicise the extent of a man's temperate authority in his private life in order to imply something about his ability to wield authority in public lies behind the characterisation of protagonists in many ancient writings.

Eusebius' own education and prolific reading habits are well known. I suggest he had a keen awareness of the value of rhetorical representation. The evidence from *The Martyrs of Palestine* above reveals a keen interest in manipulating depictions of a man's self-control and his treatment of dependents. It is precisely for a public inability to elicit willing obedience from their dependents that Eusebius condemns Urban and Firmilian, and why they resort to violent means. It is also precisely this quality that Pamphilus demonstrates so effortlessly. It is no coincidence that Eusebius repeatedly constructs martyrs and state officials around this rhetoric of the temperate *pater*; he is guiding his late antique readers in their assessments of them and their respective claims to power.

4. Literary Manipulations of Traditional Conceptions of Authority

The true aim of Eusebius' steps towards a new stylisation of martyrs and state officials becomes clearer in the light of this scholarship. His portraits of martyrs and state officials are deliberately constructed as polar opposites to demonstrate Urban and Firmilian's failure to elicit willing obedience from the martyrs. The bestial rage of Urban, Firmilian and their attendees demonstrates a complete lack of precisely that self-control which defines Apphianus, Theodosia and the companions of Pamphilus. Apphianus is self-controlled under torture, a process designed to wear away his self-possession, while Urban unexpectedly rages in a manner inappropriate to his age and station. Theodosia as a mere girl demonstrates that temperance which would mark Urban as a legitimate bearer of authority, but which he fails to demonstrate. This is a novel form of the inversion-motif found in earlier martyr narratives.

A similar inversion marks Eusebius' second shift in characterisation. The state officials' failure to elicit obedience from the martyrs is emphasised by their failure to treat them with the reciprocal respect with which good Roman men approached their dependents. The martyrs, on the other hand, do demonstrate this awareness of those around them, since Eusebius concentrates more than his literary predecessors on the martyrs' concern for others. Apphianus shows concern for

Urban's spiritual well-being, and despite Theodosia's initial request for help from other martyrs, in the event it is her martyrdom that saves their lives. Many of those surrounding Pamphilus are marked by their concern for others. Again, as with their respective demonstrations of self-control, the contrast between martyr and official is constructed to illustrate the failing of the latter as a good Roman *pater*, and thus as a good Roman leader.

Eusebius' genius is in constructing narrative scenarios which bring out the domestic overtones of these encounters, and enforce for the reader the illegitimacy of the state official's behaviour. What is implicit in the cases of the young martyrs Apphianus and Theodosia (well-educated and virginal respectively – perfect Roman children) before the powerful Roman man Urban is taken a stage further in the brilliant construction of Porphyry's confrontation with Firmilian. It is when Firmilian is presented with Porphyry, the youngest martyr and the one who most easily fits a father-son paradigm that Eusebius drives home the image of the wrathful, out-of-control governor. This comes immediately after we have been told about Pamphilus' treatment of the boy (his servant and pupil) as if he were his father. Pamphilus in treating his servant like his son elicits a public demonstration of loyal obedience which Firmilian cannot do, either from Porphyry or from his own servant, Theodolus. We cannot help but judge Firmilian next to Pamphilus. This is a clear example of Eusebius' subtle manipulation of the intertwining threads between the Roman authority figure and the Roman *pater*. Here most clearly the atmosphere of the *domus* is imposed on the courtroom.

In *The Martyrs of Palestine* then, Eusebius' first narrative about past interactions between church and state, we see the beginnings of new characterisations of both martyrs and their opponents. This takes the shape of a novel form of that inversion motif characteristic of earlier martyr literature, but based now around a manipulation of the connected themes of rational self-control and care of one's dependents. This novelty is motivated by Eusebius unique historical position.

5. Historical Motivations for Literary Manipulations of Authority Figures

In these fragments of the long recension of *The Martyrs of Palestine* the Roman governor is no longer the rational figure simply carrying out his job, characteristic of earlier martyr literature. He has become instead a feral beast incapable of controlling his emotions, unable to elicit willing obedience from his subordinates and thus unsuitable for public office. In addition and as a consequence, the martyrs are increasingly defined by their calm self-control and thoughtful interactions with other martyrs and the wider Christian community. We are witnessing here the beginning of a reworking of the medium of the martyr narrative.

These rhetorical manipulations are more than literary sophism. In an empire of such size and with a relatively small administrative network, the effects of literary depictions of authority figures could be far-reaching.[72] Eusebius' literary manipulation of his audience in assessing martyrs and officials will have influenced subsequent generations' actual attitudes. Eusebius was the first prominent writer of the peace of the church after Diocletian's Great Persecution ended, and the writer most associated with the Constantinian revolution. It is by reference to this 4th century context that I would point to the beginnings of an explanation for Eusebius' literary tactics. I suggest that he saw one of his tasks as a historian in this key moment as the re-appropriation of certain symbolic figures of preceding centuries for this new order where church and state could conceivably be aligned.

In their description of an inversion of authority, Eusebius' martyr narratives echo those of the preceding centuries. In his martyr narratives, as there, the martyrs emerge successful, and the authority of their opponents disintegrates. But Eusebius' consistent use of the particular rhetoric of the temperate Roman *pater* means that the consequences in his narratives are very different. While it is true that the Christian figures emerge as better models of authority, they no longer do so as exemplars of resistance. Their authority is not that of Christianity conceived over and above that of the Roman Empire. Instead (and this is Eusebius' true goal) they acquire precisely that type of authority which the state officials fail to demonstrate; the authority of the good Roman leader and *pater*. Their persistent self-control and positive treatment of dependents marks them as the true inheritors of the Roman ideal of legitimate authority. In short, they succeed because they embody the ideals of the Roman state better than its legal representatives do.

It is no coincidence that the figures of greatest authority in *The Martyrs of Palestine* are the most senior Christians, Pamphilus and

---

72   See e.g. Cameron, *Christianity and the Rhetoric of Empire*, 140: 'Since everything conspired to make of the fourth century a time when rhetoric did indeed convey power, Christians needed to make it their own'.

Seleucus.[73] Their authority is based on their pastoral activities, and in the case of Pamphilus his extensive education and learning as well (an education it is worth noting that Apphianus and Porphyry share; they are all examples of the Christian *literati*). These inheritors of true Roman authority are not the volatile, resistant martyrs of earlier literature; they are the educated, altruistic Christian elite. In *The Martyrs of Palestine* we see the beginnings of a transfer of authority – ideal Roman authority – from state officials to the Christian clergy.

Eusebius' motivation for the rabid characterisation of the Roman state officials is explicable in this light. In pre-Eusebian martyr literature Roman officials are good representatives of the system, and so their failure is a failure of the whole imperial criminal justice system and the ideology it supports. Eusebian officials, however, are unfit for public office and thus simply bad representatives of the state. Counter-intuitively, the state mechanisms themselves are damaged less by Eusebius' martyr stories, since they condemn examples of bad author-ity figures of preceding centuries only, not the viability of the Roman empire as a whole. As the mechanisms of the Roman administration increasingly worked in the church's favour, Eusebius would have had less and less use for a dynamic between martyrs and officials that undermined those mechanisms. Instead, he constructs narratives where those mechanisms remain intact but the Roman authority to operate them is transferred from government officials, who proved individually unworthy, to Christian clergy, who do demonstrate the necessary *romanitas*.[74] Eusebius' martyr narratives are less concerned with the triumph of the Christian martyr over the Roman state official than with the transfer of true Roman authority and the right to govern from those officials to their successors as the new Roman men, the Christian clergy.

---

73 Lawlor and Oulton claim in their commentary that Seleucus must be a member of the clergy, but since his rank is not stated they hypothesise that he may have had a role connected with the care of widows (*Eusebius* II, 332).

74 For the connections between the roles of Roman magistrates and Christian bishops see most recently Kate Cooper, Christianity, Private Power, and the Law from Decius to Constantine: The Minimalist View, *JECS* 19 (2011), 327–343, esp. 332.

PETER GEMEINHARDT

Vita Antonii oder *Passio Antonii*?

Biographisches Genre und martyrologische Topik in der ersten Asketenvita

1. Einleitung

Der Begriff des Martyriums hat das Potenzial, zu ganz unterschiedlichen Zeiten und unter wechselnden Bedingungen als Interpretament des authentischen christlichen Glaubens zu fungieren. Man könnte dies an zahlreichen Stationen der Geschichte des Christentums bis zu den Märtyrern des 20. Jahrhunderts und zum Sterben des jüngst selig gesprochenen Papstes Johannes Paul II. nachzeichnen.[1] Neben dieser Kontinuität in der Vielfalt gibt es allerdings in der Geschichte des Christentums auch Zeiträume, in denen sich signifikante Transformationen von Gegenständen und Begriffen vollziehen – so auch in Bezug auf das Verständnis des Martyriums. Hierbei zählt das 4. Jahrhundert gewiss zu den entscheidenden Epochen. Daher möchte ich den Blick auf die spätantiken Quellen richten und fragen, welche Entwicklung die Vorstellung des Martyriums in dieser Zeit genommen hat und welche Erfahrungen nun damit in Verbindung gebracht wurden, konkret: wie es dazu gekommen ist, dass auch jemand, der nicht gewaltsam gestorben war, als genuiner Nachahmer Christi angesehen werden konnte. Dass in der Zeit nach der großen Christenverfolgung unter Diokletian und seinen Mitregenten das Verständnis des Martyriums als *Blut*- (wieder) in Richtung einer *Glaubens*zeugenschaft geöffnet wurde, ist nicht strittig. Ob aber die Asketen des 4. Jahrhunderts einfach das Erbe der Märtyrer der Verfolgungszeiten antraten, wie aus einer klassischen Untersuchung von Edward Malone hervorzugehen

---

1   Vgl. Peter Gemeinhardt, *Die Heiligen. Von den frühchristlichen Märtyrern bis zur Gegenwart* (München: C.H. Beck, 2010). Zum frühchristlichen Martyriumsverständnis vgl. jetzt auch Candida R. Moss, The Other Christs. Imitating Jesus in Ancient Christian Ideologies of Martyrdom (Oxford: Oxford University Press, 2010).

scheint[2], wie sich dieser Übergang vollzogen hat und inwiefern sich Martyrologie im traditionellen und neuen Sinne begegnen, ja überlappen, scheint mir dagegen nicht völlig deutlich zu sein. Dass auch schon in vorkonstantinischer Zeit das Martyriumsverständnis asketisch konnotiert war, hat Maureen Tilley plausibel dargelegt.[3] Ich frage umgekehrt, inwieweit das asketische Ideal, das in der Spätantike rapide an Bedeutung gewinnt, martyrologisch grundiert ist und bleibt. An einem Text lässt sich diese Transformation *in nuce* nachvollziehen: an der *Vita Antonii* des Athanasius von Alexandrien. Diesen Text werde ich im Folgenden nach terminologischen und theologischen Transformation des frühchristlichen Märtyrerdiskurses befragen, was auch das Problem der literarischen Gattung dieser ersten christlichen Asketenvita einschließt.[4]

Die *Vita Antonii* steht am Beginn der christlichen Heiligenbiographie.[5] Ihr voraus gehen nur die Lebensbeschreibung des Cyprian von Karthago, die Hieronymus eine *Vita et Passio* nennt, die aber formal eine Gedenkrede ist[6] und deren Wirkung man in der hagiographischen

---

2   Edward E. Malone, The Monk and the Martyr, in: Basilius Steidle, ed., *Antonius Magnus Eremita. Studia ad antiquum monachismum spectantia*, StAns 38 (Rom: Herder, 1956), 201–228; dieser Aufsatz stellt eine gekürzte Fassung der fast gleichnamigen Monographie desselben Verfassers dar: Edward E. Malone, *The Monk and the Martyr: The Monk as Successor of the Martyr*, SCA 12 (Washington D.C.: The Catholic University of America Press, 1950).

3   Vgl. Maureen Tilley, The Ascetic Body and the (Un)Making of the World of the Martyr, *JAAR* 59 (1991), 467–479, hier 468: „Asceticism flourished within Christianity from its inception. But toward the end of the second century, when the persecution of Christianity became more intense, asceticism provided the theoretical and practical basis for heroic martyrdom." Dass Askese weit mehr ist als der Verzicht auf Nahrungsaufnahme, zeigt eine von Euseb (h.e. V 3,2) berichtete Episode: Der Bekenner Alkibiades wurde durch eine Offenbarung ermahnt, er möge durch seine radikale Verzichtsaskese nicht den anderen Anstoß geben – fortan aß er normal!

4   Die vorliegende Untersuchung steht im Kontext meines Forschungsprojekts „Religiöse und gesellschaftliche Leitbilder in spätantiken Heiligenviten", aus dem 2013 auch eine Monographie zu Antonius hervorgehen wird. Im Folgenden wird keine erschöpfende Dokumentation von Forschungsgeschichte und -stand geboten; die Anmerkungen beschränken sich auf die für die Darstellung nötigen Nachweise.

5   BHG 140; zitiert wird nach der kritischen Edition von Gerard J.M. Bartelink, ed., *Vie d'Antoine, introduction, texte critique, traduction, notes et index*, SC 400 (Paris: Editions du Cerf, 1994; ³2011); Abkürzung: VA.

6   BHL 2041; vgl. Hieronymus, vir. ill. 68; zur rhetorischen Struktur vgl. Peter Lebrecht Schmidt, Die Cyprian-Vita des Presbyters Paulinus – Biographie oder laudatio funebris?, in: Lore Benz, ed., *ScriptOralia Romana. Die römische Literatur zwischen Mündlichkeit und Schriftlichkeit*, ScriptOralia 118 (Tübingen: Narr, 2001), 305–318.

Literatur vor Augustin nicht überschätzen sollte[7], und die Kollektiv-
biographie des Euseb von Caesarea über die palästinischen Märtyrer
der diokletianischen Verfolgung (*De martyribus Palaestinae*).[8] Keiner der
beiden Texte scheint von Athanasius als literarisches Vorbild der *Vita
Antonii* herangezogen worden zu sein. Bezogen auf Antonius stehen
sich in der Forschung vielmehr zwei Interpretationsstränge gegenüber:
Zum einen wird nach gattungsgeschichtlichen Vorbildern gefragt und
dabei häufig auf Jamblichs und Porphyrius' Pythagorasviten hingewiesen, um Form und Konzept der *Vita Antonii* durch den Vergleich
mit solchen zeitgenössischen Philosophenbiographien zu erhellen. Zum
anderen wird nach der Verwandlung des Märtyrers in einen asketisch
lebenden Heiligen gefragt, womit nicht literarische, sondern inhaltliche
Vorbilder in den Blick kommen. Ich möchte im Folgenden beide
Perspektiven verbinden. Die Gattungsfrage scheint nämlich gerade
dann sinnvoll beantwortet werden zu können, wenn man nicht nur
nach ihren literatur- und philosophiegeschichtlichen, sondern ebenso
nach ihren kirchen- und theologiegeschichtlichen Kontexten fragt. Das
klingt evident, ist es aber tatsächlich nicht: Denn die Diskussion um
Abhängigkeiten der *Vita Antonii* von Pythagoras- oder anderen Viten
ist bisher nicht hinreichend mit der Werk- und Lebensgeschichte des
Verfassers verbunden worden. Athanasius war aber eben nicht nur
Apologet, Polemiker, Theologe und asketischer Autor, sondern vor

---

7   Gregor von Nazianz verwechselt in seinem Panegyricus auf Cyprian von Karthago
    (BHG 457) diesen mit seinem Namensvetter von Antiochien – die Kenntnisse über
    den afrikanischen Primas können also bei den Theologen im griechischen Osten,
    nicht allzu groß gewesen sein! Insofern geht die Einschätzung von Monique
    Alexandre, La construction d'un modèle de sainteté dans la Vie d'Antoine par
    Athanase d'Alexandrie, in: Philippe Walter, ed., *Saint Antoine entre mythe et légende*
    (Grenoble: ELLUG, Université Stendhal, 1996), 63–93, hier 68 („La forme profane de
    le biographie, lorsqu'Athanase se met à l'oeuvre, a déjà été christianisée") sowohl im
    Blick auf den Autor als auch hinsichtlich der Form zu weit. Zur *Vita Cypriani* vgl.
    Ekkehard Mühlenberg, Les débuts de la biographie chrétienne, *RThPh* 122 (1990),
    517–529; wieder in: ders., *Gott in der Geschichte. Ausgewählte Aufsätze zur Kirchen-
    geschichte*, Ute Mennecke/Stefanie Frost, eds., AKG 110 (Berlin/New York: Walter de
    Gruyter, 2008), 442–454.

8   Vgl. hierzu den Beitrag von James Corke-Webster im vorliegenden Band. Ein
    Sonderfall ist Eusebs *Vita Constantini*, die freilich kein hagiographisches, sondern ein
    panegyrisches Interesse verfolgt, möglicherweise aber auch auf die christliche
    Hagiographie Einfluss ausgeübt hat; vgl. Averil Cameron, Form and Meaning: The
    „Vita Constantini" and the „Vita Antonii", in: Thomas Hägg/Philip Rousseau, eds.,
    Greek Biography and Panegyric in Late Antiquity, The Transformation of the Classical
    Heritage 31 (Berkeley u.a.: University of California Press, 2000), 72–88; Michael S.
    Williams, *Authorised Lives in Early Christian Biography. Between Eusebius and Augustine*
    (Cambridge: Cambridge University Press, 2008), 25–57.

allem Bischof.[9] Als solcher war er *ex officio* mit dem regen Märtyrerkult in Alexandrien und Ägypten befasst und zugleich verantwortlich für eine Kirche, in der es seiner Auffassung nach keinesfalls nur für Blutzeugen und Wüstenväter, sondern auch für die „Durchschnitts-christen" Platz geben musste.[10] Insofern ist es höchst bezeichnend, dass Athanasius in einer Situation, die er als Martyrium empfand, einerseits Martyriumsterminologie aufgriff, in der *Vita Antonii* aber andererseits ein neues Leitbild entwickelte, das ohne *Sterben für Christus* auskam und stattdessen das *Leiden für Christus im Leben* in den Mittelpunkt stellte. Kurz, wir haben es hier nicht nur mit einer *Vita Antonii*, sondern auch mit einer das ganze Leben umfassenden *Passio Antonii* zu tun.

Überscharfe Alternativen zwischen *Vita* und *Passio* und zwischen Askese und Martyrium sind dabei allerdings zu vermeiden. Der βίος, als den erst die Tradition das Werk angesehen hat[11], obwohl es sich selbst als Brief ausgibt, ist keine Märtyrerakte wie in den klassischen Sammlungen. Auch von literarisch entfalteten Passionen (Polykarp oder Perpetua und Felicitas) trennt die Antoniusbiographie manches, abgesehen von dem gar nicht gewaltsam erfolgenden Tod des Asketen. Dennoch bezeugt die *Vita Antonii* eine Überlappung von Märtyrer-passion und Asketenvita – und dies in einer Situation, in der noch überhaupt nicht klar war, in welche Richtung sich der hagiographische Diskurs fortentwickeln würde. Ich werde argumentieren, dass inner-halb des Textes das Element der *Passio* dem der *Vita* vorausgeht. Darüber hinaus gibt es gute Gründe, Athanasius' Antoniusvita nicht in erster Linie als Rezeption paganer Philosophenbiographien, sondern vielmehr als eine ausgreifende Märtyrerpassion zu verstehen, die erst von späteren Generationen (zumal in ihrer lateinischen Übersetzung) als die „spirituelle Biographie" gelesen wurde, als die sie Marc van

---

9   Vgl. dazu jetzt Tobias Georges, Der Bischof, in: Peter Gemeinhardt, ed., *Athanasius Handbuch* (Tübingen: Mohr Siebeck, 2011), 82–93.

10 Peter Gemeinhardt, Kirche, in: ders., ed., *Athanasius Handbuch*, 335–343, hier 342.

11 Bartelink gibt in seiner Edition (s. Anm. 5) den Titel des prämetaphrastischen Manuskripts *D* (*). Dietmar Wyrwa, Literarische und theologische Gestaltungs-elemente der Vita Antonii des Athanasius, in: Johannes van Oort/Dietmar Wyrwa, eds., *Autobiographie und Hagiographie in der christlichen Antike*, SPA 7 (Leuven: Peeters, 2009), 12–62, hier 18 weist darauf hin, dass dies ebenso wie die Erwäh-nungen eines βίος im Text selbst auf das konkrete Leben des Antonius, nicht auf eine Gattung verweist. Vgl. aber die Formulierung in Pachomii Vita prima 99 (in: François Halkin, ed., *Le corpus athénien de Saint Pachôme*, Cahiers d'orientalisme 2 [Genf: Cramer, 1982], 66,24f.): ὁ βίος τοῦ μακαρίου Ἀντωνίου πρὸς τοὺς ἐν τῇ ξένῃ μοναχούς und die noch kürzere, vermutlich auf das griechische Original zurückgehende Angabe des Evagrius in seiner zeitgenössischen Übersetzung (BHL 609): *Athanasius episcopus ad peregrinos fratres*.

Uytfanghe – rezeptionsgeschichtlich gesehen durchaus zu Recht – klassifiziert hat.[12]

Ich will diese These in drei Schritten entfalten, indem ich zunächst einige Überlegungen zur Gattung der *Vita Antonii* anstelle und auf die oft behauptete Beeinflussung durch Pythagorasviten eingehe (2). Sodann werde ich die *Vita Antonii* daraufhin befragen, inwieweit in ihr martyrologische Topik – möglicherweise in Umformung – begegnet (3), und schließlich die Ergebnisse in die Martyriumsthematik in Athanasius' weiteres Werk, zumal im Zeitraum der Abfassung der *Vita Antonii*, einordnen (4). Am Ende steht ein kurzes Fazit (5).

2. Eine Philosophenvita? Eine ältere These und ihre neueste Reformulierung

2.1. Pythagorasviten als Vorbilder der *Vita Antonii*? Ein Rückblick

Die Erforschung der altkirchlichen Hagiographie war im 20. Jahrhundert über weite Strecken von dem Ziel geprägt, klassische literarische Vorbilder für christliche Heiligenleben zu identifizieren. Die dafür häufig in Anspruch genommene Unterscheidung eines „peripatetisch-plutarchischen" vom „alexandrinisch-suetonischen" Typ der antiken Biographie ist mittlerweile verabschiedet worden, da sich eine solche Akzentuierung nach Chronologie oder Rubriken zwar heuristisch anwenden lässt, im konkreten Fall aber kaum eine Vita trennscharf dem einen oder anderen Typ zuzurechnen ist.[13] Hier führt der von Marc van Uytfanghe im Anschluss an Michel de Certeau eingeführte Begriff des „hagiographischen Diskurses" weiter, insofern er sowohl die klassischen biographischen Gattungen als auch ganz andere Textsorten für die Beschreibung von Heiligenleben programmatisch fruchtbar macht.[14] Dennoch bleibt die Frage bestehen, ob Athanasius in der *Vita Antonii* einem konkreten Vorbild – und wenn ja, welchem –

---

12 Marc van Uytfanghe, Biographie II (spirituelle), *RAC Suppl* 1 (2001), 1088–1364, hier 1171: „Eine Annäherung an die spirituelle Biographie erfolgt, sobald auch das dem Martyrium voraufgehende Leben, der βίος πρὸ τοῦ μαρτυρίου, Beachtung und Darstellung findet, entweder als Teil der Passio oder als selbständige Ergänzung"; zur *Vita Antonii* vgl. aaO. 1181–1187.

13 Dazu Marc van Uytfanghe, Heiligenverehrung II (Hagiographie), *RAC* 14 (1988), 150–183, hier 164.

14 Zum Begriff vgl. Michel de Certeau, Eine Variante: Hagiographische Erbauung, in: ders., *Das Schreiben der Geschichte*, Historische Studien 4 (Frankfurt u.a.: Campus, 1991), 198–213; zuerst französisch: L'écriture de l'histoire (Paris: Gallimard, 1975).

folgt. Dafür gibt es eine selbst schon klassische Lösung, die kurz in Erinnerung gerufen sei.

Die Diskussion über die Gattung der *Vita Antonii* zu Beginn des 20. Jahrhunderts ging meist von den 1901 von Friedrich Leo entwickelten biographischen Typen aus (s.o.).[15] Hans Mertel identifizierte die *Vita Antonii* als „peripatetisch-plutarchisch", wenn auch nicht ohne eine gewisse Eigenständigkeit gegenüber dem Typus.[16] Karl Holl interpretierte sie dagegen als „Aufstiegsbiographie", deren Vorbilder in Antisthenes' *Herakles* oder in Philostrats *Vita Apollonii* lägen.[17] Richard Reitzenstein folgte wiederum Mertel in der Klassifizierung als „plutarchisch", ebenso – mit Differenzierungen im Detail – Anton Prießnig.[18] Akzeptiert wurde weithin – auch dort, wo man eher einen Panegyricus als *genus proximum* annehmen wollte (Johann List, Samuel Cavallin[19]) – Reitzensteins Identifizierung einer Passage aus Porphyrius' *Vita Pythagorae* als Parallele, ja möglicherweise sogar Quelle für die Beschreibung des Antonius, der nach zwanzig Jahren Abgeschiedenheit in einem verlassenen Kastell wieder an die Öffentlichkeit tritt: Weil sich viele Menschen wünschten, „seiner Askese nachzueifern" und im Übereifer sogar die Tür aufbrachen, „kam Antonius schließlich hervor wie aus einem Heiligtum, in alle Mysterien eingeweiht und für Gott begeistert."[20] Die für die Quellenfrage wichtigen Sätze lauten:

---

15   Vgl. dazu ausführlich Gerard J.M. Bartelink, Die literarische Gattung der Vita Antonii. Struktur und Motive, *VigChr* 36 (1982), 38–62; knapper ders., Introduction, in: ders., ed., *Vie d'Antoine*, 62–67; vgl. jetzt auch Dmitrij Bumazhnov, Monastische Schriften, in: Gemeinhardt, ed., *Athanasius Handbuch*, 255–265, hier 256f.

16   Hans Mertel, *Die biographische Form der griechischen Heiligenlegenden* (München: Wolf, 1909), 19.98 u.ö.

17   Vgl. Karl Holl, Die schriftstellerische Form des griechischen Heiligenlebens, in: ders., *Der Osten*, vol. 2, *Gesammelte Aufsätze zur Kirchengeschichte* (Tübingen: J.C.B. Mohr [Paul Siebeck], 1928), 249–269, hier 253f.; skeptisch hierzu Samuel Rubenson, Anthony and Pythagoras. A Reappraisal of the Appropriation of Classical Biography in Athanasius' „Vita Antonii", in: David Brakke u.a., eds., *Beyond Reception. Mutual Influences between Antique Religion, Judaism and Early Christianity* (Frankfurt: Peter Lang, 2006), 191–208, hier 200; ebenso Wyrwa, *Gestaltungselemente*, 42f.

18   Richard Reitzenstein, *Des Athanasius Werk über das Leben des Antonius. Ein philologischer Beitrag zur Geschichte des Mönchtums*, SHAW.PH 1914,8 (Heidelberg: Winter, 1914), 30; Anton Prießnig, *Die biographischen Formen der griechischen Heiligenleben* (Diss. phil. München, 1924), 23–35.

19   Johann List, *Das Antoniusleben des hl. Athanasius d. Gr. Eine literarhistorische Studie zu den Anfängen der byzantinischen Hagiographie*, TBNGP 11 (Athen: Sakellarios, 1930), 22f.; Samuel Cavallin, *Literarhistorische und textkritische Studien zur Vita S. Caesarii Arelatensis*, Lunds Universitets Årsskrift, Avd. 1, N.S. 30,7 (Lund: Gleerup, 1934).

20   VA 14,2: Μετὰ δὲ ταῦτα, πολλῶν ποθούντων καὶ ζηλῶσαι θελόντων τὴν ἄσκησιν αὐτοῦ, ἄλλων τε γνωρίμων ἐλθόντων καὶ βίᾳ τὴν θύραν καταβαλόντων καὶ

„Jene [sc. die Menschen] nun, als sie ihn sahen, wunderten sich, denn sie nahmen wahr, dass sein Leib dasselbe Aussehen hatte (wie vorher); dass er weder verfettet war aus Mangel an Bewegung, noch mürbe gemacht wie vom Fasten und vom Kampf gegen die Dämonen – sondern genauso (sah er aus), wie sie ihn vor seinem Weggang gekannt hatten. Der Zustand seiner Seele wiederum war rein. Denn weder war sie von einer Betrübnis eingehüllt, noch überströmend vor Heiterkeit, noch verwirrt von Lachen oder Scham. Weder versetzte ihn der Anblick der Menge in Unruhe, noch berührte es ihn, dass er von so vielen umarmt wurde, vielmehr war er ganz sich gleich, wie vom Logos selbst geleitet und gefestigt in der seiner Natur entsprechenden Art."[21]

Tatsächlich finden sich bei Porphyrius vergleichbare, ja teilweise identische Formulierungen: Pythagoras tritt aus einem Heiligtum (ἄδυτον) hervor, lässt keine körperlichen Veränderungen erkennen, ist weder aufgedunsen noch zermürbt von der Abgeschiedenheit und hat denselben Seelenzustand wie zuvor.[22] Er verkörpert damit perfekt das asketische Ideal, das Jamblich in seiner *Vita Pythagorica* entfaltet. [23] Während die skizzierte Passage bei Porphyrius mit einiger Wahrscheinlichkeit als Quelle der *Vita Antonii* gelten darf, haben sich dagegen andere Belege, die Reitzenstein identifizieren zu können meinte, als weit weniger einschlägig erwiesen. Über Porphyrius und Jamblich hinaus hat Oliver Overwien kürzlich Lukians *Demonax* als Vorlage einiger Stellen der *Vita Antonii* plausibel zu machen versucht[24];

ἐξεωσάντων, προῆλθεν ὁ Ἀντώνιος ὥσπερ ἔκ τινος ἀδύτου μεμυσταγωγημένος καὶ θεοφορούμενος.

21　VA 14,3f.: Ἐκεῖνοι μὲν οὖν, ὡς εἶδον, ἐθαύμαζον ὁρῶντες αὐτοῦ τό τε σῶμα τὴν αὐτὴν ἕξιν ἔχον, καὶ μήτε πιανθὲν ὡς ἀγύμναστον, μήτε ἰσχνωθὲν ὡς ἀπὸ νηστειῶν καὶ μάχης δαιμόνων, τοιοῦτον δὲ οἷον καὶ πρὸ τῆς ἀναχωρήσεως ᾔδεισαν αὐτόν. Τῆς δὲ ψυχῆς πάλιν καθαρὸν τὸ ἦθος. Οὔτε γὰρ ὡς ὑπὸ ἀνίας συνεσταλμένη ἦν, οὔτε ὑφ' ἡδονῆς διακεχυμένη οὔτε ὑπὸ γέλωτος ἢ κατηφείας συνεχομένη. Οὔτε γὰρ ἑωρακὼς τὸν ὄχλον ἐταράχθη οὔτε ὡς ὑπὸ τοσούτων κατασπαζόμενος ἐγεγήθει, ἀλλ' ὅλος ἦν ἴσος, ὡς ὑπὸ τοῦ λόγου κυβερνώμενος καὶ ἐν τῷ κατὰ φύσιν ἑστώς.

22　Porphyrius, Vita Pythagorae 35. Ob Athanasius dabei auf Porphyrius oder auf dessen mutmaßliche Quelle, die „Wunder jenseits von Thule" des Antonius Diogenes, zurückgreift – dazu Reitzenstein, *Athanasius*, 15f. und Oliver Overwien, Neues zu den Quellen der *Vita Antonii* des Athanasius, *Millennium* 3 (2006), 159–184, hier 164f. –, kann vorläufig auf sich beruhen. Entscheidend ist, ob überhaupt eine Philosophenvita dieser Art als direktes Vorbild gelten kann und muss.

23　Jamblich, De vita pythagorica, bes. Kap. 196.

24　Die Aufnahme von Lukian, Dem. 67 in VA prol. 3–5; 93,1 zeigt nach Overwien, Quellen, 171 insbesondere „die Zielsetzung des Athanasius sowie die literarischen Traditionen, in die er sein Werk eingereiht sehen will: Apomnemoneumata und Biographie, persönlicher Erfahrungsbericht und Lebensbeschreibung mit dem Ziel der Paränese."

Gerard Bartelink konnte auf Platon-Reminiszenzen hinweisen.[25] Die
Frage nach den einzelnen Quellen wäre nur durch eine minutiöse
literaturgeschichtliche Analyse der *Vita Antonii* zu beantworten, die bis
jetzt noch nicht vorliegt; diese müsste im Kontext des übrigen Werkes
des Athanasius erfolgen, das an expliziten Zitaten außerhalb der Bibel
nicht sonderlich reich ist, was sogar für das apologetische Doppelwerk
Contra Gentes / De incarnatione gilt. Die einzige „Quelle", die Athanasius
durchgehend benutzt, ist die Bibel.

Selbst wenn sich Klassiker*zitate* durch Quellenbenutzung erklären
ließen, erlaubt dies freilich noch keinen Schluss auf die der *Vita Antonii*
zugrunde liegende *Gattung*. Und in dieser Hinsicht stelt sich m.E. die
Frage, ob überhaupt *eine* Philosophenbiographie der *Vita Antonii* als
Quelle zugrunde liegt. Die Konzentration auf die Gattungsfrage und
die damit faktisch einhergehende Fixierung auf die uns heute noch
bekannten Pythagorasviten[26] führt in die Irre, weil die wirklichen
Belege selbst bei großzügiger Zählung quantitativ gering bleiben – und,
was m.E. noch wichtiger ist, weil sich auch die Makrostruktur der
neuplatonischen Philosophenviten nicht unmittelbar in der *Vita Antonii*
niedergeschlagen hat.[27]

2.2. Antonius anti-pythagoricus? Ein neuer Versuch in alten Bahnen

Einen anderen Weg schlägt Samuel Rubenson ein. Ihm zufolge ist nach
der kommunikativen Intention des Textes, nicht nach literarischen
Gattungsvorbildern zu fragen.[28] Rubenson identifiziert als die beiden

---

25 Gerard J.M. Bartelink, Echos an Platons Phaedron in der Vita Antonii, *Mn.* 37 (1984),
    145–147; ders., Eine Reminiszenz aus Platons Timaeus in der Vita Antonii, *Mn.* 40
    (1987), 150.

26 Hieran ist schon früher Kritik laut geworden: Anton Prießnig, Die biographische
    Form der Plotinvita des Porphyrios und das Antoniosleben des Athanasios, *ByZ* 64
    (1971), 1–5, hier 4 sieht nicht in Jamblichs und Porphyrius' Pythagoras- und
    Plotinbiographien, sondern in den Evangelien und in Philostrats *Vita Apollonii* die
    Vorbilder für die *Vita Antonii*. Noch schärfer urteilt Rubenson, Antony and
    Pythagoras, 202 über Reitzensteins These einer direkten Benutzung von Porphyrius'
    Vita Pythagorae: „His conclusion… lacks any substance."

27 Vgl. Alexandre, Construction, 68: „Les tentatives pour retrouver dans l'oeuvre
    d'Athanase une structure empruntée précisément aux biographies païennes,
    d'ailleurs multiformes, n'ont pas été suivies de succès, tant s'impose sa spécificité."

28 Rubenson, Antony and Pythagoras, 194: „Any attempt at discussing the *Vita Antonii*
    as an example of a Christian appropriation of classical biography must start with a
    clear idea of what the central argument of the text is, based on an analysis of its

zentralen Kennzeichen von Athanasius' Antonius, dass er einerseits alle Herausforderungen völlig „unberührt" („unaffected") übersteht (die *Vita Antonii* zeige, wie der Mensch durch Askese zu sich selbst und damit zur ἀταραξία [VA 43,3] gelange) und dass andererseits die Voraussetzung dafür die Trennung von der Welt sei.[29] Die *Vita Antonii* folge insoweit dem klassischen biographischen Schema, als sie im ersten Teil (Kap. 1–44) die Entwicklung des Antonius zum Asketen schildere und daraufhin im zweiten Teil (Kap. 45–93) thematisch gegliedert sein Leben darstelle, beginnend mit dem ihm verweigerten Martyrium in Alexandrien (46–48) und dem darauf folgenden Kampf gegen andere feindliche Mächte (Kap. 49–66), fortgeführt durch die Auseinandersetzungen mit Häretikern (67–71), paganen Philosophen (72–80) und Herrschern (81–86) und kulminierend in der Beschreibung seiner Person (87–88, 93) und seines Todes (89–92). Den entscheidenden Einschnitt sieht Rubenson zwischen Kap. 44 und 45, wobei im ersten Teil die große Rede an die Mönche (16–43) nur entfalte, was die Beschreibung des Werdens des Asketen (1–15) gezeigt habe.

Genau hier entdeckt Rubenson den Schlüssel zum Verständnis der *Vita Antonii*. Ein Vergleich mit Jamblichs *Vita Pythagorica* zeige, dass Athanasius' Vorbild nicht eine konkrete Quelle sei, sondern „an established narrative tradition that emerged in the philosophical schools of the third and fourth centuries AD regarding the lives of holy men".[30] Hierbei seien – was Reitzenstein und seine Nachfolger vernachlässigt hätten – bei der Anverwandlung der philosophischen Motive die Differenzen größer als die Gemeinsamkeiten. In diesen Differenzen liege aber die Pointe: „Athanasius uses a biography of Antony *in order to rewrite* the narrative of the ideal philosopher."[31] Das zeige besonders die Auseinandersetzung mit der Bildungsthematik: Während Pythagoras umherreist und auf diese Weise von allen Lehrern möglichst umfassende Bildung erwirbt[32], verweigert Antonius den Schulbesuch (VA 1,2), lässt sich von anderen Asketen in das monastische Leben einführen (VA 3,3–7) und mokiert sich über die „Hellenen", die um die halbe Welt reisen, um überall Bildung zu erwerben, während doch die Verstandeskraft (τὸ νοερόν) der Seele in ihrer schöpfungsgemäßen Natur liege (VA 20,4–7; vgl. 73,3). Daher sei die *Vita Antonii* insgesamt als apologetisches, ja sogar anti-neupythagoräisches Werk anzusehen

---

29 Rubenson, Antony and Pythagoras, 198f.
30 Rubenson, Antony and Pythagoras, 205.
31 Rubenson, Antony and Pythagoras, 207 (Hervorhebung P.G.).
32 Jamblich, De vita pythagorica 12.14.18f.

und entsprechend für Leser gedacht, die diesen polemischen Code entschlüsseln könnten.[33]

Rubenson gelangt also auf einem ganz anderen Weg als Reitzenstein zu einer sehr ähnlichen Schlussfolgerung: Die erste christliche Asketenvita ist auf dem Hintergrund des spätantiken philosophischen Diskurses zu interpretieren. Athanasius kennt diesen Diskurs und zögert nicht, ihn aufzugreifen, freilich in kritischer Absicht. Wie in seinem apologetischen Doppelwerk[34] erweist er sich als vertraut mit paganer Religiosität und Philosophie, ist aber nicht abhängig von ihr, sondern entwirft in kritischer Auseinandersetzung damit ein neues asketisches Leitbild. Antonius ist der bessere, weil von Gott her und nicht durch eine „weltliche" Kunst gelehrte Philosoph (VA 93,4), ja ein „Theodidakt" (VA 66,2). In Athanasius' Sicht ist der „Gottesmann" Antonius (VA 93,1) – Rubenson und auch Oliver Overwien zufolge – das Gegenbild zum pagenen ἀνὴρ ἰσόθεος[35] und anderen θεῖοι ἄνδρες der Spätantike.[36]

3. Eine Märtyrerbiographie? Martyrologische Topik in der *Vita Antonii*

3.1. Anfragen an Reitzenstein und Rubenson

Alle Ähnlichkeiten in der Figurenzeichnung zwischen Antonius und Pythagoras zugegeben – bei einem zweiten Blick auf die *prima facie* überzeugende These Rubensons (und damit auch auf Reitzensteins Impuls, überhaupt nach Philosophenviten als Vorbildern zu suchen) drängen sich von zwei Seiten her Fragen auf.

Zunächst: Rubenson betrachtet Athanasius als „a literate man educated in Alexandria", der mit Neupythagoräismus und Neuplatonismus vertraut gewesen sei und entsprechende Texte gekannt und

---

33 Overwien, Quellen, 182f. kommt in Bezug auf die Rezeption von Lukians *Demonax* zu einem ganz ähnlichen Schluss.

34 Dazu jetzt Uta Heil, Das apologetische Doppelwerk, in: Gemeinhardt, ed., *Athanasius Handbuch*, 166–175.

35 Lukian, Dem. 7.

36 Interessanterweise wird Athanasius selbst von Kaiser Konstantius II. – vor der Eskalation des Konflikts in den 350er Jahren – als „Gottesmensch" (θεοῦ ἄνθρωπος) tituliert (apol. sec. 62,7); vgl. hierzu Annick Martin, Athanase d'Alexandrie, l'Église d'Egypte et les moines: à propos de la „Vie d'Antoine", *RevSR* 71 (1997), 171–188, hier 173.

benutzt habe.[37] Auch Bartelink, der im Blick auf philosophische Quellen eher vorsichtig ist, meint, dass der Bischof Athanasius „zweifellos als gebildeter Mann die Gesetze der Rhetorik, auch aus praktischen Schulübungen, kannte"[38]. Hingegen hat Timothy Barnes betont, dass Athanasius selbst sich als primär biblisch gebildet darstellt, was sich an seinen Schriften auch bewahrheite.[39] James Ernest hat sich diesem Befund mit der pointierten These angeschlossen, Athanasius' wahre Muttersprache sei „nicht Griechisch, sondern Biblisch"[40]. Christopher Stead konnte schließlich zeigen, dass Athanasius zwar die aus den Werken des Aristoteles oder Theon bekannten rhetorischen Stilfiguren kennt und anwendet, dass man aber daraus nicht schließen dürfe, dass er diese Werke in der Hand gehabt habe, also von einem Rhetor unterwiesen worden sei; vielmehr habe er diese Kenntnisse christlichen Schriftstellern wie Irenaeus von Lyon, Origenes oder Euseb von Caesarea, zumal dessen *Praeparatio evangelica*, entnehmen können.[41]

Dies spiegelt sich schon in der Wahrnehmung der Zeitgenossen. Sozomenos nennt Athanasius einen „befähigten Redner und Denker", der dies aber als „Autodidakt" geworden sei.[42] Nach Theodoret wurde Athanasius schon „von Kindheit an in den göttlichen Lehren unterwiesen"[43]. Gregor von Nazianz erklärt in einem um 380 verfassten Panegyricus auf Athanasius den Sachverhalt differenzierter:

> „Er wurde zunächst in den göttlichen Sitten und Kenntnissen unterwiesen, während er weltliche Bildung lediglich in geringem Maße erwarb, um

---

37 Rubenson, Antony and Pythagoras, 207.

38 Bartelink, Literarische Gattung, 55; als Beleg verweist er auf Gregor von Nazianz, or. 21,6, wo aber gezielt der restringierte Erwerb paganer Bildung hervorgehoben wird. Vgl. hierzu und zum Folgenden Peter Gemeinhardt, Herkunft, Jugend und Bildung, in: ders., ed., *Athanasius Handbuch*, 75–82, bes. 79f.

39 Timothy Barnes, *Athanasius and Constantius. Theology and Politics in the Constantinian Empire* (Cambridge MA/London: Harvard University Press, 1993), 11f. mit Bezug auf Athanasius, inc. 56f.; ders., *Early Christian Hagiography and Roman History*, Tria Corda 5 (Tübingen: Mohr Siebeck, 2010), 168.

40 James Ernest, Die Heilige Schrift, in: Gemeinhardt, ed., *Athanasius Handbuch*, 282–291, hier 282.

41 George Christopher Stead, Rhetorical Method in Athanasius, *VigChr* 30 (1976), 121–137. Zu Athanasius' Rezeption apologetischer Texte vgl. Uta Heil, Athanasius und Eusebius. Zum Rückgriff des Athanasius auf Euseb von Caesarea, in: Anders-Christian Jacobsen/Jörg Ulrich, eds., *Three Greek Apologists: Origen, Eusebius, and Athanasius. Drei griechische Apologeten: Origenes, Eusebius und Athanasius*, ECCA 3 (Frankfurt/M. u.a.: Peter Lang, 2007), 189–214.

42 Sozomenos, h.e. II 17,5: λέγειν τε καὶ νοεῖν ἱκανόν... ἐκ νέου αὐτοδίδακτος τοιοῦτος φανείς.

43 Theodoret von Kyros, h.e. I 26,1: ἀνὴρ παιδόθεν μὲν τοῖς θείοις μαθήμασιν ἐντραφείς.

nicht in den Ruf zu geraten, hierin völlig unbewandert zu sein, und um wenigstens über das Bescheid zu wissen, was er zu vernachlässigen beschlossen hatte."[44]

Insofern ist es wenig wahrscheinlich, dass Athanasius ausgerechnet während der Abfassung der *Vita Antonii* – die er etwa 357 auf der Flucht schrieb – eine ganze Bibliothek zeitgenössischer Philosophie zur Hand hatte. Der Quellenbefund legt nahe, dass es sich bei den Zitaten allenfalls um Reminiszenzen an den Unterricht (nicht an die Lektüre der Philosophen selbst) handelt, was auf die Benutzung eines Florilegiums hinweisen könnte. Zwar rechnet die *Vita Antonii* zweifellos mit Lesern, die den literarischen Code der gebildeten Oberschicht kennen. Steht die apologetische, antipagane Abgrenzung aber derart im Vordergrund, dass man die (wenigen) Anspielungen auf Philosophenviten für so gewichtig halten muss? Aus meiner Sicht ist das nicht der Fall.

Sodann: David Brakke hat 2006 in seiner Monographie über „Demons and the Making of the Monk" die Verwendung philosophischer Terminologie und Motive in einen weiteren Kontext gestellt: „Athanasius self-consciously appropriates the language of paganism for the depiction of the ideal Christian. Antony the martyr has not only defeated the pagan gods but also taken on the characteristics of their inspired sages."[45] Der prototypische Christ wird mit Göttern und Dämonen fertig *und* inkorporiert die guten Seiten des paganen Weisen, weil er vor allem die Reinkarnation eines Typus des frühen Christentums ist: des Märtyrers. Natürlich bestehen auch hier Unterschiede, angefangen damit, dass Antonius nicht hingerichtet wird, sondern dem Martyrium (aufgrund von Gottes Ratschluss) entgeht. Doch spielt die Martyriumstopik m.E. in der *Vita Antonii* eine zentrale Rolle. Daher muss die Verknüpfung der literarischen Gestaltung mit der konkreten Situation, in der sich Athanasius unmittelbar nach 356 befand, und mit der Martyriumsthematik in seinem weiteren Werk beachtet werden; es wäre also eher der Kontext als der Prae- oder Intertext zu bedenken.

---

44 Gregor von Nazianz, or. 21,6: Ἐκεῖνος ἐτράφη μὲν εὐθὺς ἐν τοῖς θείοις ἤθεσι καὶ παιδεύμασιν, ὀλίγα τῶν ἐγκυκλίων φιλοσοφήσας, τοῦ μὴ δοκεῖν παντάπασι τῶν τοιούτων ἀπείρως ἔχειν, μηδὲ ἀγνοεῖν ὧν ὑπεριδεῖν ἐδοκίμασεν.

45 David Brakke, *Demons and the Making of the Monk. Spiritual Combat in Early Christianity* (Cambridge MA: Harvard University Press, 2006), 33.

3.2. Martyrologische Topik in der *Vita Antonii*

Zunächst zur Terminologie und Topik des Martyriums. Hier kann man bereits bei den ersten beiden Worten der Vita beginnen.[46] Einen „guten Wettstreit" (VA prol. 1) haben die Mönche im Westen, an die sich Athanasius brieflich wendet, mit denen in Ägypten angezettelt, um ihnen nachzueifern, ja sie nach Möglichkeit zu übertreffen. Die ἀγαθὴ ἅμιλλα steht zwar für eine eher sportliche Form des Streits, später ist aber genauso von Antonius' ἀγωνισμός (VA 10,3) bzw. vom Eremiten als ἀγωνιζόμενος (VA 13,5) die Rede wie in den Märtyrerakten z.B. von ἀγών (M. Lugd. 1,41; M. Pion. 22,1) oder *certamen* (Cyprian von Karthago, ep. 10,4). Der Protagonist Antonius wird ebenso als ἀθλητής bezeichnet (VA 12,1) wie Blandina in Lyon (M. Lugd. 1,19) oder Dasius in Durostorum (M. Dasii 9,2). Wie bei den Märtyrern der Verfolgungszeit spricht Athanasius von der ἄθλησις des Antonius (VA 10,1), bei der dieser von Christus nicht alleine gelassen wird (obwohl er diesen Eindruck durchaus gewinnt, als Heerscharen von Dämonen erbarmungslos auf ihn einstürmen). In Antonius' „erstem Kampf" (πρῶτος ἆθλος: VA 7,1) entpuppt sich dann allerdings der ihn als schwarzer Knabe heimsuchende Teufel selbst als „erbarmungswürdig" (ἄθλιος) im Hinblick auf seine Kampfestüchtigkeit (VA 5,5).

Auch im weiteren Verlauf der *Vita Antonii* wird auf das Wortfeld ἀγών rekurriert[47]: Der Asket ist immer kampfbereit (ἀγωνιῶν: VA 19,5), er muss einen Kampf führen (21,1: ἀγών; 51,4; 65,9; 66,6 u.ö.: ἀγωνίζεσθαι). Dies kann nicht anders sein, da die Dämonen in der *Vita Antonii* nicht nur böse Gedanken (λογισμοί) sind wie z.B. bei Evagrius Ponticus, in den authentischen Antoniusbriefen und in manch anderen monastischen Schriften jener Zeit.[48] Die Dämonen treten dem Asketen vielmehr handgreiflich gegenüber[49], sie sind der eigentliche Gegner in der Wüste – wie schon in den Märtyrerakten immer wieder betont wird, dass die Christen nicht eigentlich gegen die römischen Verfolger,

---

46 Zum Wortfeld ἀγών in den neutestamentlichen und frühchristlichen Schriften vgl. Uta Poplutz, Athlete of God/Christ II. New Testament and Christianity, *EBR* 3 (2011), 17–21.– Die folgenden Beispiele für martyrologische Intertexte sollen nur die seit dem 2. Jahrhundert gebräuchliche, in der Asketenvita neu besetzte Terminologie illustrieren. Die Märtyrerakten werden zitiert nach: Herbert Musurillo, ed., *The Acts of the Christian Martyrs. Texts and Translations* (Oxford: Clarendon Press 1972).

47 Vgl. den Wortindex bei Bartelink, ed., *Vie d'Antoine*, 391.

48 Vgl. Brakke, *Demons*, 3–22.48–77.

49 Das schließt freilich nicht aus, dass auch in der *Vita Antonii* die Dämonen mit Gedanken gleichgesetzt werden können: Nach VA 21,1 gelte es, einen Kampf (ἀγών) zu führen, damit nicht der Zorn uns beherrsche (τυραννεῖν) oder die Begierden Macht über uns erlangten (κρατεῖν).

sondern gegen den Teufel kämpfen (M. Lugd. 1,4f.).[50] Dafür aber muss
der Athlet trainieren: Athanasius erwägt, ob ihm der Teufel Gold auf
den Weg legt oder „eine höhere Macht, die den Athleten erproben und
dem Teufel beweisen wollte, dass er sich um derlei Versuchungen
wahrhaftig nicht schere."[51] Es ist auch gewiss kein Zufall, dass das von
Antonius ausgesuchte „Trainingsgelände" eine verlassene Festung ist
(VA 12,2: παρεμβολὴ ἔρημος).

Bis zu dem Punkt, an dem Antonius die Schwelle seines Rückzugs-
ortes erreicht, aus dem er dann zwanzig Jahre später wie Pythagoras
quasi als aus einem Heiligtum hervortreten wird, hat er ein Leben
geführt, das Athanasius in beständigem Rückgriff auf die Martyriumsterminologie beschreibt. Zwar hat sich Antonius, ähnlich wie Pythagoras, darauf vorbereitet, indem auch er von einem Lehrer zum anderen zieht (VA 3,4; 4,1); nur sind es hier eben Lehrer der Askese, die ihn
auf die Kämpfe mit den Dämonen vorbereiten, keine Lehrer der
Weisheit (Jamblich, v. Pyth. 11–12), und die zwanzig Jahre in der
Festung verbringt Antonius alleine, beschäftigt mit dem Kampf gegen
die Dämonen, nicht mit Wissenserwerb und Mysterieninitiation (v.
Pyth. 19). Rubensons These einer antineupythagoräischen Stoßrichtung
der *Vita Antonii* lässt sich mit dem Befund, der die Martyriumsterminologie und -theologie als grundlegend für die Argumentation erweist,
nicht überein bringen.[52] Das gilt auch für Antonius' lange Rede an die
Mönche, wo der bereits bewährte Dämonenkämpfer ausführt:

> „Wenn wir auf Erden gekämpft haben, werden wir nicht auf Erden unser
> Erbteil haben, sondern im Himmel erhalten, was [uns] verheißen ist.
> Wiederum: Wenn wir unseren vergänglichen Leib aufgeben, werden wir
> ihn unvergänglich zurück erhalten."[53]

Den himmlischen Lohn für den irdischen Kampf zu erhalten und sich
durch Askese darauf vorzubereiten – das ist das Thema im ersten Teil
der *Vita Antonii*, also in den Kapiteln, die sich seinem Aufstieg zum

---

50 Vgl. Paul Middleton, *Radical Martyrdom and Cosmic Conflict in Early Christianity*,
    Library of New Testament Studies 307 (London: T & T Clark, 2006), 134; Peter
    Gemeinhardt, Märtyrer und Martyriumsdeutungen von der Antike bis zur
    Reformation, *ZKG* 120 (2009), 289–322, hier 292.

51 VA 12,1: Εἴτε δὲ τοῦ ἐχθροῦ δείξαντος, εἴτε τινὸς κρείττονος δυνάμεως
    γυμναζούσης τὸν ἀθλητὴν καὶ δεικνυούσης τῷ διαβόλῳ, ὅτι μηδὲ τῶν ἀληθῶς
    φροντίζει χρημάτων.

52 Die Tabelle bei Rubenson, Antony and Pythagoras, 204 weist zwar formale Struktur-
    und Begriffsähnlichkeiten aus, differenziert aber nicht, welche dieser Elemente die
    postulierte *anti*-neupythagoräische Stoßrichtung der *Vita Antonii* konkret belegen.

53 VA 16,8: Καὶ ἐπὶ γῆς ἀγωνισάμενοι, οὐκ ἐν γῇ κληρονομοῦμεν, ἀλλ' ἐν οὐρανοῖς
    ἔχομεν τὰς ἐπαγγελίας. Πάλιν δὲ φθαρτὸν ἀποθέμενοι τὸ σῶμα, ἄφθαρτον
    ἀπολαμβάνομεν αὐτό.

Asketen und zugleich seinem Rückzug in die Wüste widmen.[54] Der Heilige, als der Antonius fortan anerkannt ist, hat nicht nur ein philosophisches Leben unter christlichen Vorzeichen geführt, sondern sich diesen Status regelrecht erkämpft und sich als den verehrten Märtyrern ebenbürtig erwiesen.

Die Martyriumsthematik spielt aber auch darüber hinaus eine entscheidende Rolle in der *Vita Antonii.* Traditionell wird von zwei großen Teilen ausgegangen, innerhalb derer sich jeweils eine umfangreiche Rede findet (die sicher von Athanasius komponiert sind, auch wenn nicht ganz auszuschließen ist, dass sie der Sache nach auf Antonius zurückgehen könnten[55]). Wo ist aber der Einschnitt bzw. Übergang zu lokalisieren?[56] Rubenson lokalisiert den Abschluss des

---

54 Nach Alexandre, Construction, 72 spiegelt sich in der Zweiteilung der VA „[la] tension entre royaume des cieux et médiation humaine". Tilley, Ascetic Body, 472 betont, dass die für die Zugehörigkeit zum Himmelreich nötige Reinheit nur durch Askese erreicht und bewahrt werden könne, wie Acta Pauli et Theclae 3,12 (AAAp I, 244,3f. Lipsius) zeige: Ἄλλως ἀνάστασιν ὑμῖν οὐκ ἔστιν, ἐὰν μὴ ἁγνοὶ μείνητε καὶ τὴν σάρκα μὴ μολύνητε ἀλλὰ τηρήσητε ἁγνήν. AaO. 474 bietet sie eine originelle Erklärung für die oftmals heftige Ablehnung von freiwilligen Martyrien: „Ascesis necessarily took time. This is why voluntary martyrdom could not be approved." Die spontanen Martyrien hat Geoffrey de Ste. Croix, *Christian Persecution, Martyrdom, and Orthodoxy*, Michael Whitby/Joseph Streeter, eds. (Oxford: Oxford University Press, 2006), 129–133 als Hauptgrund für Beginn und Intensivierung der Christenverfolgungen dargestellt; diese sachlich nicht zutreffende, aber gleichwohl immer noch einflussreiche These wäre von hier aus noch einmal neu als Teil des asketischen Diskurses im frühen Christentum zu bedenken.

55 Ein Urteil in dieser Sache hängt von der Einschätzung der Antoniusbriefe als authentisch ab. Samuel Rubenson, *The Letters of Antony. Monasticism and the Making of a Saint* (Minneapolis: Fortress Press, ²1995) votiert positiv und nimmt die von ihm rekonstruierten Briefe als Kriterium für eine Unterscheidung von antonianischem und athanasianischem Gut in der *Vita Antonii.* Nachdem sich die Authentizität der Briefe durchgesetzt zu haben schien, hat jüngst Dmitrij Bumazhnov, *Visio mystica im Spannungsfeld frühchristlicher Überlieferungen. Die Lehre der sogenannten Antoniosbriefe von der Gottes- und Engelschau und das Problem unterschiedlicher spiritueller Traditionen im frühen ägyptischen Mönchtum*, STAC 52 (Tübingen: Mohr Siebeck, 2009) Widerspruch erhoben; er will aufgrund inhaltlicher Beobachtungen allenfalls den ersten Brief auf den Einsiedler selbst zurückführen. Damit würde das Unterscheidungskriterium Rubensons im Grunde entfallen, und es wäre aus den zweifelsfrei bestehenden Übereinstimmungen zwischen Terminologie und Theologie der Reden mit den anderen Schriften des Athanasius nicht mehr so umstandslos auf dessen Verfasserschaft zu schließen. Insofern es im vorliegenden Beitrag vorrangig um das *athanasianische Bild* von Antonius gilt, kann die Frage hier auf sich beruhen.

56 Die folgenden Überlegungen haben wesentlich von Diskussionen mit Yorick Schulz-Wackerbarth profitiert, in dessen Vortrag „Die Wüste: Ort der Heiligung – heiliger Ort? Stimmen aus dem christlichen Eremitentum" (in: Peter Gemeinhardt/Katharina Heyden, eds., *Heilige, Heiliges und Heiligkeit in spätantiken Religionskulturen*, RGVV

ersten Teils in dem Summarium des erblühenden monastischen Lebens in VA 44, wo die zahlreichen neuen μοναστήρια als Zeichen einer „Landschaft der Frömmigkeit und Gerechtigkeit" gewürdigt werden.[57] Der zweite Teil begänne demnach mit Antonius' intensivierter Askese, motiviert durch seine Sehnsucht nach dem Himmelreich und der bedrückenden Einsicht in die Vergänglichkeit und Begrenztheit des menschlichen Lebens.[58] Rubenson setzt also „Antony's development and teaching" (Kap. 1–44) von „Antony and the world" (Kap. 45–93) ab, wobei der letztere Teil nochmals in „Antony's victories over the evil powers" (Kap. 46–66) und „Antony's victories over his opponents" (Kap. 67–88) und einen kurzen Schlussteil über seinen Tod (Kap. 89–93) zerfalle.[59] Kap. 45 – der Rückzug vom öffentlichen Wirken – gehört demnach als Übergang zum zweiten Teil, der mit der Erzählung von Antonius' Reise nach Alexandrien während der Verfolgung unter Maximinus Daja (311) beginnt.

Mir scheint es hingegen plausibler, den ersten Teil der Vita erst mit dem vergeblichen Versuch, das Martyrium zu erlangen, abzuschließen – nach dem klassischen biographischen Schema wären das die *acta*, denen dann die *virtutes* folgen. Die Sorge, sich zu viel um den Körper anstatt um die Seele zu kümmern (VA 45,5), mündet direkt in Antonius' Entschluss, in Alexandrien den „Kämpfen der heiligen Märtyrer" beizuwohnen, „damit wir, sofern wir dazu berufen werden, (wie diese) kämpfen oder (wenigstens) die Kämpfenden sehen".[60] Das erwähnte Kampfmotiv bestimmt also weiterhin das Geschehen, und die Sehnsucht nach dem Martyrium schließt unmittelbar an die Gedanken über die Kurzlebigkeit des Menschen an, so dass Antonius – da ihm selbst das Martyrium verwehrt wird – wenigstens den „zum Kampf Berufenen" zur Seite zu stehen und sie beim „Zeugnisgeben" zu begleiten,

---

[Berlin/New York: de Gruyter, 2012], im Druck) aus VA 46,6 ein dreigliedriges Modell der *Vita Antonii* entwickelt wird: Gott habe Antonius „zu *unserem* Heil und zu dem der *anderen*" vor dem Martyrium bewahrt – ersteres beziehe sich auf die Rede an die Mönche (VA 16–43), die sich bereits auf dem Heilsweg befänden, letzteres auf die noch noch auf diesem Weg befindliche Welt samt den Heiden und Häretikern (VA 44–93). Doch ist m.E. die Wendung εἰς τὴν ἡμῶν καὶ τῶν ἑτέρων ὠφήλειαν eher auf die folgenden Kapitel (47ff.) zu beziehen, in denen es um das Heil der Kirche, ihrer Bischöfe und Gläubigen geht und zugleich um das Heil der (noch) nicht gläubigen Welt, während Kap. 1–45 unter dem Stichwort „Theorie und Praxis der monastischen Existenz" eine Einheit bilden.

57 VA 44,3: ὥσπερ χώραν τινὰ καθ᾽ ἑαυτὴν οὖσαν θεοσεβείας καὶ δικαιοσύνης.

58 VA 45,1: τὸ ἐφήμερος τῶν ἀνθρώπων βίος.

59 Rubenson, Antony and Pythagoras, 194–197.

60 VA 46,1: Ἀπέλθωμεν, ἵνα ἀγωνισώμεθα κληθέντες, ἢ θεωρήσωμεν τοὺς ἀγωνιζομένους.

„bis sie vollendet waren".[61] Dass er freilich nicht bloß einer der Gaffer, sondern selbst ein potenzieller Bekenner ist, erkennt schnell auch der Richter, der gleich allen Mönchen den Zutritt zum Gericht verwehrt (VA 46,3). Antonius aber ist „furchtlos" (ἄφοβος) und zeigt sich auch weiterhin öffentlich als Christ, ja er wäscht dafür sogar sein Gewand – in wohl eher unfreiwilligem Widerspruch zu Athanasius' späterer Bemerkung, der Eremit habe nie auch nur ein Körperteil gewaschen (VA 93,1)! Für das Martyrium, möchte man sagen, war er also zum Äußersten bereit. Er gibt dadurch ein Beispiel für den Mut bzw. die Kampfbereitschaft (προθυμία) der Christen (VA 46,5), jedoch ganz vergeblich: Trotz seines sehnlichen Wunsches, „Zeugnis abzulegen" (μαρτυρῆσαι), wird ihm selbst das *Blut*-Zeugnis verwehrt (μὴ μεμαρτύρηκεν: VA 46,6). Es bleibt ihm nicht anderes übrig, als den Bekennern zu dienen, „als ob er mit ihnen gefangen wäre" (VA 46,7: ὡς συνδεδεμένος αὐτοῖς).

Genau an dieser Stelle erfolgt der entscheidende Umschwung:

> „Als dann aber die Verfolgung aufgehört hatte und auch der selige Bischof Petrus durch sein Blut Zeugnis abgelegt hatte (μεμαρτύρηκεν), entfernte sich auch Antonius und zog sich wieder in seine monastische Wohnstatt zurück. Und er verbrachte dort jeden Tag als einer, der im Gewissen Zeugnis ablegt (μαρτυρῶν τῇ συνειδέσει) und die Kämpfe des Glaubens bestreitet. Er unterwarf sich nämlich noch mehr und in noch strengerer Form der Askese."[62]

Zunächst ist dieser Abschnitt das Präludium zu Antonius' gefestigtem asketischen Leben, in dem ihm die Dämonen nichts mehr anhaben können, während er selbst andere Menschen heilt und schützt und schließlich auch belehrt – also zu den biographischen *loci*, die den zweiten Teil der *Vita Antonii* prägen und für die spätere christliche Hagiographie stilbildend geworden sind. Darüber hinaus erfolgt hier zugleich eine Umwertung des Martyriumsverständnisses und – mehr noch – eine historische Ortsangabe, unter welchen Voraussetzungen dieses unblutige Martyrium möglich und geboten ist. Der verhinderte Blutzeuge wird zum Glaubenszeugen, der nun im Gewissen kämpft – wieder wird das Wortfeld ἀγωνίζειν aufgerufen – und seinen Kampf nicht vor dem Richterstuhl, sondern im Glauben durchficht; aber weiterhin ist es ein ἄθλος, und der Glaubenszeuge ist durch seine

---

61 VA 46,2: ἀγωνιζομένους μὲν τοὺς καλουμένους ἐπαλείφειν εἰς προθυμίαν, μαρτυροῦντας δὲ αὐτοὺς ἀπολαμβάνειν καὶ προπέμπειν ἕως τελειωθῶσιν.

62 VA 47,1: Ἐπειδὴ δὲ λοιπὸν ὁ διωγμὸς ἐπαύσατο, καὶ μεμαρτύρηκεν ὁ μακαρίτης ἐπίσκοπος Πέτρος, ἀπεδήμησε, καὶ πάλιν εἰς τὸ μοναστήριον ἀνεχώρει, καὶ ἦν ἐκεῖ καθ' ἡμέραν μαρτυρῶν τῇ συνειδήσει καὶ ἀγωνιζόμενος τοῖς τῆς πίστεως ἄθλοις. Καὶ γὰρ καὶ ἀσκήσει πολλῇ καὶ συντονωτέρᾳ ἐκέχρητο.

Askese ebenso ein ἀθλητής wie der Märtyrer. Das kann nun aber nur geschehen, weil die Verfolgungen durch die paganen Kaiser aufgehört haben (was tatsächlich mit dem Sieg von Licinius über Maximinus Daja erfolgt war) – was zur Situation der Adressaten der *Vita Antonii* überleitet: Denn auch sie werden nicht mehr von nichtchristlichen Kaisern verfolgt. Ihnen droht nicht mehr (oder jedenfalls nicht unmittelbar), was dem großen Vorgänger des Athanasius auf dem alexandrinischen Bischofsstuhl, Petrus, widerfahren war: das blutige Martyrium. Diese Zeit ist vorbei, und damit hat eine neue Zeit begonnen, in der der Asket an die Stelle des Märtyrers tritt. Bis zu Kap. 46 war ja noch nicht klar, ob Antonius das Martyrium erleiden und den Kranz des Märtyrers erringen würde. Nun ist eindeutig: Die Wüste wird zum Ort des Zeugnisses. Wie Antonius nach Alexandrien gegangen war, kommen nun die Menschen zu ihm, um seine Form des Martyriums anzusehen und davon – durch Belehrung und Heilung – zu profitieren.

Wie das aber aussehen würde, wurde bereits zum Abschluss des ersten Teils erklärt: Antonius verpasst das Martyrium ja nicht zufällig, sondern wird von Gott selbst gezielt davor bewahrt, „zu unserem und anderer Nutzen, damit er in Bezug auf die Askese, die er selbst aus der Schrift gelernt hatte, für viele andere ein Lehrer würde."[63] Hier geht die Martyriums- in die Bildungsthematik über: Der wahre, durch Askese vorbereitete Bekenner ist der rechtmäßige Lehrer (wie später auch die Souveränität des Antonius im Umgang mit den sich für gebildet haltenden Philosophen zeigen wird)! Zum Lehrer der in Friedenszeiten lebenden Asketen und Christen insgesamt wird also einer, der in Verfolgungszeiten rückhaltlos zum Martyrium bereit gewesen wäre. Der Asket ist genau der Märtyrer und Lehrer, den die Gegenwart benötigt.[64] Ich meine, dass genau diese Verschränkung den sachlichen Mittelpunkt und zugleich die Scheidelinie zwischen den zwei großen Teilen der *Vita Antonii* markiert: Wird in Kap. 46 die Bereitschaft zum Martyrium dokumentiert und dessen Ausbleiben heilsgeschichtlich gedeutet, weshalb Antonius hinter keinem der hingerichteten Märtyrer zurückzustehen braucht, so leitet Kap. 47 dazu über, dass das asketische Leben insgesamt als Substitution, ja sogar als Überbietung des Blutzeugnisses angesehen werden kann.

---

63 VA 46,6: ὁ δὲ Κύριος ἦν αὐτὸν φυλάττων εἰς τὴν ἡμῶν καὶ τὴν ἑτέρων ὠφέλειαν, ἵνα καὶ ἐν τῇ ἀσκήσει, ἣν αὐτὸς ἐκ τῶν γραφῶν μεμάθηκεν, πολλοῖς διδάσκαλος γένηται.

64 Vgl. Bartelink, Literarische Gattung, 51: Trotz des Rückzugs in die Wüste und auch nach seinem Ausflug nach Alexandrien anno 311 „nimmt [Antonius] teil am Kampf der Märtyrer".

Die Martyriumsterminologie steht im zweiten Teil nicht mehr so im Vordergrund, kommt aber immer wieder zum Vorschein. Als Mönch zu leben heißt, zu leben, als könne man täglich sterben.[65] Das schließt wiederum ein, gegen die Dämonen zu kämpfen (51,4), aber auch um den Fortschritt in der Vollkommenheit (66,6; beide Male steht ἠγωνίζετο). Das einfache Christusbekenntnis der Märtyrer (Χριστοῦ γὰρ δοῦλός εἰμι) vertreibt Dämonen (52,3) sowie ein Fabelwesen, das daraufhin flieht und verstirbt, wodurch die Wüste insgesamt von den Dämonen befreit wird (53,2). Das Bekenntnis der Märtyrer behält also in der Wüste Gültigkeit! Auch den paganen Philosophen hält Antonius entgegen: Hätte er selbst sie aufgesucht, würde er sie nachahmen (ἐμιμνησάμην); nun seien sie zu ihm gekommen, und das bedeute: „Werdet wie ich, denn ich bin Christ."[66] Eine besondere Reminiszenz an die Märtyrer erfolgt schließlich in Kap. 65, wo Antonius in einer Vision seine Seele auf dem Weg zum Himmel erblickt, die die dämonischen Wesen aber am Aufstieg zu hindern versuchen. Die Engelwesen, die ihn begleiten, stellen klar, dass Gott Antonius' „Schuld von Geburt her" getilgt habe (65,4); zu urteilen sei nur noch darüber, ob er als Asket sündlos gelebt habe und deshalb gleich in den Himmel einziehen dürfe. Nicht nur die Vision als solche erinnert an Entrückungsberichte von Märtyrern[67]: Entscheidend ist ja gerade, dass der „Schlüssel zum Paradies" nicht mehr (ausschließlich) das Blut des Märtyrers ist, sondern dass auch die Askese zum sofortigen Eintritt in das Himmelreich qualifiziert. Das Blut- wird durch ein Lebenszeugnis ersetzt, die *Vita* substituiert die *Passio*. Darum ist Antonius ein Lehrer und Vorbild für den asketischen Kampf, sieht er sich doch selbst in der Luft kämpfen, bis er frei ist[68]: Der Himmel steht ihm offen.

3.3. Vita oder Passio Antonii? Ein Vorschlag zur Gliederung

Ich meine, dass man die *Vita Antonii* aufgrund dieser Beobachtungen vor dem Hintergrund der Märtyrerakten und -passionen betrachten sollte und erst in zweiter Linie vor dem der neuplatonischen Philosophenviten. Die terminologischen und theologischen Akzent-

---

65 VA 89,4: ὡς καθ᾽ ἡμέραν ἀποθνῄσκοντας ζῆν.

66 VA 72,5: γίνεσθε ὡς ἐγώ, Χριστιανὸς γὰρ εἰμι.

67 Peter Gemeinhardt, „Tota paradisi clauis tuus sanguis est". Die Blutzeugen und ihre Auferstehung in der frühchristlichen Märtyrerliteratur, in: Tobias Nicklas u.a., eds., *Gelitten – Gestorben – Auferstanden. Passions- und Ostertraditionen im frühen Christentum*, WUNT II, 273 (Tübingen: Mohr Siebeck, 2010), 97–122, hier 105–109.

68 VA 65,9: καὶ ἀγωνισάμενον ἕως ἐλεύθερος φανῇ.

setzungen sprechen eher für den martyrologischen Diskurs als *cantus firmus* der Asketenvita. Im Prolog ist zwar von der ἄσκησις, den μοναχοί und den μοναστήρια die Rede (prol. 3), und nicht zu Unrecht spricht Gregor von Nazianz davon, Athanasius habe die Regeln des Mönchslebens in narrativer Form aufgeschrieben.[69] Nur erfolgte das eben in einer Zeit, in der diese Begriffe erst ihre technische Bedeutung gewannen und in der das neue Leitbild entwickelt, begründet und von einem älteren Ideal abgesetzt werden musste. Vereinfachend könnte man den ersten Teil (Kap. 1–46) als *passio* bezeichnen – denn hier leidet Antonius; zwar behütet ihn im Prinzip Christus, dessen Passion er aber am eigenen Leibe nachahmen muss. Der zweite Teil (Kap. 47–88) wäre dann die *vita*, und zwar eine *vita contemplativa et activa*, in der nach wie vor Christus der Akteur ist, was Wunder und Heilungen angeht, in der der Asket aber zu seinem eigenen Lebensrhythmus gefunden hat, so dass ihm Dämonen, Häretiker und heidnische Philosophen nichts mehr anhaben können. Vielmehr kann nun er belehren und heilen. Diese Idiorhythmie erreicht man aber durch die Bereitschaft zum Martyrium. Diese zeichnet Antonius vor allen anderen Christen und Asketen aus. Aus diesen Überlegungen ergibt sich die folgende Gliederung der VA:

Prolog
1–46 Passio Antonii
    1–15   *passiones* als Weg zur Askese
        1–4   Kindheit, Berufung und asketische Bildung
        5–7   Dämonenkämpfe im Dorf
        8–10   Das Grab in der Wüste
        11–15 Zwei Jahrzehnte in der verlassenen Festung
    16–43 Theorie der monastischen Praxis: Antonius' Rede an die Mönche
    44–46 Abschluss der *passiones* samt der Verweigerung des Martyriums durch Gottes Ratschluss
        44   Ausbreitung des Eremitentums
        45   Antonius' Sorge aufgrund der Bedürfnisse seines Leibes
        46   Reise nach Alexandrien während der maximinischen Verfolgung

---

69 Gregor von Nazianz, or. 21,5: τοῦ μοναδικοῦ βίου νομοθεσίαν ἐν πλάσματι διηγήσεως. M.E. unzutreffend sieht Wyrwa, Gestaltungselemente, 19, hiernach die διήγησις (ebenso in VA prol. 3) als Gattung der gesamten *Vita Antonii*.

4. Märtyrerverehrung in Alexandrien und Ägypten zur Zeit des Athanasius

4.1. Athanasius und Petrus von Alexandrien

Wenn die Martyriumsthematik in der *Vita Antonii* eine derart zentrale Rolle spielt, stellt sich die Frage, welches kommunikative Ziel Athanasius damit verfolgt. Hierfür ist zunächst zu klären, wo das Martyrium im Werk und Umfeld des Autors eine Rolle spielt. Ich gehe dabei davon aus, dass die *Vita Antonii* insgesamt ein Werk des Athanasius ist, auch wenn er darin Quellenstücke verarbeitet haben mag. Gerade die Verknüpfung der narrativen Struktur der *Vita Antonii* mit dem Kontext der späten 350er Jahre spricht dafür, dass wir mit Athanasius als Autor zu rechnen haben.[70] Martin Tetz' These, dass Serapion von Thmuis der eigentliche Autor und Athanasius nur ein Redaktor sei, hat sich ebenso wenig durchsetzen können wie die Bestreitung der Autorschaft des Athanasius auf der Basis von rein lexikalischen Beobachtungen.[71] Die

---

70 Dass Athanasius seit seinem Amtsantritt Verbindungen zum Mönchtum knüpfte, die in seiner Beschreibung des Antonius zusammenlaufen, zeigt Martin, Athanase, l'Église et les moines, 174–179.

71 Für eine kritische Einschätzung der athanasianischen Verfasserschaft vgl. zuletzt Barnes, *Early Christian Hagiography*, 160–170 im Anschluss an die Argumentation von

semantischen und argumentativen Relationen zu anderen Schriften des
Athanasius wie dem apologetischen Doppelwerk sind, gerade in Bezug
auf das Martyrium, unübersehbar. In gewisser Analogie zur Forschung
an den synoptischen Evangelien wird der Komposition der *Vita Antonii*
heute mehr Aufmerksamkeit geschenkt als der Quellenverarbeitung.[72]
Damit ist aber auch die Frage nach der historischen Gestalt des
Antonius und ihrer athanasianischen Bearbeitung neu gestellt: Hatte
Hermann Dörries noch in den Apophthegmata Patrum „die Wirklichkeit des Mönchsvaters" erfassen zu können geglaubt[73], so hat Michael
Williams zu Recht betont, dass Athanasius nicht einfach die Biographie
einer Persönlichkeit schreibt und dabei das Faktengerüst ausmalt und
idealisiert, sondern dass er ein spezifisches Antonius-Bild neben – und
in Auseinandersetzung mit – anderen Bildern entwirft.[74] Die zentrale
Frage ist daher, mit welcher Absicht Athanasius dieses Bild anderen
Antonius- oder Asketen-Bildern zur Seite oder sogar entgegen gestellt
hat; darüber hinaus wäre zu fragen, warum der Antonius der *Vita* „zu
einer Macht im Leben der Kirche und der Völker" anancieren konnte.[75]

Für Athanasius war die Martyriumsthematik in den späten 350er
Jahren vor allem insofern relevant, als er seinen Vorgänger Petrus, der
311 das Martyrium erlitten hatte, als Leitbild in Anspruch zu nehmen
versuchte. Den Hintergrund bildete die Konkurrenz zur melitianischen

---

Martin Tetz, Athanasius und die Vita Antonii. Literarische und theologische
Relationen, in: ders., *Athanasiana. Zu Leben und Lehre des Athanasius*, Wilhelm
Geerlings/Dietmar Wyrwa, eds., BZNW 78 (Berlin/New York: Walter de Gruyter,
1995), 155–184; dessen These einer Autorschaft des Serapion von Thmuis ist von
Klaus Fitschen, *Serapion von Thmuis. Echte und unechte Schriften sowie die Zeugnisse des
Athanasius und anderer*, PTS 37 (Berlin/New York: Walter de Gruyter, 1992), m.E.
überzeugend widerlegt worden.

72 Michael A. Williams, The Life of Antony and the Domestication of Charismatic
Wisdom, in: ders., ed., *Charisma and Sacred Biography*, JAAR Thematic Studies 48,3/4
(Chambersburg: American Academy of Religion, 1982), 23–45, hier 23f. zieht explizit
die Analogie zwischen der *Vita Antonii* und dem Markusevangelium.

73 Hermann Dörries, Die Vita Antonii als Geschichtsquelle, in: ders., *Gesammelte
Studien zur Kirchengeschichte des 4. Jahrhunderts*, vol. 1, *Wort und Stunde*, (Göttingen:
Vandenhoeck & Ruprecht, 1966), 145–224, hier 147. Athanasius habe hingegen in der
Vita Antonii „eine geschichtliche Größe in ein neues Licht" gerückt, da er überzeugt
gewesen sei, „damit die Wirklichkeit nicht zu verfälschen, sondern ihre tiefere
Wahrheit aufzuzeigen" (aaO. 178). Vgl. Christel Butterweck, *„Martyriumssucht" in
der Alten Kirche? Studien zur Darstellung und Deutung frühchristlicher Martyrien*, BHTh
87 (Tübingen: J.C.B. Mohr [Paul Siebeck], 1995), 80.

74 Williams, Charismatic Wisdom, 34–38. Die Unterscheidung zwischen „history" and
„legend" oder zwischen verlässlichen Märtyrerakten und „fictitious hagiography",
die Barnes, *Early Christian Hagiography* vornimmt, erweist sich demgegenüber als
nicht hinreichend, um Eigenart und Wirkung der *Vita Antonii* zu erklären.

75 Dörries, Geschichtsquelle, 199.

Kirche, die sich selbst als „Kirche der Märtyrer" darstellte[76], war sie doch im Streit um die Frage entstanden, ob Petrus zu Recht in der Verfolgung zweimal geflohen und sich erst später den Verfolgern gestellt hatte – mit der Frage, ob nur ein toter Bischof ein guter Bischof sei, hatte sich schon Cyprian von Karthago ein Jahrhundert zuvor konfrontiert gesehen.[77] Die Flucht des Athanasius aus Alexandrien im Jahr 356 hatte diese Frage wieder aktuell werden lassen, freilich unter anderen Vorzeichen, da nun nicht mehr Christen von „Heiden" verfolgt wurden, sondern „orthodoxe" (nizänische) Christen von „häretischen" (homöischen) Kaisern. In Frage stand also nicht nur, ob man in der Verfolgung ausharren müsse, sondern auch, wer überhaupt der rechte Bischof und damit der Garant der Orthodoxie sei. In der *Vita Antonii* lassen sich verschiedene Hinweise darauf finden, dass und wie Athanasius in diese Debatte eingreifen wollte. Ich beschränke mich aus Raumgründen auf wenige Aspekte.

In Athanasius' Episkopat fungierte der Bischof und Märtyrer Petrus von Alexandrien als Vorbild des Kampfes gegen Schismatiker und Irrlehrer.[78] „Als ein prächtiges Volksfest begehen noch jetzt die Alexandriner den alljährlichen Gedenktag an das Martyrium ihres ehemaligen Bischofs Petrus", so der Kirchenhistoriker Sozomenos im zweiten Viertel des 5. Jahrhunderts[79], und es gibt gute Gründe anzunehmen, dass auch schon im 4. Jahrhundert an Petrus' Grab in der westlichen Nekropole vor dem Stadttor dessen Gedenktag gefeiert wurde.[80] Das

---

76 Zum Selbstverständnis der Melitianer als ἐκκλησία μαρτύρων im Gegenüber zu der ἐκκλησία καθολική unter den Nachfolgern des Petrus, zumal unter Alexander, vgl. Epiphanius, haer. 68,3,7; vgl. Theofried Baumeister, Vorchristliche Bestattungssitten und die Entstehung des Märtyrerkultes in Ägypten, in: ders., *Martyrium, Hagiographie und Heiligenverehrung im christlichen Altertum*, RQ.S 61 (Rom u.a.: Herder, 2009), 269–275, hier 271 sowie jetzt auch Andreas Müller, Athanasius und die Melitianer, in: Gemeinhardt, ed., *Athanasius Handbuch*, 122–126.

77 Vgl. Gemeinhardt, Märtyrer und Martyriumsdeutungen, 301f.

78 Zum Folgenden, zumal zur verwickelten Überlieferungsgeschichte der *Passio(nes) Petri*, vgl. grundlegend Tim Vivian, *St. Peter of Alexandria. Bishop and Martyr* (Philadelphia: Fortress Press, 1988).

79 Sozomenos, h.e. II 17,6: δημοτελῆ καὶ σφόδρα λαμπρὰν πανήγυριν εἰσέτι νῦν ἄγουσιν Ἀλεξανδρεῖς τὴν ἐτησίαν ἡμέραν τῆς μαρτυρίας Πέτρου τοῦ γενομένου παρ᾽ αὐτοῖς ἐπισκόπου. Übers.: Günter Christian Hansen, tr., Sozomenos, Historia ecclesiastica. Kirchengeschichte, vol. 1, FC 73/1 (Turnhout: Brepols, 2004), 261.

80 So die griechische Langfassung und die lateinische Übersetzung der im Original verlorenen *Passio Petri* nach der Edition von Paul Devos, Une passion grecque inédite de S. Pierre d'Alexandrie et sa traduction par Anastase le Bibliothécaire, *AnBoll* 83 (1965), 157–187, hier 177.187 (cap. 18). Die griechische prämetaphrastische Vita (BHG 1502a) ist nicht näher datierbar: ihre lateinische Übersetzung wurde wohl

belegt eine von Rufin (h.e. X 15) nach Gelasius von Caesarea (frg. 27 Winkelmann) überlieferte Episode aus Athanasius' Kindheit: Am Tag des Märtyrerbischofs Petrus verfolgt dessen Nachfolger Alexander ein Spiel von Kindern, die kirchliche Ämter und Riten imitieren, bis dahin, dass Athanasius als Bischof einige andere Kinder als „Katechumenen" tauft, womit er sich selbst als Bischof designiert – was Alexander nach eingehender Untersuchung akzeptiert und Athanasius' Eltern aufträgt, ihren Jungen „für die Kirche aufzuziehen".[81] Der Wahrheitsgehalt dieser Erzählung mag hier auf sich beruhen; wichtig ist vor allem, dass bereits für Athanasius' Lebzeiten, als Gelasius sein Kirchengeschichtswerk verfasste, die Petrusverehrung als bekannt gelten kann. Das bestätigen Nachrichten der hagiographischen Tradition, wonach diese Verehrung direkt nach seinem Tod eingesetzt habe, und Athanasius' *Apologia secunda* bezeugt diese Gedenkpraxis bereits für die 350er Jahren.[82] Die Hochschätzung des Märtyrerbischofs in der späteren Tradition kommt in einer griechischen Fassung der *Passio Petri* aus prämetaphrastischer Zeit zum Ausdruck: „Petrus war der erste der Apostel, Petrus möge der letzte der Märtyrer sein!"[83]

Der Bischof wurde der Tradition nach am 25. November 311 unter Maximinus Daja hingerichtet. Von Euseb erfahren wir lediglich, dass er „sich strenger Askese widmete und dabei offen für das gemeinsame Wohl der Kirchen sorgte. Dafür wurde er im neunten Jahre der Verfolgung enthauptet und so mit der Krone des Martyriums geschmückt."[84] Die hier genannte asketische Qualifikation – was immer das konkret bedeuten mag – ist ebenso für Athanasius bezeugt.[85] Petrus

---

unzutreffend Anastasius Bibliothecarius zugeschrieben (BHL 6698b); vgl. Vivian, *St. Peter of Alexandria*, 65f.

81 Athanasius' Selbstdesignation zum Bischof ist auch in die weitere historiographische und hagiographische Tradition eingegangen; vgl. Peter Gemeinhardt, Spätantike Historiographie und Hagiographie, in: ders., ed., *Athanasius Handbuch*, 371–378, hier 373.

82 Apol. sec. 59,1: Πέτρος παρ' ἡμῖν πρὸ μὲν τοῦ διωγμοῦ γέγονεν ἐπίσκοπος, ἐν δὲ τῷ διωγμῷ καὶ ἐμαρτύρησεν.

83 Passio Petri 13 (Devos, Une passion grecque inédite, 172): Πέτρος ἀρχὴ ἀποστόλων, Πέτρος τέλος μαρτύρων.

84 Euseb von Caesarea, h.e. VII 32,31: τὸν λοιπὸν τοῦ βίου χρόνου εὐτονωτέρᾳ τῇ συνασκήσει ἑαυτόν τε ἦγεν καὶ τῆς κοινῆς τῶν ἐκκλησιῶν ὠφελείας οὐκ ἀφανῶς ἐπεμέλετο. ταύτῃ δ' οὖν ἐνάτῳ ἔτει τοῦ διωγμοῦ τὴν κεφαλὴν ἀποτμηθεὶς τῷ τοῦ μαρτυρίου κατεκοσμήθη στεφάνῳ. Übers.: Philipp Haeuser/Hans Armin Gärtner, tr., *Eusebius von Caesarea, Kirchengeschichte* (Darmstadt: Wissenschaftliche Buchgesellschaft, ³1989), 357.

85 Athanasius, apol. sec. 6,5: σπουδαῖος, εὐλαβῆ, Χριστιανόν, ἕνα τῶν ἀσκητῶν, ἀληθῶς ἐπίσκοπον. Zur Bedeutung asketischer Vorbildung von Bischöfen des 4. Jahrhunderts vgl. Andrea Sterk, *Renouncing the World Yet Leading the Church. The*

kam nach dem Galerius-Edikt von 311, als in Ägypten eine erneute
Verfolgungswelle aufflammte, ums Leben (Euseb, h.e. IX 6,2). Er hinter-
ließ der ägyptischen Kirche den seit 304 schwelenden Konflikt mit den
Melitianern[86], der auch zu Athanasius' Zeit noch nicht gelöst war. Die
Auseinandersetzung um die Theologie des Arius begann dagegen erst
nach Petrus' Tod, wurde aber in der Tradition auch mit seinem Namen
verbunden, wohl um die Liste der sowohl den Meletianern als auch
den Arianern Widerstand leistenden Bischöfen von Athanasius über
Alexander bis hin zu Petrus selbst zu erweitern. Sein Grab wurde zum
Treffpunkt für die Anhänger des am 9. Februar 356 aus Alexandrien
vertriebenen Athanasius und damit zum Ärgernis für den Kaiser und
und den homöischen Gegenbischof Georg. Die staatliche Obrigkeit
reagierte mit Repressionen: Die Versammlung wurde am 18. Mai 357
gewaltsam aufgelöst (Athanasius, apol. Const. 27).[87]

4.2. Athanasius als „Märtyrer im Gewissen"

In dieser doppelten Frontstellung gegen Arianer und Melitianer[88] wird
nun die Terminologie und Theologie des Martyriums für Athanasius
wichtig – also genau in der Zeit, als er sich im Hinterland von
Alexandrien und in der Wüste versteckt halten musste.[89] Der Konflikt
mit den Arianern begegnet in der *Epistula ad episcopos Aegypti et Libyae*
in derselben Kampfterminologie, die auch die *Vita Antonii* durchzieht:
Die Väter von Nizäa hätten bereits ein Beispiel gegeben, wie „gegen die

---

Monk-Bishop in Late Antiquity (Cambridge MA/London: Harvard University Press,
2004). Zu weit geht die These von Martin, Athanase, l'Église et les moines, 171f.:
„Tous deux ont reçu une éducation comparable, même si celle de l'Alexandrin est,
par tradition, plus approfondie: c'est-à-dire non tant profane qu'essentiellement
biblique et ascétique." Vgl. dazu oben bei Anm. 41 die Hinweise zur Bildung des
Athanasius, die sich von der des Antonius doch erheblich unterschied!

86 Vgl. dazu Vivian, *St. Peter of Alexandria*, 15–40.

87 Vgl. Winrich Löhr, Athanasius und Alexandrien, in: Gemeinhardt, ed., *Athanasius
Handbuch*, 113–122, hier 119.

88 Ein Beispiel für die Verknüpfung dieser Konfliktkonstellationen in seinen eigenen
Schriften bietet Athanasius, ep. Aeg. Lib. 21,5.

89 Einen Wüstenaufenthalt in den Jahren 356/57 erwähnt Athanasius selbst in apol.
Const. 27,2; 32,1; 34,2. Die hagiographische Tradition schrieb ihm ein Versteck bei
einer Jungfrau in Alexandrien zu, so Palladius (h. Laus. 63), hiernach Sozomenos
(h.e. V 6,4f.) und die prämetaphrastische *Vita Athanasii III* (BHG 185). Der Index zu
den Osterfestbriefen notiert für 358, Athanasius habe sich in Alexandrien versteckt
(SC 317, 259) – was er allerdings kaum sechs Jahre lang getan haben dürfte. Vgl.
Gemeinhardt, Historiographie und Hagiographie, 374.

Häresie um der Wahrheit willen der Kampf zu führen" sei.[90] Insbesondere müsse man auf den „seligen Alexander" blicken, der „bis zum Tod gegen diese Häresie kämpfte" (ep. Aeg. Lib. 21,4: ἠγωνίσατο). Die Väter seien, so Athanasius, keineswegs nur deshalb Märtyrer, weil sie trotz Drohungen keinen Weihrauch geopfert hätten: „Auch wer den Glauben nicht verleugnet, vollbringt ein glanzvolles Zeugnis des Gewissens!"[91] Ein solches μαρτύριον τῆς συνειδέσεως finden wir fast wortgleich auch in VA 47,1 – also genau an dem Punkt, an dem die Zeit der Asketen beginnt, nachdem Petrus als der letzte Märtyrer genannt worden ist.[92]

Die Märtyrerbischöfe (unter die auch Alexander in diesem Sinne gezählt werden kann) und der Asket als Zeuge im Leben sind gemeinsam die Schirmherren von Athanasius' Kampf gegen die Arianer. Darum ist es wichtig, dass Antonius der kirchlichen Hierarchie gegenüber demütig (VA 67,1f.) und im Glauben orthodox und standfest ist (so VA 68,1) und sich weder mit Melitianern oder Manichäern, vor allem aber nicht mit der „Häresie der Arianer" (68,2) einlässt![93] Auf die akute Verfolgungssituation deutet auch die Vision von den Greueltaten der Arianer hin (VA 82,6–8), die Antonius zwei Jahre vor dem, „was wir

---

90 Athanasius, ep. Aeg. Lib. 21,1: δεικνύντες ἀγῶνα προκεῖσθαι νῦν πρὸς τὴν αἵρεσιν ὑπὲρ τῆς ἀληθείας.

91 Athanasius, ep. Aeg. Lib. 21,2: Οὐ γὰρ μόνον τὸ μὴ θῦσαι λίβανον δείκνυσι μάρτυρας· ἀλλὰ καὶ τὸ μὴ ἀρνήσασθαι τὴν πίστιν, ποιεῖ τὸ μαρτύριον τῆς συνειδήσεως λαμπρόν.

92 Nach Vivian, St. Peter of Alexandria, 4 ist Petrus der koptischen Kirche vor allem als Märtyrer im Gedächtnis geblieben, der griechischen Tradition dagegen vor allem als antiorigenistischer Theologe. Das „Zeugnis des Gewissens" kennt auch schon Origenes, hom. Num. 10,2: „Ego non dubito et in hoc conventu esse aliquos ipsi soli cognitos, qui iam apud eum martyres sint testimonio conscientiae, parati, si quis exposcat, effundere sanguinem suum pro nomine Domini nostri Iesu Christi"; er verbindet es bereits mit der Vorbereitung durch Askese (hom. Gen. 8,8–10); vgl. Malone, The Monk and the Martyr, 207–209.

93 Vgl. Alexandre, Construction, 85: „Dans son exil aux déserts d'Égypte, Athanase, combattant de la foi, revoit la vie d'Antoine comme centrée sur la foi et la piété, au service de l'orthodoxie militante." Dass Antonius eingedenk seines Versuchs, das Martyrium zu erlangen, von der melitianischen Märtyrerkirche vereinnahmt worden sei, weshalb Athanasius ihn davor retten musste – so Brian R. Brennan, Athanasius' „Vita Antonii": a Sociological Introduction, VigChr 39 (1985), 209–227, hier 218 –, ist nicht mehr als eine Spekulation. Dass die Arianer Antonius als einen der Ihren bezeichnet hätten (VA 69,1), kann mangels unabhängiger Belege weder verifiziert noch bestritten werden. Die mit der VA zeitgleiche Epistula ad monachos (CPG 2126; vgl. jetzt Blossom Stefaniw, Epistula ad monachos, in: Gemeinhardt, ed., Athanasius Handbuch, 206–208) sollte jedenfalls nicht dazu verwendet werden, aus Athanasius' Werben um die Mönche in seinem dritten Exil die Rolle des Antonius in der arianischen Propaganda um 338 zu rekonstruieren (so aber Brennan, aaO. 219).

jetzt erleben", zuteil wurde, so dass auf die Auseinandersetzung in den Jahren 356/57 in Alexandrien angespielt wird. Doch wird dies Episode bleiben: Die Kirche wird bald wieder neu erstrahlen und zur Ordnung zurückkehren; daher halte man sich von den Arianern fern (VA 82,12) und bewahre treu die παράδοσις τῶν πατέρων, d.h. den Glauben an Christus, wie er aus der Heiligen Schrift hervorgehe und wie ihn schon Antonius seinen Brüdern eingeschärft habe (VA 89,5f.). Denn nichts anderes tut ja der vertriebene und verfolgte Bischof, der sich dadurch selbst die Rolle eines „Märtyrers im Gewissen" zuschreibt und sich in die wahre episkopale wie in die asketische Tradition stellt. Athanasius inszenierte sich selbst als Märtyrer der Orthodoxie[94] und wurde von seiner Mit- und Nachwelt auch als solcher akzeptiert, wie die Kirchengeschichtswerke der Spätantike zeigen. Und schon die *Vita prima* des Pachomius bezeugt diese Wahrnehmung: Der Klostergründer, der dem Bischof begegnete, erkannte diesen „als heiligen Diener Gottes, da er von den Prüfungen gehört hatte, die Athanasius um des Evangeliums willen erduldet hatte und um seines rechten Glaubens willen, für den er auch in Zukunft würde leiden müssen."[95]

4.3. Doppelte Apologetik: Martyriumssucht und -flucht

Diese Wahrnehmung war freilich zu Athanasius' Lebzeiten nicht unbestritten. Wie er selbst berichtet (fug. 1,1), wurde die knapp geglückte Flucht aus Alexandrien von homöischer Seite als Feigheit denunziert, da er dem Martyrium ausgewichen sei. Eine solche Kritik hätte sich z.B. darauf stützen können, dass für Athanasius andernorts die Vielzahl der Blutzeugen als heilsgeschichtlichen Beweis für die Wahrheit des christlichen Glaubens in Anspruch nimmt. Diese traditionelle apologetische Position findet sich nicht nur in *De incarnatione* (Kap. 48,2), sondern auch in der *Vita Antonii* (79,3–6): Obwohl der heidnische

---

94 Vgl. David Brakke, *Athanasius and the Politics of Asceticism* (Oxford: Oxford University Press, 1995), 165f. mit Verweis auf Athanasius' *Apologia de fuga sua* und auf ep. fest. (copt.) 29 (CSCO 150, 53,18f. Lefort; Übers.: Rosario Pius Merendino, tr., *Osterfestbriefe des Apa Athanasios*, Düsseldorf: Patmos 1965, 75): „Nun wollen auch wir in ähnlicher Weise [sc. wie die biblischen Heiligen] ausharren, um Anteil an ihrem Leiden zu gewinnen." Als ägyptisches Vorbild verweist er auf die koptische Elia-Apokalypse; dazu David Frankfurter, The Cult of the Martyrs in Egypt before Constantine, *VigChr* 48 (1994), 25–47, bes. 26–32.
95 Pachomii Vita prima 30: Ὅμως δὲ μακρόθεν ἐπέγνω τὸν μέγαν Ἀθανάσιον ἐν τῷ πλοίῳ ὑπάρχειν καὶ δοῦλον τοῦ θεοῦ, μάλιστα τοὺς ποικίλους πειρασμοὺς ἀκούων οὓς ὑπέμεινεν κατὰ τὸ εὐαγγέλιον, καὶ τὴν ὀρθὴν αὐτοῦ πίστιν ἧς ἕνεκεν καὶ μετὰ ταῦτα ἔπασχεν. Vgl. dazu Vivian, *St. Peter of Alexandria*, 5.

Glaube sich weiterhin unbedrängt entfalten könne, erblühe der Glaube
der verfolgten Christen; die christliche Lehre werde – anders als die
Philosophie – verspottet und verfolgt, erfülle dennoch die Welt (vgl.
inc. 28,4; 47,5; 52,5). Es leuchte nun die θεογνωσία, es prosperierten die
σωφροσύνη ἀρετὴ und die παρθενία, auf der ganzen Welt bekannt sei
die θανάτου καταφρόνησις der Christen (vgl. inc. 38,6; 46,1–4).[96] Die
Märtyrer mit ihrer Todesverachtung und die Jungfrauen mit ihrer
Bewahrung der Reinheit des Leibes seien somit Zeichen der Weltver-
änderung seit dem Erscheinen des Kreuzes Christi.

Wird hier also das Martyrium für die Apologetik in Dienst genom-
men, so wehrt Athanasius in anderem Zusammenhang – besonders in
eigener Sache – der Forderung, man müsse das Martyrium suchen.
Liegt hier eine Spannung im Verständnis des Autors, ja sogar im selben
Text vor? Es sei, so betont Athanasius, zu unterscheiden, ob von Gottes
Providenz als Grund des Leidens oder von einem mutwillig gesuchten
Martyrium die Rede sei. Letzteres kritisiert Athanasius scharf. Johan
Leemans[97] hat gezeigt, dass Athanasius in *De fuga sua* ein Arsenal von
Argumenten einsetzt, das der alexandrinischen Tradition von den
Apologeten Clemens und Origenes bis zu den Bischöfen Dionysius und
Petrus entstammt. Hier sei nur auf drei signifikante Übereinstimmun-
gen mit der *Vita Antonii* hingewiesen.

Erstens ist hierfür das Konzept des καιρός zu nennen: Gott habe
jedem Menschen seine individuelle Todesstunde zugewiesen, die bei
Athanasius offensichtlich noch nicht gekommen sei – nun trotzdem
mutwillig den Tod zu suchen, entspreche nicht dem Beispiel Jesu und
der Heiligen (fug. 13–15). Ebenso wird ja auch Antonius der Märtyrer-
tod verwehrt: Sein καιρός, also seine Zeit zum Sterben, ist erst viele
Jahre später gekommen (VA 89,3). Hinzu kommt zweitens Gottes
πρόνοια: Wiederholt weist Athanasius in *De fuga sua* darauf hin, dass
der Mensch in Übereinstimmung mit Gottes Heilsplan agieren muss.[98]
Auch Antonius wird das Martyrium ja nicht aus einer Laune des
Schicksals heraus verwehrt, sondern weil Gott mit ihm anderes vor hat
(VA 46,6).[99] Daher wird die Souveränität Gottes missachtet, wenn man
ausschließlich das *brutum factum* des Todes zum Kriterium der wahren
Zeugenschaft macht. Schließlich und drittens betont Athanasius, dass

---

96 Parallelen nach Bartelink, ed., *Vie d'Antoine*, 337.
97 Johan Leemans, The Idea of „Flight for Persecution" in the Alexandrian Tradition
 from Clement to Athanasius, in: Lorenzo Perrone, ed., *Origeniana Octava. Origen and
 the Alexandrian Tradition. Origene e la tradizione alessandrina*, vol. 2, BEThL 164 B
 (Leuven: Peeters, 2003), 901–910.
98 Vgl. die Belege bei Leemans, „Flight for Persecution", 909.
99 Vgl. Malone, The Monk and the Martyr, 214.

nicht der Tod an sich das Zeugnis ist, sondern das Tun des Willens Gottes, das im Erleiden des Martyriums bestehen kann, aber nicht muss. Vielmehr gibt es, wie die *Vita Antonii* verdeutlicht, den Weg der Askese, der das Martyrium sogar dahingehend übertrifft, dass der Eremit „ein Lehrer für viele" sein kann (VA 46,6). Aber auch die Flucht kann eine Form sein, den Willen Gottes zu erfüllen: Denn auch dafür braucht man großen Mut, da sie zu unermesslichem Leiden führen kann – daher erhält auch, wer auf der Flucht stirbt, „den Ruhm des Martyriums".[100] In einer Situation, in der für Athanasius selbst noch gar nicht absehbar war, ob, wann und wie seine Flucht enden würde, gibt er seinem Exil einen tieferen Sinn.

Angesichts dieses biographischen und zeitgeschichtlichen Hintergrundes erstaunt es nicht, wie Athanasius seine Reflexion in *De fuga sua* als Maxime formuliert: Entscheidend sei, zu tun, was Gott befiehlt – „das ist die Regel, die die Menschen zur Vollkommenheit führt!"[101] Genau dafür ist Antonius das beste Beispiel, der aus dem ihm nicht zugestandenen blutigen Martyrium ein „Martyrium im Gewissen" macht (VA 47,1) und dessen Leben in zuvor gar nicht intendierter Weise zur „Begründung des asketischen Lebens" schlechthin wird.[102] Durch die Übersendung von Antonius' Gewand an den Bischof von Alexandrien (VA 91,8) wird dieser symbolisch zum legitimen Erben[103] dessen, der Märtyrer hätte werden können, es aber dank Gottes Providenz nicht wurde, der vielmehr eine andere Lebensweise begründete, durch die man auch in Friedenszeiten den Glauben bezeugen konnte.

4.4. Lebende Märtyrer, verstorbene Heilige und hoffende Gläubige

Die Sterbeszene des Antonius enthält kompendienhaft die Botschaft, die der Asket der Nachwelt und Athanasius seinen Lesern übermitteln wollte. Erneut spielt hier die Abgrenzung gegenüber Melitianern und

---

100 Athanasius, fug. 17,3: ὥστε καὶ τοὺς ἐν τῇ φυγῇ τελειωθέντας μὴ ἀκλεῶς ἀποθνήσκειν, ἀλλ᾽ ἔχειν καὶ αὐτοὺς τοῦ μαρτυρίου τὸ καύχημα. Vgl. schon Dionysius' Brief an Fabius von Antiochien bei Eus. h.e. VI 42,2; dazu Leemans, „Flight for Persecution", 907f.

101 Fug. 11,5: καὶ ἔστιν οὗτος ὅρος ἀνθρώποις εἰς τελειότητα φέρων, ὃ δ᾽ ἂν ὁ θεὸς προστάξῃ τοῦτο ποιεῖν.

102 VA 93,1: ἡ ἀρχὴ τῆς ἀσκήσεως.

103 Vgl. Brennan, Athanasius' „Vita Antonii", 210f., verbunden mit der These, dass Athanasius mit dem Erbe auch die Kontrolle über das Antonius-Bild empfängt bzw. sich aneignet und in der VA die Weber'sche „routinization of charisma" für die Integration des Mönchtums in die Kirche fruchtbar macht.

Arianern eine zentrale Rolle. Darüber hinaus verleiht Antonius der
Sorge Ausdruck, man könne seinen Leichnam mumifiziert in einem
Privathaus zur Schau stellen. Dies spiegelt altägyptische, aber offenbar
weiterhin praktizierte Begräbnissitten wider, gegen die Athanasius
auch in seinem 41. Osterfestbrief für das Jahr 369 zu Felde zieht.[104]
Theofried Baumeister hat gezeigt, dass es sich nicht nur um von den
Melitianern gepflegte Bräuche handelte.[105] Offensichtlich folgten auch
in der Kirche der Bischöfe Petrus, Alexander und Athanasius viele
Gläubige dieser Tradition – und es war unzweifelhaft zu befürchten,
dass sie ihn von den alten Märtyrern auf die Asketen als neue Heilige
übertragen würden.[106] Antonius selbst lehnte ein sichtbares Grab als
Ziel für Besucherströme ab, und nur seine zwei letzten Gefährten, die
ihn begruben, kannten den Ort seiner Grabstätte (VA 92,2).

Angesichts eines blühenden Märtyrerkults in Alexandrien (s.o.)
und eingedenk der nur wenig später beginnenden Praxis der
Reliquientranslationen erstaunt diese Weigerung, dem Gedenken des
Heiligen einen Ort zu geben. David Brakke hat im Anschluss an diese
Beobachtungen die einfache, aber wichtige Frage gestellt: Wo sind die
Heiligen? Für Athanasius, von seinem Bischofssitz vertrieben und auf
unbestimmte Zeit zur Flucht in die Wüste gezwungen, konnte es nur
eine Antwort geben: Heiligkeit ist nicht an Orte, sondern an Menschen
gebunden.[107] Nicht die Wüste *an sich* ist ein Ort der Heiligkeit, sie ist
vielmehr zuerst das Herrschaftsgebiet der Dämonen und muss durch
die Eremiten erst zivilisiert werden. Aber auch Kirchen und Grabmäler
sind nicht *eo ipso* heiligen Stätten, sondern nur dann, wenn dort die
richtigen Heiligen in korrekter Weise verehrt werden, d.h. wenn wie
bei Antonius die μνήμη τῶν ἁγίων dem Glaubens- und Lebensvorbild

---

104 Athanasius, ep. fest. (copt.) 41 (CSCO 150, 62,23–28 Lefort; Übers. Merendino,
    Osterfestbriefe, 114).
105 Baumeister, Bestattungssitten, 269–275. Frankfurter, Cult of the Martyrs, zeigt
    anhand der koptischen Apokalypse des Elia, dass zwischen dem alexandrinischen
    und dem ländlich-ägyptischen Milieu und den jeweiligen martyrologischen Idealen
    Unterschiede bestehen, und folgert im Blick auf das Hinterland (aaO. 25): „Egyptian
    Christianity here becomes, essentially, Christianized Egyptian religion" – was sich
    eben an dem von Antonius zurückgewiesenen Begräbnisbrauch zeige (aaO. 31f.).
106 Vgl. Malone, The Monk and the Martyr, 216.
107 David Brakke, Athanasius of Alexandria and the Cult of the Holy Dead, StPatr 32
    (1997), 12–18, hier 15; vgl. auch ders., „Outside the Places, Within the Truth":
    Athanasius of Alexandria and the Localization of the Holy, in: David Frankfurter,
    ed., *Pilgrimage and Holy Space in Late Antique Egypt*, RGRW 134 (Leiden/Boston: Brill,
    1998), 445–481, hier 446: „Athanasius, who battled all his life for certain ideas,
    mapped holiness cognitively, as a function of right belief in the incarnate Word, not
    locatively, as a function of God's continued presence on earth."

der biblischen Heiligen gilt und zu einem gottgefälligen Leben führt. Daher ermutigt der exilierte Bischof seine Anhänger: Mögen auch jetzt die Arianer dank kaiserlicher Protektion die Kirchen in Alexandrien besitzen – „ihr besitzt den apostolischen Glauben!"[108] Und wenn Athanasius rhetorisch fragt, ob denn dem *locus* oder der *fides* der Vorrang gebühre, ist die Antwort eindeutig: „Gut ist ein Ort, wenn dort der apostolische Glaube gepredigt wird; heilig ist er, wenn der Heilige dort weilt."[109] Die *Vita Antonii* leitet dazu an, Heiligkeit anhand des zeitgenössischen Vorbilds des Antonius in dieser Weise aufzufassen. Die Fortführung ägyptischer Bestattungsriten wird dagegen kritisiert, weil sie gerade nicht dem christlichen Glauben und Leben dient und zudem den Märtyrern der falschen episkopalen Sukzession zu Gute kommt – sie ist also doppelt verdammenswert und erweist die Melitianer als die Kirche der *falschen* Märtyrer.

Wenn also das Martyrium ins Leben verlagert wird, ist es nur konsequent, dass auch sein Ort nicht mehr fixiert werden kann. Wer von den Märtyrern der Gegenwart profitieren will, muss sich auf den Weg in die Wüste machen – sei es, um dort zu leben, sei es, um dort Hilfe zu erlangen und gestärkt ins Leben in der Zivilisation zurückzukehren. Das schreibt ein Bischof, der noch auf unbestimmte Zeit in der Wüste zu „überwintern" hat, der aber – seiner eigenen Darstellung zufolge – das Erbe des prototypischen Eremiten antritt, indem dieser Athanasius und dessen Weggefährten Serapion von Thmuis seine Gewänder vermacht (VA 91,8f.).[110] Das Gedenken der Märtyrer wird entsprechend dynamisiert: Ausschlaggebend ist nicht mehr der *Ort* des Gedenkens, sondern der *Zeugnisakt* selbst. In gewisser Weise restituiert Athanasius damit den ursprünglichen, biblischen Sinn von μαρτύριον als eines in vielfältiger Weise zu leistenden Zeugnisses, wobei das Blutzeugnis nur eine unter vielen Möglichkeiten ist, ein Zeuge (Märtyrer) zu werden. Der Asket auf dem inneren Berg kann es ebenso sein wie der Bischof, der um der Orthodoxie willen verfolgt wird. Athanasius stellt nicht nur Antonius explizit in die Nachfolge der biblischen Heiligen, sondern reiht sich selbst implizit in die illustre Schar der Glaubenszeugen ein.

Ist also die *Vita Antonii* ein Aufruf an *alle* Christen, in die Wüste zu gehen? Ganz sicher nicht – genauso wie bereits die Märtyrerakten aus vorkonstantinischer Zeit nicht das Ziel verfolgten, alle Christen für den

---

108 PG 26, 1189: „*Illi enim loca, vos vero habetis apostolicam fidem.*" Vgl. Brakke, „Outside the Places, Within the Truth", 451f. zu diesem auf ca. 356 zu datierenden, lateinisch überlieferten Brieffragment.

109 PG 26, 1189: „*Bonus quidem locus est. quando illic apostolica fides praedicatur; sanctus est, si ibi habitat sanctus.*"

110 Vgl. Brennan, Athanasius' „Vita Antonii", 224f.

Weg zur eigenen Hinrichtung zu begeistern. Vielmehr dient die *Vita Antonii* gerade dazu, allzu radikales Asketentum kirchlich einzuhegen, indem sie Antonius in die soeben beschriebene Sukzession stellt: „Die biblischen Heiligen relativieren ein sich wunderlich etablierendes Mönchtum."[111] Zu der Dynamisierung und Mobilisierung des Heiligen durch Athanasius tritt mit der Abfassung und Verbreitung der *Vita Antonii* weiterhin seine Literarisierung: Gelesen werden sollte (und wurde) die *Vita Antonii* ja gerade von „Brüdern" oder Mönchen „in der Fremde", die mit denen „in Ägypten" in einen asketischen Wettstreit eingetreten sind.[112] Die Vita ist also von vorneherein darauf angelegt, in anderen Kontexten gelesen, verstanden und umgesetzt zu werden. Wie Antonius die Imitation der biblischen Heiligen zum Ausgangspunkt seiner asketischen Existanz macht, so leitet seine Vita dazu an, nun wiederum Antonius selbst – und dadurch vermittelt die Heiligen der christlichen Frühzeit – nachzuahmen.[113] Dass dies nicht in der Wüste erfolgen muss, zeigt schon das Vorbild des Hagiographen, der ja alles daran setzte, seine Wüstenexistenz bald wieder zu beenden und sein „Zeugnis im Gewissen" an seinem Bischofssitz zu erbringen. Daher mahnte er den der Bischofsweihe widerstrebenden Mönch Dracontius, er werde gerade in diesem Amt ein „Nachahmer aller Heiligen" sein.[114]

Wie also das Heilige für Athanasius grundsätzlich nicht lokal fixiert werden kann, so eröffnet die *Vita Antonii* eine Vielzahl möglicher Orte, Zeiten und Gelegenheiten des Martyriums.[115] Diese hagiographische Konzeption des Athanasius ist aus seiner inkarnationstheologischen Konzeption zu erklären[116] – ob auch eine bewusste Abgrenzung gegen

---

111 Tetz, Athanasius und die Vita Antonii, 179. Dass zum Hintergrund der *Vita Antonii* auch die Texte von Nag Hammadi gehören, so dass Athanasius sein gemäßigtes asketisches Ideal in Auseinandersetzung mit den weit radikaleren Mönchen Oberägyptens entwickelt habe, vermutet Williams, Charismatic Wisdom, 25f.

112 VA prooem. 1: Ἀγαθὴν ἄμιλλαν ἐνεστήσασθε πρὸς τοὺς ἐν Αἰγύπτῳ μοναχοὺς ἤτοι παρισωθῆναι ἢ καὶ ὑπερβαλέσθαι τούτους προελόμενοι τῇ κατ' ἀρετὴν ὑμῶν ἀσκήσει. Zum Titel vgl. oben Anm. 11.

113 VA prooem. 3: θελήσετε καὶ ζηλῶσαι τὴν ἐκείνου πρόθεσιν.

114 Athanasius, ep. Drac. 5: Ἐγὼ μὲν εὔχομαί σε καὶ ἐμαυτὸν πάντων τῶν ἁγίων μιμητὴν γενέσθαι.

115 Vgl. Butterweck, „Martyriumssucht", 81: „Für Athanasius ist die Bereitwilligkeit zum Martyrium auch hier eine ‚für uns Christen' charakteristische Einstellung, die gerade nicht zu einem selbstgesuchten Bekenntnistod führt, sondern dazu, auch gegen den eigenen Willen die Aufgaben zu übernehmen, die der Herr im Blick auf die anderen Gemeindeglieder gestellt hat. Dabei kann diese Berufung im äußersten Fall auch im Tod um des Glaubens willen bestehen, obwohl Athanasius in erster Linie an den Kampf des täglichen Lebens denkt."

116 Vgl. hierzu Johannes Roldanus, Die Vita Antonii als Spiegel der Theologie des Athanasius und ihr Weiterwirken bis ins 5. Jahrhundert, *ThPh* 58 (1983), 194–216,

die Sakraltopographie Alexandriens hierbei eine Rolle spielte, wäre zu untersuchen.[117] Entscheidend ist, dass die Bezugnahme auf Antonius eine gerade Linie von Bischöfen, Mönchen und Christen der Gegenwart zu den biblischen Heiligen zu ziehen erlaubt. Dass die Märtyrer dabei eine Scharnierfunktion einnehmen, ist besonders zu unterstreichen.[118]

5. Fazit: Auf dem Weg zum lebenden Märtyrer

Am Leben des Antonius setzt Athanasius den Übergang vom Märtyrer im Tode zum Märtyrer im Leben in Szene. Er gibt damit auch eine Antwort auf die Frage: Wer sind in der Gegenwart der Kirche ihre Leitbilder, die Heiligen? Antonius' asketische Karriere beginnt damit, dass er der Heiligen gedenkt, womit die Jerusalemer Urgemeinde gemeint ist.[119] Die Lebenspraxis der Mönche schließt das Gedenken der Heiligen ein, um dadurch die Seele in ihren Rhythmus zu bringen (VA 55,3). Auch im Umgang mit Dämonen soll man ihren Mut nachahmen (VA 27,1), den Heiligen – gemeint sind hier nun die Engel (VA 35,6f.) – dagegen unbefangen gegenübertreten: Ihre Erscheinung bewirkt ja nicht Furcht, sondern Freude (VA 43,2). Heilig sind schließlich auch die Märtyrer der Verfolgungszeit (VA 46,1; 90,2), und sie sind gemeint, wenn Antonius an seinem Lebensende seine Gefährten ermahnt, „sich darum zu bemühen, die Seele vor unreinen Gedanken zu bewahren und Eifer im Blick auf die Heiligen zu üben, sich weder mit den schismatischen Meletianern zu vereinen noch Gemeinschaft mit den Arianern zu haben."[120] Damit konkretisiert Athanasius, was es heißt, als

---

hier 198–211; ähnlich Tetz, Athanasius und die Vita Antonii, 180. Vgl. Williams, Charismatic Wisdom, 36: „Athanasius's real task was not to elevate Antony but to humanize him, not to make Antony into a charismatic figure but to translate a charismatic authority which was already possessed into a wider social context whose values and expectations called for the articulation of controls."

117 Vgl. Christopher Haas, *Alexandria in Late Antiquity. Topography and Social Conflict* (Baltimore: Johns Hopkins University Press, 1997); zuletzt Stefan Schmidt, Der Sturz des Serapis. Zur Bedeutung paganer Götterbilder im spätantiken Alexandria, in: Reinhard Feldmeier u.a., eds., *Alexandria – Stadt der Bildung und der Religion*, vol. 1, BN N.F. 147 (Freiburg u.a.: Herder, 2010), 127–146.

118 Dieser Aspekt fehlt in der ansonsten treffenden Beschreibung bei Martin, Athanase, l'Église et les moines, 187: Athanasius' Ziel sei es, „ne plus former qu'une seule figure exemplaire, celle du chrétien véritable, capable de résister, par grâce divine, aux adversaires du Christ, modèle donné à imiter à toute la chrétienté."

119 VA 2,4: μνήμη τῶν ἁγίων.

120 VA 89,4: Καὶ καθὰ προεῖπον σπουδάζειν τὴν ψυχὴν φυλάττειν ἀπὸ ῥυπαρῶν λογισμῶν καὶ τὸν ζῆλον ἔχειν πρὸς τοὺς ἁγίους, μὴ ἐγγίζειν τε Μελετιανοῖς τοῖς

täglich Sterbender zu leben und d.h.: ein Märtyrer zu sein. Asketisches Leben, Gehorsam gegenüber dem rechten Bischof und theologische Orthodoxie fallen – auch wenn der Abstand zu den biblischen und urchristlichen Heiligen gewahrt bleibt – in einem Leitbild zusammen.[121] Solche Märtyrer, die sich an den Kyrios und an die Heiligen halten, können mit Recht darauf hoffen, von letzteren „nach dem Tod in die ewigen Wohnstätten als Freunde und Verwandte aufgenommen zu werden."[122]

In den Grundzügen und auch in Details entspricht das Martyriumsverständnis in der *Vita Antonii* dem Befund im weiteren Werk des Athanasius. Die *Vita Antonii* ist Zeuge einer „théologie en recherche": Das klassische Ideal des Märtyrers ist (noch) dominant, der (über-) lebende Asket muss (noch) gegenüber den „echten", hingerichteten Märtyrern gerechtfertigt werden, und seine Lebensbeschreibung ist von Martyriumstopik regelrecht durchzogen. Wenige Jahre später sollte das Konzept des *martyrium sine sanguine* seinen Siegeszug in der christlichen Frömmigkeit antreten[123], freilich flankiert vom Erblühen des Kultes der „alten" Märtyrer (zu denen viele neue hinzukamen). Den Titel eines *martyr vivus* kannte Athanasius noch nicht. Was er aber deutlich sah, war die Herausforderung, dem Christentum ein neues Leitbild zu geben, als die Zeit der Verfolgungen von Staats wegen vorbei war. Das musste ein Glaubenszeuge sein, bei dem die *Vita* nicht nur das Vorspiel zur *Passio* ist, sondern selbst zum Schauplatz des

---

σχισματικοῖς οἴδατε γὰρ αὐτῶν τὴν πονηρὰν καὶ βέβηλον προαίρεσιν μηδὲ κοινωνίαν ἔχειν τινὰ πρὸς τοὺς Ἀρειανούς. Nach Roldanus, Vita Antonii, 208 ist die Reinheit und Ruhe der Seele, die in der VA wiederholt angeführt wird, ein Grundmerkmal von Athanasius' Christologie, insofern durch die Inkarnation den Märtyrern ihre „Schwachheiten" (πάθη) genommen und so ihre Unerschrockenheit erst ermöglicht wurde (Ar. III 57; vgl. inc. 27,1f.; 48,2; 50,4).

121 Wyrwa, Gestaltungselemente, 24f. hat darin Recht, dass Athanasius damit nicht eine Kult des Antonius begründen, sondern einen solchen vielmehr unterbinden wolle. Es müsse „der unverrückbare und bleibende Abstand zu den Heiligen, d.h. zu den Engeln, den biblischen Heiligen, den erstberufenen Jüngern und Aposteln und den Märtyrern gewahrt bleiben" (aaO. 53). Daher heiße Antonius μακάριος in Bezug auf seinen Tod (prol. 2; 92,3 sowie schon 66,2), aber nie ἅγιος wie die Engel (35,4.7; 43,2), die biblischen Heiligen (27,1; 55,3; 89,4; 91,5), die Apostel und die Urgemeinde (2,4) und die Märtyrer (46,1; 90,2.5). Vgl. auch Alexandre, Construction, 67. Dennoch wird Antonius eindeutig den Märtyrern angenähert und mit ihnen in eine Reihe gestellt; er soll aber nicht kultisch verehrt, sondern vielmehr glaubens- und lebenspraktisch nachgeahmt werden.

122 VA 91,5: Σπουδάζετε δὲ μᾶλλον καὶ ὑμεῖς ἀεὶ συνάπτειν ἑαυτούς, προηγουμένως μὲν τῷ Κυρίῳ, ἔπειτα δὲ τοῖς ἁγίοις, ἵνα μετὰ θάνατον ὑμᾶς εἰς τοὺς αἰωνίους σκηνάς, ὡς φίλους καὶ γνωρίμους, δέξωνται.

123 Vgl. Gemeinhardt, Märtyrer und Martyriumsdeutungen, 307f.

Leidens wird.[124] Mit dieser Einsicht wurde Athanasius stilbildend für die christliche Hagiographie, und sei es in kreativer Fortschreibung und Abgrenzung wie in der *Vita Martini* des Sulpicius Severus, dessen „Held" ganz anders agiert, aber in der Sache vergleichbar und sogar explizit als *lebender* Märtyrer dargestellt wird.[125] Wie am Beispiel des Antonius zu einer neuen (und potenziell vielgestaltigen) Form heiligen Lebens aufgerufen werden sollte, so zeitigte auch die *Vita Antonii* selbst eine breite Palette literarischer Inszenierungen christlicher Heiligkeit. Produktiv missverstanden zu werden ist freilich das Schicksal (und das Potenzial) jeder Schrift, wie schon Ambrosius von Mailand beklagte: „Schlecht ergeht es einem Buch, das sich ohne Beschützer nicht verteidigen kann. Also möge für sich sprechen, wer ohne Dolmetscher in die Welt hinausgeht!"[126]

Hier gilt es nicht zu verteidigen, sondern lediglich das hagiographische Profil der *Vita Antonii* kurz zusammenzufassen. Martyrium und Askese überlappen sich darin. Man könnte (wie Hieronymus mit Bezug auf Pontius' Cyprianbiographie) von einer *Vita et Passio* oder, wie oben erläutert, von einer *Passio et Vita* sprechen. Diese Einsicht sollte für die Interpretation der *Vita Antonii* fruchtbar gemacht werden. Die Martyriumstopik wird in das biographische Genre übernommen und damit verwoben. Das erstaunt insofern nicht, da der Märtyrerkult in Ägypten und anderswo in der Mitte des 4. Jahrhunderts blühte und auch zur Deutung der Gegenwart genutzt werden konnte. Die Zeit der Märtyrer war noch nicht lange vorbei; ob sich nochmals Verfolgungen ereignen würden, war noch keineswegs ausgemacht. Niemand konnte sicher vorhersagen, ob die heidnische Restauration, die Kaiser Julian ab 361 initiierte, tatsächlich „wie ein Wölkchen"[127] vorübergehen und sich nie wiederholen würde. Das bedeutet freilich nicht, dass die antipagane Polemik der entscheidende Subtext der *Vita Antonii* sei. Diese sollte zwar auch den „Heiden" vorgelesen werden (VA 94,2), in erster Linie aber ein Vorbild für Mönche sein (VA prol. 3). Die *Vita Antonii* bot die außergewöhnliche Chance, Märtyrertum und Askese in einem Ideal zu vereinen und damit anschlussfähig zu sein sowohl für das Gedenken

---

124 Brakke, *Politics of Asceticism*, 245: „Antony's authority, as Athanasius views it, is moral; it resides in his entire way of life, which constitutes a model for others to imitate. By writing the *Life of Antony*, Athanasius hopes to contribute to the formation of a Christian πολιτεία by fostering an ethic of imitation that reflects his own programm of self-formation through imitation of the saints."

125 Vgl. nur Sulpicius Severus, ep. 2,12f.; dazu Gemeinhardt, *Heilige*, 26f.

126 Ambrosius, ep. 32(48),3: *„male habet liber, qui sine adsertore non defenditur. Ipse igitur pro se loquatur, qui procedit sine interpraete."*

127 So Athanasius nach Rufin, h.e. X 35; Sokrates, h.e. III 14,1; Sozomenos, h.e. V 15,3.

der Opfer der Verfolgungen als auch für die Frage, was Christsein unter den Bedingungen der Legalität ausmache. In dieser Dynamik steht sie gewissermaßen „zwischen den Zeiten".

Obwohl das Antonius-Gedenken also dynamisiert und delokalisiert wurde, blieb dem ersten Eremiten das Schicksal des typischen Heiligen doch nicht erspart: Seine Reliquien, deren Ort nach VA 92,2 unbekannt war, wurden im Jahr 561 aufgefunden und zunächst nach Alexandrien, später nach Konstantinopel und schließlich nach Südfrankreich (Motte-Saint-Didier) verbracht.[128] Doch schuf Athanasius auf der anderen Seite mit einer Biographie, deren ostentative Kritik an lokal fixierten Kulten als „out of step with where world Christianity was going" erscheinen musste[129], den Klassiker der spätantiken hagiographischen Literatur schlechthin. Man könnte diesbezüglich die Vermutung wagen, dass die kommunikative Strategie einer flexiblen Verortung des Heiligen sich schon wenige Jahre nach der Abfassung der *Vita Antonii* durch die Wiedereinsetzung des Autors in sein Bischofsamt erübrigt hatte. Athanasius war und blieb ein lebender „Märtyrer" und förderte im Übrigen den Kult seines dritten Vorgängers Petrus nach Kräften (s.o.). Die *Vita Antonii* trat unterdessen in der Übersetzung des Evagrius von Antiochien ihren Siegeszug im Westen an, aber nicht mehr als Dokument der Résistance gegen „Heiden", Melitianer und Arianer, sondern als spirituelle Biographie (die Hieronymus, Sulpicius Severus und andere zur literarischen *imitatio* inspirierte). Sie blieb aber *Passio et Vita* zugleich und schlug damit die Brücke von den Märtyrern zu den Asketen – und von beiden zu den „normalen" Christen vor und nach der „Konstantinischen Wende". Insofern erscheint es möglich und sinnvoll, die *Vita Antonii* als Darstellung eines Glaubens- und Lebensvorbildes zu lesen, das gewiss zur Blutzeugenschaft hätte führen können, zugleich aber auch denjenigen Wege zur authentischen Glaubenszeugenschaft vor Augen stellte, denen das Martyrium – aus welchem Grund auch immer – verwehrt blieb. Aus dieser Perspektive dürfte sich die literarische Gestalt und auch der Publikumserfolg der *Vita Antonii* m.E. plausibler erklären lassen als durch den Vergleich mit den spätantiken Philosophenviten.

---

128 Bartelink, Introduction, 75.
129 Brakke, Cult of the Holy Dead, 18; vgl. schon Tetz, Athanasius und die Vita Antonii, 182.

EKKEHARD MÜHLENBERG

Gregor von Nyssa über die Vierzig und den ersten Märtyrer (Stephanus)*

Die ältesten Reden zu Märtyrerfesten finden wir bei Basilius von Caesarea und seinem jüngeren Bruder Gregor von Nyssa. Dadurch haben
wir handfeste Fixpunkte für das Genre. Es handelt sich um die Zeit
zwischen 370 n.Chr. (Bischofsweihe des Basilius) und Mitte 380 n.Chr.,
in der Tat noch vor Johannes Chrysostomus. Das Gedenken der Märtyrer an den Jahrestagen ihrer Hinrichtung beginnt wohl im 2. Jahrhundert; schriftliche Berichte über Prozess und Hinrichtung, die zum Vor-
lesen zirkulierten, gab es ebenfalls seit der zweiten Hälfte des 2. Jahrhunderts.[1] Die Art und Weise der Feiern, wie Christen der Märtyrer
gedachten, ist Gegenstand erfinderischer Rekonstruktion; verlässliche
Daten gibt es erst ab Mitte des 4. Jahrhunderts. Die Vorstellung von
Reliquien ist so alt wie das Märtyrergedenken; für deren Aufbewah-
rung gibt es vor dem 4. Jahrhundert nur Spekulationen. Die Martyrien-
berichte (*passiones*) und die Reden bei Märtyrerfeiern sind historisch[2],
rhetorisch[3], hagiographisch[4] und homiletisch[5] untersucht worden; seit

---

*   Die Vortragsform ist weitgehend beibehalten, um eine Linie in einiger Ausgewo-
     genheit zu präsentieren. Die Anmerkungen tragen die Belegstellen, zusätzliche Fra-
     gen und Literatur nach.
1   Zu Übersichtsliteratur vgl. Jan W. van Henten, Martyrium II, *RAC* 24 (2010-2011),
     300–325. Der Autor arbeitet kräftig daran mit, jegliche klare Begrifflichkeit aufzuhe-
     ben. Es geht doch kein Weg an der Tatsache vorbei, dass die Christen den Ausdruck
     „Märtyrer" gefunden und geprägt haben. Wer die Religionsgeschichte einbeziehen
     will, muss wenigstens genau wissen, an welchem Ort er in das uferlose Meer
     springt.
2   Zu den XL Märtyrern vgl. Pio Franchi de' Cavalieri, *I Santi Quaranta martiri di Seba-
     stia,* Note agiografiche, fascicolo 7, Studi e Testi 49 (Rom: Tipographia Poliglotta Va-
     ticana, 1928), 155–184.
3   Vgl. Louis Méridier, *L'influence de la seconde sophistique sur l'oeuvre de Grégoire de
     Nysse* (Rennes: Imprimerie Brevetée Francis Simon, 1906).
4   Vgl. Hippolyte Delehaye, *Les origines du culte des martyrs,* SHG 20 (Brüssel: Société
     des Bollandistes, ²1933); ders., *Les passions des martyrs et les genres littéraires,* SHG 13
     (Brüssel: Société des Bollandistes, 1921; ²1966).

Peter Brown[6] gibt es den wissenschaftssoziologischen Zugriff, und jüngst hat der Identitätsverlust zu neuen Untersuchungen angeregt.[7] Ich will einen kleinen Ausschnitt ein wenig analysieren und hoffe auf diskutable Ergebnisse.

Mein Ausschnitt ist das Gedenken der XL Märtyrer von Sebaste. Die erste erhaltene Rede hat Basilius von Caesarea gehalten und schriftlich verbreitet; das geschah zwischen 370 und 379 n.Chr.[8] Gregor von Nyssa hielt in Kenntnis der Rede seines Bruders 379 am traditionellen Gedenktag der XL Märtyrer – überliefert ist der 9. März – eine Rede (II)[9] im Martyrium der Vierzig in Caesarea, eine zweite Rede auf sie im Jahr 383 in Sebaste (I a+b)[10]. Durch Vergleichen der Texte können einige Züge der Frömmigkeit sichtbar werden, und zwar bei Rednern, denen wir theologische Reflexion zuerkennen. Im Jahr 386 n.Chr. hat Gregor von Nyssa die wohl tatsächlich erste Rede auf den Protomärtyrer Stephanus[11] gehalten; ich will skizzieren, wie er diese Figur mit ihrem vorgegebenen Bibeltext ausgestaltet.

1. Basilii Caesariensis Oratio in XL martyres

Basilius hat bekanntlich Rhetorik studiert, und so sind ihm die rhetorischen Grundmuster vollkommen geläufig.[12] Er weiß genau, dass er sich bei den XL Märtyrern auf ein Encomium, eine Lobrede, in dem Geden-

---

5   Vgl. Jean Bernardi, *La prédication des pères cappadociens. Le prédicateur et son auditoire*, Publications de la Faculté des Lettres et Sciences Humaines 30 (Paris: Presses Universitaires de France, 1968), 77–85 (Basilius), 303–307 (Gregor von Nyssa).

6   Peter Brown, *The Cult of the Saints. Its Rise and Function in Latin Christianity*, The Haskell Lectures on History of Religions. New Series 2 (Chicago: University of Chicago Press, 1981); deutsch: *Die Heiligenverehrung. Ihre Entstehung und Funktion in der lateinischen Christenheit* (Leipzig: Benno Verlag, 1991).

7   Vgl. z.B. Johan Leemans, Grégoire de Nysse et Julien l'Apostat. Polémique anti-païenne et identité chrétienne dans le Panégyrique de Théodore, *REAug* 53 (2007), 15–33.

8   CPG 2863 (BHG 1205): PG 31,508–525 (der gedruckte Text lässt viele Fragen offen; es fehlt eine kritische Edition).

9   CPG 3189 (BHG 1208): II = GNO X/1 (1990), 159–169 (ed. Otto Lendle).

10 CPG 3188 (BHG 1206+1207): Ia = GNO X/1 (1990), 137–142 (ed. Lendle) und Ib = GNO X/1 (1990), 145–156 (ed. Lendle).

11 CPG 3186 (BHG 1654): I = GNO X/1 (1990), 75–94 (ed. Lendle).

12 Mario Girardi, *Basilio di Cesare e il culto dei martiri nel IV secolo. Scritture e tradizione*, Quaderni di Vetera Christianorum 21 (Bari: Istituto di studi classici e cristiani, Università di Bari, 1990) behandelt diese Rede in seinem dritten Kapitel (121–136). Der Text ist nach grober Einteilung paraphrasiert; ein Beitrag liegt in dem Aufspüren von biblischen Sprachassoziationen.

ken an Menschen einlässt.[13] Er setzt auch voraus, dass Märtyrer-gedenken oft stattfinden. Und wohl auch den rhetorischen Regeln fol-gend reflektiert er über die Form seines Tuns. Er hält am Beginn fest, dass die Ehrung der Märtyrer mit dem Gottesglauben verbunden sei; denn man zeige bei der Ehrung der Märtyrer die „Zuneigung zum gemeinsamen Herrn". Damit endet das explizite Gotteslob, bis auf die Doxologie an Jesus Christus zum Abschluss. Nachdem sich Basilius des Gotteslobes entledigt hat, teilt er den Hörern mit, was er von ihnen erwartet. Er sagt: „Wer die edlen Männer anerkennt, wird sie in ähnli-chen Situationen auch nachahmen." Das heißt in emphatischer Formu-lierung: „Preise aufrichtig den Märtyrer, damit du durch deinen wil-lentlichen Entschluss ein Märtyrer wirst" (Μακάρισον γνησίως τὸν μαρτυρήσαντα, ἵνα γένῃ μάρτυς τῇ προαιρέσει...). Er gibt auch an, wie er sich vorstellt, dass jemand durch einen willentlichen Entschluss zum Märtyrer wird, nämlich in negativer Beschreibung: „[dass du] ohne Verfolgung, ohne Feuer und ohne Folterungen den gleichen Lohn wie sie erhältst."[14] Und wie sieht das positiv aus? Worin besteht der Willensentschluss? In direkter Anrede sagt es Basilius nirgends; im Schlussabschnitt bleibt es bei der Ermahnung, sie nachzuahmen.[15] Er verpackt es in die Antwort der Märtyrer auf den Befehl, der besagt, „dass – wie Basilius es formuliert – Christus nicht bekannt werden darf oder schlimme Folgen zu ertragen sind".[16] In einer langen Rede[17] lässt Basilius die Märtyrer ihren Grundsatz, Christen zu sein und trotz des Angebotes von weltlichen Vorteilen und auch trotz der Drohung mit unerträglichen Qualen zu bleiben, vortragen. Tenor: „Die ganze Welt

---

13 Die tradierte Überschrift ist aus Migne, PG 31, 508A nicht zu erschließen. Das rheto-rische Kennwort ἐγκώμιον begegnet in 509A11. Die rhetorische Gattung ‚Enkomion' wird zumeist der Beschreibung in Menander über den Basilikos Logos entnommen; siehe *Menander Rhetor, edited with translation and commentary by D.A. Russell and N.G. Wilson* (Oxford: Clarendon Press, 1981), 368–377. Einen Überblick gab schon Richard Volkmann, *Die Rhetorik der Römer und Griechen in systematischer Übersicht dargestellt* (Leipzig: B.G. Teubner, ²1885 = Hildesheim: Georg Olms, 1963), 338–341. Vgl. auch Theresia Payr, Enkomion, *RAC* 5 (1962), 332–343, bes. B.II. Märtyrer-Enkomion, 338–342; Delehaye, *Les passions*, Kapitel 2 (133–169, zum Aufbau 141–143). Wichtig ist bei Menander die anfängliche Bemerkung (331), dass das Lob der Götter „Hymnen" sind; die Heiligen der Christen sind ja nicht einfach sterbliche Menschen, sondern im göttlichen Bereich, und vielleicht erklären sich so die hymnischen Einschübe.

14 Μακάρισον γνησίως τὸν μαρτυρήσαντα, ἵνα γένῃ μάρτυς τῇ προαιρέσει, καὶ ἐκβῇς χωρὶς διωγμοῦ, χωρὶς πυρός, χωρὶς μαστίγων, τῶν αὐτῶν ἐκείνοις μισθῶν ἠξιωμένος (PG 31, 508B6–9).

15 Siehe PG 31, 524A12–15.

16 Ἐπειδὴ δὲ περιηγγέλη τὸ ἄθεον ἐκεῖνο καὶ ἀσεβὲς κήρυγμα, μὴ ὁμολογεῖν τὸν Χριστὸν, ἢ κινδύνους ἐκδέχεσθαι (PG 31, 509D1–512A1).

17 PG 31, 513A6–C10.

ist uns verachtet." Griechisch muss man es hören: Ὅλος ἡμῖν ὁ κόσμος καταπεφρόνηται. Jetzt ist die Urform erkennbar, die Basilius über sein Enkomion setzt: „denen die Welt gekreuzigt ist" (οἷς δὲ ὁ κόσμος ἐσταύρωται).[18] Der Apostel Paulus hat den Ausdruck geprägt (Gal 6,14), und dieser Ausdruck kennzeichnet die christliche Lebenshaltung, wie es schon der Christenfeind Celsus feststellte.[19] Aus dem Enkomion auf die XL Märtyrer ergibt sich, dass Mut und Tapferkeit (ἀνδρεία) nötig sind, um den Lebensgrundsatz der Weltverachtung zu leben. Denn seine Rede will zur „Tapferkeit" aufrufen; das Enkomion versteht Basilius als „Aufruf an die Versammelten zur Tugend".[20] Basilius will das bewerkstelligen, indem er mittels des Hörens die Tugend der Märtyrer vor Augen stellt, d.h. deren Taten erinnert.

Die Taten selber, d.h. das Faktische ist in ein paar kurzen Sätzen in die Rede eingestreut. Ich benenne es und gebe damit die Daten zum

---

18 „Ein Enkomion auf Märtyrer besteht nämlich darin, die Versammelten zur Tugend aufzurufen. Reden über Heilige unterliegen ja nicht den Gesetzen von Lobreden. Die Lobredner nehmen die Gründe für ihr Loben aus weltlichen Anlässen. Aber ‚denen die Welt gekreuzigt ist', wie kann etwas Weltliches Stoff für Berühmtheit sein?" (PG 31, 509A10–B2). Gal 6,14: Ἐμοὶ δὲ μὴ γένοιτο καυχᾶσθαι εἰ μὴ ἐν τῷ σταυρῷ τοῦ κυρίου ἡμῶν Ἰησοῦ Χριστοῦ, δι' οὗ ἐμοὶ κόσμος ἐσταύρωται κἀγὼ κόσμῳ.

19 Origenes zitiert Kelsos (Contra Celsum V 64).

20 Monique Alexandre hat für das Thema der „martyrs par le témoignage de leur conscience" auf Origenes, In Numeros homilia X 2 verwiesen: Les nouveaux martyrs. Motifs martyrologiques dans la vie des saints et thèmes hagiographiques dans l'éloge chez Grégoire de Nysse, in: Andreas Spira, ed., The Biographical Works of Gregory of Nyssa. Proceedings of the Fifth International Colloquium on Gregory of Nyssa (Mainz, 6-10 September 1982), PatMS 12 (Cambridge/Mass.: The Philadelphia Patristic Foundation, Ltd., 1984), 33–70, dort 42. Origenes verbindet den asketischen Kampf, den der ‚Gerechte' im Verborgenen des Herzens gegen unsichtbare Feinde führt, mit 2Kor 1,12. Der eindeutige Beleg ist allerdings des Origenes Kommentar zu Ps 118,157, wie er in der Katenenüberlieferung aufbewahrt ist. Ich zitiere daraus: ἐὰν γὰρ μὴ ἀγωνίσωμαι ἵν᾽ ὁμολογήσω τὸν Θεὸν διὰ τῆς σωφροσύνης καὶ τῶν λοιπῶν ἀρετῶν, ἀρνησίθεος γίνομαι· ὥσπερ καὶ γεγόνασί τινες μάρτυρες, – οὕτω δὲ λέγω, ὡς ἔθος τῇ Ἐκκλησίᾳ ὀνομάζειν –, οὕτως μάρτυς τοσαυτάκις γίνεται τοῦ θεοῦ ὁσάκις διώκεται ὑπὸ δυνάμεων ἀντικειμένων καὶ οὐ νικᾶται οὐδὲ ἡττᾶται πάθει τινὶ ἀτιμίας· ὁ οὖν δίκαιος οὐκ ἔστιν ὅτε οὐ διώκεται, οὐκ ἔστιν ὅτε οὐ μαρτυρεῖ ἐπὶ ἀοράτων δυνάμεων ἐν τῷ κρυπτῷ τῆς καρδίας. περὶ τούτου τοῦ μαρτυρίου φησὶ ὁ Ἀπόστολος· Τοῦτο γάρ ἐστι τὸ καύχημα ἡμῶν, τὸ μαρτύριον τῆς συνειδήσεως ἡμῶν (2Kor 1,12), aus: Marguerite Harl avec la collaboration de Gilles Dorival, La chaîne palestinienne sur le psaume 118, tome I, SC 189 (Paris: Les Éditions du Cerf, 1972), 436,12–21. Monique Alexandre verweist auch auf Athanasius, Vita Antonii 47, wo es von Antonius heißt: Ἐπειδὴ δὲ λοιπὸν ὁ διωγμὸς ἐπαύσατο, καὶ μεμαρτύρηκεν ὁ μακαρίτης ἐπίσκοπος Πέτρος, ἀπεδήμησε, καὶ πάλιν εἰς τὸ μοναστήριον ἀνεχώρει, καὶ ἦν ἐκεῖ καθ' ἡμέραν μαρτυρῶν τῇ συνειδήσει καὶ ἀγωνιζόμενος τοῖς τῆς πίστεως ἄθλοις. Καὶ γὰρ καὶ ἀσκήσει πολλῇ καὶ συντονωτέρᾳ ἐκέχρητο.

Martyrium der XL Märtyrer. Es sind Soldaten, die ins römische Heer konskribiert worden waren. Am Anfang steht das Edikt, Christus nicht zu bekennen. Das Edikt ist an das stationäre Militär gerichtet. Aus den Reihen der Soldaten treten vierzig (XL) hervor und legen öffentlich das Bekenntnis ab: „Ich bin Christ!" Damit, so sagt Basilius, haben die Vierzig den Kampfplatz betreten. Es folgt eine Konfrontation mit Zureden und Drohen. Der „Machthaber", wohl Statthalter oder Kommandant, ersinnt als Strafe, dass „alle nackt unter freiem Himmel mitten in der Stadt durch Erfrieren sterben sollen". Die Vierzig ziehen sich aus „und gingen dem frostigen Tod durch Erfrieren entgegen". Ein warmes Badehaus ist als Köder für Überläufer in der Nähe; einer läuft dorthin, und der vor Kälte Starre stirbt sofort: „bei der Berührung mit der Wärme löst sich sein Fleisch auf". Der Aufseher im Badehaus wird durch eine Vision bekehrt, „wirft seine Bekleidung ab und mischt sich unter die Nackten und ruft: ‚Ich bin Christ!'." Am nächsten Morgen werden die Erfrorenen zur Verbrennung gekarrt und „die Überreste des Feuers (τὰ λείψανα τοῦ πυρός) in den Fluss geworfen". Zusatz: Einer wird nicht auf den Karren zur Verbrennung geworfen, weil er noch atmet. Dessen Mutter tritt vor und hievt ihn zu den Übrigen auf den Karren – soweit die Fakten, die Basilius mitteilt.

Exkurs

Außer den Reden auf die XL Märtyrer, die in den Anmerkungen 8–10 genannt sind, gibt es noch folgende Überlieferungen:
– Eine Rede, die unter dem Namen Ephraem überliefert ist (CPG 3962). Der Verfasser sagt selber, dass Basilius von Caesarea ihm von dem Martyrium der XL Märtyrer berichtet habe; das kann die Kenntnis der Rede des Basilius meinen.[21] Jedenfalls können alle mitgeteilten Fakten aus Basilius entnommen sein bis auf drei Überschüsse: 1) Es wird die Zeit mit Kaiser Licinius angegeben; 2) es wird Sebaste genannt. 3) Es wird Erfrieren auf dem See angenommen, während Basilius explizit sagte: „mitten in der Stadt" und den gefrorenen See nur

---

21   Die Belege hierfür sind: In XL martyres, in: *Ephraem Syri opera omnia quae exstant Graece, Syriace, Latine in sex tomos distributa. Tomus secundus: graece et latine*, ed. Josephus S. Assemani (Rom: Typographia Pontifica Vaticana, 1743), 341–356, dort 341EF; Encomium in S. Basilium Magnum, in: Sylvius Ioseph Mercati (ed.), *S. Ephraem Syri Opera, tomus I*, Monumenta Biblica et Ecclesiastica 1 (Rom: Pontificus Institutus Biblicus, 1915), 113–188, Strophen 98–105.

als Beispiel für den starken Frost anführte; es könnte bei „Ephraem" ein rheto-
risches „Missverständnis" vorliegen.[22]
– Johannes Chrysostomus bei Photius, Bibliotheca codex 274; Photius exzerpiert
nur die Partien, die allgemein über Märtyrer und Martyrium handeln.
– Gaudentius, Tractatus XVII 4–36. Seine Erzählung über das Martyrium der
XL Märtyrer hat als einzige Vorlage die Rede des Basilius, wie Gaudentius
selber sagt (§ 17).
– Außerdem ist überliefert eine *Passio XL martyrum*.[23] Über deren Entstehungs-
zeit ist nichts bekannt. Auf jeden Fall ist die *Passio* sekundär und für historische
Fakten unbrauchbar, trotz des Ausgleichsversuches von Pio Franchi de' Cavalieri.[24] Jedoch muss vermerkt werden, dass die *Passio XL martyrum* den Provinzstatthalter Ἀγρικόλαος nennt. Ein Provinzstatthalter ist für Armenia minor
im Jahre 303 möglicherweise ein historisches Faktum.[25] Dux ist in der *Passio XL*
martyrum Lysias.[26] Beide Namen und Ämter erscheinen auch in der *Passio*
Eustratii, die ihren Bericht in die Zeit des Kaisers Diokletian datiert.[27] Die *Passio*
XL martyrum gibt das Datum mit Kaiser Licinius, also zwanzig Jahre später. Wo
setzt die Fiktivität ein? Die *Passio XL martyrum* lässt das Erfrieren auf dem See
vor der Stadt Sebaste stattfinden. Gregor von Nyssa dagegen nennt die Ther-
men in der Stadt und sagt dies vor den Sebastenern. Basilius sagt: „mitten in
der Stadt."[28]

---

22   Franchi de' Cavalieri, *I santi quaranta martiri* versucht nachzuweisen, dass Basilius,
     Gregor von Nyssa (In XL martyres Ia+b) und Ephraem Graecus alle eine schriftliche
     Vorlage hatten (160–164 und 172). Diese Vorlage habe verschiedene Formen gehabt,
     aber alle Formen bezeichnet er als Vorformen der legendären *Passio*. Der Einzelver-
     gleich der Fakten in den Reden ist sehr ausführlich, ausführlicher als meine Über-
     sicht. Ich halte es für erwägenswert, Ephraem Graecus als eine Quelle der *Passio* ein-
     zuordnen.
23   Text: Oscar von Gebhardt, *Acta martyrum selecta. Ausgewählte Märtyreracten und*
     andere Urkunden aus der Verfolgungszeit der christlichen Kirche (Berlin: Verlag von Ale-
     xander Duncker, 1902), 170–181 nach drei Handschriften. Bei Albert Ehrhardt †, *Ü-*
     berlieferung und Bestand der hagiographischen und homiletischen Literatur der griechischen
     Kirche von den Anfängen bis zum Ende des 16. Jahrhunderts. Erster Teil: Die Überlieferung
     III. Band 1. Hälfte, TU 52 (Leipzig: J.C. Hinrichs, 1943), 310/r nennt eine Handschrift
     A.D. 1607. Von Gebhardt benutzt drei ältere Handschriften.
24   De' Cavalieri, *I santi quaranta martiri* (siehe Anm. 2).
25   Siehe Pierre Maraval, *La passion inédite de s. Athénogène en Cappadoce*, SHG 75 (Brüs-
     sel: Société des Bollandistes, 1990), 19 note 71; Christopher P. Jones, Rezension zu
     Maraval, JThS.NS 43 (1992), 245–248 – bestätigt von Timothy D. Barnes, *Early Chri-*
     stian Hagiography and Roman History, Tria Corda 5 (Tübingen: Mohr Siebeck, 2010),
     147–148.
26   175,30 ed. Gebhardt.
27   PG 116, 469AB, worauf Jones hinweist.
28   PG 31, 516A3. Patricia Karlin-Hayter, Passio of the XL Martyrs of Sebasteia. The
     Greek Tradition: The Earliest Account (BHG 1201), *AnBoll* 109 (1991), 249–304 ver-

– Historisch auch nicht verwertbar ist das *Testamentum XL martyrum*. Dessen Text hat Nathanael Bonwetsch ediert.[29] Bonwetsch verteidigt die Echtheit; sie wird noch heute für möglich gehalten.[30]

Nach meinem Urteil bleibt des Basilius' Rede die überlieferte Faktengrundlage. Somit ist die Nennung des Kaisers Licinius (so „Ephraem", aber auch Sozomenus, H.E. IX 2) eine wahrscheinliche Einordnung. Sie könnte gedeckt sein durch Eusebius von Caesarea (H.E. X 8,10), der über Licinius schreibt: τῇ κεφαλῇ τοὺς κατὰ πόλιν στρατιώτας ἡγεμονικῶν ταγμάτων ἀποβάλλεσθαι, εἰ μὴ τοῖς δαίμοσιν αἱροῖντο θύειν, παρεκελεύετο (vgl. Vita Constantini I 54,1). Eusebius sagt dazu sonst nichts; ihm sind also (?) keine Hinrichtungen bekannt. Die Zeit des Ediktes fiele in die Jahre 321-323 n.Chr.[31]

Sebaste als der Ort des Martyriums („Ephraim", Sozomenus) ist offenbar Tradition; dazu stimmt Gregor von Nyssa in einem Brief.[32] Die Lokalisierung von Gregors *In XL martyres* Ia + b in Sebaste ist eine Wahrscheinlichkeitsannahme.[33]

Der Befehl zum Opfern ist bei „Ephraem" und Gaudentius eine evidente Auslegung von des Basilius Formulierung.[34]

Kerkerhaft steht nicht bei Basilius, auch nicht in Gregors erster Rede (II); jedoch spricht er in seiner späteren Rede von einer „langen Kerkerhaft", wodurch sie für den Hauptkampf trainiert werden.[35] Es ist nicht zu entscheiden, ob Gregor die Kerkerhaft aus Basilius[36] herausgesponnen oder ob er eine neue Information (z.B. in Sebaste) erhalten hat.

---

sucht die Passio als die historische Grundlage für die Predigten zu retten. Sie rekonstruiert eine Urgestalt, indem sie Interpolationen identifiziert. Die Interpolationen erkennt sie mithilfe eines religionswissenschaftlichen Modells über Wunder. Mich hat sie gar nicht überzeugt.

29 Nathanael Bonwetsch, *Das Testament der vierzig Märtyrer*, SGTK I.1 (Leipzig: A. Deichert'sche Verlagsbuchhandlung Nachf., 1897), 71–95, dort 75–80.

30 Siehe Herbert Musurillo, *The Acts of the Christian Martyrs. Introduction, Texts, and Translations*, OECT (Oxford: Oxford University Press, 1972), XLIX–L (Text 354–361 nach Bonwetsch).

31 Siehe Timothy D. Barnes, *Constantine and Eusebius* (Cambridge: Mass./London: Harvard University Press, 1991), 71.

32 Ep. 1,5 nach einer genialen Konjektur von Werner Jaeger; siehe GNO VIII/2, 4,14 und vgl. Paul Devos, Saint Pierre Ier, évêque de Sébastée, dans uns lettre de Grégoire de Nazianze, *AnBoll* 79 (1961), 346–360.

33 Siehe Ia (GNO X/1, 141,8.12–13): Versammlungsort = Martyriumsort; Ib (GNO X/1, 153,14–15): auf dem Thermengelände.

34 Siehe Anm. 51. Bei Gregor vgl. II (GNO X/1, 160,27) und Ib (GNO X/1, 148,2–5).

35 In XL martyres Ib (GNO X/1, 150,6–16).

36 Vgl. PG 31, 513A6–C10.

Das Testament enthält keine Zeitangabe, nennt aber in der Überschrift Sebaste. Die namentlich genannten vierzig Märtyrer legen testamentarisch ihren Willen fest, an einem einzigen Ort beerdigt zu werden, und bedrohen den mit der Strafe Gottes, der sich einen Überrest privat aneignet. Sie sind eingekerkert und erwarten einen Tod durch Verbrennung. Vorstellbar ist die Abfassung eines derartigen Testamentes der Eingekerkerten, und der Tod durch Erfrieren wäre also als eine noch nicht beschlossene Maßnahme zu werten. Auffällig ist jedoch, dass ihr Soldatenberuf nicht angedeutet wird. Es fällt ebenfalls auf, dass nach aller sonstigen Überlieferung – dem Testament zuwider – sich Reliquien weit verbreitet haben und die im Testament genannte „Ruhestätte" nirgendwo erwähnt wird.

Was die vierzig Märtyrer zu erdulden hatten und worin ihre Tapferkeit und ἀρετή besteht, stellt Basilius so dar: Erstens gibt er eine medizinische Beschreibung, wie durch Erfrieren der Tod eintritt; zweitens schildert er den damaligen Frost durch Verweis auf den See bei der Stadt, der total zugefroren sei.[37] Und drittens schaltet er eine *adhortatio*, eine Aufmunterungsrede der nackt in Nacht und Frost Stehenden ein, in welcher es unter anderem heißt: „Für eine Nacht tauschen wir die ganze Ewigkeit. Der Fuß soll abgetrennt werden, damit er auf Dauer mit den Engeln wandelt. Die Hand soll abfallen, damit sie frei ist, sich zum Herrn zu erheben."[38] Der Todeskampf wird nicht als Fakt ausgebreitet, sondern insinuiert (vorweg die medizinische Beschreibung einerseits und die Aufmunterungsrede andererseits).

Die sog. Paränese, der Epilog, an die Zuhörer besteht in drei Punkten: Erstens, dass (Teile der) Überreste der Märtyrer immer alle Vierzig einschließen; denn das Feuer habe sie miteinander vermischt.[39] Zweitens, dass diese „heilige Truppe" „die mächtigsten Anwälte" bei Gott seien,[40] Adressaten beim Gebet „in Not", beim Gebet für die Heimkehr des Mannes, bei Krankheit, und für Bitten, es ihnen gleichzutun.[41] Implizit ergibt sich drittens: „Sie haben euch die Pforten des Paradieses geöffnet." Wodurch? „Weil sie in der Blüte der Jugend das Leben verachteten und den Herrn mehr liebten als die Eltern, als die Kinder."[42] Für die Kirche sind sie ein „Siegesmal für die Frömmigkeit".[43]

---

37 Oratio in XL martyres (PG 31, 516A4–B6 und B6–C1).
38 PG 31, 517B1–4.
39 PG 31, 521B8–C3.
40 PG 31, 524C6–10.
41 PG 31, 524 A5–14.
42 PG 31, 524C11–D1. Hören soll man in der hymnischen Anrede an Märtyrer die implizite Ermahnung.
43 PG 31, 525A6.

2. Gregorii Nysseni In XL martyres II

Gregor von Nyssa hält sein Enkomion auf die XL Märtyrer nach dem Tod des Basilius in Caesarea, im dortigen Martyrium[44] und unter explizierter Berufung auf des Basilius' Rede. Die Rede ist am Jahrestag der XL Märtyrer gehalten; die Jaeger-Edition (GNO X/1) bezeichnet sie als II; ich übernehme die Datierung von Jean Daniélou[45] auf den 9. März 379.

Ich beginne mit ein paar Beobachtungen zum Aufbau des Enkomions. Basilius setzte mit der rhetorischen Frage ein: „Welcher Märtyrerfreund könnte je des Gedenkens der Märtyrer überdrüssig werden?" und antwortet mit der Begründung: Weil im Ehren der Märtyrer der gemeinsame Gott geehrt wird und weil das Preisen der Märtyrer deren Nachahmung einschließt und so den gleichen Lohn verheißt. Dann gibt Basilius an, dass nicht einer, sondern vierzig zu preisen seien, und er macht Sprüche wie: Schon einen Märtyrer zu bewundern, überfordere seine Redekunst; aber diese Phalanx von Soldaten, diese unschlagbare Truppe, sei „wie im Kämpfen unbesiegbar, so im Loben unerreichbar". Dann sagt Basilius: „Wohlan, durch Erinnern bringen wir sie [zu uns] herein." Und dies geschehe mit derselben Wirkung, zur Tapferkeit zu erwecken, wie in Schrift und in Gemälden, nämlich durch das Hören des gesprochenen Wortes würden sie uns vor Augen gestellt. Dann greift Basilius auf die Phrase der Rhetorik zurück, dass ein Enkomion bei Christen nicht weltliche Vorzüge als Stoff benutzen könne, wie die Vierzig ja auch keine gemeinsame irdische Vaterstadt haben – der erste rhetorische Topos in einem Encomium -, sondern die Gottesstadt dort oben.[46] Soweit die Einleitung, danach beginnt die Kampfesschilderung.

Gregor dagegen beginnt mit dem Hinweis, dass das römische Militär den Tag des Jahresbeginns mit Kampfübungen feiere, er selber dagegen den Redekampf aufnehme, um die XL Soldaten Christi seinen Zuhörern zur Bewunderung vorzuführen. Denn Erzählungen von Tugend (ἀρετή) haben erzieherische Wirkung und zwar besonders die durch Hören aufgenommene Erzählung.[47] Dann lässt Gregor eine kurze Abhandlung zur Handlungspsychologie folgen: was durchs Hören in

---

44 Einer der beiden Zeugen der handschriftlichen Überlieferung überliefert den Titel wie folgt: τοῦ αὐτοῦ εἰς τοὺς αὐτοὺς λόγος ἐγκωμιαστικὸς ῥηθεὶς ἐν τῷ μαρτυρίῳ (GNO X/1, 159,2–3 mit Apparat für den Codex Venetus Marcianus graecus 69, saeculo XII).

45 Jean Daniélou, La chronologie des sermons de Grégoire de Nysse, RevSR 29 (1955), 346–372, dort 346–348.

46 Oratio in XL martyres (PG 31, 508B1–C14).

47 In XL martyres II (GNO X/1, 159,4–17).

die Seele eindringe, baue Vorstellungen auf und löse so das Streben zum Tun aus.[48] Als Ziel nennt er die Erziehung zu Frömmigkeit und Gottesfreundschaft.[49] Dann stellt er sich selber dar als in einem doppelten Kampf befindlich, einmal der Größe der Sache in einer Rede nicht gerecht werden zu können, zum andern hinter dem Enkomion des berühmten Basilius zurückbleiben zu müssen. Aber er wolle weder schweigen noch in einen Wettkampf mit seinem Vorredner eintreten, „sondern ich will euch, meinen Hörern, zu Nutzen sein. Jeder zieht ja Nutzen daraus, dass er das Größere von reicher Begabten ausnutzt."[50] Dann beginnt die Kampfesschilderung, in der gleichen Satzkonstruktion wie Basilius: ein langes Ἐπειδὴ = „Als der gottlose Befehl ... – τότε = „zu dem Zeitpunkt begannen die Seligen ihre Heldentat ...".[51]

Basilius flicht vier Reden ein: (1) Die Köderrede des Machthabers mit der (2) langen Antwort der XL Märtyrer, (3) die lange adhortatio, Aufmunterungsrede, der in Nacht und Frost Stehenden, (4) eine Rede der Mutter an den zurückgelassenen Märtyrer.[52] Darauf lässt sich Gregor nicht ein. Er gestaltet das Emphatische anders und verschiebt dadurch die Akzente. Basilius hatte durch eine lange Antwort der Märtyrer auf das Zureden und Drohen, ihr Christusbekenntnis aufzugeben, den Bibelspruch eingeschärft: „Die Welt ist mir gekreuzigt" (Gal 6,14). Gregor verkürzt auf den Satz: „Sie bekundeten laut unseren Glauben und sagten dabei, dass sie dieses vergängliche Leben gering achteten und ihre Körper der Bestrafung, welcher Art auch immer, preisgäben."[53] Darauf gibt Gregor der Erfindung der neuen Todesart, nämlich durch Erfrieren, eine besondere Emphase; er lässt den Machthaber ein Selbstgespräch führen.[54] Und wie Kälte und Frost die Natur pervertie-

---

48 In XL martyres II (GNO X/1, 159,17–160,3).

49 ... καὶ ὑμεῖς διὰ τῆς μνήμης παιδευθῆτε τὸ εὐσεβὲς καὶ φιλόθεον (GNO X/1, 160,2–3).

50 In XL martyres II (GNO X/1, 160,4–21; Zitat: 19–21).

51 Basilius, Oratio in XL martyres: Ἐπειδὴ δὲ περιηγγέλη τὸ ἄθεον ἐκεῖνο καὶ ἀσεβὲς κήρυγμα... (PG 31, 509D1) – τότε δὴ οὗτοι, οἱ ἀήττητοι καὶ γενναῖοι τοῦ Χριστοῦ στρατιῶται... (PG 31, 512A15). Gregor, In XL martyres II: ἐπειδὴ δὲ ὁ τηνικαῦτα κρατῶν εἷς ὢν τῶν πολυθέων... (GNO X/1, 160,24) – τότε δὴ τότε τὴν τυραννικὴν ὠμότητα καὶ τὸν μισόθεον νόμον ἀνδραγαθίαν ἑαυτῶν οἱ μακάριοι ποιησάμενοι ... (GNO X/1, 160,29–30).

52 Oratio in XL martyres (PG 31, 512C12–D2); Antwort (PG 31, 513A6–C10): ὥσπερ ἐν σκύλων διαρπαγῇ ἀλλήλοις ἐγκελευόμενοι· Μὴ γὰρ ἱμάτιον, φησίν... (PG 31, 517A1–C3; Mutter in PG 31, 524B10–13).

53 ... τὴν πίστιν ἡμῶν ἐξεβόησαν μικρὸν φροντίζειν λέγοντες τῆς προσκαίρου ταύτης ζωῆς καὶ παρέχειν ἔκδοτα τὰ σώματα ποικίλαις κολάσεων ἰδέαις (GNO X/1, 161,1–3).

54 In XL martyres II (GNO X/1, 161,6–13).

ren, führt Gregor ausführlicher vor, um, wie er sagt, über das Durchhaltevermögen (καρτερία) der Märtyrer bei frostigem Tod durch Erfrieren zu belehren.[55] Basilius berichtet: „Als die Märtyrer den Befehl (zur Hinrichtung durch Erfrieren) hörten, rissen sie freudig das letzte Hemd vom Leib und gingen dem Erfrierungstod durch Frost entgegen."[56] Was sie erlitten, fängt Basilius in einer langen *adhortatio* auf; er legt sie den Märtyrern in den Mund. Gregor dagegen: „Da standen sie also und wurden zu Eis. Ihre Glieder zitterten, aber ihre Gesinnung blieb unbewegt."[57] Den Verlauf des Sterbens gestaltet Gregor als einen Schaukampf vor Engeln, Menschen und Dämonen. Aus dieser Zuschauerperspektive erzählt er. Die Engel warten mit ausgebreiteten Händen auf die Loslösung der Seelen. Die Menschen sind gespannt, ob die übermenschlichen Schmerzen ertragen werden. „Die Dämonen folgten dem Geschehen besonders gespannt, da sie so gerne den Fall der Kämpfer und ihr feiges Einknicken vor der Gefahr sehen wollten. Aber ihre Hoffnung wurde zuschanden, weil Gott seine Kämpfer stärkte. – Die Seligen sahen also ihre Extremitäten, jeder seine eigenen und jeder die der übrigen. Dem einen ging der Fuß ab oder fielen die Zähne heraus; ein anderer lag da, weil ihm jegliche Wärme ausgekältet war. Wie Stürme auf einen Wald treffen und die höchsten Bäume entwurzeln, so wurde die Frontlinie der Seligen von der Winterkälte umgelegt....Angetreten zum Kampf gegen die Barbaren kämpften sie am Ende gegen den Feind der ganzen Menschheit."[58]

Die örtliche Nähe des Erfrierungsortes zu einem warmen Badehaus, die Basilius ungeschickt einführt, nutzt Gregor, um die Freiwilligkeit der Märtyrer zu betonen.[59] Sie hatten die Alternative der Straffreiheit, falls sie opferten. Durch sein Opfer an die „Götter" löschte ein Christ sein Christsein aus. Dieses Grundelement des christlichen Märtyrerverständnisses ist in den besprochenen Predigten klar ausgebreitet.

Das irdische Ende der Märtyrer beschreibt Basilius und hebt es durch ein deutendes Bild heraus: „Als schließlich der Tag anbrach,

---

55 In XL martyres II (GNO X/1, 162,1–27): ταῦτα δὲ ὑμῖν οὐκ ἀπὸ καιροῦ ἐφυσιολόγησα, ἀλλ' ἵνα τὴν καρτερίαν τῶν ἀνδρῶν καταμάθητε τὸν τρόπον τῆς τιμωρίας ἐπισκεψάμενοι. (162,11–13).

56 Oratio in XL martyres (PG 31, 515C2–5).

57 In XL martyres II: Ἔστησαν οὖν καὶ ἐπήγνυντο τὰ μέλη τρέμοντες καὶ τὴν γνώμην ἀκλόνητοι (GNO X/1, 162,31–163,1).

58 In XL martyres II: ... θέαν παρέχοντες ἐναγώνιον ἀγγέλοις ἀνθρώποις δαίμοσι – οἱ κατὰ βαρβάρων ὁπλιτεύειν ἀπογραψάμενοι καὶ πρὸς τὸν κοινὸν ἐχθρὸν τῆς ἀνθρωπότητος τὸν ἀγῶνα τελέσαντες (GNO X/1, 163,1–19).

59 GNO X/1, 163,20–164,8.

wurden sie dem Feuer übergeben, auch wenn noch jemand atmete, und die Feuerüberbleibsel wurden in den Fluss geworfen. Folglich durchlief ihr Kampf die ganze Schöpfung." Auf die vier Elemente Erde, Luft, Feuer und Wasser verweist er.[60] Gregor dagegen hält die Verbrennung der Leichen für eine besondere Untat des Machthabers und unterstreicht das nicht nur durch den Vergleich mit wilden Tieren, sondern zusätzlich mit einer fiktiven Rede: „Und einer der Märtyrer könnte zu Recht dem Machthaber sagen: ‚Du Nichtiger, ich fürchte deine Grausamkeit nicht mehr. Solange die Seelen in den Erstarrenden anwesend waren, war ich in Furcht, ob die übergroße Folter die Tapferkeit der Frommen besiegen würde…'".[61]

Gregor beschließt seine Rede ganz eigenwillig. Er erzählt zwei Geschichten aus seinem eigenen Leben. In der ersten Geschichte berichtet er, dass es bei ihm zu Hause Überreste der XL Märtyrer gebe. Ins Grab seiner Eltern habe er Partikel gelegt, damit die Eltern am Jüngsten Tage zusammen mit den mächtigen Fürsprechern auferweckt werden.[62] (Ich merke an: es sind also nur die Seelen der Märtyrer im Himmel.) Und aus einer eigenen Begegnung könne er, Gregor, bezeugen, dass die XL Märtyrer Anwälte von Menschen in Not seien und freien Zugang zu Gott haben. Er selber habe einen Soldaten berichten hören, wie ihm im Martyrium der XL Märtyrer, auf dem Familiengut, während eines Traumgesichtes sein lahmer Fuß geheilt wurde.[63] Ob Gregor diesen Wunderbericht Zweifeln über die Wirksamkeit dieser Märtyrerreliquien entgegensetzt oder ob die Wunder bei Märtyrerreliquien überhaupt ein neues Phänomen sind, mag offen bleiben. Übrigens hatte Basilius an der entsprechenden Stelle die gewisse Gegenwart Gottes mit dem Jesusspruch Mt 18,20 bewiesen: „Wo zwei oder drei in meinem Namen versammelt sind, da bin ich mitten unter ihnen." Ja, sagt Basilius, hier haben wir XL.[64]

In einem zweiten Eigenbericht setzt Gregor seine eigene Mutter an die Stelle, wo Basilius die Mutter eines der Märtyrer eingeführt hatte. Seine eigene Mutter habe vor vierzig Jahren[65] die erste Gedenkfeier der XL Märtyrer zu einem Termin, der ihm gar nicht passte, festgelegt, und er habe sich in jugendlicher Unvernunft mit der Mutter über die verbindliche Einladung gestritten. Er erzählt, dass die Märtyrer ihm,

---

60   Oratio in XL martyres (PG 31, 521A10–B2; Zitat A10–13).
61   In XL martyres II (GNO X/1, 165,19–166,6; Zitat 165,26–166,1).
62   In XL martyres II (GNO X/1, 166,7–12).
63   In XL martyres II (GNO X/1, 166,12–167,9).
64   Oratio in XL martyres (PG 31, 524A2–5).
65   GNO X/1, 168,7–8; dafür wäre das Jahr 339 n.Chr. anzunehmen.

nachdem er eine bittere Reueträne auf ihr Reliquienbehältnis in seinem Hause habe fallen lassen, eine Untat vergeben haben.[66] Und so bildet – wie bei Basilius – der Verweis auf die Anwaltschaft der XL Märtyrer vor Gott den Schluss, aber obenan und an erster Stelle: der mit Sünden beladene Mensch – wenn er sein Bittgebet spricht und diese XL Märtyrer als Fürbitter bei Gott hat, dann wird sein Gebet erfüllt werden.[67] Bei Abraham, sagt Gregor, hatte sich Gott auf zehn Gerechte in Sodom eingelassen (Gen 18,32), hier aber sind vierzig, „eine starke Leibgarde gegen Feinde, vertrauenswürdige Fürbitter beim Herrn. Mit solcher Hoffnung soll sich der Christ mutig erweisen gegen den Teufel, der Versuchungen ausheckt… gegen Naturgewalten. Denn für Not und für jedes Missgeschick genügt die Kraft der Märtyrer, da Christus sie mit reichlicher Gnade beschenkt. Dem sei Ehre von Ewigkeit zu Ewigkeit. Amen."[68]

Man kann sicher fragen, warum nicht Christus selber als Gnadengeber angesprochen wird, warum die Bitten und das Beten nicht an Christus gerichtet werden – das lehrte doch deutlich der Hebräerbrief –, warum stattdessen vermittelnde Mittler eingeführt werden. Aber zu beachten ist Gregors Hinwendung zur Sünde des Menschen, das Gebet um Vergebung, die Bitte um die Bewahrung vor den Versuchungen des Teufels.

3. Gregorii Nysseni In XL martyres Ia+b

Gregor hielt ein zweites Enkomion auf die XL Märtyrer, vermutlich im Jahr 383 n.Chr., jedenfalls in Sebaste. Er begann im Martyriumsgebäude, aber wegen Überfüllung und Lärm musste er die Rede abbrechen I(a). Er setzt das Enkomion I(b) am nächsten Tag im Kirchengebäude fort. Da er in Sebaste auftritt, weiß er, dass die versammelten Hörer die Geschichte eigentlich kennen. Aber die Ehrung geschieht eben im Erzählen der Heldentat. Gregor vollbringt das Wunder, dass er die be-

---

66   In XL martyres II (GNO X/1, 167,10–168,4).

67   In XL martyres II: ὁ γὰρ τοσούτους ἔχων πρεσβευτὰς οὔποτ' ἂν ἄπρακτος ἀπέλθοι προσευχῆς καὶ δεήσεως, κἂν σφόδρα βεβαρημένος ὑπάχῃ τοῖς ἁμαρτήμασι (GNO X/1, 169,8–10).

68   In XL martyres II: Τεσσαράκοντα γὰρ μάρτυρες, ἰσχυροὶ μὲν κατὰ τῶν ἐχθρῶν ὑπασπισταί, ἀξιόπιστοι δὲ τῆς πρὸς τὸν δεσπότην ἱκεσίας παράκλητοι· μετὰ τῆς τούτων ἐλπίδος καταθαρρείτω Χριστιανὸς καὶ τοῦ διαβόλου πειρασμοὺς ῥάπτοντος καὶ… πρὸς πᾶσαν γὰρ χρείαν καὶ περίστασιν ἡ τούτων δύναμις ἐξαρκεῖ πλουσίαν παρὰ Χριστοῦ λαβοῦσα τὴν χάριν· ᾧ πρέπει πᾶσα δόξα εἰς τοὺς αἰῶνας τῶν αἰώνων. ἀμήν. (GNO X/1, 169,16–25).

kannten Tatsachen, verflochten mit einigen christlichen Grundsätzen, zu einer fulminanten Lobrede macht, dabei allerdings die Grenzen des Anstandes überschreitet. Des Basilius´ Rede liefert ihm das Wissen wie auch die Ansätze zur rhetorischen Ausmalung. Das versammelte Volk soll durch eine rhetorische Darbietung beeindruckt werden. Die Hörer will er zu Zuschauern machen, seine Rede lässt den Kampf in der Arena vor ihren Augen entstehen.[69] Es wird zu einer dramatischen bis burlesken Erzählung. Wie in der Hiobgeschichte, deren Anfang die Schriftlesung war, zieht „der Widersacher des menschlichen Lebens" umher und „ertrug es nicht, gereifte Haltung in der Jugend zu sehen", „schöne Körper mit Enthaltsamkeit geschmückt", „einen bewaffneten Chor durch den Heeresdienst vor Gott tanzend."[70] Tugend erregt seinen Neid.[71] Dem Militärkommandanten flüstert der Teufel ein, die Christen müssten geopfert werden, sonst könne er gegen die Barbaren nicht siegen.[72] Erster Teil der Strafe für das „gute Bekenntnis" (vgl. 1Tim 6,12–13) sind eiserne Ketten. „Welch anmutiger Anblick für die Augen der Christen."[73] Das eine Wort: "Christus", im Munde der Bekenner, „verwundete das Herz des Widersachers",[74] im Himmel aber löste es Beifall und Freudengeschrei aus.[75] Und Gregor will sich noch weiter in die Überwelt vorwagen[76]: „der gerechte Kampfrichter bot die Siegeskränze an, der Oberfeldherr der göttlichen Macht hielt die Preise für die Sieger bereit, und der Heilige Geist sorgte für die Empfangsgeschenke."[77] (Nota: Die Trinitätslehre stand 383 n.Chr. kirchenpolitisch zur Debatte). Gregor kommt aber wieder ins Irdische zurück und fährt

---

69 In XL martyres Ib: Καὶ εἰ δοκεῖ ὡς ἂν ἡδίους γενοίμεθα, πάντα τὰ τῶν μαρτύρων ἐφεξῆς ἀναλαβῶμεν οἷον ὑπ' ὄψιν ἄγοντες τῷ παρόντι θεάτρῳ τὴν ἄθλησιν (GNO X/1, 146,6–8).

70 In XL martyres Ib (GNO X/1, 147,18–24).

71 In XL martyres Ib: ὥστε τῷ περιόντι τῆς ἀρετῆς καθ' ἑαυτῶν ἀναστῆσαι τὸν φθόνον (GNO X/1, 147,15–16).

72 In XL martyres Ib (GNO X/1, 148,2–5).

73 In XL martyres Ib: τοῖς δὲ ἦν ἄρα καὶ ὁ δεσμὸς ἐγκαλλώπισμα καὶ θέαμα γλαφυρὸν καὶ ἡδὺ Χριστιανῶν ὀφθαλμοῖς (GNO X/1, 148,10–11).

74 In XL martyres Ib (GNO X/1, 149,25–150,2).

75 In XL martyres Ib (GNO X/1, 150,7–10).

76 In XL martyres Ib: ἔτι ὁ λόγος κατὰ τῶν ἀτολμήτων θρασύνεται, ἔτι τολμᾷ διηγεῖσθαι τὰ ὑπερκόσμια ὅτι... (GNO X/1, 150,23–24); vgl. ebd. (150,5–7): ἀλλὰ παρηνέχθη ἀφηνιάσας ὁ λόγος καὶ ὑπὲρ τοὺς ὅρους ἐξάλλεται καὶ τῶν ἀρρήτων κατατολμᾷ καὶ λέγειν προάγεται, ὡσπερεὶ θεάτης τῶν ἀοράτων γενόμενος...

77 In XL martyres Ib: ... ὁ δίκαιος ἀγωνοθέτης τοὺς ἐπὶ τῇ νίκῃ στεφάνους προέτεινεν, καὶ ὁ ἀρχιστράτηγος τῆς θείας δυνάμεως τὰ ἀριστεῖα τοῖς νικηταῖς παρεσκεύαζεν, καὶ τὸ πνεῦμα τὸ ἅγιον τοῖς παντοδαποῖς ἐδεξιοῦτο χαρίσμασιν (GNO X/1, 150,25–151,1).

fort: „Denn da das Bekenntnis [der Märtyrer] der Glaube an die Trinität war, teilt die Trinität ihnen die Gnade zu." Sofort kann Gregor zum Predigtstoff wechseln. Er fragt: „Was war die Gnade?" und antwortet: „Sie war der manifeste Nachweis, wie überlegen diese XL Kämpfer den ersten Kämpfern, Adam und Eva, sind."[78] Der theologische Kern des predigtartigen Abschnitts ist die gewagte Aussage, dass die Märtyrer dem Tod seine Waffe wegnahmen. Denn stark waren sie, hielten trotz Todesqualen an ihrem Bekenntnis fest. Wo keine Sünde ist, hat der Tod seinen Stachel verloren, entsprechend dem Apostelwort: „Tod, wo ist dein Stachel?" 1Kor 15,55).[79]

Den Schluss[80] seiner Rede leitet Gregor mit dem Hinweis ein, er wolle ein Problem aufgreifen, über das er mit den Zuhörern am Vortage gesprochen habe. „Erinnert euch der Frage! Erinnert euch, wie vergeblich wir nach einer Antwort suchten!" Nach weiteren aufhaltenden Worten nennt er das Problem: Wenn das Paradies durch ein sich drehendes Feuerschwert verschlossen worden sei, wie denn die Heiligen hineinkommen könnten, insbesondere die Märtyrerathleten. Basilius hatte seine Rede mit dem hymnischen Ausruf beendet: O ihr Seligen! „Die Erde hat euch nicht verborgen, sondern der Himmel hat euch aufgenommen. Für Euch stehen die Tore des Paradieses offen." Gregor verkündet jetzt eine Lösung; sie findet sich übrigens in einer anderen Basiliuspredigt. Es sei doch in dem Genesisbericht (Gen 3,24) ausdrücklich mitgeteilt, dass sich das Schwert drehe. Daraus ergebe sich, dass das Schwert den Unwürdigen die scharfe Seite, den Würdigen aber die stumpfe Seite zuwende, „ihnen den Eingang zum Leben öffnend". Die Märtyrer kamen also ins ewige Leben, und wir gelangen durch ihre Fürbitte auch hinein.[81]

---

78 In XL martyres Ib (GNO X/1, 151,1–8).

79 In XL martyres Ib: ἐκεῖνοι [sc. Adam und Eva] καθ' ἑαυτῶν τὸν θάνατον ὥπλισαν (ὅπλον γὰρ θανάτου ἡ ἁμαρτία, φησίν), οὗτοι καθωπλισμένον τῇ ἁμαρτίᾳ τὸν θάνατον διὰ τῆς ἑαυτῶν ἀνδρείας ἠχρείωσαν τῇ ὑπομονῇ τῶν παθημάτων τοῦ κέντρου τὴν ἀκμὴν ἀπαμβλύναντες, ὥστε εἰπεῖν καλῶς· Ποῦ σου, θάνατε, τὸ κέντρον; ποῦ σου, ᾅδη, τὸ νῖκος; (GNO X/1, 151,8–13). Das Zitat (φησίν) ist bisher nicht nachgewiesen. Zu der einmaligen Metapher, dass die Sünde die Waffe des Todes sei, kann man vergleichen *De virginitate* (GNO VIII/1, 306,24–307,1), *In sanctum et salutare Pascha* (GNO IX, 310,20), *In illud Tunc et ipse filius* (GNO III/2, 14,16–17 et 16,7–8).

80 GNO X/1, 155,20–156,20.

81 Basilius, Oratio in XL martyres (PG 31, 524C10–12) und *In sanctum baptisma* (PG 31, 428C1–9). Auf diese Auslegung hat hingewiesen Monique Alexandre, *Le commencement du livre Genèse I–V. La version grecque de la Septante et sa réception*, CAnt 3 (Paris: Beauchesne, 1988), 339.

Jedoch verleitet ein Grundzug der Theologie Gregors dann wieder zu enkomiastischer Rhetorik. Es ist die Unterscheidung von Körper und Seele. Sie tendiert zur Trennung, und rhetorisch nutzt Gregor das so: Der Körper erleidet die Todesqualen des Erfrierens und empfindet richtig unerträgliche Schmerzen, aber die Kraft der Seele wird größer.[82] So weit, so gut. Grenzwertig wird der Spruch Hiobs, den Gregor ihnen beim Ausziehen der Kleider in der frostigen Kälte unter eisigem Himmel in den Mund legt: „Bereitwillig legten sie ihre Bekleidung ab und deklamierten: «Nackt sind wir in die Welt gekommen, nackt kehren wir zurück zu dem, der uns hereingebracht hat.» (vgl. Hi 1,21).[83] Aber dies? „Die selige Jugendtruppe begab sich unter Lachen und Scherzen und in Heiterkeit zum Bestrafungsort" – zum Tod durch Erfrieren.[84] Die Rede Gregors gleitet aus und wird zur Darbietung, wie ein Gladiatorenkampf fesselnd, aber auf Zuschauerseite.

4. Gregorii Nysseni In sanctum Stephanum I

Die Reden Gregors an den Gedenktagen der Märtyrer sind nicht als Predigten konzipiert, sondern als Lobreden, Enkomia. Sie preisen die Tugend der Märtyrer, sie wollen zur Nachahmung anreizen und bewegen. Auf einige könnte der Spruch aus einer Buchbesprechung zutreffen: „Klingt nicht gerade neu, macht aber nichts. Vielleicht müsste man es nur noch mal rumerzählen. Vielleicht mit ein paar mehr Verben, Tu-Wörtern. Damit das auch mal jemand macht."[85] Das Enkomion[86] Gregors auf den Protomärtyrer Stephanus beruht auf allgemein bekanntem Stoff, der Apostelgeschichte Kapitel 6 und 7. Gregor kennt keinen an-

---

82 Vgl. H. Delehaye, Les passions, 147–150 unter der Überschrift: Abus de l'hyperbole. Vgl. In XL martyres Ib: ἡ μὲν γὰρ δύναμις κατὰ μικρὸν διελύετο μαραινιμένη καὶ δαπανωμένη διὰ τῆς πήξεως, ὁ δὲ τῆς ψυχῆς τόνος μείζων ἐγίνετο (GNO X/1 153,26–27); kurz vorher: μᾶλλον δὲ ἡ μὲν φύσις τὸ οἰκεῖον ἔπασχε καὶ τὰ ἀλγεινὰ παρεδέχετο... (ebd. 153,24–25).

83 In XL martyres Ib (GNO X/1, 153,16–19).

84 In XL martyres Ib: καὶ ἡ μακαρία νεότης ἐν γέλωτι καὶ παιδιᾷ καὶ φαιδρότητι τὸν τῆς τιμωρίας κατελάμβανε τόπον (GNO X/1, 153,9–11).

85 Claudia Kohlhase in der Frankfurter Allgemeinen Zeitung (31.5.1995), 13.

86 Im Titel steht ἐγκώμιον, was gemäß der Stemmatik der Zeugen zur ältesten erreichbaren Schicht gehört. In s. Stephanum II wird diese Gattungsbezeichnung im Titel wie auch im Text angegeben (GNO X/1, 98,23; 104,1). Das Datum ist der 26. Dezember 386; der Nachweis steht bei Jean Daniélou, La chronologie, 367. In s. Stephanum II ist einen Tag nach In s. Stephanum I vorgetragen worden. Ich kann die zweite Rede vernachlässigen, da sie nach dem Protomärtyrer sehr schnell auf die Apostel Petrus, Jakobus und Johannes übergeht.

deren Stoff; seine Rede ist die erste uns bekannte rhetorische Bearbeitung des Stephanusmartyriums.[87] Gregor lässt also die körperlichen Qualen, einen Topos in den Märtyrerpredigten aber in der biblischen Geschichte nicht vorkommend, aus. Seine Rhetorik gestaltet die biblische Geschichte um, wie er selber sagt: „Aber lasst uns, Brüder, mittels der Rede in die Arena eilen, wo der große Athlet sich in der Arena des Bekennens bereit macht und gegen den bösen Widersacher des menschlichen Lebens kämpft."[88]

Gregor nutzt das Bild vom Wettkampf in der Arena zur Dramatisierung des biblischen Textes. Das gelingt mit der Figur des Teufels. Der Teufel, „der Vater der Lüge", kämpft also gegen den Glaubensbekenner.[89] Erst mobilisiert der Widersacher die vermeintliche Wahrheit griechischer Bildung,[90] dann das Rechtsinstitut der Juden[91] – aber Ste-

---

87 Zur Behandlung des Stephanus in der frühchristlichen Literatur vgl. François Bovon, *The Dossier on Stephen, the First Martyr*, HThR 96 (2003), 279–315, besonders 289. – Der Editor Otto Lendle hatte zwei Jahrzehnte vor GNO X/1 (1990) seine Textrekonstruktion von *In s. Stephanum I* in der Monographie *Gregorius Nyssenus: Encomium in sanctum Stephanum protomartyrem. Griechischer Text, eingeleitet und herausgegeben mit apparatus criticus und Übersetzung* (Leiden: E.J. Brill, 1968) veröffentlicht. Ich benutze seine Übersetzung, aber ich übersetze meist anders.

88 In s. Stephanum I (GNO X/1, 75,13–72,2).

89 In s. Stephanum I: ὅπλα δὲ κατ' ἀλλήλων ἀμφοτέροις ἦν, τῷ μὲν μαθητῇ τῆς ζωῆς ἡ ὁμολογία τῆς πίστεως (GNO X/1, 76,17–19). ... τὸ δὲ διὰ τοῦ φαινομένου νοούμενον ὁ πατὴρ τοῦ ψεύδος (Joh 8,44) ἦν, δι' ἀνθρωπίνων προσώπων πρὸς τὴν ἐν τῷ Στεφάνῳ λαλουμένην ἀλήθειαν ἑαυτὸν ἀντεγείρων (ebd. 79,14–16).

90 In s. Stephanum I (GNO X/1, 79,4–80,10). Aus Act 6,8–10 macht Gregor: „Gleichwie das Feuer, wenn es das nötige Brennholz ergriffen hat, die Flamme auflodern lässt und den Lichtschein heller macht, so machte der Heilige Geist, nachdem er Stephanus inspiriert hatte, die Strahlen der Gnade sichtbarer. Deswegen blickten alle auf ihn, die Erkenntnis und Bildung besaßen. Und wer von den übrigen meinte, weiser zu sein, die rotteten sich zusammen wie zu geschlossenen Schlachtreihen und versuchten auf diese Weise, dem Angriff des Stephanus standzuhalten. Der aber blieb allen gegenüber unüberwindbar, ob er mit vielen oder mit wenigen zusammentraf. Dem Anschein nach waren es Alexandriner, Libertiner, Kyrenäer und Menschen von überall her, die gegen den Kämpfer für die Wahrheit antraten, aber wer das Erscheinungsbild durchschaut, sieht ‚den Vater der Lüge' (Joh 8,44) sich mittels menschlicher Personen gegen die durch Stephanus redende Wahrheit erheben" (79,4–16). Es ist „die falsche Weisheit" gegen „die wahre Weisheit" (85,22–86,2).

91 Das von den Juden vor dem Synhedrium angezettelte Verfahren (Act 6,11–7,60) dramatisiert Gregor so: „Da also die Lüge durch die wirkliche Wahrheit widerlegt worden war und der Teufel keinen weiteren Vorkämpfer für den Trug finden konnte, weil sich alle der Offenbarung der Wahrheit zuwandten, erinnerte er sich seines besonderen Kunstgriffes und verteilte seine Kraft auf Ankläger und Richter und, tätig in beiden, schickte er die einen vor, Lügen gegen Stephanus auszusagen, die anderen, die Verleumdung aufzugreifen und zornig auf sie zu reagieren. Er schwängerte die Juden mannigfach, so dass er für Stephanus alles in einem wurde, Anklä-

phanus, der Weise (vgl. Act 6,3), weiß seine Lügen aufzudecken. Und Stephanus lässt sich im Kampf für die Wahrheit nicht durch Todesdrohungen einschüchtern. Gregor schiebt christliche Gehalte in Anlehnung an die biblische Apostelgeschichte herein, so dass die enkomiastische Rede zu einer Predigt wird, gipfelnd in der Vergebungsbitte des Stephanus: «Herr, rechne ihnen diese Sünde nicht an!» (Act 7,60).[92]

Eine zweifache Lehre packt Gregor in diese Lobpredigt auf den gesteinigten Stephanus hinein.

Erstens leitet er zu einem dogmatischen Angriff auf Pneumatomachen und Arianer über; denn in verschiedener Weise nutzten beide Gruppen die Vision des Stephanus gegen die Nicäner: „Ich sah den Sohn des Menschen zur Rechten Gottes stehen" (Act 7,56).[93] Menschliches Lob, sagt Gregor zur Überleitung, wollte Stephanus nicht haben. Uns jedoch, so Gregor, ist er nützlich; denn er trainiert uns zur Abwehr falscher Glaubenslehren.[94]

Zweitens fasst Gregor in eine Formulierung, was die Botschaft des Martyriums ist: Unter der Todesdrohung gegen das Christusbekenntnis handelnd wurde Stephanus durch seinen Tod zum Verkünder des verborgenen Lebens. „Denn dieses Leben bereitwillig aufzugeben, beweist für die recht Urteilenden, dass das aufgegebene Leben gegen ein wertvolleres Leben eingetauscht wird."[95] Ich halte eine engere Formulierung für besser: „nicht von Christus getrennt werden wollen."[96] Sie steht in der von mir gerügten zweiten Rede auf die XL Märtyrer.

---

ger, Richter, Vollstrecker und die übrige Hilfstruppe des Todes…" (GNO X/1, 80,8–16).

92　In s. Stephanum I (GNO X/1, 84,15–16; vgl. 88,17).

93　In s. Stephanum I (GNO X/1, 89,7–91,9 gegen Pneumatomachen; ebd. 91,10–94,7 gegen Arianer).

94　In s. Stephanum I (GNO X/1, 88,17–22 und 88,23–89,7).

95　In s. Stephanum I: τίς γὰρ οὐκ ἂν ἠγάσθη τὸ καινὸν τοῦτο τῆς ἀγωνίας εἶδος, ὅτε ζωῇ καὶ θανάτῳ ἡ ἀλήθεια διεκρίνετο καὶ ἀπόδειξις ἐγίνετο τῆς ἀληθείας ὁ θάνατος; ὁ γὰρ κῆρυξ τῆς κεκρυμμένης τέως καὶ ἀγνοουμένης ζωῆς ἔργῳ διήγγελλε τοῖς ἀνθρώποις τὸ κήρυγμα· τὸ γὰρ ἑτοίμως τοῦτον καταλιπεῖν τὸν βίον ἀπόδειξις τοῖς ὀρθῶς κρίνουσιν ἦν τοῦ τὴν προτιμοτέραν ζωὴν ἀντὶ τῆς καταλειπομένης ἀλλάξασθαι (GNO X/1, 76,19 – 77,5).

96　In XL martyres Ib: Bei den XL Märtyrern ἐπὶ τούτων δὲ πάντα ἦν ἀργὰ καὶ ἄπρακτα τοῦ ἐχθροῦ τὰ παλαίσματα. ἐλπίδας προέτεινεν, οἱ δὲ κατεπάτουν· φόβους ἠπείλει, οἱ δὲ κατεγέλων. ἓν φοβερὸν ἦν μόνον αὐτοῖς τὸ τοῦ Χριστοῦ χωρισθῆναι· ἓν ἀγαθὸν τὸ μετὰ Χριστοῦ εἶναι μόνου· τὰ δὲ ἄλλα πάντα γέλως καὶ σκιὰ καὶ φλυαρία καὶ ὀνειρώδη φαντάσματα. (GNO X/1, 150,16–21).

C. Latin Martyrology

Peter Kuhlmann

Christliche Märtyrer als Träger römischer Identität

Das *Peristephanon* des Prudentius und sein kultureller Kontext

In der römischen Literatur um ca. 400 n.Chr. lässt sich eine Art kultureller Synthese zwischen paganer und christlicher Kultur beobachten.[1] Besonders der aus Spanien stammende Dichter Prudentius[2] hat in dieser Zeit versucht, eine neuartige Synthese zwischen traditionellen römischen Werten und christlichem Weltbild zu schaffen.[3] Er hat den aristokratischen Wertekanon in das Christentum integriert und auf diese Weise eine Art christlichen *mos maiorum* konstituiert.[4] In diesem Beitrag wird untersucht, wie Prudentius den paganen und primär aristokratischen Wertekanon (*virtutes*) in ein christliches System transformiert und welche Funktion dabei speziell der Märtyrerverehrung zukommt. Dabei wird auch Prudentius' Verhältnis zur paganen

---

1   Knapper, aber treffender Überblick hierzu bei Helmut Krasser, Pilgerreisen im Text. Das Peristephanon des Prudenz als religiös-performativer Erfahrungsraum, *Millennium* 7 (2010), 205–209. Siehe auch Siegmar Döpp, Die Blütezeit der lateinischen Literatur in der Spätantike, *Ph.* 132 (1988), 19–52, 25–43; zur Romanisierung der christlichen Kultur vgl. Ramsay MacMullen, *Christianity and Paganism in the Fourth to the Eigth Century* (New Haven: Yale University Press, 1997), 103–151.

2   Zur Person Prudentius siehe Anne-Marie Palmer, *Prudentius on the martyrs* (Oxford: Clarendon Press, 1989), 6–31.

3   Ettore Paratore, Prudenzio fra antico e nuovo, in: *Da Teodosio a San Gregorio Magno* (Rom: Accademia nazionale dei Lincei, 1980), 51–86; Maria Kah, *Die Welt der Römer mit der Seele suchend. Die Religiosität des Prudentius* (Bonn: Borengässer, 1990); Willy Evenepoel, Le Martyre dans le libre Peristephanon de Prudence, *SE* 36 (1996); Paul-Augustin DeProost, *Le martyre chez Prudence. Sagesse et tragédie*, *Ph.* 143 (1999), 161–180.

4   Zu dem Prozess dieser Identitätsstiftung Bernhard Giesen, Kollektive Identität. Die Intellektuellen und die Nation (Frankfurt a.M.: Suhrkamp, 1999), 119.

Literatur und Kultur[5] sowie seine Auffassung von römischer Herrschaft im christlichen Kontext auf der Grundlage seiner Märtyrerhymnen *Peristephanon* analysiert. Im Ergebnis lässt sich dabei ein vielfältiges paganes Substrat auf kultureller und literarischer Ebene aus Prudentius' Werk herausarbeiten, das eine wichtige Grundlage für die mit dem *Peristephanon* offenbar intendierte Neukonstruktion christlicher Identität auf altrömischer Grundlage bildet.

Innerhalb des 4. Jahrhunderts n. Chr., also in den Jahrzehnten vor Prudentius' literarischem Wirken, vollzieht sich innerhalb des Imperium Romanum ein grundlegender kultureller und religiöser Wandel: Kaiser Konstantin beginnt das Römische Reich zu christianisieren und verlegt die kaiserliche Residenz von Rom nach Byzanz, der νέα Ῥώμη. Vor der konstantinischen Wende war das Christentum lediglich eine minoritäre Religion innerhalb des Reiches, nun wurde es jedoch von der Kaiserdynastie besonders gefördert.[6]

Römische Identität – speziell innerhalb der Nobilität – war ursprünglich untrennbar an den polytheistischen Götterkult sowie an ein spezifisches Wertesystem gebunden:[7] Ein zentraler Wert ist die *pietas*, d.h. die Bindung der Römer an die Götter als Fundament römischer Staatlichkeit und Herrschaft. Dazu kommen weitere Wertbegriffe wie Sieghaftigkeit (*victoria*) im Rahmen des typisch aristokratischen Wertekanons (*virtus*); hierzu gehören militärische Tüchtigkeit, Selbstverleugnung und politisches Engagement im Dienst an der *res publica*. Aufgrund dieser Werte oder „Tugenden" (*virtutes*) erlangen die Mitglieder der Nobilität wiederum Ruhm (*gloria*) zu Lebzeiten und Nachruhm (*memoria*) als Ansporn für weitere Leistungen für Staat und Gesellschaft. Nach paganer Vorstellung trägt die Festigung und Ausweitung römischer Herrschaft über die *Oikumene* zur römischen Iden-

---

5   Giesen, *Identität*, stellt eine Typologie zur semantischen Rekonstruktion von kulturellen Codes auf, welche die Identitäten von Gesellschaften bestimmen.

6   Ein Überblick findet sich bei MacMullen, *Christianity*; Charles Piétri et al., *Die Geschichte des Christentums*, 2 (Freiburg u.a.: Herder, 2005), 193–237; Peter Gemeinhardt, *Das lateinische Christentum und die antike pagane Bildung*, STAC 41 (Tübingen: Mohr Siebeck, 2007), 129–137.

7   Generell dazu Maximilian Braun/Andreas Haltenhoff/Fritz-Heiner Mutschler, *Moribus antiquis res stat Romana*, BzA 134 (München: Walter de Gruyter, 2000); zu dem spezifischen Wertesystem vgl. die Beiträge von Andreas Haltenhoff in: Braun/Haltenhoff/Mutschler, *Res stat Romana*, 15–30 sowie 81–106; zum *mos maiorum* Maurizio Bettini, mos, mores und mos maiorum. Die Erfahrung der „Sittlichkeit" in der römischen Kultur, in: Braun/Haltenhoff/Mutschler, *Res stat Romana*, 303–351.

tität innerhalb der Oberschicht bei. Eine wichtige Basis dieser Herrschaft ist das Streben nach Ruhm als gesellschaftlicher Norm.[8] Durch die Christianisierung gerät dieses traditionelle Wertesystem in Gefahr: Die Ablehnung des polytheistischen Götterkultes im Sinne einer Polis-Religion stellte das kulturelle System Roms in Frage, denn die paganen Götter garantierten den Römern *salus* und *victoria* als Gegenleistung für den Kult.[9] Seit dem 4. Jahrhundert waren die führenden Christen im Staat (z.B. Ambrosius und Augustinus) nicht mehr bereit, pagane Kulte zu tolerieren: Die neue monotheistische Universalreligion beanspruchte eine Monopolstellung im römischen Staat und gefährdete damit nach paganer Auffassung die *salus rei publicae*.[10] Bei den Christen wurde das Heil für den Staat durch das individuelle Seelenheil im Jenseits ersetzt. Die politische römische Universalherrschaft wurde durch eine geistliche Universalherrschaft, d.h. eine christliche *fides catholica* ersetzt. Durch diesen Paradigmenwechsel schien auch das traditionelle Wertesystem der Nobilität seinen Sinn zu verlieren, denn für die Christen bedeutete das Engagement für einen diesseitigen Staat und seine Herrschaft ursprünglich nichts. Diese kulturellen Gegensätze bildeten für Prudentius den Kontext, in dem seine Werke entstanden. Zugleich lieferten diese kulturellen Voraussetzungen Prudentius die Themen, an denen er seine neue Konzeption eines spezifisch römischen Christentums entwickeln konnte.

Über Prudentius als Person ist nur wenig bekannt. Er hat seinem Gesamtwerk eine kurze poetische *Praefatio* vorangestellt, aus der wir einige wenige Lebensdaten kennen. Die Werke des Prudentius sind allesamt Gedichte und behandeln den christlichen Glauben: In den Gedichten *Contra Symmachum* verurteilt Prudentius den Glauben an die polytheistischen Götter, in seinen epischen Werken *Apotheosis* und *Hamartigenia* verteidigt er den wahren katholischen Glauben gegen zeitgenössische Häresien. Das Epos *Psychomachia* beschreibt einen erbarmungslosen Krieg der Tugenden gegen die Laster, bei dessen Lektüre der Rezipient fast Mitleid mit den meist grausam verstümmelten Lastern bekommen könnte.

---

8   Zur *memoria* besonders Uwe Walter, *Memoria und res publica. Zur Geschichtskultur im republikanischen Rom* (Frankfurt/M.: Verlag Antike 2004), 26–37 und 118–130. Die Verbindung zwischen Erinnerungskultur und Identität wird umfassend diskutiert von Giesen, *Identität*.

9   Antonie Wlosok, *Rom und die Christen* (Stuttgart: Klett, 1970), 54f.

10 Wlosok, *Rom*, 53–67; Pedro Barceló/Gunther Gottlieb, *Christen und Heiden in Staat und Gesellschaft* (München: Vögel 1992), 3–59; Peter Kuhlmann, *Religion und Erinnerung. Die Religionspolitik Kaiser Hadrians und ihre Rezeption in der antiken Literatur* (Göttingen: Vandenhoeck & Ruprecht, 2002), 173–176.

Bei dem hier näher untersuchten Textkorpus des *Peristephanon* handelt es sich um eine Sammlung von 14 Märtyrerhymnen, die Prudentius wohl kurz nach 400 verfasst oder zumindest als Gesamtedition publiziert hat.[11] Diese Hymnen zeichnen sich durch eine durchweg plastische Darstellung der jeweiligen Martyrien aus: Zungen oder Brüste werden von lebendigen Körpern abgetrennt, Eingeweide aus dem Körper herausgerissen, Märtyrer werden ertränkt, verbrannt oder geköpft. Besonders auffällig an diesen Schilderungen ist die oft detailverliebte Präzision in der Beschreibung grausiger Szenen, die stark an Senecas Tragödien oder Lucan erinnert. Im Barockzeitalter dienten diese Darstellungen vielfach als Vorbilder für plastische Gemälde von Martyrien. Der wohl bekannteste Hymnus, der hier den Basistext für die Untersuchung bildet, schildert das Martyrium des Heiligen Laurentius (*Pe.* 2), eines Stadtpatrons von Rom, der Mitte des 3. Jahrhunderts lebte und Diakon unter dem römischen Bischof (bzw. „Papst") Sixtus II. war. Laurentius wurde von dem paganen *praefectus urbi* gezwungen, die Schätze der römischen Kirche herauszugeben und versammelte daraufhin alle Bettler, Kranken und Bedürftigen, die unter dem Schutz der Kirche standen. Am festgesetzten Tag zeigte er sie dem Präfekten mit den Worten: „Sieh hier die Schätze unserer Kirche." Der wütende Präfekt verurteilte daraufhin Laurentius dazu, lebendig gegrillt zu werden. Doch noch kurz vor seinem Tod war Laurentius zu Scherzen aufgelegt und forderte vom Grill aus den Präfekten auf: „Die eine Seite ist jetzt gar; dreh mich um und koste, ob mein Fleisch roh oder durchgebraten besser schmeckt."[12]

Insgesamt sind die Texte des Prudentius nicht nur Beispiele eines grimmigen frühchristlichen Humors, sie zeigen auch eine für viele christliche Texte dieser Zeit typische Einseitigkeit der Darstellung, in der die Christen und Märtyrer durchweg positiv, die Heiden hingegen dezidiert negativ charakterisiert werden. Die Handlungsfiguren des *Peristephanon* erinnern in ihrer schematischen Eindimensionalität bisweilen an die Typen der römischen Komödie. Die in den Hymnen auftretenden Heiden entstammen in der Regel der römischen Nobilität in der Gestalt von Stadtpräfekten, Provinzverwaltern und Richtern. Die Frage, wie in diesem scheinbar dualistischen Weltbild eine Synthese zwischen paganen und christlichen Werten möglich ist, wird im Folgenden unter den drei Aspekten der Sprache, der Kultur und des Raumes untersucht.

---

11 Manfred Fuhrmann, *Rom in der Spätantike* (München/Zürich: Artemis & Winkler 1994), 232–235.

12 *Pe.* 2,401–404.

Sprachliche Aspekte: Semantische Felder, Intertextualität und Metrik

Zunächst soll der Eingang des Laurentius-Hymnus (*Pe.* 2,1–20) unter sprachlich-stilistischen Aspekten betrachtet werden. Auffällig sind in diesem Textabschnitt die vielen Ausdrücke aus dem semantischen Feld „Krieg" bzw. „Militär", die im Textzitat entsprechend markiert sind. In diesen Versen hebt Prudentius zunächst die Macht und den Ruhm der Stadt Rom hervor, die mittlerweile christlich geworden ist:[13]

Antiqua fanorum parens,
iam Roma Christo dedita,
Laurentio uictrix duce
ritum triumphas barbarum.

Reges superbos uiceras   5
populosque frenis presseras,
nunc monstruosis idolis
inponis imperii iugum.

Haec sola derat gloria
urbis togatae insignibus,   10
feritate capta gentium,
domaret ut spurcum Iouem,

non turbulentis uiribus
Cossi, Camilli aut Caesaris,
sed martyris Laurentii   15
non incruento proelio.

Armata pugnauit Fides
proprii cruoris prodiga;
nam morte mortem diruit
ac semet inpendit sibi.   20

Würde man in dem zweiten Vers das Wort *Christo* und in Vers 15 *martyris Laurentii* durch pagane Götter- oder Heroennamen ersetzen, könnte es sich hier um die pagane Beschreibung eines siegreichen Krieges der Stadt Rom gegen äußere Feinde aus einem klassischen Text wie Horaz oder – mit anderem Metrum – Vergil handeln. Das handelnde Subjekt ist in den ersten vier Strophen *Roma*, in der fünften Strophe ist es die *Fides*. Erst hier wird klar, dass es sich um einen primär christlich-

---

13   *Pe.* 2,1–20.

religiösen Text handelt, obwohl *fides* natürlich im Sinne von „Vertrau-
en(sverhältnis)" oder „Zuverlässigkeit" auch ein typischer Wertebegriff
der paganen römischen Kultur ist. Allerdings bedeutet es in den christlichen Texten meist „christlicher Glaube".[14] Dieser christliche Glaube
hat bei Prudentius einen evident militärischen Charakter: Die *Fides* ist
bei ihm bewaffnet und kann kämpfen. Das handelnde Subjekt *Fides* tritt
hier also als Personifizierung und Allegorie auf wie bei Ovid oder
Vergil z.B. auch die *Fama*.[15] Wie ein Soldat wird auch der Heilige
Laurentius vorgestellt: Sein Martyrium ist hier eine blutige Schlacht.
Dieses Bild des kriegerischen Heiligen taucht auch sonst oft in den
Texten auf[16], im Laurentius-Hymnus z.B. noch in Vers 501–508:

> Sic <u>dimicans</u> Laurentius
> non <u>ense</u> praecinxit latus,
> hostile sed <u>ferrum</u> retro
> torquens in auctorem tulit.
>
> Dum daemon inuictum Dei   505
> testem lacessit <u>proelio,</u>
> <u>perfossus</u> ipse concidit
> et <u>stratus</u> aeternum iacet.

Der Märtyrer hat also gegen den Feind bzw. den bösen Dämon des
Heidentums einen Krieg geführt und ihn besiegt. Auch hier benutzt
Prudentius militärisches Vokabular, um den Sieg des christlichen
Glaubens über die paganen Kulte zu illustrieren.

Den römischen Leser erinnert diese Wortwahl deutlich an
literarische Vorbilder aus der paganen Literatur mit echten militärischen Inhalten. Eine besonders instruktive Stelle ist in diesem Kontext
ein Abschnitt aus dem ersten Hymnus, der den spanischen Soldaten-
Märtyrern Emeterius und Chelidonius gewidmet ist (*Pe.* 1,24–30 u. 51);
darin wird die Bereitschaft, auch ein gewaltsames Martyrium zu
erleiden, als besonders ruhmvoll angepriesen. Offenbar handelt es sich
um einen intertextuellen Bezug zu der thematisch verwandten Horaz-
Ode 3,2,13–16 mit dem berühmten Vers *dulce et decorum est pro patria
mori*[17], der in Anlehnung an einen Alkaios-Vers (Frg. 57) den Tod im

---

14   Thesaurus Linguae Latinae s.v. „fides" (besonders unter III: „fides Christiana").
15   Verg. *Aen.* 4,174–197; Ov. *Met.* 12,39–63.
16   Die eindrucksvollsten Beispiele sind die Märtyrertode der Soldaten Emeterius und
      Chelidonius im ersten Hymnus (*Pe.* 1).
17   Hor. c. 3,2,13–16; zu den intertextuellen Bezügen siehe Maria Lühken, *Christianorum
      Maro et Flaccus. Zur Vergil- und Horazrezeption bei Prudentius*, Hyp. 141 (Göttingen:
      Vandenhoeck & Ruprecht, 2002), 243f.

Kampf für das Vaterland als große Ehre propagiert. In dem folgenden Prudentius-Zitat sind die intertextuellen Referenzen fett markiert (*Pe.* 1,24–28 u. 51):

> hoc genus **mortis decorum** est. hoc probris dignum uiris,
> membra morbis exedenda, texta uenis languidis,   25
> hostico donare ferro, **morte** et hostem uincere.
> **pulchra** res ictum sub ense persecutoris pati.
> nobilis per uulnus amplum porta iustis panditur
>   (...)
> **dulce** tunc iustis cremari, **dulce** ferrum perpeti.   51

Wie bei Horaz oder in der frühgriechischen Elegie wird auch hier der Tod als unausweichlich für den Menschen präsentiert; ein Tod in der Schlacht bringt ewigen Ruhm und nobilitiert so den, der sich für den Staat bzw. die *patria* oder den Glauben opfert. Die beiden realen Soldaten Emeterius und Chelidonius werden durch ihr Martyrium in der christlichen Bildersprache zu Soldaten Christi, die analog zumindest in der Vorstellung des gebildeten und mit der Horazstelle vertrauten Rezipienten für eine wie immer geartete *civitas Christiana* ihr Leben opfern würden. Diese *militia Christi* kommt zwar auch bei anderen christlichen Autoren vor[18], aber Prudentius verwendet diese militärische Bildsprache besonders konsequent.

Der gebildete Leser wird zugleich hier und an vielen anderen Stellen an den paganen Prätext Horaz erinnert. Hier handelt es sich speziell um eine der Römer-Oden, die besonders die Themen bzw. Sachfelder: römischer Staat und römische Werte reflektieren. Vergleichbare intertextuelle Anspielungen auf die Römer-Oden finden sich noch an vielen anderen Stellen im Werk des Prudentius.[19]

Den Bezug speziell zu Horaz zeigen im Übrigen auch schon die Metren in den Hymnen des Prudentius. Anders als andere zeitgenössische christliche Lyriker verwendet Prudentius noch die klassischen, rein quantitierenden Versmaße, die meist aus den Epoden und Oden des Horaz stammen, weswegen man ihn auch gern den „christlichen Horaz" nennt.[20] Die Verwendung solcher Metren ist auffällig, weil um 400 n.Chr. bereits die Quantitäten der Vokale kollabierten, d.h. die meisten lateinischen Muttersprachler konnten nicht mehr akustisch

---

18   Dieses Konzept tritt schon auf bei 2Tim 2,3–5; 1Clem 37; bekannt auch aus den Werken von Tertullian und Cyprian; Hanns Christof Brennecke, Militia Christi, *RGG*⁴ 5 (2002), 1231–1233.

19   Übersicht bei Lühken, *Vergil- und Horazrezeption*, 320.

20   Palmer, *Prudentius*, 58–67.

genau zwischen langen und kurzen Vokalen unterscheiden, wodurch auch die Silbenquantität instabil wurde. Daher verwendete z.B. Ambrosius in seinen Dichtungen Versmaße, in denen der natürliche Iktus bzw. Druckakzent mit dem Versakzent weitgehend übereinstimmte. Die mittelalterliche lateinische Lyrik richtete sich dann ausschließlich nach dem Naturakzent der Wörter wie auch in den meisten modernen Sprachen. Prudentius ist also unter sprachlichen Aspekten ein Dichter, der für ein gebildetes Publikum schreibt, das die klassische Metrik noch gut kennt und auch eine sehr sorgfältige lateinische Aussprache bei der mündlichen Rezitation verwendet haben muss.

Bei Prudentius ist anders als bei Ambrosius die Koinzidenz von natürlichen Wort-Akzenten und den festen *elementa longa* der Versmaße (modern gesprochen: „Hebungen") offensichtlich eher zufällig[21], wenn nicht sogar gemieden, wie zwei willkürlich herausgegriffene Beispiele in jambischen Dimetern und (katalektischen) trochäischen Tetrametern zeigen – hier ist der natürliche Druckakzent mit Akzent, die „Hebung" im Vers durch Unterstreichung markiert:

> Antíqua fanórum párens,
> iam Róma Chrísto dédita,
> Lauréntio uíctrix dúce
> rítum triúmphas bárbarum.   (2 ia)

> hoc génus mórtis decórum (e)st. hoc próbris dígnum uíris   (4 tro ^)

Für den richtigen akustischen Eindruck ist eine sorgfältige Realisierung der Verse nach den phonologischen Regeln des klassischen Lateins relevant: Die jambischen Dimeter haben einen einhämmernden und martialischen Rhythmus; die trochäischen Tetrameter kommen aus der Triumphal-Dichtung und evozieren einen Triumphzug beim Hörer.

Die bisher behandelten Textbeispiele haben auf verschiedenen Ebenen gezeigt, in wie hohem Maße Prudentius auf der sprachlichen Ebene bis ins kleinste Detail gezielte Signale sendet, die bei den Rezipienten die Welt der klassischen paganen Dichtung und ihrer sprachlichen Normen reaktivieren. Zugleich entfaltet die Sprache des Prudentius ihre intendierte Wirkung vollständig nur bei solchen Rezipienten, die diese poetische Sprache zumindest rezeptiv noch sicher beherrschen.

---

21 Fuhrmann, *Rom*, 239–241.

Kulturelle Identität: Gesellschaft, römische Werte und Religion

Wie die Bemerkungen zur sprachlichen Gestaltung gezeigt haben, verwendet Prudentius in seiner Dichtung Formen, die dem literarischen Geschmack eines adligen Publikums entsprechen. Hierzu gehört natürlich schon die Wahl bestimmter Gattungen: Die Gattung Epos mit dem Versmaß Hexameter z.B. verleiht der *Psychomachia* einen eminent heroischen Charakter wie die griechische *Ilias* oder die römische *Aeneis.*[22] Poetische Texte dieser Art sind in der Zeit um 400 fast nur noch für ein hochgebildetes Publikum voll verständlich, das mit diesen Formen aufgrund seiner aristokratischen Ausbildung vertraut ist.

Aristokratische und christliche Normen

Zu diesem aristokratischen Habitus der Gedichte gehören auch die in allen Hymnen des *Peristephanon* auftretenden typisch römischen, aristokratisch konnotierten Wertbegriffe wie *virtus* oder *gloria* und die damit zusammenhängenden Eigenschaften und Konkretisierungen.[23] Oben wurde bereits auf die Dominanz militärischer Begriffe und Vorstellungen verwiesen. In der gesellschaftlichen Elite des paganen Rom gehörte die militärische Karriere zu einer obligatorischen Station im Leben eines Mannes von Stand. Der Begriff *vir-tus* bezeichnet ursprünglich genau die Eigenschaften, die einen Mann ausmachen, wozu in Rom vor allem auch Leistungen auf dem Schlachtfeld gehörten. Durch diese Leistungen erwarb sich der Mann der Oberschicht *gloria*, das heißt Ruhm in der Erinnerung der Nachwelt. Ein Nichtadliger konnte in diesem Sinne kaum *virtus* erwerben, der Begriff der *gloria* passt nach dem traditionellen *mos maiorum* überhaupt nur für die soziale Gruppe der *nobiles*.

Anteil an diesem Wertesystem haben in den Gedichten des Prudentius jedoch interessanterweise auch Christus oder Gott selber: Im ersten Hymnus befehligt Christus als Feldherr die Kohorten des Glaubens (*Pe.* 1,67). Im Laurentius-Hymnus dagegen ist der Märtyrer

---

22 Zur *Psychomachia* Martha A. Malamud, *A Poetics of Transformation. Prudentius and Classical Mythology* (Ithaca: Cornell University Press, 1989), 47–77.

23 Zu dem Ausdruck *virtus* bei Prudentius Lühken, *Vergil- und Horazrezeption*, 242–246; Palmer, *Prudentius*, 140; Michael Roberts, *Poetry and the Cult of Martyrs* (Ann Arbor: University of Michigan Press, 1993), 182–187; Francois Paschoud, *Roma Aeterna*, BHRom 7 (Rom: Institut Suisse de Rome 1967), 227.

ein Feldherr im Kampf des Christentums gegen die Heiden (*Laurentio duce*: *Pe.* 2,3). Die *virtus* ist eine Eigenschaft, die sowohl Gott als auch die Märtyrer oder auch nichtadlige Menschen besitzen: So ist im Hymnus für den Heiligen Vincenz die Rede von der *virtus Dei* (*Pe.* 5,473); im Hippolytus-Hymnus sagt eine Mutter zu ihrem kleinen Sohn (*Pe.* 10,743f.), dass alle Altersgruppen – Erwachsene und Kinder – im christlichen Sinne *virtus* erwerben können:[24]

> omnes capaces esse virtutum Deus
> mandavit annos.

Dieses letzte Beispiel zeigt die Umdeutung römischer Werte bei Prudentius. Auf der einen Seite ist das tradierte System von *virtus* und *gloria* in Form seiner Termini voll präsent, auf der anderen Seite ist es aber offensichtlich nicht unbedingt an die gesellschaftliche Gruppe der römischen *nobiles* gebunden. Dies bestätigt sich, wenn man die Handlungsfiguren in den Hymnen und deren Charaktere und Verhaltensweisen untersucht. Wie bereits eingangs angedeutet, zeichnet Prudentius die Figuren in den Hymnen einseitig und holzschnittartig: Die Märtyrer sind die Guten, die paganen römischen Beamten hingegen die Bösen. Die christlichen Märtyrer besitzen genau die Eigenschaften, die eigentlich die Nobilität nach antiken Wertvorstellungen haben sollte: Sie besitzen das, was man im Griechischen ἐγκράτεια nennt, d.h. „Selbstbeherrschung" in allen Lebenslagen; sie verlieren nie ihre *serenitas* – selbst wenn sie bei lebendigem Leibe gegrillt, zerstückelt oder auf andere Weise gefoltert werden; und schließlich besitzen sie die Fähigkeit, genau zwischen wahren und falschen Gütern im Leben zu unterscheiden. Im Laurentius-Hymnus kann man dies gut an der berühmten Szene sehen, wo Laurentius den makabren Scherz macht, der bereits am Anfang dieses Beitrags kurz angedeutet wurde (*Pe.* 2,397–409):

> Postquam uapor diutinus
> decoxit exustum latus,
> ultro e catasta iudicem
> conpellat adfatu breui: 400
>
> 'Conuerte partem corporis
> satis crematam iugiter
> et fac periclum, quid tuus
> Vulcanus ardens egerit.'

---

24 Zum Aspekt der christlichen *virtus* siehe auch Krasser, Pilgerreisen, 205f.

Praefectus inuerti iubet,   405
tunc ille: 'coctum est, deuora
et experimentum cape,
sit crudum an assum suauius!'

Haec ludibundus dixerat...

Die römischen Beamten dagegen kennen diese heitere Gelassenheit auch in schwierigsten Situationen nicht, sondern lassen sich in ihrem Handeln von negativen Affekten leiten: Ihr Verhalten beschreibt Prudentius mit den Ausdrücken *ira, furor* oder *furere*. Als der Präfekt im Laurentius-Hymnus in der Erwartung großer Goldschätze die versammelte Schar der Bettler und Kranken sieht, verliert er die Selbstkontrolle und beschimpft den Priester Laurentius (*Pe.* 2,313–320):

'Ridemur', exclamat furens
praefectus, 'et miris modis
per tot figuras ludimur,   315
et uiuit insanum caput!

Inpune tantas, furcifer,
strophas cauillo mimico
te nexuisse existimas,
dum scurra saltas fabulam?   320

Ähnlich unbeherrscht reagieren die Beamten auch im Eulalia- und im Agnes-Hymnus auf die christliche Gesinnung dieser beiden jungen Mädchen. Die noch jungfräuliche Eulalia möchte nicht heiraten, sondern ihr Leben als keusche Jungfrau Christus weihen. Daraufhin befiehlt der von Furien getriebene römische Richter, das Mädchen zu foltern, um sie zu einer Hochzeit und den Freuden der Ehe zu zwingen (*Pe.* 3,95–105), was natürlich ohne Erfolg bleibt. Die Heilige Agnes wiederum – auch sie noch ein junges Mädchen – weigert sich, den Kult für die paganen Götter zu verrichten. Trotz ihrer Jugend steht sie fest zum christlichen Glauben. Daraufhin gerät der Richter in Raserei und schickt das Mädchen ins Bordell (*Pe.* 14,10–30). Mit Gottes Hilfe kann Agnes ihre Jungfräulichkeit auch im Bordell bewahren, woraus der Leser als Botschaft entnehmen soll, dass am Ende stets Gottes Wille über die moralische Verworfenheit der Heiden obsiegt.

Die römischen Richter in den Hymnen üben ihr Amt entweder als Verwalter ganzer Provinzen (*Pe.* 3: Spanien) oder als Stadtpräfekten (*Pe.* 14) aus und gehören somit zur höchsten römischen Nobilität. Ihr Verhalten im *Peristephanon* entspricht aber aufgrund fehlender Affektkontrolle in keiner Weise dem überlieferten aristokratischen Verhaltenskodex.[25] Im Laurentius- und im Eulalia-Hymnus sehen wir zudem römische Beamte, die äußere Güter der *fortuna* wie Gold oder auch die Ehe höher schätzen als die wahren, unverlierbaren Güter im Leben. Die Märtyrer erkennen hingegen nicht nur, was wahre und falsche Güter sind, sondern sind auch bereit, für ihren als richtig empfundenen Glauben zu sterben. Sie sind sogar auf der Folterbank glückselig, wie es die pagane Philosophie – insbesondere die Stoa – in dem bekannten Gemeinplatz vom idealen Weisen fordert. Das Verhalten der christlichen Märtyrer entspricht somit ziemlich genau der stoischen Güterlehre: Die Märtyrer erkennen das Leben als ein bloßes Adiaphoron und haben durch ihr Verhalten die *virtus* als *summum bonum* und somit auch *gloria* erreicht. Interessant ist dies deswegen, weil die Stoa unter den Angehörigen der römischen Nobilität mindestens bis in die hohe Kaiserzeit eine Art Mode-Philosophie war und die römische Oberschicht auch in der Spätantike durch ihre rhetorisch-philosophische Ausbildung mit den Leitsätzen der wichtigen philosophischen Systeme vertraut war.[26] Insbesondere die Stoa mit ihrer *virtus*-Lehre besaß große Übereinstimmungen mit dem Ehrenkodex der Nobilität. Auf der anderen Seite wurde speziell die stoische Güterlehre auch bei den christlichen Kirchenvätern vielfach rezipiert und ist in der Spätantike besonders im zweiten Buch von Boethius' Werk *De consolatione philosophiae* präsent.[27]

Nebenbei bemerkt entsprechen die Märtyrer auch in einer auf den ersten Blick äußerlichen Weise den aristokratischen Normen der römischen Oberschicht: Sie besitzen *eloquentia*. Indirekt lässt sich das an den sehr langen Reden der Märtyrer in den Hymnen ablesen. Diese Reden haben einen doppelten Adressaten: Zum einen richten sie sich auf der intratextuellen Ebene an die römischen Beamten, zum anderen aber natürlich außerhalb des Textes an das Lesepublikum der Hymnen. In diesen sorgfältig ausgefeilten Reden erläutern die Märtyrer Grundsätze ihres Glaubens und ihres Handelns. Ganz direkt bezeichnet der Erzähler in Hymnus XIII den karthagischen Kirchenvater Cyprian mehrfach als *facundus* (*Pe.* 13,10–20) und *eloquens* (*Pe.* 13,97). Diese

---

25 Engelbert Prolingheuer, *Zur literarischen Technik bei Prudentius' Peristephanon* (Hamburg: Kovač, 2008), 155–160.

26 Die wichtigste Philosophie der Spätantike war allerdings der Neoplatonismus; zur Rolle des Stoizismus siehe Fuhrmann, *Rom* ,135–156.

27 Zum Einfluss des Stoizismus auf die christlichen Autoren der Spätantike vgl. Fuhrmann, *Rom*, 178, 184–186; zu den stoischen Elementen in der Philosophie des Augustinus und des Boethius Kurt Flasch, *Das philosophische Denken im Mittelalter* (Stuttgart: Reclam, 2000), 44–52 und 82–84.

facundia oder *eloquentia* verbindet sich bei dem Heiligen Cyprian mit seiner großen Weisheit und Gelehrsamkeit (*Pe.* 13,15–20), so dass hier entsprechend das ciceronische Ideal der Verbindung von *sapientia* und *eloquentia*[28] in einem Märtyrer der christlichen Kirche verwirklicht ist.

Zusammenfassend könnte man formulieren: Prudentius schafft den traditionellen römischen Wertekanon keineswegs ab, sondern behält ihn im Gegenteil weitgehend unverändert bei. Er überträgt ihn jedoch auf die christliche Kirche und zeigt, dass gerade die pagane Oberschicht ihre *virtus* und die Werte des *mos maiorum* verloren hat. In christianisierter Form führen die Märtyrer der Kirche diese Werte fort. Auch der Begriff des Adels existiert fort; aber nicht Herkunft oder Reichtum nobilieren den Menschen, sondern christlicher Glaube und Martyrium. So belehrt der Märtyrer Romanus seinen paganen römischen Richter im 10. Hymnus (*Pe.* 10,123–125):

> (...) absit, ut me nobilem
> sanguis parentum praestet aut lex curiae:
> <u>generosa Christi secta nobilitat viros.</u>   125

Das Konzept einer Nobilitierung nicht durch Herkunft, sondern durch die richtige innere Einstellung, ist übrigens auch wieder in der lateinischen Stoa verankert, wie insbesondere Seneca im 44. Brief seiner *Epistulae morales* ausführlich darlegt. Dort (Sen. ep. 44,3) bezeichnet er die großen philosophischen Lehrer Sokrates, Platon, Kleanthes u.a. als die eigentlichen *maiores* eines Philosophen und die *virtus* als entscheidendes Merkmal des Adels.[29] Ähnlich wie später bei Prudentius zeigt sich sich auch bereits hier bei Seneca die Tendenz, zum einen durchaus Werte eines nobilitären Lesepublikums zur Grundlage der Textgestaltung zu machen, auf der anderen Seite aber durch das stoische, teilweise dem eigentlichen oberschichtlichen Wertekanon fernstehende Gedankengut genau diese Werte zu konterkarieren.

---

28 Z.B. in Cic. de inv. 1–5; de orat. 1,1–23; or. 11–19.
29 Vgl. etwa Sen. ep. 44,2: *bona mens omnibus patet: omnes ad hoc sumus nobiles;* Sen. ep. 44,5: *quis est generosus: ad virtutem bene compositus ... animus facit nobilem.*

Orthopraxie und Kultkontinuität

Ein anderer Komplex, der ebenfalls zur römischen Werte-Kultur im weiteren Sinne gehört, ist der Bereich Kult und Religion.[30] Christen können laut Prudentius aufgrund ihrer neu definierten *virtus* nicht nur zu *nobiles* aufsteigen, sondern durch ihren Tod als Märtyrer sogar ewige *gloria* erwerben und entsprechend wie pagane Heroen kultisch verehrt werden. Diese Parallele zwischen Heroen und Märtyrern macht z.B. der Laurentius-Hymnus durch einen expliziten Vergleich deutlich; dort werden vergöttlichte oder heroisierte Personen der römischen (Früh-) Geschichte wie etwa Cossus, Camillus oder Caesar in einen Gegensatz – damit aber auch in einen direkten Kontext – mit dem christlichen Märtyrer Laurentius gestellt. Dabei misst Prudentius dem christlichen Heldentum einen höheren Wert als dem paganen Heroentum bei (*Pe.* 2,13–16):[31]

> (...)
> non turbulentis uiribus
> <u>Cossi</u>, <u>Camilli</u> aut <u>Caesaris</u>,
> sed <u>martyris Laurentii</u>   15
> non incruento proelio.

Durch diesen sozialen und geistlichen Aufstieg können die Märtyrer auch als Fürsprecher der Menschen im Himmel fungieren und dem Menschen helfen, das Heil zu erlangen.[32] Die Märtyrer werden von Prudentius mit dem römischen Rechtsterminus *patronus* benannt, so dass sie Funktionen erhalten, die in etwa denen bestimmter Heroen oder Gottheiten als Patrone einer paganen Kultgemeinde entsprechen; dazu heißt es am Ende des Laurentius-Hymnus (*Pe.* 2,579f.):

> (...) per patronos martyras
> potest medellam consequi.   580

Ebenso wie beim paganen Vorbild ist aber offenbar auch im Christentum die richtige kultische Verehrung für die heiligen Märtyrer

---

30 Zu einigen archäologischen Befunden der Romanisierung im christlichen Kult vgl. Stefan Heid, The Romanness of Roman Christianity, in: Jörg Rüpke, ed., *A Companion to Roman Religion* (Oxford: Blackwell, 2007), 406–424.

31 Siehe auch Rainer Henke, *Studien zum Romanushymnus des Prudentius* (Frankfurt a. M.: Peter Lang, 1983), 155–163.

32 Allgemein zum Konzept der Heiligen als Fürsprecher Peter Brown, *The Cult of the Saints* (Chicago: University of Chicago Press, 1981), 54–64.

notwendig, wie der Erzähler im Hymnus an den Heiligen Vinzenz dem
Leser erklärt (*Pe.* 5,545–568):

adesto nunc et percipe   545
voces precantum supplices
nostri reatus efficax
orator ad thronum Patris.

(...)

si rite sollemnem diem   561
veneramur ore et pectore.
si sub tuorum gaudio
vestigiorum sternimur.

Die Textpassage macht klar, dass die Einhaltung der Feiertage für die
Märtyrer und die Verehrung der Reliquien zu dieser richtigen
Kultausübung (*rite ... veneramur*) gehören. In gewisser Weise hat sich
also nicht viel gegenüber dem paganen Kult verändert: Der christliche
Märtyrerkult weist zum einen deutliche orthopraxe Züge auf; zum
anderen besteht eine Art Klientelverhältnis zwischen den Märtyrern
bzw. Göttern und Heroen auf der einen Seite und den im Diesseits
lebenden Menschen auf der anderen Seite. Die Menschen als Klienten
der Götter und Märtyrer verrichten den Kult korrekt und erhalten
dafür von ihren himmlischen *patroni* entsprechende Wohltaten. Der
Märtyrerkult ist wie der traditionelle Götter- und Heroenkult lokal
organisiert, d.h. ein Gott oder Heros war zunächst für seine Stadt
zuständig. Dies bleibt in der Welt des Prudentius auch bei den Märtyrern in ähnlicher Weise bestehen, wie er selbst im letzten Hymnus am
Beispiel der Heiligen Agnes von Rom erläutert (*Pe.* 14,1–4):

Agnes sepulcrum est Romulea in domo
fortis puellae, martyris inclytae,
conspectu in ipso condita turrium
servat salutem virgo Quiritium.   4

So wie die paganen Götter und Heroen für die *salus rei publicae*
zuständig sind, beschützen auch die Lokalheiligen ihre jeweilige Stadt;
hier ist die Heilige Agnes als Patronin der Stadt Rom auch explizit für
die salus „ihrer" *civitas* zuständig. Die Wortwahl *Romulea domus* für
Rom, *inclyta* für Sankt Agnes und *Quirites* für die römischen Bürger
verleihen diesem christlichen Textabschnitt übrigens eine altrömisch-
pagane und zugleich heroisch-aristokratische Konnotation.

Aspekte des Raums: Rom und das Reich

Der letzte Textabschnitt berührte bereits Aspekte des Raums. Eigentlich handelt es sich bei dem paulinischen Christentum im religionswissenschaftlichen Sinne um eine sog. „Universalreligion", d.h. es ist nicht an einen bestimmten Raum im Sinne einer Stadt oder einer Nation gebunden. Ganz anders funktionieren das Judentum oder die paganen Kulte im antiken Rom, Griechenland und im übrigen mediterranen Raum der Alten Welt. Diese Kulte sind prinzipiell an eine bestimmte, teilweise ethnisch definierte Kultgemeinde oder Polis gebunden. Besonders im Laurentius-Hymnus aber hat die Stadt Rom doch eine herausgehobene Bedeutung. Dies ist auffällig, weil Prudentius selbst aus Spanien stammt und auch die meisten Märtyrer aus dem *Peristephanon* Spanier waren. Die Paradoxie zwischen lokalen Bezügen und römischem Zentralismus löst Prudentius auf, indem er die in Vergils *Aeneis* entwickelte Rom-Idee übernimmt und christianisiert. Im Werk des Prudentius gibt es an mehreren Stellen für den gebildeten Leser erkennbare intertextuelle Bezüge z.B. zur Anchises-Rede im 6. Buch der *Aeneis*. So ist die schon behandelte Passage aus dem Laurentius-Hymnus, die die Sieghaftigkeit Roms über andere Völker schildert, (*Pe.* 2,5–12) mit Vergil (*Aen.* 6,851–853) zu vergleichen:[33]

> Reges superbos uiceras   5
> populosque frenis presseras,
> nunc monstruosis idolis
> inponis imperii iugum.
>
> Haec sola derat gloria
> urbis togatae insignibus,   10
> feritate capta gentium
> domaret ut spurcum Iouem (...).

Hierzu bietet die berühmte Passage aus Vergils *Aeneis* das Vorbild, in der Äeneas' Vater Anchises die römische Suprematie über die Welt programmatisch als „Sendung Roms" verkündet:

> tu regere imperio populos, Romane, memento,
> hae tibi erunt artes, pacique imponere morem,
> parcere subiectis et debellare superbos.

---

33   Zu den Parallelen ausführlich Vinzenz Buchheit, Christliche Romideologie im Laurentius-Hymnus des Prudentius, in: Peter Wirth, ed., *Polychronion. FS Dölger* (Heidelberg: Winter, 1966), 121–144; Albertus Mahoney, *Virgil in the Works of Prudentius* (Diss., The Catholic University of America, Washington D.C. 1934), 31; Palmer, *Prudentius*, 128f.; Lühken, *Vergil- und Horazrezeption*, 172–184.

Die Vorstellungen sind bei beiden Autoren ähnlich: Die vielen Völker auf der Welt sind durch die römische Oberherrschaft mit Rom verbunden. Dies fügt sich auch gut zu dem martialischen Konzept, das Prudentius vom Christentum entwickelt. Bei ihm ist Rom christlich geworden und hat nun die Aufgabe, durch die Herrschaft über die Welt den christlichen Glauben in der Welt zu verbreiten und zu schützen. Denkt man diese programmatischen intertextuellen Bezüge weiter, ergibt sich auch eine Parallelisierung des römischen Gründungsheros Anchises mit dem römischen Märtyrer und Lokalheiligen Laurentius, der in der Tat für das christliche Rom eine wichtige Identifikationsfigur bildete und heute noch bildet. Somit eröffnet sich auch hier für den literarisch vorgebildeten Leser, der aus dem Schulunterricht die *Aeneis* mehr oder weniger auswendig kannte, eine weitere Verständnisebene, die durch die Art der Textdarstellung klare kulturelle Analogien zwischen paganen Heroen und den Begründern des christlichen Rom beim Rezipienten evoziert.

Einen zweiten wichtigen Punkt, der gerade auch in Form der Hymnen literarisch manifest ist, bildet die physische Präsenz bestimmter kultisch verehrter Märtyrer bzw. ihrer Gräber in Rom: Dort sind die zentralen Märtyrer Petrus und Paulus bestattet, die neben Jesus die beiden wichtigsten Gründungsfiguren des Christentums darstellen. Das Martyrium dieser beiden Heroen des Christentums und die Anwesenheit ihrer Reliquien macht die Stadt Rom geradezu zu einer sakralen Gedächtnislandschaft,[34] wie besonders der Hymnus auf die beiden Apostel (*Pe.* 12,7f.; 29f.) verdeutlicht. Auch im Eingang des Laurentius-Hymnus preist Prudentius die Stadt Rom wegen der vielen dort befindlichen Heiligtümer als einen heiligen Raum.[35]

Die beiden Apostel Petrus und Paulus stammen allerdings natürlich nicht aus Rom, sondern haben die Stadt erst durch ihre Präsenz sekundär geheiligt. Rom ist also eine zentrale Anziehungsstätte für Märtyrer aus der ganzen Welt und vereint somit Fremdes und Lokalrömisches innerhalb derselben Stadtmauern. Diese integrierende Kraft der Stadt Rom erläutert Prudentius besonders im Hymnus auf den Heiligen Romanus (*Pe.* 10) – *nomen est omen*. Dieser Diakon stammt eigentlich aus Antiochia und wirkte lange als Priester in

---

34 Zum Terminus vgl. Hubert Cancik, Rome as a Sacred Landscape, *VisRel* 4/5 (1985/6), 250–256; Krasser, Pilgerreisen, 208 spricht hier von Rom als einem religiösen „Erinnerungsort".

35 Zu dem allgemeinen Konzept des „lieux de mémoire" als Teil der Erinnerungskultur Pierre Nora, *Zwischen Geschichte und Gedächtnis* (Berlin: Wagenbach, 1990) und Aleida Assmann, *Erinnerungsräume. Formen und Wandlungen des kulturellen Gedächtnisses* (München: C.H. Beck, 1999), die den Begriff „Erinnerungsräume" benutzt.

Caesarea. In der langen Rede an seinen Richter bezeichnet Romanus Rom als Haupt der Welt (*Pe.* 10,167: *saeculi summum caput*). Weiter am Anfang wird der Märtyrer als Anführer des christlichen Heeres bezeichnet, zu dem alle Menschengruppen gehören (*Pe.* 10, 57f. u. 62):

> grex christianus, agmen imperterritum   57
> matrum, virorum, parvulorum, virginum
> (...)
> plebis rebellis esse <u>Romanum</u> ducem.   62

Der Rezipient des lateinischen Textes kann rein sprachlich in Vers 62 und sonst im Text nicht unterscheiden, ob es sich bei dem ambiguen *Romanus* um einen Eigennamen oder ein ethnisches Appellativum „der/ein Römer" handelt: Der Satz könnte theoretisch auch wie folgt übersetzt werden: „Anführer dieses aufständischen Volkes sei ein <u>Römer</u>". Aufgrund dieser semantischen Ambiguität kann der muttersprachliche Leser immer auch die Konnotation „Römer" haben, wenn er *Romanus* liest. Dieser Romanus ist insofern eine Art Prototyp für den idealen Christen nach Prudentius' Maßstäben: Seine lokale Herkunft ist gleichgültig; durch sein Christsein und seine Teilhabe an den wahren christlich-römischen Werten wird er zum Römer.

Wie bei Livius oder auch im vierten Buch des Properz[36] wird Rom als Stadt und auch als Imperium zu einem Schmelztiegel verschiedener Ethnien, die alle durch die Teilhabe an denselben Werten Römer sind. Die Stadt Rom hat eine herausgehobene Funktion, weil sie der lokale Ursprung dieser Werte ist und weil sie durch ihre militärische Macht die Gründung und Vergrößerung des Imperiums ermöglicht hat. Das Bestehen des Imperium Romanum wiederum hat die Ausbreitung des Christentums überhaupt erst ermöglicht, wie es schon der Kirchenvater Meliton von Sardes oder Eusebius von Caesarea gedeutet haben.[37] Insofern besitzt die Macht Roms auch eine wichtige heilsgeschichtliche Bedeutung.[38] Vor allem aber ist für Prudentius die Stadt Rom die Raum gewordene Trägerin eines ganz bestimmten Wertekanons, der wesentlich zur Identitätsstiftung der christlichen Bürger des Römischen Reiches beiträgt. Prudentius hat in seinem Werk das Christentum romanisiert und er hat auf dem Wege der Literatur mitgeholfen, aus der christlichen Kirche eine römische Kirche zu machen.

---

36 Zur Abstammung der Römer von verschiedenen Ethnien (*Troiani, Aborigines, Latini, Sabini, Etrusci*): Liv. 1,1–13; Prop. 4,1; 2; 4.

37 Eus. laud. Const. K 16; theoph. 3.1f.

38 Dazu Buchheit, Romideologie ‚129.

Der intendierte Rezipientenkreis

Zum Schluss stellt sich die Frage, wer das intendierte Lesepublikum der Märtyrer-Hymnen war. Auf der Grundlage der bisherigen Ausführungen lassen sich hierzu einige Hypothesen aufstellen:

Auf der einen Seite scheint sich das im *Peristephanon* behandelte Thema des Märtyrerkultes an ein breites, auch nicht-aristokratisches Publikum zu richten: Für auch ungebildete Rezipienten boten die Märtyrer mit ihren neuen Kultorten in jedem Fall willkommene Objekte religiöser Verehrung in der Tradition der paganen Orthopraxie. Zudem machen die Hymnen sogar klare Identifikations- und Integrationsangebote für die unterschiedlichen sozialen Gruppen in Rom: Dies zeigen zumindest die Stellen im Werk, in denen die integrierende Kraft der geistlichen Nobilitierung aller sozialen Gruppen unter dem Dach des Glaubens und – zumindest in der mythisch verklärten Zeit der Verfolgungen – des Martyriums beschworen wird. Dies bildet eine gewisse Analogie zum Ideal der bei Cicero, Livius und anderen klassischen Autoren inszenierten *concordia ordinum* in der Gemeinschaft von *plebs* und *nobiles* als Ideal der römischen *res publica*. Es kommt hinzu, dass nicht alle Gedichte des *Peristephanon* sprachlich gleich schwer zugänglich sind: Ein ungebildetes Publikum konnte sicher nicht alle metrischen und sprachlichen Raffinessen im Detail verstehen, aber doch Gefallen an den plastischen und spektakulären Martyrien haben.

Auf der anderen Seite richteten sich die Hymnen aber offensichtlich speziell an ein Lesepublikum, das aufgrund seiner Ausbildung ein Bedürfnis nach anspruchsvoller Dichtung hatte. Für dieses Publikum gab es vor Prudentius nur wenig Literatur mit christlichen Inhalten wie z.B. die Bibelepik des Iuvencus. Es muss also mit einem christlichen Rezipientenkreis mit einer entsprechenden aristokratischen Ausbildung gerechnet werden, für den ein eher populär erscheinender Stoff wie die kultische Verehrung von Märtyrern attraktiv gemacht werden sollte. Nach der konstantinischen Wende seit dem 4. Jahrhundert dürfte es innerhalb der Aristokratie viele Christen ohne besondere christliche Überzeugung gegeben haben; zumindest muss die Bandbreite zwischen (nach moderner Terminologie) fundamentalistischen Bekennerchristen und religiös eher indifferenten Angehörigen der Oberschicht groß gewesen sein.[39] Ein wichtiges bekanntes Beispiel für einen gebildeten Christen ohne erkennbaren Glaubenseifer noch aus der Zeit

---

39 Insgesamt zu dem Phänomen vgl. die differenzierten Ausführungen von Gemeinhardt, *Christentum*, 137–152 mit einer ausführlichen Diskussion früherer Forschungsansätze.

deutlich nach Prudentius ist etwa der gallische Bischof und Schrift-
steller Apollinaris Sidonius.[40] Besonders in der Zeit des Prudentius
selbst gab es viele in der paganen Literatur gebildete Autoren, für die
ihre literarische Bildung ein höheres Gut als ihr (offizielles) Christentum darstellte. Zu nennen sind hier bedeutende Autoren wie Claudian,
Ausonius oder der Verfasser der *Historia Augusta*: Die alten römischen
Kulte waren nicht mehr erlaubt, das Christentum in der Ausprägung
eines Paulus oder Augustinus mit seinem vielfach romfernen und
antiaristokratischen Weltbild war für die römischen Eliten zunächst
unattraktiv. Die Neukonstruktion eines römisch-christlichen Weltbildes
auf der Grundlage des Märtyrerkultes in den Hymnen des Prudentius
bot dieser Gruppe Möglichkeiten zu einer Identifikation mit einem
christlichen Glauben in römischem Gewand. Dieses Gewand in Gestalt
einer anspruchsvollen literarischen Form nach den Normen und
Konventionen der paganen Klassiker, kam dem verwöhnten poetischen
Geschmack der römischen Elite entgegen und konnte so für Akzeptanz
bei diesem an Vergil und Horaz geschulten Publikum sorgen. Auch für
die vielen Angehörigen der Oberschicht, die nicht von römisch-
italischer Herkunft waren, waren die christlichen Rom-Konzeptionen
des Prudentius attraktiv: Der Spanier und römische Magistrat
Prudentius ist selbst ein einschlägiges Beispiel für die Identifikation
eines Provinzialen mit der christlichen Romidee.

---

40   Hierzu ausführlich Jochem Küppers, Autobiographisches in den Briefen des Apolli-
     naris Sidonius, in: Michael Reichel, ed., *Antike Autobiographien. Werke – Epochen –
     Gattungen* (Köln: Böhlau, 2005), 251–277.

ANTHONY DUPONT

Augustine's Homiletic Definition of Martyrdom

The Centrality of the Martyr's Grace in his Anti-Donatist and Anti-Pelagian *Sermones ad Populum*

The martyr cult proved to be very popular in Augustine's North Africa. This article will focus on the martyrology the *Doctor Gratiae* developed, and this from a particular angle, namely how he preached about martyrs in his anti-Donatist and anti-Pelagian *sermones ad populum*, the way in which he linked this theme with grace. The article consists of three parts. Firstly, Augustine's general thoughts on the martyrs will be summarized, which will, at the same time, provide us with a *status quaestionis* on the studies on his martyrology. This first part will also present an analysis of the martyr theme in the whole *corpus* of Augustine's *sermones*. The second part will examine how Augustine dealt with this subject matter in his anti-Donatist *sermones*, while the third will do the same for the anti-Pelagian *sermones*. The key issue here will be whether Augustine links martyrs with the central discussion topic in the category of anti-Pelagian *sermones*: grace. Grace was central in the Pelagian controversy, but the topic of martyrs was not really debated. On the other hand, martyrology was very much an issue in the Donatist debate, but the topic of grace seems not to be central in this controversy. Here, the question will be how the topic of grace is linked with Augustine's anti-Donatist treatment of martyrs.

Augustine's Thinking and Preaching on Martyrs

Several studies elaborated on Augustine's martyrology.[1] These studies can be summarized by stating that Augustine's view on martyrs was

---

1   Tars-Jan van Bavel, The Cult of the Martyrs in St. Augustine. Theology versus Popular Religion?, in: Mathijs Lamberigts/Peter Van Deun, eds., *Martyrium in Multidisci-*

determined by two main concerns. By stressing that martyrs do not exist outside the church and that only the true *causa* (which is to die for Christ) constitutes genuine martyrship, he wanted to react against the Donatist appropriation of martyrdom. Donatists sometimes provoked their own death or described the imperial/legal actions undertaken against them as martyrship. The latter is according to Augustine their just *poena*, but it is not the right *causa* that makes real martyrs.[2] Secondly, Augustine attempted to direct the enthusiasm of his flock for the veneration of martyrs to God and to Christ. Hans von Campenhausen pointed out that Augustine first and foremost wanted to avoid that the martyr cult replaced the worship of Christ.[3] In every study about Augustine's martyrology this concern is emphasised. The confession of Christ is according to Augustine the central element in martyrdom. Augustine considers martyrdom to be an imitation of Christ and a testimony of the love for Christ. Martyrs themselves called for everyone to pray to Christ, and refused any personal veneration. They longed for the future life with and in Christ. Christ assists the martyrs and is present within the martyrs.[4] Martyrs are friends of Christ. There exists a unity between Christ and the martyrs, a unity so strong that Christ suffers and dies again in the passion of the martyrs. Martyrdom is repeating the sacrifice of Christ and giving it back to him. God's grace makes martyrs into martyrs, He gives them the capacity to suffer.[5] With this Christological focus, Augustine wanted to prevent the veneration

---

plinary Perspective. Memorial Louis Reekmans, BEThL 117 (Leuven: Peeters, 1995), 351–361; Michele Pellegrino, *Chiesa e martirio in Sant' Agostino*, Ricerche Patristiche, vol. 1 (Torino: Bottega d'Erasmo, 1982), 597–633; Michele Pellegrino, *Cristo e il martire nel pensiero di Sant' Agostino*, Ricerche Patristiche, vol. 1 (Torino: Bottego d'Erasmo, 1982), 635–668; Victor Saxer, *Morts, martyrs, reliques en Afrique chrétienne aux premiers siècles. Les témoignages de Tertullien, Cyprien et Augustin à la lumière de l'archéologie africaine* (Paris: Editions Beauchesne, 1980), 124–149, 170–229; Frederik van der Meer, *Augustine the Bishop: the Life and Work of a Father of the Church* (London: Sheed and Ward, 1961), 471–497.

2   Pellegrino, *Chiesa e martirio in Sant' Agostino*.

3   Hans Freiherr von Campenhausen, *Die Idee des Martyriums in der alten Kirche* (Göttingen: Vandenhoeck & Ruprecht, 1936), 101–106. Martyrs imitate Christ. Augustine however strongly opposes an identification of Christ and the martyrs: they are inferior to Christ. Cf. Candida R. Moss, *The Other Christs: Imitating Jesus in Ancient Christian Ideologies of Martyrdom* (Oxford/New York: Oxford University Press, 2010).

4   Pellegrino, *Cristo e il martire nel pensiero di Sant' Agostino*.

5   Carole Straw, Martyrdom, in: Allen D. Fitzgerald, ed., *Augustine through the Ages. An Encyclopedia* (Grand Rapids/Cambridge: Eerdmans, 1999), 538–542.

of martyrs from becoming a sort of polytheism. This focus also clearly illustrates the centrality of grace in his martyrology.[6]

The presence of the martyr theme is also well studied in Augustine's sermons.[7] This is not surprising, since many of his sermons were

6   Scholars tend to distinguish three periods in the evolution of Augustine's ideas on the cult of martyrs: (1) Originally, Augustine was not interested in the subject of martyrdom. Three factors made him considering the topic, namely the very popular veneration of the martyrs; Faustus' accusation that the Christians simply replaced the pagan sacrifices and idols by their veneration of martyrs; and the pride of the Donatists of their martyrs. Augustine answers Faustus that Christians want to imitate the example of the martyrs, they want to connect themselves with the merits of the martyrs, they want to be helped by the intercession of the martyrs, they venerate God and not the martyrs (*Contra Faustum Manicheum* 20, 4–21). (2) Augustine replies the Donatists that not the suffering *in se* makes the martyr, but the suffering for the just cause. (3) From 415 onwards (the discovery of the relics of Stephen) Augustine accepted the cult of martyrs. Tars van Bavel points out that, despite this change in attitude, Augustine's concern to aim the attention of the faithful to God and Christ remains the same. Augustine was originally convinced that no miracles took place anymore after the era of the New Testament. His scepsis about the contemporary miracles by intercession of martyrs made place for an acceptance of those martyr miracles. The bottom line however remains unchanged: Christ is central. See van Bavel, *The Cult of the Martyrs in St. Augustine*; Jan den Boeft, "Martyres sunt, sed homines fuerunt". Augustine on Martyrdom, in: A.A.R. Bastiaensen/Anthony Hilhorst/C. H. Kneepkens, eds., *Fructus Centesimus. Mélanges offerts à Gerard J. M. Bartelink à l'occasion de son soixante-cinquième anniversaire*, IPM 29 (Steenbrugge/Dordrecht: Brepols, 1989), 115–124; Cornelius P. Mayer, "Attende Stephanum conservum tuum" (Serm. 317, 2, 3). Sinn und Wert der Märtyrerverehrung nach den Stephanuspredigten Augustins, in: Bastiaensen/Hilhorst/Kneepkens, eds., *Fructus Centesimus*, 217–237, 221–224; Saxer, *Morts, martyrs, reliques en Afrique chrétienne aux premiers siècles*, 124; Straw, Martyrdom. Cf. Paul de Vooght, *La notion philosophique du miracle chez saint Augustin*, RThAM 10 (1938), 317–343 ; id., *La théologie du miracle selon saint Augustin*, RThAM 11 (1939) 197–222 ; Serge Lancel, La tardive acceptation du miracle, in: Id., *Saint Augustin* (Paris: Fayard, 1999), 648–658.

7   Den Boeft, "Martyres sunt, sed homines fuerunt"; Anthony Dupont, Imitatio Christi, Imitatio Stephani. Augustine's Thinking on Martyrdom. The Case Study of Augustine's Sermons on the Protomartyr Stephanus, *Augustiniana* 56/1–2 (2006), 29–61; id., Augustine's Anti-Pelagian Interpretation of Two Martyr Sermons. Sermones 299 and 335B on the Unnaturalness of Human Death, in: Johan Leemans, ed., *Martyrdom and Persecution in Late Antique Christianity (100–700) AD. Essays in Honour of Boudewijn Dehandschutter on the Occasion of His Retirement as Professor of Greek and Oriental Patrology at the Faculty of Theology of the K.U. Leuven*, BETL 241 (Leuven: Peeters, 2010), 87–102; Anne-Marie La Bonnardière, Les 'Enarrationes in Psalmos' prêchées par saint Augustin à l'occasion de fêtes de martyrs, RechAug 7 (1971), 73–103; Cyrille Lambot, Les sermons de saint Augustin pour les fêtes des martyrs, AnBoll 67 (1949), 249–266; Guy Lapointe, *La célébration des martyrs en Afrique d'après les sermons de Saint Augustin*, Cahiers de Communauté Chrétienne 8 (Montréal: Communauté Chrétienne, 1972); Mayer, "Attende Stephanum conservum tuum".

held on feast days of martyrs.[8] Guy Lapointe observes that according to
Augustine the real celebration of the martyrs is to imitate their virtu-
ous, concrete example of a life solely aimed at reaching moral happi-
ness and eternal life (and to hold the temporary, the earthly and the
visible in contempt). The martyrs are *exempla* because they followed the
supreme *exemplum*, the passion of Christ. Christ is thus imitated by
imitating the martyrs. Augustine also considers the intercession made
by the martyrs as intrinsically linked with the idea of imitation of the
martyrs, for they pray that their example would be followed. Lapointe
concludes that the martyr theology of Augustine's sermons is based
upon a threefold principle. Firstly, martyrs are celebrated, but only God
is worshipped. Martyrs identify themselves with God, to the degree
that praising martyrs is the same as praising God. Since martyrdom is
the work of God, tribute to the martyrs is tribute to God. Secondly,
Augustine emphasises the Christocentric dimension of martyrdom.
Christ is the *caput et princeps martyrum*. He did not only give the martyrs an exemplary model through his own passion, but he also assists
the martyrs permanently in their sufferings. He makes them strong
enough to endure their passion. Thirdly, Augustine perceives an eccle-
siological dimension in martyrdom. Martyrs are the building blocks of
the church, their blood is the seed for the growth of the church.[9] Jan
den Boeft gives an overview of the recurring themes in Augustine's
martyr sermons: call to imitate the martyrs; contemplation on their
suffering, death, and glorious crown; stressing that genuine martyrdom

---

8   For an overview of Augustine's ca. 100 *sermones* on saints and martyrs, with their
     possible dates and places of predication, see: Lapointe, *La célébration des martyrs*, 73–
     76. During the liturgy of martyrs, their acts were read. This tradition was allowed in
     the liturgy by the councils of Hippo (October 8, 393) and of Carthago (August 397).
     The *responsorium* was often selected in accordance with a theme from the *passio*. The
     first reading was often 1John 3:16 or 2Tim 3:12 and the gospel Mt 5, or 10, or 19.
     Margoni-Kögler deepens, elaborates and critically evaluates the previous research in
     this regard of Willis, Lapointe and Saxer by listing possible lectures (First Reading,
     Psalm, Gospel/Acta/Passio) for each celebration of a specific saint/martyr (and the
     sermones in which this happens) and subsequently substantiating the information
     given in this list with extensive notes. Michael Margoni-Kögler, *Die Perikopen im Got-
     tesdienst bei Augustinus. Ein Beitrag zur Erforschung der liturgischen Schriftlesung in der
     frühen Kirche*, Österreichische Akademie der Wissenschaften. Philosophisch-
     historische Klasse. Sitzungsberichte 810, VKCLK 29 (Wien: Verlag der Österreichi-
     schen Akademie der Wissenschaften, 2010), 143–170; cf. Baudouin de Gaiffier, La lec-
     ture des Actes des martyrs dans la prière liturgique en occident, *AnBoll* 72 (1954),
     134–166; La Bonnardière, Les 'Enarrationes in Psalmos', 98–104; Lapointe, *La célébra-
     tion des martyrs*, 104–112; Saxer, *Morts, martyrs, reliques*, 200–229; Geoffrey C. Willis,
     St. Augustine's Lectionary, ACC 44 (London: S.P.C.K., 1962).
9   Lapointe, *La célébration des martyrs*.

only results from love and that it is based not on human decisions, but is made possible by divine grace and Christ's co-suffering within the passion of the martyrs; reflection that martyrdom is a testimony of truth, faith and eternal life.[10]

Augustine's *sermones ad populum* emphasise that not the *poena* but the correct *causa* constitutes genuine martyrdom: to die for the truth, for Christ.[11] The preacher describes martyrs as the building blocks of the church, the seed and grain of the church.[12] Martyrs are not afraid of physical threats, they prefer the eternal above the temporary, they chose for the inner richness, they gain (eternal) life by dying (the physical death).[13] Martyrs are strengthened by God. He gives them the confidence and the courage to endure the pain, the patience and endurance to suffer, the capacity to fight against the devil, the faith and wisdom to withstand their persecutors.[14] Christ suffers together with the martyrs,[15] and gave them himself as example.[16] Not the martyrs should be venerated, but God because He made their martyrship possible. This, according to Augustine, is indicated by the martyrs themselves.[17] There is only one way to pay homage to the martyrs: thanking God for them and imitating their virtues, fighting against sin and temptation (as martyrs had to fight their persecutors), to prefer the Creator above creatures.[18] Augustine's sermons on the feast of Saint Stephen, the first mar-

---

10   Den Boeft, "Martyres sunt, sed homines fuerunt".

11   *S.* 53A, 13; 94A, 1–4; 128, 3; 138, 3; 169, 15; 275, 1; 285, 2; 299F, 3–4; 300, 5; 304, 1; 306, 2.10; 306A, 1; 311, 1–2; 313B, 2; 313E, 5; 319, 1; 325, 1; 327, 1–2; 328, 2.7; 331, 2; 335, 2; 335A, 1; 335C, 5.12; 335G, 2; 380, 8; 359B, 17.

12   *S.* 116, 7; 286, 3; 305, 1; 306C, 1; 306D, 1; 313G, 3; 329, 1; 335A, 2; 335E, 2.

13   *S.* 20B, 10; 36, 11; 62, 14; 64A, 1–3; 65, 3.7–8; 94A, 3–4; 159, 1; 174, 2; 273, 1–2; 277, 1–3; 280, 4–5; 283, 3; 286, 1; 297, 3; 299, 8; 299B, 3; 299D, 1.4–5; 299E, 1–2; 299F, 1–3; 302, 1–2; 303, 1–2; 306, 10; 306C, 1; 306E, 1; 311, 3; 313B, 2; 313C, 1; 318, 2; 319A; 326, 1–2; 330, 3–4; 335A, 2; 335C, 4; 335G, 1; 335J, 1; 344, 3; 345, 1; 368, 3; 394.

14   *S.* 4, 2; 37, 1; 128, 3; 198, 3; 274, 1; 275, 1; 276, 1–2; 277A, 2; 280, 4; 281, 1; 283, 2; 284, 1–3.5–6; 285, 1.4; 286, 1; 299, 3; 299B, 4; 299E, 1; 305A, 2; 313, 3; 313A, 1; 313G, 1–2; 314, 1; 316, 1; 329, 2; 331, 1; 332, 3; 333, 1–2; 335E, 2; 335F, 2; 375B, 1; 394.

15   *S.* 31, 3; 37, 1.

16   *S.* 273, 1; 277A, 2; 398, 9.

17   *S.* 198, 12.46–47; 273, 3.7–9; 283, 1; 312, 1; 313, 2; 313A, 5; 318, 1.3; 319, 7; 335H, 2.

18   *S.* 4, 36–37; 64, 8; 64A, 1; 65A, 9; 96, 4; 159, 1; 159A, 1; 260E, 2; 273, 9; 280, 6; 282, 1; 284, 6; 285, 7; 299A, 1; 299D, 1; 299F, 4; 300, 6; 301A, 7; 302, 1.9; 303, 2; 304, 2; 305A, 1–2.4–5; 306, 10; 306E, 1.6–7; 311, 1; 315, 10; 318, 3; 325, 1–2; 328, 7; 335, 2; 335G, 2; 345, 6; 351, 11; 382, 5.
      Augustine does not emphasize the 'bloody death' of martyrs, but rather their moral example, and exhorts his audience to imitate their example of authentic Christian life. "Today the martyr's battle continues inwardly: trials are not wanting, the battle and the crown are prepared. Now, 'the Christian soul is tried; and with God's help,

tyr, received ample attention.[19] Augustine states that the authentic way to celebrate a feast of a martyr consists in looking to what the martyr placed in his passion as an example to imitate, to believe and fulfil that.[20] The most recurring point throughout the *sermones* on Stephen is Augustine's call to follow his example. Stephen gave an example of the struggle we too have to fight in our heart,[21] against the same temptation to deny Christ.[22] The crown reached by Stephen and several martyrs after him, is still hanging intact for everybody who desires it.[23] Everybody who longs for that crown, has to step into Stephen's footsteps. It is especially in the love for the enemy that Stephen has to be imitated.[24]

---

it conquers and wins a great victory enclosed in the body, with no one watching. One fights in the heart, and is crowned in the heart, but by him who sees in the heart' (s. 328; cf. s. 335D). Christians can do nothing better than lead lives of virtue, imitating the martyrs (s. 300, 6). The abnegation of the historic martyrs justifies contemporary asceticism. The martyrs' sacrifice is now interpreted more generally as contempt for the present life and desire for the future resurrection (s. 335H, 1). Now temptations are persecutions. The 'good soldiers' of today merit reward 'non saltando, sed orando; non potando, sed jejunando; non rixando, sed tolerando' (s. 326, 1). To die daily means to do charitable works (s. 335C). One can even be a martyr dying in one's bed (s. 286, 7; s. 335D). Above all, martyrs teach patience and self-sacrifice, 'to endure all hard things' (s. 335C)." Straw, Martyrdom, 541.

In this perspective, for Augustine, the thesis of Malone that monasticism is the successor of martyrdom, can be broadened: all Christians who battle against sin are the imitators and successors of the martyrs according to Augustine. Edward E. Malone, *The Monk and the Martyr: the Monk as the Successor of the Martyr*, SCA 12 (Washington D.C.: The Catholic University of America Press, 1950).

19   Dupont, Imitatio Christi, Imitatio Stephani. Mayer, "Attende Stephanum conservum tuum".

20   *S.* 317, 1 (Hill: 425, Rebillard: 26/12/425, Gryson: 26/12/425).

Even though there exists much literature on the dating of specific *sermones*, we refer at each dating of a *sermo* to four recent chronological overviews, i.e. of Hill, Rebillard, Hombert and Gryson. Roger Gryson, Bonifatius Fischer, Herman Josef Frede, *Répertoire général des auteurs ecclésiastiques Latins de l'Antiquité et du Haut moyen âge* (5e édition mise à jour du Verzeichnis der Sigel für Kirchenschriftsteller), Vetus Latina. Die Reste der altlateinischen Bibel 1/1 (Freiburg: Herder, 2007); John E. Rotelle, ed., Edmund Hill, trans. and notes, *Sermons I–XI*, The Works of Saint Augustine. A translation for the 21st Century III/1–11 (New York: New City Press, 1990–1997); Pierre-Marie Hombert, *Nouvelles recherches de chronologie augustinienne*, Collection des Études Augustiniennes, Série Antiquité 163 (Paris: Études Augustiniennes, 2000); Éric Rebillard, Sermones, in: Fitzgerald, ed., *Augustine through the Ages*, 773–792.

21   *S.* 315, 10 (Hill: 416/417, Rebillard: 26/12/416–417, Gryson: feast of Stephen, 26/12/ 416–417).

22   *S.* 318, 3 (Hill: 425, Rebillard: 26/12/425, Gryson: 425, arrival of Stephen's relics).

23   *S.* 314, 2 (Hill: 415–425, Rebillard: 26/12 before 425, Gryson: feast of Stephen, 26/12/ 415/425.).

24   *S.* 314, 2.

As human, Stephen forgave his enemies, showing that it is an example which can be imitated.[25] Moreover, what Stephen did was a gift from God. That grace is still available.[26] This group of sermons illustrates the fact that Augustine perceives grace in the life of martyrs. Augustine for example explains that Stephen received the martyrdom as a *beneficium* from God.[27] In this context Augustine also notices that martyrs did not achieve martyrdom through their own powers. Their ability to endure martyrdom is a gift from God, God gave them the opportunity of martyrdom.[28]

Anti-Donatist *sermones ad populum*

Circa 40 *sermones ad populum* are considered to have an anti-Donatist intent (ss. 3, 4, 10, 33, 37, 45–47, 71, 88, 90, 129, 137, 138, 147A, 159B, 162A, 164, 182, 183, 197, 198, 202, 223, 252, 266, 269, 271, 275, 292, 293A, 295, 313E, 327, 340A, 357–359, 359B, 360, 360A, 360C, 400). Recently, Ivonne Tholen studied Augustine's anti-Donatist homiletic discourses. She concluded that the sermons regarding the Donatist controversy show us not so much Augustine the theologian, but the bishop of Hippo as caretaker of souls. His caring of souls includes the explanation of why a heretical position is wrong and should be condemned. Augustine is aware of the double fear Donatism could instill in his flock: the fear of losing salvation and the fear of being contaminated by the sins of others. The idea of complete sanctity could be attractive to his community. The fear of his community, the attraction of Donatism and

---

25   *S.* 315, 3–4.8.

26   *S.* 315, 4.8.

The emphasis on the imitation of Stephen clearly shows the moralising and pastoral intentions of Augustine's sermons on Stephen. Forgiveness of the enemy seems to be very important. Jean Lafitte, Pardon des offenses et amour des ennemis dans "Les Sermones" de Saint Augustin, *Anthropotes 16* (2000), 69–103.

27   *S.* 317, 4.

28   *S.* 318, 1: "Reddiderunt uicem, sed non de suo: ut enim hoc possent, ille donauit; et ut fieret quod ab ipsis fieri potuit, ille donauit. Ehibendo dignationem, dedit occasionem." PL 38, 1438. Cf. *s.* 319, 1 (Hill: 426, Rebillard: 26/12 not before 425, Gryson: not before 425, feast of consecration of *memoria* of Stephen): "Donet mihi Dominus pauca dicere salubriter, qui donauit sancto Stephano tanta dicere fortiter." PL 38, 1440.

"Reddiderunt uicem" out of *s.* 318, 1 confirms the mutual character perceived by Straw in Augustine's thinking about martyrdom. The martyrdom is a second movement, an answer to and a giving back of Christ's sacrifice from the martyrs to Christ who himself gave away his life. Straw, Martyrdom, 538.

Augustine's reaction in his sermons deal with the question of salvation: how can one reach it, who can administer it, what determines it, can one lose it? His sermons are orientated at his community. For this reason he does not deal with Donatism in an abstract or historical-critical way, but very concretely: 'what does a Donatist say and do (now)?' He approaches them in his sermons from the perspective found in the contemporary scene, from the specific questions and concrete fears his audience is struggling with.[29]

Our research confirms that two issues are of priority in Augustine's preaching against the Donatists: ecclesiology and harmatology. Firstly, he constantly repeats that the Catholic church is universal, not limited to Africa,[30] and that unity (of *caritas, pax*) is one of the most essential characteristics of the church. With this he reproaches most of all the Donatists for destroying the said ecclesial unity.[31] Secondly, in this earthly church, sinners and saints live and should live together, it is a *mixtum*. Only God can separate the chaff from the wheat. Sinners have to be tolerated. Moreover, sin is not something contagious.[32] This is the core of his anti-Donatist *sermones ad populum*, and he hardly if ever seems to refute the Donatist martyr theology in his sermons.

The anti-Donatist thesis that martyrdom is not constituted by *poena*, but by the correct *causa* is not absent in the anti-Donatist *sermones*, but is at the same time not prominently present. In the above mentioned list, we find this theme in five *sermones*.

In *sermo* 138, on the feast of the martyr Vincent, on the *boni pastoris officium* of John 10:11–16, Augustine preaches that Christ himself is the good shepherd. Peter, Paul, all the apostles, the martyrs and saints (such as Cyprian), who gave their life, are good shepherds, not only because they spilt their blood, but because they did so on behalf of the flock: not out of self-esteem, but out of love.[33] Martyrdom should arise

---

29   Ivonne Tholen, *Die Donatisten in den Predigten Augustins. Kommunikationslinien des Bischofs von Hippo mit seinen Predigthörern* (Berlin: Lit, 2010).

30   *S.* 46, 147A, 159B, 162A, 340A, 358, 359, 360A.

31   *S.* 3, 33, 37, 47, 88, 90, 137, 138, 147A, 162A, 164, 202, 252, 266, 269, 271, 313E, 340A, 357, 358, 359, 360A, 360C, 400. Cf. Emilien Lamirande, *La situation ecclésiologique des Donatistes d'après saint Augustin* (Ottawa: Éditions de l'université d'Ottawa, 1972).

32   *S.* 4, 10, 47, 88, 90, 164, 223, 252, 266. Cf. in this context the Donatist opinion on baptism: *s.* 33, 269, 292.

33   *S.* 138, 1 (Hill: 411–412, Rebillard: 411–412, Gryson: 'wohl im Sommer 411').
     Cf. *s.* 137 (Hill: 400–405, Rebillard: 408–411, Hombert: 410–420, Gryson: 410–420, rather 412–416) on John 10:1–16: on earth, Christ suffers everything what the members of his body suffer (*s.* 137, 2). Those who enter the door (John 10:1–16), are the shepherds, are Christ and all who imitate his passion, understand his *humilitas*, admit their own sinfulness and weakness (*s.* 137, 4).

from the correct reasons. *Molestiae* as such do not make martyrs, because also *haeretici* have to suffer such trials. All who spilt their blood against the flocks instead of on behalf of them, are not martyrs, because they do not have *caritas*.[34] All good works should be done because of *caritas*, and not for any other reasons.

Sermo 275 is preached on the feast of the same martyr Vincent. The preacher explicitly reacts against the Donatists: not the *poena* but the *causa* makes martyrs. "Scilicet ut uictores non tolerantia faciat, sed iustitia. Quoniam martyres discernit causa, non poena."[35] *Mutatis mutandis*, a lot of people suffer because of their vices and not because of their virtues, while the devil is not their persecutor but their possessor. Augustine adds that it was not Vincent himself who spoke, but God speaking through him.[36]

Sermo 359B is devoted to the topic of obedience. Augustine refers to martyrs, especially to Vincent, as examples of obedience. Vincent was a true martyr because he placed God's commandment above the emperor's decree to make sacrifices to the idols.[37] Augustine adds that it is not because the emperors are now catholic, that the church no longer suffers persecutions.[38] Augustine here refers to the Donatists. While the devil in the era of the imperial persecution of Christians made false gods, he now makes false martyrs. Christ, by his example and teaching, taught that saints have to die, if necessary, for the truth that there is only one God to be venerated.[39] The true *causa*, and not the *poena*, makes the real martyrs, crowns them. The correct cause of martyrship is *iustitia*,[40] to die for Christ.[41] Confessing Christ – the bridegroom – implies also confessing his bride, the church. A true martyr thus recognizes the church: he spills his blood in and for the church.[42] A true mar-

---

Cf. *s.* 147A, 2 (Denis 12. Hill: 409–410, Rebillard: Saturday after Easter, 409–410, Gryson: Saturday after Easter, 409–410): The false shepherds led the sheep out of the one flock (Donatists). There is only one shepherd, the Lord, who paid his blood as price for his flock.

34   *S.* 138, 2.

35   *S.* 275, 1. PL 38, 1254 (Hill: 411, feast of Vincent, Rebillard: 22/01/410–412, Gryson: 22/01/410–412).

36   *S.* 275, 1.
      S. 275, 3: God even takes care of the remains of the martyrs, testifying that what dies does not perish.

37   *S.* 359B, 14 (Dolbeau 2. Hill: 411, Rebillard: 411/412, Gryson: 411/412).

38   *S.* 359B, 15.

39   *S.* 359B, 16.

40   *S.* 359B, 17.

41   *S.* 359B, 18.

42   *S.* 359B, 19.

tyr refuses to offer incense to the idols, a false martyr – the Donatist – refuses to make peace with his brother – the Catholic.[43]

Sermo 327, delivered on the feast of 'some martyrs', deals very clearly with the issue of authentic martyrship. Many people suffer, but not all because of the same *causa*. Criminals could suffer the same *poena* as martyrs, but not due to the same cause. *Haeretici* could also suffer, often from their own hand, and also wish to be considered to be martyrs. "Non fecit martyrem poena, sed causa."[44] Christ and the two robbers on the cross received the same punishment, but because of a different cause. Christ did not suffer for his own crimes, but actually for theirs – a reality which the 'good' thief accepted.[45] Augustine also adds that God himself gave to the martyrs what pleases him.[46]

Sermo 313E is held on the feast of Cyprian and connects grace with Cyprian, an authority to whom the Donatists appealed.[47] Augustine preaches that Cyprian lived as a man confident of death and died confident of rising again. He won God's favour with a twofold grace, the grace he received from God who was pleased with him, he pleased God through God's own gift to him. Previously Cyprian, before his conversion, had only sin in him. This he confessed in his writings. He did not forget what he once had been, so as not be ungrateful to the one who caused him to cease from sinning. He won God's favour with a double grace: through the way in which he was a bishop, and the way in which he was a martyr. As bishop he held on to unity, as martyr he gave an example of *confessio*.[48] The Donatists, who falsely boast that Cyprian belongs to them, do not look at his episcopal office (directed at

---

43   *S.* 359B, 20. Cf. *s.* 90, 9 (Hill: 411–412, Rebillard: 411–416, Gryson: 411), a sermon against the Donatists, on *caritas* and forgiveness, against their rejection of sinners: Augustine invites to follow the example of Christ and the martyr Stephen, who forgave their own persecutors.

44   *S.* 327, 1. PL 38, 1451 (Hill: 405–411, Rebillard: 405–411, Gryson: 405–411).

45   *S.* 327, 2.

46   *S.* 327, 1.

47   *S.* 313E, 1 (Guelf. 28. Hill: 410, feast of Cyprian, Rebillard: 14 September 410, Gryson: feast of Cyprian 14/09/395–396).

48   *S.* 313E, 1. "Itaque numero, quos hoc docuit, eminuit beatus Cyprianus: sic uiuens tamquam sciens se moriturum, et sic moriens tamquam certum habens resurrecturum; gemina gratia commendatus Deo, ea utique gratia, quam sumpsit ab illo cui placuit. Placuit autem illi ex dono eius: quod enim ad ipsum attinebat, unde displiceret habebat, non unde placeret; sed quemadmodum scriptum est, *ubi abundauit peccatum, superabundauit gratia* [Rom 5:20]. Ille ipse ueridicus et uerax martyr seruus Dei, uerax munere Dei, confitetur in scripturis suis, qualis antea fuisset: non obliuiscitur qualis fuerit, ne ingratus sit ei, per quem talis esse cessauit. Gemina ergo gratia commendatur Deo, episcopatu et martyrio. Episcopatus eius defendit et tenuit unitatem; martyrium eius docuit et impleuit confessionem." MA 1, 536.

unity) and his martyr death (because of the right *causa*, and not like jumping off a cliff).[49] The Donatists who look for their own death do not listen to the Lord but to the devil when he tempted Christ to jump off the temple roof. They are not bad Christians, but simply no Christians at all, since they listen to the devil and not to Christ's reply to the devil.[50] Cyprian, imitating the example of Christ, did not deliberately look for his death, but accepted it because of the correct *causa*: the confession of his faith in Christ. The Donatists actually commit murder.[51]

The topic of martyrs recurs in the anti-Donatist *sermones ad populum* in *Sermo* 295 which discusses the martyrhood of Peter and Paul. Opening his sermon, Augustine says the two apostles died for the truth.[52] They were, in their *passiones*, tested and trained by Christ.[53] In *sermo* 198, parallel to his rejection of pagan idolatry (which replaces the Creator with creatures), he explains that the holy martyrs and angels do not wish to be venerated themselves but desire that the one whom they venerate, should be venerated, namely God.[54] Martyrs should not be venerated instead of God – martyrs themselves despise this – God should be venerated in the martyrs.[55] The examples of Paul, Barnabas and Peter (Acts 14:15; 14:18; 3:12–13) show that people wanted to venerate them because of the miracles they performed, but they strongly rejected this and wished that God instead was venerated.[56] *Mutatis mutandis*, the good angel does not want to be venerated instead of God

---

49   S. 313E, 2.

50   S. 313E, 4. Augustine adds that the Donatists opt to jump off cliffs, but not to hang themselves, because Judas did the latter. Augustine reacts rhetorically: 'you refuse to do what the traitor did, but you listen to his master, the devil'.

51   S. 313E, 5. The devil convinced the *haeretici* to break away, the Donatists to jump, Judas to commit treason and suicide. S. 313E, 6. "So then, observe the branch that has been pruned, the martyr Cyprian; observe the branches that have been cut off, the heretics and Donatists. Why do you people say you belong to this man, this man who bore fruit of peace and unity, who was pruned by the pruning hook of martyrdom, to obtain the crown of eternal salvation? Why do you compare yourselves to this man, heretics and Donatists, cut off from the vine by separation, defiled by your habit of headlong self-destruction." John E. Rotelle, ed., Edmund Hill, trans., *Sermons III/9 (306–340A), On the Saints*, The Works of Saint Augustine, A translation for the 21st Century III/9 (Hyde Park/New York: New City Press, 1994), 114.

52   S. 295, 1 (Hill: 29/06/410, Peter and Paul, Rebillard: 29/06/405–411, Hombert: 400–410, Gryson: 29/06/400–410, Peter and Paul).

53   S. 295, 7.

54   S. 198, 46 (Dolbeau 26. Hill: 420–425, January 1, Rebillard: –, Gryson: 404).

55   S. 198, 12.

56   S. 198, 13.

(Jes 14:13–14).[57] Angels and martyrs do not wish to be venerated, only that He is venerated whom they themselves venerate, namely God.[58] At the *memoria* of martyrs, there are no sacrifices made to the martyrs, but only one sacrifice to the Lord, in which also the martyrs are venerated, not in or because of themselves, but in and because of the One who helped them to defeat the devil.[59] *Sermo* 4 is a call to imitate the example of the martyrs.[60] The fight against the temptations of the devil is parallel to the battle the martyrs had to fight against their persecutors, and also leads to a *corona* as for the martyrs.[61] Augustine adds that Peter – just like all martyrs – was prepared to die because the coming of the Spirit filled him with spiritual confidence.[62]

To conclude, the issue of martyrship seems not to have been an issue of great importance in Augustine's *sermones* situated in the Donatist controversy. However, whenever it is dealt with, his treatment is identical to his anti-Donatist writings, stressing the correct *causa*. While grace is not central to the said controversy, we observed that its essence is far from absent: it is Christ and not the human person who 'graciously' guarantees the perseverance of martyrs.

Anti-Pelagian *sermones ad populum*

The following *sermones ad populum* have an anti-Pelagian intent, or are at least situated in the Pelagian controversy: *ss.* 26, 30, 71, 72A, 100, 114, 115, 125(?), 125 A, 128, 131, 137, 142(?), 143, 144, 145(?), 151-156, 154A, 158, 159, 160(?), 163, 163A, 165, 166, 168, 169, 170, 174, 176, 181, 183, 193, 214(?), 250, 260D, 270, 272B, 283(?), 290, 293, 294, 299, 333, 335B, 348A, 351(?), 363, 365(?). Without discussing the content of the said *sermones* in detail, we can describe them nevertheless as a series of anti-Pelagian broadsides in line with Augustine's anti-Pelagian polemical discourses. The *gratia* themes characteristic of this polemic literature are also to be found in these *sermones*. The fall is the result of the *liberum arbitrium*, of the *uoluptates* of humankind, the human *superbia*. As a result of the *peccatum originale* the will was disordered, humanity lost its capacity to do

---

57   *S.* 198, 14–16; 46–48. This is precisely the error of the *haeretici* – who desire Christ's name changed for theirs (*s.* 198, 15) – and of the Donatists in particular, who perversely replaced Christ by Donatus (*s.* 198, 45).

58   *S.* 198, 46.

59   *S.* 198, 47.

60   *S.* 4, 37 (Hill: before 420, Rebillard: 22/01/410–419, Gryson: 22/01/403).

61   *S.* 4, 36.

62   *S.* 4, 2.

the good and death came into the world. Human nature is thus sick, *uitiata*, and human beings are incapable of healing themselves. Only the sinless Christ *medicus* can bring about this healing. Having been born outside the domain of the *uoluptas* and the *libido carnalis*, Christ alone is without sin. Augustine underlines here that Christ took the punishment due for sin upon himself when he died on the cross and not sin itself. Every human being thus remains sinful in two ways: they have their own personal sin and they inherit Adam's sin. We all sin in Adam, moreover, and the transmission of this original sin is brought about in fleshly procreation. It is because of this sin of Adam that infant baptism is necessary for the redemption of such children and not only because it grants them access to the kingdom of heaven as the Pelagians – according to Augustine – claimed. Augustine returns time and again to humility. The faithful are to accept redemption as a gift of God and should not ascribe it in pride to their own merits. Augustine's primary argument against the 'Pelagians' is that they set out to establish their own righteousness, refuse to subject themselves to the righteousness of God, arrogantly insist that a life without sin is possible, and thus deny the power of prayer (post-baptismal, especially the prayer of Mt 6:12-13) and the necessity of grace (baptismal and post-baptismal). Recurring themes include the necessity of infant baptism on account of original sin, the need to have original sin and our own personal sins forgiven by Christ *medicus*, the sin-disclosing function of the as such insufficient (and sin-multiplying) law, inner disharmony between the spirit and the flesh (*concupiscentia carnalis*), the insufficiency of the human free will and the law of Moses, and the relationship between Adam and Christ.

Despite the fact that martyr theology is not an issue debated upon during the Pelagian controversy, the language used by Augustine, especially in his *sermones*, hold some similarities with his martyrology. He constantly stresses that (baptized) Christians have to fight, to battle against *concupiscentia carnis*, and that the capacity to fight and to triumph is only possible thanks to Christ's grace,[63] that actually everything one achieves is the result of God's gifts.[64] Salvation is brought about, because Christ spilled his blood. He is the sacrifice for human

---

63   Combat (*bellum*) against *concupiscentia carnis*: s. 26, 30, 125, 128, 145, 151, 152, 153, 154, 154A, 155, 156, 163, 163A, 169, 170, 193, 348A, 351, 363.
      Victory/*corona* thanks to God's grace and Christ's assistance, constant need of God's grace in this combat: s. 30, 128, 145, 151, 152, 153, 154, 154A, 155, 156, 163A, 169, 170, 351, 363.

64   All things in man that are good (esp. *iustitia*), come from God, it are not own merits but grace: s. 26, 71, 115, 131, 144, 158, 165, 166, 169, 176, 250, 260D, 270, 348A, 365. God crowns his own gifts: s. 131.

sin.[65] This language and these ideas are similar to how Augustine describes martyrdom, he however very rarely makes such a link in his anti-Pelagian *sermones*. Nevertheless, the theme of martyrs is not absent in this *corpus*, and has some significant occurrences.

Some sermons deal with the issue of martyrs in passing. *Sermo* 158, dealing with the topic of predestination in the larger framework of faith, hope and love, makes clear that within this earthly life we have to hope not for a temporary reward, but for God since He offers the only true fulfilment.[66] This hope comforts us during our journey. The object hoped for – God – cannot yet be seen. Otherwise, it would not be hope. This was precisely the hope of the martyrs.[67] *Sermo* 159 invites to love (*amare, delectare*) *iustitia*. Despite the fact that all what is longed for here on earth in faith, will be fulfilled in heaven, a certain degree of perfection can also be reached in this life. This is what the martyrs did: they fought against sin to the extreme of spilling their blood.[68] For this reason, they are perfect lovers of *iustitia*.[69] *Sermo* 169, an anti-Pelagian discourse on *concupiscentia*, states that the genuine martyrship can only proceed from *caritas*. One needs *caritas* to partake in Christ's suffering and this *caritas* can only be given by God.[70] *Sermo* 137, which is sometimes believed to be anti-Donatist, declares that Christ suffers everything the members of his body suffer.[71] As already mentioned, when explaining John 10:1-16, Augustine states that the good *pastor* imitates Christ's passion.[72]

---

65   S. 125, 152, 155, 163, 163A, 214, 294, 348A, 365.

Forgiving sins in baptism is grace, help against sins is grace: s. 71, 72A, 125, 143, 144, 170, 174, 176, 181, 211, 270, 272B, 293, 294, 351, 363. Parallel to his anti-Donatist harmatology, Augustine preaches in s. 181, 214, 250, 270, 351 that the church on earth is not without sins, and that sinners within the church should be tolerated.

Augustine calls to imitate Christ (his forgivingness, humility): s. 114, 142. Cf. s. 100, 4: to be *imitator sanctorum* is gratis grace, no merit.

66   S. 158, 7 (Hill: 417, Rebillard: not before 418, Gryson: around 418).

67   S. 158, 8.

68   S. 159, 1 (Hill: 417, Rebillard: not before 418?, Gryson: 418/420?, Hombert: 418–420).

69   S. 159, 8. Cf. s. 142, 13–14 (Wilmart 11 + Dolbeau 7. Hill: 413–417, Rebillard: 404, Gryson: 404/406): calls to imitate the Lord, to do everything what one does for the Lord – giving one's possessions to the poor, surrendering one's body to fire (1Cor 13:3) with *caritas*.

70   S. 169, 15 (Hill: 416, Rebillard: 416, Gryson: September 416).

71   S. 137, 2 (Hill: 400–405, Rebillard: 408–411, Gryson: Lent 410/420, rather 412/416, Hombert: 410–420).

72   S. 137, 4.

Cf. s. 137, 9: Some proclaim the gospel out of love, others because of external reasons ("alios annuntiare Euangelium per caritatem, alios per occasionem", PL 38, 759). In

Other anti-Pelagian sermons, most often linked to the liturgical celebration of martyrs, deal more extensively and more specifically with several aspects of Augustine's martyrology.

Sermo 128, dealing with the theme of John the Baptist as a witness of Christ (John 5:31-35) and elaborating on the struggle against *concupiscentia carnis*, states that martyrs are witnesses of Christ, of the truth. It is Christ who resides (*perhibere*) in them and renders them capable to testify. In them, Christ gives testimony of himself. God is God, also without them, they however are nothing without God.[73]

Sermo 283, on the feast of the martyrs of Maxula, opens with:

> "Fortitudinem sanctorum martyrum sic in eorum passione miremur, ut gratiam Dei praedicemus. Neque enim et ipsi in seipsis laudari uolunt, sed in illo cui dicitur: "in Domino laudabitur anima mea" [Ps 33:3]. Hoc qui intellegunt, non superbiunt. Cum tremore petunt, cum gaudio accipiunt; perseuerant, non amittunt. Quia enim non superbiunt, mites sunt."[74]

The martyrs are not to be praised, but God. The virtue which made it possible for them to tolerate what was done against them is *patientia*. The preacher Augustine lists two sources of sin, namely *uoluptas* and *dolor*. Against *uoluptas* one needs *continentia*, against *dolor patientia*. The first temptation works via promises, the second by threats. God however supersedes both: He gives the sweetest good (sweeter than any *uoluptas*) and also the most severe threat, namely eternal fire.[75] *Continentia* and *patientia* are both gifts of God, and have to be recognised as such (in gratitude). The commandment 'non concupisces' (Rom 7:7) forbids *uoluptas* and the fear for pain. The martyrs did not have this longing for an earthly, bodily life (*uoluptas*), but longed for the eternal life.[76] Without the help of *Deus adiutor* one is nothing,[77] and precisely this *adiutor* the martyr needed to win. Without this helper, the martyr could not have triumphed. Perhaps he could have conquered the pain, but not the devil. In this case, he would have achieved insensitivity to

---

the case of the latter: their message is real, they themselves however are not, because they do not look for God but for something else.

73   *S*. 128, 3 (Hill: Saturday, 412–416, Rebillard: 412–416, Gryson: 416). Cf. *s*. 290, 2 (Hill: John the Baptist, 414, Rebillard: 24/06/412–416, Gryson: 24/06/412–416) notices that only from John the Baptist and Christ the anniversary of both their physical birth and their martyrship is celebrated. Other saints are only commemorated on the day of their death.

74   *S*. 283, 1. PL 38, 1286 (Dolbeau 14. Mainz 45. Hill: 414, Rebillard: 397, Gryson: 22/07/ 412).

75   *S*. 283, 1.

76   *S*. 283, 3.

77   *S*. 283, 2–3.

pain, but not yet *patientia*. For *patientia* comes from the Helper, who provides the martyr with real faith, a good *causa* and *patientia* for this cause. True *patientia* is preceeded by a good *causa*. Faith too is given by God. This is the patience of martyrs which encourages us.[78] Only the cause of suffering counts: because of faith and justice. Adulterers, thieves, murderers, *haeretici* suffer persecution, but not while striving for a just cause. To tolerate pain because of a bad cause, is no *patientia*, but *duritia*. The real *patientia* is given by God.[79]

Sermo 333, preached on the feast of 'some martyrs', elaborates on the theme of martyrs. Christ promised to assist martyrs, and prepared their will for martyrdom. Also our *patientia* to bear suffering is given to us by God, and should therefore not be ascribed to ourselves. Martyrs are brave and strong, but it is Christ who makes the human heart strong.[80] Paul admits that the crown he will receive from God is given to him precisely because God always assisted him. God gives us what makes us capable of receiving a reward from him.[81] God gave Paul a reward for the good things He himself previously gave Saul/Paul. Because of this gift, Paul was able to fight the good battle, to end the race, to keep his faith. When God crowned Paul's merits, He is actually crowning his own merits.[82]

In the anti-Pelagian *sermones* discussed above, we noticed a great emphasis on grace. Grace is a crucial theme in the Pelagian controversy. The stress however on Christ's assistance during the martyr sermons was also noticeable in the anti-Donatist *sermones*, and should not *per se* be read as specifically anti-Pelagian. *Sermones* 299 and 333B link

---

78   *S.* 283, 4: Martyrs are God's soldiers, they also undergo dangers, worries and wounds. After the hard work of the military service, they are granted their pension. Soldiers however can die in battle before receiving that pension. Martyrs on the other hand do not lose their reward by dying in battle, but win it. This heavenly reward is eternal and unchangeable rest.

79   *S.* 283, 6: "Elige causam, ne inaniter sufferas poenam. Et cum elegeris causam, et ipsam Deo commenda et dic illi: «iudica me, Deus, et discerne causam meam a gente non sancta». Ab illo discernitur causa tua, a quo est patientia tua. Veram quippe donat patientiam. Nam pro causa mala duritia est, non patientia." *AnBoll* 110 (1992) 286. *s.* 283, 7: there is a difference between a criminal who does not want to *confiteri* his crimes and a believer who under torture confesses Christ.

80   *S.* 333, 1 (Hill: feast of some martyrs, Rebillard: –, Gryson: –).

81   *S.* 333, 2.

82   *S.* 333, 5. Cf. *s.* 168, 6 (Hill: 416, Rebillard: just before 416, Gryson: around 416) – in the context of the necessity and effectiveness of prayer – Augustine declares that Saul was converted to Paul thanks to the prayers of Stephen at the moment of his martyr death.

the topic of martyrdom with specific aspects of Augustine's anti-Pelagian doctrine.

Sermo 299

Sermo 299 was preached on the feast of the martyrs Peter and Paul.[83] At the outset, Augustine seems to remain with the general *gratia* discourse characteristic of martyr homilies. The Lord bears the suffering of martyrs and thus makes it possible. The sacrifice of the martyrs is thus a reimbursement of what they had already received from Christ (1Cor 4:7). Christ has spilt his blood for us. For this reason, we are indebted to him: we have to offer ourselves as sacrifice. Christ provided himself the sacrifices, He devoted them to himself, He filled the martyrs with the Spirit, He gave them strength.[84] The appeal to follow the martyrs as examples is also typical of the genre. Furthermore, believers should follow the example of the martyrs in spite of the fact that when compared to the number of believers, martyrs are few and far between: we are not all expected to spill our blood, "pauci martyres, sed multi fideles."[85] Every human merit, crowned by God with the *corona iustitiae*, was in the first instance granted by God (1Cor 4:7). God has a debt to pay to humanity in the sense that He promised to reward such merits (which He himself granted). In other words, God rewards that which comes from God. God crowns his own gifts (cf. 2Tim 4:6–8). The Spirit fills the martyr with strength as a sign of divine *gratia*.[86] The martyr's *uirtus* and *patientia* are a gift of *gratia*.[87]

When Augustine turns his attention to the significance of death, to the relationship between death and human nature, and to the role of Adam in this regard, the *gratia* of the martyr is given an anti-Pelagian interpretation. He begins by insisting that death cannot be loved. All living beings shun and fear death. Death has to be endured, tolerated. "Amari mors non potest, tolerari potest."[88] If death was something to be embraced, loved, enjoyed, then the martyrs would not have been considered great and would not have been praised for their courage and patience. Augustine argues that Peter and Paul had an aversion to

---

83   Hill: 418, feast Peter and Paul, Rebillard: 29/06/418, Gryson: Peter and Paul, 29/06/413, Hombert: 29/06/413.
84   *S.* 299, 3.
85   *S.* 299, 4. PL 38, 1369.
86   *S.* 299, 5–6.
87   *S.* 299, 8.
88   *S.* 299, 8. PL 38, 1373.

death, but embraced martyrdom because of a higher ideal. In so doing, he underlines the fact that only what comes after death is to be loved.[89] Death is a punishment, inherited from Adam. Adam was the first to face death as a punishment for his sin (Sir 25:24; Rom 5:12).[90]

Augustine then goes on to explain the difference between *culpa* and *poena*:

> "Ergo in nostra natura et culpa et poena. Deus naturam sine culpa fecit, et si sine culpa persisteret, nec poena utique sequebatur. Inde uenimus, inde utrumque traximus, et hinc multa contraximus. In nostra igitur natura et culpa et poena: in Iesu carne et poena sine culpa, ut et culpa sanaretur et poena. *Alter te*, inquit, *cinget, et feret quo tu non uis* [John 21:18]. Poena est haec: sed per poenam tenditur ad coronam."[91]

---

89 *S.* 299, 8. *S.* 299, 9 refers to 2Cor 5:4 and 1Cor 15:53–56 as evidence for Paul's aversion to death. Based on the example of Peter and Paul, Augustine discusses our natural fear of death in *s.* 299, 8–9. Van Bavel has demonstrated that Augustine considered this natural aversion to death as an integral part of our human weakness. Since the said aversion was not a sin, it was also possible for Christ – who took human *infirmitas* upon himself and did not sin – to fear death. Augustine only develops this perspective after 415. Prior to this he considered fear of death to be a sign of human imperfection rooted in the enormity of our worldly orientation. Christians, however, must be able to overcome this anxiety. Christ was thus distressed prior to his death. *s.* 299, 8 describes this as follows: "Hanc nostrae infirmitatis naturam in se ipse Dominus transfigurauit, cum passurus ait Patri: *Pater, si fieri potest, transeat a me calix iste* [Mt 26:39]." PL 38, 1373. Christ was not distressed on his own account but on account of all of those who were unable to conquer their fear out of weakness. Rebillard concludes in regard to *s.* 299: "Voilà donc un sermon anti-pélagien tout entier construit autour du thème de l'origine de la nature de la mort. Puisque la mort est refusée par la nature humaine, qu'elle est un mal, elle ne peut être qu'un châtiment, le châtiment du péché originel dont les Pélagiens ne peuvent nier l'existence sans fair mentir l'Ecriture." Éric Rebillard, *In hora mortis. Evolution de la pastorale chrétienne de la mort aux IVe et Ve siècles*, BEFAR 283 (Rome: École Française de Rome, 1994), 43–44 (nn. 92–95); 55 (n. 18); 57 (n. 25); 58 (nn. 35–36); 79 (n. 156). Tars-Jan van Bavel, *Recherches sur la christologie de saint Augustin. L'humain et le divin dans le Christ d'après Saint Augustin*, Par. 10 (Fribourg: Editions Universitaires Fribourg, 1954), 137 (n. 61, n. 63), 138 (n. 65).

90 *S.* 299, 8.

91 *S.* 299, 8. PL 38, 1373–1374. Paul considered the punishment of death to be insignificant because it led to the crown. The same holds for humanity as a whole. Our journey is difficult, but our destination is great. Peter was fully aware of his destination and was able to submit to his sufferings with complete engagement and devotion. He was thus able to endure martyrdom. He did not love martyrdom; rather he loved his final goal and willingly endured the journey that would lead him to it.

Augustine continues to insist that death is not a natural reality. Sin is the cause of death and not vice versa. Death is the consequence of sin.[92] The Lord puts an end to the punishment of death through the resurrection. While God could have done away with death by justifying humanity, He chose nevertheless to leave it unperturbed as something believers and saints must struggle with (*contemnere*) on account of their faith. God chose to dispense with death for certain individuals, however, because He so willed it. Enoch and Elijah were taken up alive into heaven. Augustine makes it clear, nevertheless, that this did not have anything to do with their personal merits or their *iustitia*, but God's *gratia* alone.[93]

---

92   *S.* 299, 10. "Peccatum aculeus mortis, quo aculeo facta est mors, non quem aculeum fecit mors: quomodo uenenum poculum mortis, quia facit mortem, non quia fit a morte." PL 38, 1375.

93   *S.* 299, 10. "Dominus ergo in resurrectione finit hanc poenam: mortem autem etiam et fidelibus et sanctis relinquit ad luctam. Ad agonem tibi mors dimissa est. Nam poterat Deus iustificato tibi auferre mortem, sed dimisit ad certamen, ut esset quod pro fide contemneres. Nam de quibus uoluit, fecit. Enoch translatus est, et Elias translatus est, et uiuunt. Iustitia ipsorum meruit hoc? An Dei gratia et Dei beneficium et speciale concessum? Vt creator ostendat in omnibus potestatem, commendauit nobis quid possit." PL 38, 1375.

S. 299, 11: Augustine employs the *casus* of Enoch and Elijah to refute the suggestion that death is a natural reality and that human beings do not die on account of sin. He reacts against the argument that Adam would also have died in spite of the fact that he had not sinned. Fictional adversaries ask in the sermon why Elijah and Enoch did not die if death is the consequence of sin. According to Augustine, this contention implies that death must be rooted in human nature, since the said (Pelagian) claim implies that it is not the consequence of sin. He explains to his opponents that physical death is only rooted in our *natura* in the sense that it is a *natura uitiata*, a nature already condemned to the punishment of death.

S. 299, 12. "Cauti et circumspecti simus aduersus nouitates disputationum, humanarum utique, non diuinarum." PL 38, 1376.

The sermon ends with a warning against a certain group of people – who remain nevertheless unnamed – who are undermining the stability of the faith by calling it into question. Adam is dead, but the serpent (the devil) continues to live. The latter persists with his insinuations and is incessantly on the lookout for companions to share his condemnation. Augustine points out that the followers of the group in question are increasing in number. He asks his community to be patient and cautious in face of these new arguments, which are of purely human origin and definitely do not come from God. The fact that the warning at the end of his sermon remains 'anonymous' might suggest that it should be located at the beginning of the controversy, at a time when Augustine still approached his adversaries with a degree of courtesy.

Sermo 335B

Sermo 335B is a martyr homily, during the liturgy of not explicated martyrs.[94] The sermon opens with the classic theme of the martyrs' willingness to accept even their own death – spilling their blood – in their struggle against sin. They underwent death because of the truth, in dying they discovered life. Augustine relates this to his anti-Pelagian discourse on death as a consequence of sin. He points out that the martyrs would not have died if the human person – Adam – had not sinned. Indeed, if human beings had been obedient to God's command they would have lived. God's threat of death is directed against sin, but the human person appears to have preferred the deception of the serpent instead of listening to the warning from the Creator. "Natura ergo ui sua incurrit in mortem: et, quantum in illa est, obluctatur, ne moriatur; sed moritur nolens, quia peccauit uolens."[95] People are no longer born in the state in which they were originally created by God. Rather they are born, contaminated by the sin of the first transgressor, with both *culpa* and *poena*.[96] Augustine thus argues that death does not belong to (original) human nature, that it is a punishment for sin, and that every person is born with the guilt of Adam and its associated punishment.

"Venit ergo unus contra unum."[97] Here Augustine uses 1Cor 15:21–22 to introduce a first contrast, namely that between Adam and Christ. Christ came to counter Adam (*uenire contra*), which brings Augustine to the difference between Christ and humanity. Christ did not come in the same way as those He came to save. He was born of a virgin without *libido*, "conceptus non cupiditate sed fide."[98] In order to redeem humankind, he took on something of our nature but not all of it. He took the punishment due for our sins upon himself and set humanity free from both its failure and the associated punishment.[99]

Augustine then discusses a second contrast, this time between Adam and the martyrs. With his own words and deeds, Christ encouraged

---

94 *S. Guelf.* 31. Hill: 410–412, Rebillard: 410–412, Gryson: 415–420, Hombert: 415–420.

95 *S.* 335B, 1. MA 1, 558. The serpent is well aware of humanity's aversion to death and makes no effort to convince humanity that death is not an evil. It succeeds, however, in convincing humanity that it shall not die (Gn 3:4).

96 *S.* 335B, 1: "Secuta est mors peccantem: genuit nos, non qualis creatus erat, sed qualis peccando factus fuerat. Nati sumus, de transgressore trahentes culpam et poenam." MA 1, 558.

97 *S.* 335B, 1. MA 1, 558.

98 *S.* 335B, 1. MA 1, 558.

99 *S.* 335B, 1.

martyrs not to fear their own death. The snake said: 'if you sin, you will not die.' Christ on the contrary said: 'if you deny me – and even if you do not deny me – you will die, but do not fear those who only kill the body'. Before the fall, Christ said: 'by sinning you will die'. Now, He says (to the martyrs): 'die, in order to not sin, and by dying you will reach life'. Previously, the first men died by listening to the devil. Now, the martyrs conquer the devil by dying on behalf of the truth. The martyrs died, not because they loved death, but because they loved eternal life.[100] Adam was thus told not to sin in order to avoid death. The martyrs, on the other hand, were urged to accept death in order to avoid sin. Indeed, by denying Christ and succumbing to sin they would have saved their lives. The first human beings died because they listened to the devil, while the martyrs (and humanity today) defeat the devil by dying for the truth. The human person who accepts death can no longer be made to fear by the devil.[101] Martyrs refuse to deny Christ, eternal life, in order to prolong their earthly existence.[102]

Augustine insists here that death is far from easy and that it is even unnatural, thereby intensifying the meritorious character of the martyr's death. Martyrs refuse to deny Christ – eternal life – in order to extend their earthly (and finite) existence. Augustine admits that death is difficult and points out that on the Mount of Olives Christ himself was distressed (Mk 14:34)[103], the moment at which He said to Peter: "someone else [...] will take you where you do not wish to go" (John 21:18).[104] According to Augustine, it is precisely because the martyrs loved life that they were willing to endure death.[105]

The topic of the martyr's death leads Augustine to reflect on his understanding of grace. The martyrs would not have held their earthly existence in disdain and accepted physical death on account of the truth were it not for the help they received from God. Human beings often run the risk of death, but not due to their love for God as was the case with the martyrs. On the contrary, they do so for the sake of worldly *cupiditas*, the *concupiscentia carnis*, the *concupiscentia oculorum*, the *ambitio saeculi*. Augustine rejects this worldly orientation (1John 2:15–16). At the same time, he notes that salvation does not come from our fellow human beings (Ps (145) 146:3–4) but only from the Lord (Ps

---

100 *S.* 335B, 2.
101 *S.* 335B, 2.
102 *S.* 335B, 3.
103 See *s.* 299, 3; 8–9 for Christ's distress prior to his death on the cross.
104 *S.* 335B, 3. See *s.* 299, 7–8 for Peter's fear of his impending death.
105 *S.* 335B, 4.

3:8 (9)).[106] Augustine is convinced that a human being has a natural aversion to death. Martyrs love eternal life and the truth (Christ), and it is for this reason that they hold their earthly existence in disdain. But they cannot do this without the help of the one who commands that they should despise this life.[107] Augustine's emphasis on the working of divine grace, does not set out to deny our personal, human contribution. The fact that God helps us through his grace does not mean that we ourselves do not carry out what He is helping us to do.[108]

To conclude, martyrology was not at the centre of the Pelagian debate, as is illustrated by the *sermones*. Augustine however seizes the occasion of the liturgical feasts of martyrs to deliver an anti-Pelagian homily, using the theme of martyrs to illustrate the priority of God's all-inclusive grace, particularly in the struggle against sin. The difference between *causa* and *poena* we found explicitly in *sermo* 283 and implicitly in *sermones* 299 and 335B. *Sermo* 299 was delivered during the feast of a martyr at the beginning of the Pelagian controversy and Augustine realigns the martyrdom theme to locate it within an anti-Pelagian discourse. Courageous submission to a martyr's death points to the unnaturalness of death and our natural aversion to it. Inspired no doubt by the (anti-Donatist) distinction between *causa* and *poena* in relation to true martyrdom, Augustine establishes a distinction be-

---

106 S. 335B, 4.

107 In s. 335B, 3–4.

108 S. 335B, 5. "Responde nunc, et dic mihi: si non fido in me, non ergo ego contemno mortem; non ego impleo praeceptum, ne Christum negem. *Beatus, cuius Deus Iacob adiutor est* [Ps 145:5]. Tu quidem mortem contemnis: tu credis, et praeceptum imples: tu minas persecutorum calcas: tu uitam aeternam ardentissime diligis et desideras. Verum est quia tu: sed *beatus, cuius Deus Iacob adiutor est* [Ps 145:5]. Tolle adiutorem, non inuenio nisi desertorem. Desertor Adam, adiutor Christus." MA 1, 561–562.

S. 335B, 5: At the end of his *sermo*, Augustine repeats that our (first) death is a consequence of the sin of the first human being. In parallel to this, he warns that for everyone who sins this first (temporary) death – which all people must endure – will evolve into a second (permanent) death. He goes on to argue that physical death is a consequence of the prior death of the soul. The death of the soul signifies that people have turned their back on God and their sin thus leads to (the punishment of) physical death. The soul deserted God of its own free will, but did not freely desert the flesh. The Lord, by contrast, did not desert the flesh against his will. He died when He chose to die because He was born when He chose to be born. He died so that people would no longer be afraid. In our fear of death, we strive to avoid it and give the impression that it is avoidable. Augustine advises rather that we should fear what we can in fact avoid, namely sin. We should not fear death, because we cannot avoid it. He appeals to the faithful by way of conclusion, not to rely on their own human capacities (Jer 17:5) and urges them in the first instance to pray that they will not succumb to temptation. We should not put our trust in ourselves – mankind – but in the *Adiutor*.

tween *culpa* and *poena* in relation to human mortality. Prior to the fall, humanity was free of *culpa*. Because of Adam's sin, however, this *culpa* and its ally death were passed on to humanity as a whole in the form of *poena*. *Sermo* 335B uses the theme of martyrdom to engage in an anti-Pelagian discourse on human death. The martyrs – humanity in general – are mortal as a (punitive) consequence of the sin of Adam. Bearing this in mind, Augustine draws attention to the contrast between Adam and a martyr. The former died because he chose sin, the latter dies because he refuses sin. The martyrs' need for divine grace in this struggle demonstrates humanity's need for grace in the context of its struggle against *concupiscentia*. Augustine concludes by insisting on the basis of the greatness of the martyrs – who enjoyed enormous respect among his listeners – that our aversion to death is natural, but death itself is unnatural. The martyrs in this perspective serve as an example and an *auctoritas* in his anti-Pelagian analysis of human *mortalitas*.

General Conclusion

Although Augustine reflected often on the issue of the meaning and the true cause of martyrdom – which he considered to be an expression of divine grace – he does not often mention the topic in the here studied polemical *sermones*. This seems to be a constant factor both in the anti-Donatist and the anti-Pelagian *sermones*. We also observed that Augustine does not put the emphasis on the physical death of the martyrs (the martyr's death as such is not important, a much repeated anti-Donatist refrain), but on their choice for eternal life – an example which can be imitated by all Christians by fighting – helped by God – against sin and by leading an ethical Christian life. Another parallel between these two collections of polemical *sermones* is that when he preaches on this topic, this is most often occasioned by the fact that he delivers his sermon during the liturgical celebration of the feast of martyrs. During the Donatist controversy he seizes this liturgical occasion to explain the difference between *causa* and *poena*, while in the Pelagian controversy he does this to emphasize that God's *gratia* constitutes martyrdom. The topic of grace is present in Augustine's anti-Donatist homiletic treatment of martyrdom, but in an implicit way. He rather stresses the distinction *causa-poena*. The latter distinction is not completely absent in his anti-Pelagian *sermones*, the emphasis here however is on *gratia*. Concerning the issue of *martyres* and their definition, one can thus contend that there is a continuity in the anti-Donatist and anti-Pelagian *sermones*, and this continuity can be explained by the liturgical occasion and evolves – regarding their content – around God's helping grace, implicit in the anti-Donatist and explicit in the anti-Pelagian *sermones*.

HAJNALKA TAMAS

"Eloquia Divina Populis Legere"

Bible, Apologetics and Asceticism in the *Passio Pollionis*

"Dans l'Antiquité chrétienne, on ne devient un martyr
que parce que les autres ont fait de vous un martyr."[1]

Audience-oriented methodologies of textual interpretation are leaving their imprint also on hagiographic research, where the many cases of hagiographic fiction (within reasonable limits) offer a gold-mine for the scholar. The *passiones*, in particular, raise multiple interests. Being Christian re-editings of the proconsular acts, often eluding the conventional rhetoricity characteristic to the hagiographic legends, they preserve a modicum of historical truth in the events they narrate, but are also representative for the social and cultural landscape of the community that generated them. In that, they contribute to a better understanding of the history of Christianity on two fronts: by the value of the narrated events and by the value of the narration itself, as a historical product.

In the following, I shall attempt to pursue such an analysis on a late 4th century Pannonian hagiographic text, the Passio Pollionis (BHL 6869)[2], containing the trial and martyrdom of Pollio, *primicerius lectorum*

---

1   Marie-Françoise Baslez, *Les persécutions dans l'Antiquité: victimes, héros, martyrs* (Paris: Fayard, 2007), 257.

2   Godefridus Henschenius, *De S. Eusebio episcopo, Pollione lectore, et Tiballo, martyribus in Pannonia*, ActaSS Aprilis, vol. 3 (Paris and Rome: Apud Victorem Palmé, 1866), 571–573. Subsequent editions reprint the Bollandist recension: Thierry Ruinart, ed., *Acta primorum martyrum sincera et selecta* (Amsterdam: ex Officina Wetsteniana, 1713), 403-405; Daniel Ruiz-Bueno, ed., *Actas de los mártires*, (Madrid: Biblioteca de auctores cristianos, 1951), 1045–1050. The Passio was translated in Spanish by the same Ruiz-Bueno (*loc. cit.*) and into Italian by Giuliana Caldarelli, ed, *Atti dei martiri* (Milan: Paoline Editoriale Libri, ²1985, reprint 1996), 675–679, who used the Latin text published by Ruiz-Bueno. Based on a single (and not the best) manuscript, the Bollandist edition is faulty; yet, this article will quote the text published by Hen-

in Cibalae.[3] The text enjoyed a long-standing reputation of reliability, stemming from its status as one of the few sources (all hagiographic) documenting the history of the Great Persecution in Pannonia. Its structure, evading hagiographic conventions, its textual connections with the Passio Irenaei Sirmiensis (BHL 4466)[4], considered equally reliable, further strengthened the confident attitude of scholars. The present article will argue against its use as a source for the Great Persecution:

---

schen, as the critical edition that I am preparing is still unpublished; where the Bollandist text differs substantially from the new edition, the quotations will be taken from the manuscript closest to the original: Clm 4531, Bayerische Staatsbibliothek München, f. 74r – 75r.

3   Feast-day: 28th of April. Main sources attesting Pollio's cult: Martyrologium Hieronymianum ("In Pannonia Cibalis Eusebii episcopi, Pollionis lectoris"), Hippolyte Delehaye, *Commentarius perpetuum in martyrologium Hieronymianum*, ActaSS Novembris, vol. 2, pars 2 (Brussels: Société des Bollandistes, 1931), 215 (see also 208, 211 and 280); several 7th century Roman *itineraria* (the most complete is Notitia ecclesiarum urbis Romae, which reads in the cemetery of Pontianus: "Tunc ascendis et pervenies ad Sanctum Anastasium papam et martirem, et in alio Pollion martir quiescit"), Pasquale Testini, *Archeologia cristiana: nozioni generali dalle origini alla fine del sec. VI; propedeutica – topografia cimiteriale; epigrafia – edifici di culto* (Rome: Editori Pontifici, 1958), 58; Agnellus of Ravenna, *Liber pontificalis* 22 ([Liberius III] "Sepultusque est in monasterio sancti Pullionis, quem suis temporibus aedificatum est, non longe a porta quae vocatur Nova, cuius sepulcrum nobis cognitum est"), Agnellus Ravennatis, *Liber pontificalis ecclesiae Ravennatis*, cura et studio Deborah Mauskopf Deliyannis, CChr.CM 199 (Turnhout: Brepols, 2006), 169. The *monasterium* Agnellus mentions was likely an oratory or chapel: Hippolyte Delehaye, *L'hagiographie ancienne de Ravenne*, AnBoll 47 (1929), 8; for other interpretations on the shape of the construction, see: Agnellus von Ravenna, *Liber pontificalis – Bischofsbuch. Übersetzt und eingeleitet von Claudia Nauerth*, vol. 1, FC 21/1 (Freiburg: Herder, 1996), 134, n. 53, and Hans Reinhard Seeliger, Pollio(n), *LThK* 8 (³1999), 397 (mausoleum); Agostino Amore, Pollio, *LThK* 8 (²1963), 592 (basilica). A hypothetic *martyrion* of Pollio whose ruins were unearthed in the architectural complex of Kamenica (1,5 kilometers eastwards outside Vinkovci, the ancient Cibalae, thus corresponding to the location where Pollio was martyred according to the Passio), was catalogued by Branka Migotti, *Evidence for Christianity in Roman Southern Pannonia (Northern Croatia): A Catalogue of Finds and Sites*, BAR International Series 684 (Oxford: Archaeopress, 1997), 22. The construction, consisting of two unidentified graves with a hypothetical basilica above them, knew intense cultic activity in the late 4th and the entire 5th century. Based on these sources, the history of Pollio's relics can be retraced with some degree of certainty: first deposed outside Cibalae, they were moved at the end of the 4th century in Ravenna and from there (in early 5th century?) they took the path to Rome, where they found a resting-place in the cemetery of Pontianus.

4   Herbert Musurillo, ed., *The Acts of the Christian Martyrs* (Oxford: Oxford University Press, 1972, reprint 1979), 294–301. A revised dossier, accompanied by a new critical edition of the Passio was published by François Dolbeau, Le dossier hagiographique d'Irénée, évêque de Sirmium, *Antiquité Tardive* 7 (1999), 205–214. Unless otherwise noted, references to the Passio Irenaei are given throughout this article according to Dolbeau's edition.

apart from the martyr's name and the place of his execution, there is little useful information. I shall address two aspects in support of my claim – these will serve at the same time to establish the chronological framework in which the Passio was written. I shall try then to highlight the insights that the text offers about its compositional milieu. The guiding presumption is that the Passio surprises a state of facts which it then attempts to mold. This section, the result of an unprecedented research, is the first tentative to observe the relevance of the Passio Pollionis for the cultural, social and religious landscape of Pannonia in late 4th century.

1. *Passio Pollionis:* Chronological and Compositional Setting

The little-known Passio Pollionis opens with an introduction cataloguing the many ecclesiastics who were sentenced to death by the persecutor Probus. After martyring clerics from Singidunum and Sirmium, Probus headed for Cibalae, birthplace of Valentinian, "christianissimus imperator", and famous for the martyrdom of its bishop, Eusebius, occurring in a previous persecution.[5] Here, by the will of God, he proceeded to the interrogation of Pollio. The accused identifies himself as a Christian and as "primicerius" of the readers who "eloquia divina populis legere consueverunt."[6] These *eloquia* proclaim one God, creator of all, as opposed to the woods and stones the pagans call gods; next, they take the shape of normative statements guiding the social behavior of Christians in public and in private, vis-à-vis different social classes.[7] However, Pollio's theological and socio-ethical statement bears little fruit as far as Probus's attitude is concerned. Following his obstinate refusals to sacrifice to the emperors, the judge condemns him to be burnt alive, a sentence immediately carried out[8]. The epilogue refers to the celebration of Pollio's *dies natalis*, suggesting that the text was composed for liturgical usage.

---

5 *Pass. Poll.* 1.
6 *Pass. Poll.* 2.
7 *Pass. Poll.* 2.
8 *Pass. Poll.* 3.

1.1.

The Passio is void of miracles or torture; though we are informed that the martyr prays before his execution, we do not know what prayer he uttered[9]. The focus is on the dialogue with Probus, which occasions a lengthy confession in the form of socio-ethical propositions with apologetic undertone. Nothing is said about the fate of Pollio's relics. It is legitimate to conclude, therefore, that the narrative eludes conventional hagiographic structuring. That is not to say that it is a uniquely original document. The immediate observation is that a number of passages depend on the Passio Irenaei Sirmiensis in such a way as to ascertain that the Passio Pollionis was composed after it. Furthermore, Manlio Simonetti showed, using comparative analysis, that both the Passio Irenaei Sirmiensis and the Passio Pollionis are patchworks of hagiographic *topoi*. Even in Pollio's confession Simonetti saw nothing more than an apologetic influx aiming to exploit at the maximum the martyr's being *primicerius lectorum*.[10] The pertinent observations of the Italian scholar, however, did not affect ulterior reflections, whereby the text was treated as a reliable, albeit literary, document. In what little scholarly work addressed the topic, the Passio was regarded as the Christian re-editing of the proconsular acts, carried out during the reign of Valentinian I.[11] Certainly, hagiographic comparativism has its weakness. Even the most reliable martyr-acts contain hagiographic clichés. It is nothing less than their audiences expected. Therefore, no charges could be laid against the compiler of this hagiographic narrative, were it not for the fact that his creative ardor left some para-

---

9   Hagiographic custom often recorded the martyr's last prayer. See, for example, *Mart. Polyc.* 14, in: Musurillo, *Acts*, 12; *Pass. Iren.* 5.2–5; *Pass. Felicis* 30, in: Musurillo, *Acts*, 270.

10 Manlio Simonetti, Sugli atti di due martiri della Pannonia, in: Id., *Studi Agiografici*, 53–79.

11 Jacques Zeiller, *Les origines chrétiennes dans les provinces Danubiennes de l'Empire Romain* (Paris: De Boccard, 1918), 74; Amore, Pollio, 592; Seeliger, Pollio(n), 397; Ireneo Daniele, Pollione, *BSS* 10 (1982), 1001–1003; Ruiz-Bueno, *Actas*, 1045; Caldarelli, *Atti*, 675, 676n2; Migotti, *Evidence*, 21. Mirja Jarak, Martyres Pannoniae: The Chronological Position of the Pannonian Martyrs in the Course of Diocletian's Persecution, in: Rajko Bratož, ed., *Westillyricum und Nordostitalien in der spätrömischen Zeit* (Ljubljana: Narodni Muzej, 1996), 277–278 maintains that the editor knew and consulted the original acts, but leaves open the possibility that the Passio was written in the 5th century. Reserve, although unargued, was expressed by Musurillo, *The Acts*, XLIII. Similarly to Musurillo, Reinhart Herzog, ed., *Handbuch der lateinischen Literatur der Antike*, vol. 4: *Restauration und Erneuerung. Die lateinische Literatur von 284 bis 374 n. Chr.* (München: C.H. Beck, 1989), 528–532 (especially 529), while conceding authentic elements to the Passio Irenaei, does not even mention the Passio Pollionis.

doxes – whose solution appears evident once the compiler's immediate context is examined. The ensuing challenges passed unnoticed both by Simonetti and all modern authors who dealt with the Passio Pollionis.

1.2.

Should Pollio claim to hold merely the office of a *lector*, the authenticity of this narrative still had some chances of success. In the first centuries of our era, readers were also catechists. Besides reading the Word of God during liturgy, they assisted converts in the preparation for baptism: a certain competence in apologetic argumentation was thus involved in the process, to which Pollio's skills can offer a dignified answer. However, Pollio is *primicerius lectorum*. Courtesy of the Liber Pontificalis, we know of a college of *notarii* led by a *primicerius* in 4th century Rome.[12] We may suspect that large episcopal sees had a college of readers too, either headed or instructed by a *primicerius*. But we should be careful in projecting it to the situation of a small provincial church[13]. And this during the Great Persecution, in a town that did not produce Christian monumental architectonic evidence but starting from the second half of the 4th century![14] This complex ecclesiastical

---

12   Louis Duchesne, *Le liber pontificalis*, vol. 1 (Paris: De Boccard, 1955), 205 under the pontificate of Iulius, 337–352.

13   Granted, this church has – at least according to the text – already distinguished itself with a bishop-martyr: Eusebius. According to the Passio Pollionis, he suffered during a previous persecution and was martyred on the same day as Pollio. The Martyrologium Hieronymianum (perhaps based on the Passio Pollionis?) attests the cult of the bishop celebrated together with Pollio. See Delehaye, *Commentarius*, 215 (quotation in note 2). Zeiller, *Les origines*, 48–49, however intricate might be his explanation, has already dismissed the information as a fictitious entry. Yet, other scholars readily accepted its authenticity, placing Eusebius' martyrdom during Valerian's persecution. See Ruiz-Bueno, *Actas*, 1045; Caldarelli, *Atti*, 675; Mirja Jarak, The History of the Early Christian Communities in Continental Croatia, in: Branka Migotti, ed., *Od nepobjedivog sunca do sunca pravde: Rano kršćanstvo u kontinentalnoj Hrvatskoj – From the Invincible Sun to the Sun of Justice: Early Christianity in Continental Croatia* (Zagreb: Arheološki Muzej, 1994), 169–170; Jarak, Martyres, 278. On the contrary, Simonetti, Sugli atti, 73 maintains that Eusebius' character is another hagiographic convention. The lack of sources makes it impossible to confirm the existence of Eusebius. Either way, this detail is far too insecure to deduct from it the existence of a long-standing bishopric with a complex clerical hierarchy.

14   See Migotti, *Evidence*, 21–22; 32–33. Smaller archeological findings for Cibalae range from the late 3rd century onwards, the earliest elements being two inscriptions displaying (probable) Gnostic features (Migotti, *Evidence*, 14–15, second half of the 3rd century, and 16–17, 3rd century/first half of the 4th century; none of the two inscriptions have been interpreted at the time Migotti published her book); a sarcophagus

organization is unrealistic for the time and place in which Pollio's martyrdom is set. It rather befits a late 4th century bishopric[15]. It shows, at
the same time, a corrupted historical reality even in that part of the
Passio which should be based on the proconsular acts.

1.3.

That the text reflects socio-ecclesiastical realities specific to the last
quarter of the 4th century is verified by the case of the presiding official,
Probus. The same persecutor was responsible also for the martyrdom of
Irenaeus, in Sirmium.[16] François Dolbeau, commenting on the Passio
Irenaei Sirmiensis, already allowed for the possibility that the model
and name-giver of the persecuting magistrate might be Sextus Claudius
Petronius Probus[17], repeatedly praetorian prefect of Illyricum, Italy and
Africa under Valentinian I and his successors.[18] Several arguments con-
cur to uphold this theory. Albeit most scholars readily accept Probus as
governor of Pannonia during the Great Persecution[19], they cannot offer

dating from the beginning of the 4th century (Migotti, *Evidence*, 42–43); and a ring
with inscription from the 3rd/4th century (Migotti, *Evidence*, 72). Other findings: fragment of vessel with a cross graffiti, 3rd century (Migotti, *Evidence*, 88: uncertain; the
argument that it is Christian revolves around the episcopate of Eusebius as a historical fact); tombstone with epitaph, second half of the 4th century (Migotti, *Evidence*,
45–46); several stone slabs, 4th/5th century (Migotti, *Evidence*, 50–51); and a lamp, 5th
century (Migotti, *Evidence*, 83). The meagerness of sources is explained by Migotti,
Evidence, 104 on account of the Arian neglect of Christian symbolism.

15   Rajko Bratož, *Il cristianesimo in Slovenia nella Tarda Antichità: un abrozzo storico*, in: Atti
e memorie della Società Istriana di Archeologia e Storia Patria.NS 29-30 (1981/1982),
28 maintains that the evangelization of the region happened mostly in the first half
of the 4th century – which is highly contradictory with the idealized picture of a
complex Cibalitan bishopric with its beginnings dating from the mid-3rd century.

16   *Pass. Iren.* 2.1; 5.1; 6.

17   Dolbeau, Le dossier, 207 n. 17.

18   PPO Illyrici in 364; PPO Illyrici, Italiae et Africae in 368-375 and 383. PLRE I, 736–
740, Probus 5. Overview of sources and of laws he received in Jenő Fitz, *Die Verwaltung Pannoniens in der Römerzeit*, vol. 3, (Budapest: Encyclopedia, 1994), 1215–1219.

19   PLRE I, 736, Probus 2: *praeses* of Pannonia Inferior for 303/305, with the reserve that
he is known only from the Passio Irenaei Sirmiensis and the Passio Pollionis. Zeiller,
Les origines, 80, knowing the former text only from the Bollandist edition, explained
Probus' double function (*praeses* and prefect, see below, note 21) thus: "il n'est pas
du tout impossible qu'un gouverneur de la Basse Pannonie, dont le chef-lieu était
Sirmium, ait monentanément géré la prefecture du prétoire". More recent historical
accounts refer to Probus only as governor of Pannonia Secunda: Norman H. Baynes,
Two Notes on the Great Persecution, *CQ* 18/3 (July-October 1924) 192; Jenő Fitz,
L'administration des provinces pannoniennes sous le Bas-Empire romain, Latomus 181

any other support for the conjecture apart from the two already-mentioned hagiographic narratives.[20] On the contrary, the administration of the late 4th century *praefectus*[21] Sextus Petronius Probus, whom we know as residing in Sirmium[22], made him in all likelihood hateful to Pannonian memory: he implemented with brutal efficiency the taxation policy of Valentinian I[23] and, in 372, when faced with barbarian invasions, he firstly thought about escaping before he proceeded to a hasty defense of Sirmium.[24] The city miraculously escaped, but the province

---

(Brussels: Latomus, 1983), 49 and 93 (with commentary on the years of office forwarded by PLRE I); Fitz, *Die Verwaltung*, 1258; Rajko Bratož, Die diokletianische Christenverfolgung in den Donau- und Balkanprovinzen, in: Alexander Demandt / Andreas Goltz / Heinrich Schlange-Schöningen, eds., *Diokletian und die Tetrarchie: Aspekte einer Zeitenwende* (Berlin/New York: Walter de Gruyter, 2004), 134 (only for 304). Even Musurillo, *The Acts*, XLIII, allows for the existence of Probus. None of these authors seems to mind that in the *Pass. Iren.* 2.1, Probus' administration covers the entire Pannonia. Cf. Dolbeau, Le dossier, 211 n. 45.

20 Probus – having a different function – is a recurrent figure in Illyricum-related hagiography. Apart from Pollio's and Irenaeus' accounts, Bratož, Die diokletianische Christenverfolgung, 134 lists the Passio Anastasiae (as *praefectus*) and the Passio Ursicini.

21 Several manuscript witnesses of both *passiones* attribute to Probus also the function of *praefectus*. For Irenaeus, see the Bollandist edition in the ActaSS Martii, vol. 3 (Antwerp: Apud Iacobum Merusium, 1668), 557: "Martyrizatus est ... S. Irenaeus ... agente praefecturam Probo Praeside". The five manuscripts of the Pollio text belonging to the Magnum Legendarium Austriacum all mention Probus as prefect during the interrogations: "Probus praefectus dixit: Quorum lectorum?" (Heiligenkreuz, Stiftsbibl. H 12, f. 99r; Zwettl, Stiftsbibl. 24, f. 112v; Admont, Stiftsbibl. 24, f. 103r; Wien, ÖNB 336, f. 133v; Melk, Stiftsbibl. 97 [old 674, M. 4], f. 265r). The passages could be the result of contamination with the Passio Anastasiae: recognizing the same name throughout several martyr-texts relating to Pannonia, a copyist could have easily concluded (in this case, not without grounds) that the same name corresponds to the same person – thus, the amalgam of functions.

22 Ammianus, *Hist.* 29.9: "praefectus praetorio agens tunc apud Sirmium Probus".

23 Hieronymus, *Chron. ad annum* 372: "Probus praefectus Illyrici iniquissimus tributorum exactionibus ante provincias quas regebat, quam a barbaris vastarentur, erasit". On Pseudo-Augustinus, *Quaest.* 115.49 as source for Jerome's *erasit*, see László Várady, *Das letzte Jahrhundert Pannoniens, 376-476* (Budapest: Akadémiai Kiadó, 1969), 34–35.

24 Ammianus, *Hist.* 29.9–12. What is known of the affairs of Probus is owed mostly to authors (esp. Ammianus) who had their own motives to hate both Valentinian I and those employed in his administrative apparatus; cf. Várady, *Das Letzte Jahrhundert*, 36. But at this instance, there is no reason to doubt his account: the troubles of those times, the general imperial lack of interest in Pannonia, corroborated with the events of 372 and beyond, could have easily been attributed to Probus' ill-management of the province, whether he was in fact guilty of it or not. Later, Paulinus of Milan depicts Probus in a somewhat positive light. It is the powerful magnate who patronizes over Ambrose' secular career (*Vit. Ambr.* 5); when Ambrose was elected bishop, Pro-

was devastated by the raids[25], and 372 marked the beginning of barbarian presence within the confines of the province.

Overall, it seems much more probable that when naming the persecuting official Probus, the compiler of our text was referring, in fact, to Valentinian's prefect. In this context, Pollio's emphasis on socio-ethical norms receives a new dimension. In the same light, the address that concludes his confession, "haec si displicent, optime cognitor, iudicio tuo, poteris derogare"[26], becomes less an appeal to the prosecutor's common sense and more an ironic remark which the intelligent ears must have perceived: by his political behavior, Probus failed to realize precisely what Pollio considered to be the essence of Christianity.

1.4.

This being said, it is time to sum up the considerations regarding the chronological framework. For the *terminus post quem*, Probus' name indicates a date after A.D. 364. But we can set it at a later date on the basis of the epithet "christianissimus imperator"[27], addressing Valentinian. The emperor in question is Valentinian I, born in Cibalae. Yet the epithet *christianissimus* has not been applied to him in any written source, not even post-mortem. The Passio therefore could not have been written during his reign.

Although infrequent in the 4th century, the epithet is used in the account which forms the object of this study as a regular apostrophe of the emperors. Such usage is indeed verified for the last decades of the

---

bus rejoices "quod verbum eius inpleretur in Ambrosio", for he had instructed Ambrose to govern his province "non ut iudex sed ut episcopus" (*Vit. Ambr.* 8). This information alone contradicts all knowledge about Probus from contemporary sources. Moreover, if such were his relations to Probus, one might wonder why is Ambrose himself entirely silent about it. In fact, the prefect is never mentioned in the bishop's extensive writings. One is left to think that Ambrose had serious reasons to avoid mentioning him – and that these reasons were not at all positive in their nature. Ambrose, if he was indeed in Probus'service, he must have been in Pannonia during the ominous events of 372. Should the animosity towards the prefect make itself felt at that time, Ambrose might have decided for a cautious management of their relation.

25   András Mócsy, *Pannonia and Upper Moesia: A History of the Middle Danube Provinces of the Roman Empire* (London/Boston: Routledge and Kegan Paul, 1974), 294 and 310 believes that Ammianus' account refers to events taking place in 374. The date of 372 is supported in PLRE I, 737, by Libanius, *Or.*, 24.12.

26   *Pass. Poll.* 2.

27   *Pass. Poll.* 1.

4th century, when it is extended from the letters of Ambrose[28] to the official panegyrics.[29] The first documented occurrence of the word is the letter Ambrose addressed to Gratian in A.D. 380.[30] Two years earlier, in 378, the Milanese bishop – who, as Paulinus relates, served several years in Pannonia, in the employment of Probus – spent some time in Sirmium. The highly productive sojourn included a meeting with Gratian, participation to an anti-Arian council, and even an intervention in the election of a new bishop – ultimately Anemius, thought to be Ambrose's Nicene candidate, obtained the see.[31] It is more likely that Ambrose invented the word[32] and used it at the opportune moment at the court in Sirmium[33] rather than encountering

---

28 Mary Bridget O'Brien, *Titles of Address in Christian Latin Epistolography to 543 A.D.*, The Catholic Universtiy of America Patristic Studies 21 (Washington D.C.: The Catholic University of America, 1930), 129.

29 Heinz Bellen, Christianissimus imperator: Zur Christianisierung der römischen Kaiserideologie von Constantin bis Theodosius, in: Id., *Politik – Recht – Gesellschaft: Studien zu Alten Geschichte*, Hist.E 115 (Stuttgart: Franz Steiner, 1997), 150–151.

30 Ambrose, *Ep.* 1.1: "Non mihi affectus defuit, christianissime principum" (title: "Beatissimo augusto Gratiano et christianissimo principi Ambrosius episcopus"). Cf. Bellen, Christianissimus imperator, 150. In 385 the Milanese bishop resorts again to the term, this time investing it with binding consequences, in a letter addressed to Valentinian II, *Ep.* 17.3: "Ergo cum a te, imperator christianissime, fides Deo vero sit exhibenda, cum ipsius fidei studium, cautio atque devotio, miror quomodo aliquibus in spem venerit, quod debeas aras diis gentium tuo instaurare praecepto" (title: "Ambrosius episcopus beatissimo principi et christianissimo imperatori Valentiniano").

31 Roger Gryson, *Scholies Ariennes sur le concile d'Aquilée* (Paris: Cerf, 1980), 107–121.

32 Bellen, Christianissimus imperator, 149 is of the opinion that *christianissimus* is a neologism imported by Ambrose. See also Bellen's note 1, on the same page, for literature supporting this assumption. The claim forwarded by Walter Woodburn Hyde, *Paganism to Christianity in the Roman Empire* (Philadelphia, Pa: University of Pennsylvania Press, 1946, reprint New York: Octagon Books, 1970), 210, that Jovian was named *christianissimus imperator* on account of his restoring the privileges Christians enjoyed before Julian, has no grounds. The reference he gives in note 60 on the same page (Sozomen, *Hist. eccl.* 6.4) is incorrect. Sozomen, indeed, quotes a letter sent by the synod of Antioch in 363, in which Jovian is addressed as θεοφιλεστάτῳ δεσπότῃ (*Hist. eccl.* 6.4.7). However, while it is true that this formula translates at times the Latin "christianissimus imperator", the reverse is not applicable, as the corresponding Greek formulae are not translated, in general, with *christianissimus*. See Gerhard Rösch, *Onoma Basileias* (Wien: Verlag der Österreichisches Akademie der Wissenschaften, 1978), 65–66.

33 In both instances when the epithet occurs, it is directed to one emperor, singled out, and fulfills manipulative functions. Ambrose might have used it *viva voce* to achieve similar purposes.

it there[34]. Ambrose's *Ep.* 1 and the date 380 seem thus a secure milestone for the *terminus post quem*.[35]

When looking at the *terminus ante quem*, the attention is captured immediately by the Passio Donati, Venusti et Hermogenis (BHL 2309)[36]. Since it mentions Pollio by name and borrows passages from his Passio, it must have been written later. Debate surrounds this neglected martyr-account too. Some consider it compiled immediately after the Passio Pollionis (in the time of Valentinian I).[37] Rajko Bratož suggested, with stronger arguments, that its composition, in Aquileia, was occasioned by the transfer of relics, occurring in circa A.D. 409-410.[38] Perhaps it was written at a slightly earlier date. The creedal elements in Venustus' confession integrate it in the anti-Arian struggle which has seen its last battles in Northern Italy (see, for example, the council of Aquileia in 381, or Ambrose's troubles with the Arians in Milan, in 385). The last decade of the 4th century seems suitable also because in this period the intense Aquileian relic-trade sought to impose the city's prestige and ecclesiastical hegemony over Illyricum against other centers such as Ravenna and Milan. Ravenna in particular offers an attractive aspect, as we know that Pollio's cult was celebrated there at the time[39]. Therefore, it is safe to presume that the Passio Pollionis must have been written prior to the end of the 4th century.

To conclude, our text was composed in the last two decades of the 4th century, in Pannonia (in Cibalae or perhaps even Sirmium), as the sensitivity to Probus, the proud display of Christian personalities of

---

34 The epithet helps elucidate one other problem posed by Simonetti, Sugli atti, 76: the Italian scholar argued, based on the presence of Grecisms – similar in occurrence with the Passio Irenaei – that the Latin version of the Passio Pollionis is a translation from a lost Greek original. If so, the epithet *christianissimus* is an aberration in our text. In fact, the Greek equivalent for this apostrophe is φιλόχριστος, which in turn is rendered in Latin as "Deo amabilis". Cf. Rösch, *Onoma*, 65–66.

35 That the text does not distinguish between two Valentinians should not deceive. After all, for locals, even for Pannonian provincials, it must have been clear which Valentinian was born in Cibalae. Rather curious is the fact that the exact construction, "christianissimus imperator" occurs both in Pollio's passion and in Ambrosius, *Ep.*, 17, each time attributed to a Valentinian.

36 Published with lacunae in ActaSS Augusti, vol. 4 (Antwerp: Apud Bernardum Albertum vander Plassche, 1739), 412–413.

37 Svetozar Ritig, *Martyrologij srijemsko-pannonske metropolije*, Bogoslavska Smotra 2/4 (1911), 355.

38 Rajko Bratož, Verzeichnis der Opfer der Christenverfolgungen in den Donau- und Balkanprovinzen, in: Demandt / Goltz / Schlange-Schöningen, eds., *Diokletian und die Tetrarchie* (Berlin/New York: Walter de Gruyter, 2004), 217.

39 Liberius III, who dedicated the oratory to Pollio, was bishop roughly around 380–399.

local origin, and the liturgical dimension of the Passio suggest.[40] It was used in local liturgy while the relics were in Pannonia, and maybe even later. Its spread in Northern Italy at the turn of the 5th century was occasioned by the translation of Pollio's relics.

2. Bible and Apologetics: The Functions of Pollio's Confession

At this point, one must ask what was the reason that caused the composition of Pollio's acts? Was it a desire to record in written form the deeds of the martyr so that the account might travel with his relics? Or should it be seen rather as a text fulfilling multiple functions, as most martyr-acts do?[41] In accordance with the argumentation above, the second option is by far preferable. In fact, Pollio's exhortations cannot be appreciated at their full value unless one assumes an audience for whom they were written in the first place. My reading, therefore, understands the text as an intentional discourse aiming to produce an immediate impact on the community which heard it during the liturgical celebrations dedicated to the saint.

2.1.

Given Pollio's being a *primicerius lectorum*, a vocation centered on close knowledge of the Scripture, the reader would expect an influx of biblical passages to illustrate the martyr's belief in the one God. Pollio himself entertains this hope in the beginning: when asked about his profession, the martyr answers: "primicerius lectorum... qui eloquia divina populis legere consueverunt."[42] Nevertheless, as soon as he sets out to

---

40 The remarks above on the *terminus ante quem* were not available to me when the paper was presented. I owe gratitude to Prof. Kate Cooper, Prof. Steffen Diefenbach and Dr. Anthony Dupont for their observations and questions which prompted further reflection on the topic. Among others, the possibility that the Passio was composed in Rome, by Pannonian immigrants, was debated. That hypothesis can no longer be sustained.

41 See, for example, *Pass. Perpetuae* 1, in: Musurillo, *Acts*, 106–108; and *Pass. Montani et Lucii* 23.7, in: Musurillo, *Acts*, 238.

42 *Pass. Poll.* 2. The past tense, *consueverunt*, could be related to the fact that, as a consequence of Diocletian's first edict, the sacred books were confiscated, and thus, at the moment of Pollio's trial there was nothing to read from anymore. However, I wonder whether a more subtle interpretation is possible. Towards the end of the 4th cen-

summarize the *eloquia*, disappointment is instilled upon the reader. Not only does Pollio make little use of Scriptural quotations or paraphrases, but, as Simonetti rightly observed[43], Pollio's entire exposition of Christianity employs the arguments and methods of apologetics.[44]

A first striking feature is the absence of doctrinal tenets. The discourse concentrates on orthopraxis, summarizing in a series of normative statements the desirable behavior of Christians belonging to all social strata. This disproportion corresponds to the use of apologetic formulae against scriptural texts. There are merely two recognizable Biblical passages in the entire Passio, both pronounced by Pollio and both expressing what one should believe. The first is a vetero-testamentary epithet of God: "unum Deum in caelo intonantem"[45]. Though used here as a scriptural term, *intonantem* recalls one of the epithets attributed to the pagan god Iupiter (*Iupiter tonans*). The quotation thus communicates monotheism in terms familiar to a pagan/recently converted audience – a favored method of apologetic argumentation. The second Scriptural quotation, equally from the Old Testament, "sacrificans daemoniis eradicabitur"[46], carries the same apologetic spirit. Being the preferred justification of many martyrs for their refusal to perform the requested sacrifice,[47] it can be counted as a hagiographic commonplace; the compiler found it in the Passio Irenaei Sirmiensis.[48] In addition to these two references, an allusion to John 1:9 can be retraced in Pollio's reply: "Quia hac brevi melior est lux illa perpetua, et dulciora sunt quae permanent quam quae pereunt bona"[49]. But it can equally function simply as a philosophical assertion acceptable for pagans as well, and its continuation proves such understanding: "nec est pruden-

---

tury, we assist to a change in the attributions of the lectors, who are recruited from very young age and are involved more in the chanting of psalms – whereas the readings from Scripture become the responsibility of the deacon. The readers are trained in special schools having as teacher the *primicerius lectorum*. The past tense in Pollio's *consueverunt* denotes in this case the awareness of the compiler – and implicitly of his audience – that the readers are no longer in charge of the sacred books.

43   Simonetti, Sugli atti, 73.

44   As opposed to the Passio Irenaei, which is, by far, better supplied with Scriptural quotations (eight places, with crushing preference for the New Testament, over three; the texts are similar in length).

45   *Pass. Poll.* 2. Cf. Ps 18:13; 2Sam 22:14.

46   *Pass. Poll.* 3. Cf. Ex 22:20.

47   *Pass. Iren.* 2.1; *Pass Montani et Lucii* 14.1, in: Musurillo, *Acts*, 226. Simonetti, Sugli atti, 62, gives the following examples: Passio Petri Balsami, Passio Phileae et Philoromi.

48   *Pass. Iren.* 2.1.

49   *Pass. Poll.* 3. Cf. *Mart. Pionii* 5.4–5, in: Musurillo, *The Acts*, 142.

tiae caducis postponere sempiterna."[50] The mentality behind its use is the same as in the case of *intonantem*.

Pollio's recommendations concerning the right behavior, though biblically inspired, are never phrased using quotations or even paraphrases. Certainly, the scriptural undertone cannot be denied: Pollio's confession is built around commonplaces of ethical reflection scattered all over the New Testament. But Pollio seems to re-work this material in a concise synthesis of orthodoxy and orthopraxis. One example will suffice to illustrate the process. At the peak of a climactic exposition on orthopraxis, Pollio affirms that the 'divine sayings' teach: "suis bonis cedere, aliena nec oculorum quidem delectatione concupiscere."[51] The passage interestingly blends in one original unit the commandment to share one's goods (as a consequence to the love commandment) and the tenth commandment of the Decalogue. The statement forms the summit of authentic Christian behavior, in Pollio's (or, rather, the compiler's) view.

2.2.

If Pollio doesn't demonstrate keenness in quoting from Scripture, his familiarity with apologetics is all the more prevalent. This is visible both in the dogmatic and in the ethical section. When asked which are the sayings, he is reading to the people, the saint enumerates them focusing initially on monotheism: "Quae unum Deum in caelis indicant intonantem; quae non posse dici deos ligna et lapides salutifera admonitione testantur."[52] The topic of pagan gods being merely stone and wood is characteristic to the apologetic literature.[53] The two tenets invoked by Pollio express the basic creedal changes involved in the act of conversion. Christian identity, however, is not reduced to them. They are quickly dismissed, despite being central for the martyr's refusal to sacrifice. It is not by chance that the only dogmatic contents proclaim God the creator and Christ the king (no word about Christ as God!). The compiler is perhaps avoiding troublesome dogmatic issues still under debate with the Arian party.[54] But, more importantly, his

---

50   *Pass. Poll.* 3.

51   *Pass. Poll.* 2.

52   *Pass. Poll.* ms., f. 74v.

53   Cf., e.g., Theophilus, *Ad Autolycum* 1.10; Tertullianus, *Apol.* 22, *De idol.* 3; Minucius Felix, *Oct.* 23.

54   Although Arianism was at this time on the defensive in Illyricum, it was far from creating trouble. Two late 4th century councils addressed the problem, in 378 in Sir-

focus is not on what a Christian should believe – that is almost a datum. His attention is captured instead by the everyday manifestation of this faith. Ultimately, what Pollio dies for is not just the belief in one God, but also the behavioral ideals inherent to that belief.

These ideals are exposed in the following section, dedicated to the Christian social ethos, that is, how a Christian should live out his/her faith on the level of the community. It is useful to quote the entire passage:

> "quae [Christi ... mandata] corrigunt noxios et emendant; quae innocentes in propositi sui perseverantia et observatione corroborant; quae virgines integritatis suae docent obtinere fastigia, coniuges pudicam in creandis filiis conscientiam custodire; quae dominos servis plus pietate quam furore persuadent unius conditionis contemplatione dominari; quae servos hortantur debitam fidem dominis plus amore quam timore persolvere; quae docent regibus iusta praecipientibus oboedire, sublimioribus potestatibus bona obtemperare cum iusserint; quae praecipiunt parentibus honorem, amicis fidem, inimicis veniam, affectum civibus, hospitibus humanitatem, pauperibus misericordiam, caritatem cunctis, malum nemini; accipere illatas patienter iniurias, facere omnino nullas; suis bonis cedere, aliena nec oculorum quidem delectatione concupiscere."[55]

We are told that those who comply with these precepts are steadfast and constant in faith – Pollio included. Some aspects deserve further attention.

Firstly, obedience to secular authority has been claimed on Christian side as early as Justin Martyr.[56] For the apologists, it served as an exoneration of their refusal to participate in the pagan devotion. At the same time, they hoped to attract a more benevolent attitude on the part of the authorities, by contradicting the obvious charge: that Christians are traitors to the cause of the emperor and state. The apologists argued that, although the true faith makes it impossible for them to offer sacrifice to the emperor's *genius*, Christians obey him in every other respect.[57] Such sense is impossible to maintain in the case of the Passio Pollionis. What lesson was its audience to learn from this "divine saying"? Certainly, it does not command blind obedience to the emperor;

---

mium, and in 381 in Aquileia. The latter, probably projected by the emperors as an ecumenical council, but orchestrated by Ambrose as a local council, condemned the Arian bishops Palladius and Secundianus and the priest Attalus. Cf. Gryson, *Scholies*, 121–143.

55   *Pass. Poll.* ms., f. 74v–75r. The corresponding passage in the ActaSS is *Pass. Poll.* 2. I chose to reproduce the manuscript because the Bollandist text has lacunae and presents, in places, distortions.

56   *Apol.* 1.17: worship to God alone, and only obedience to the emperor.

57   See also Theophilus, *Ad Autol.* 1.17; Irenaeus, *Adv. Haer.* 5.27.

instead, it calls for discrimination in obedience[58]: only the kings who issue just commandments should be hearkened to. The text implies – if only on a hypothetical level – the possibility that kings may not always be just in their rule. Such moderate perception on imperial authority, befitting the imperial dynamics in the late 4th century, is far from Eusebius' idealized view of the Christian emperor. It rather agrees with the conceptions on secular rule expressed by Athanasius and Ambrose.[59] The emperor should constantly work so that he might be truly a Christian ruler; at the other end of the social chain, the common Christian should not be accomplice to the sin which results from an unjust rule.

The second observation concerns the quoted fragment as a whole. It provides the mass-converts with a set of guidelines about what a Christian should do, giving to all the authority of a commandment issued by Christ himself[60]. In this sense, the absence of traditional hagiographic structures receives a new meaning. We do not hear Pollio's prayers[61]; we do not witness any miracles, any scenes of torture or attempts to bribe the saint with religious or secular offices. The redactor of the Passio is not interested with the short moments before the martyr's death, but with the life whose summit it forms. A different kind of sacrifice for Christ's sake, yet one which should be desired and performed by all who call themselves Christian. That its parameters are pronounced by a martyr, a hero of the past, a favorite of God in heavens, who has conformed to them and therefore received eternal life only gives them prestige and authority, as well as a guarantee of success. This is the way in which salvation is earned.

---

58 Several biblical passages (Rom 13:1–7; Tit 3:1; 1Tim 2:1–2; 1Pet 2:13–17) recommend obedience to secular authority in every respect except those which interfere with one's faith in God. Just like the apologists, they do not reflect on the possibility that a monarch issues unjust commandments.

59 Kenneth M. Setton, *Christian Attitude towards the Emperor in the Fourth Century* (New York: AMS Press, 1967), 78–108 (Athanasius and his supporters); 109–152 (Ambrose).

60 All the statements pronounced by Pollio are brought together under the heading "Christi regis pia et sancta mandata" (*Pass. Poll.* 2).

61 In the conclusion, the redactor notes: [Pollio] "agonem suum laudans, et benedicens et glorificans Deum implevit martyrium intrepidus" (*Pass. Poll.* 3). This is the closest indication of a prayer pronounced by Pollio. The editor wanted to maintain the focus on Pollio's dialogue with Probus, conceived as a legacy that the martyr leaves behind.

2.3.

This interpretative direction is verified by the reflections on the constancy in faith, which enclose Pollio's confession in a circular structure. The martyr claims: "devoti et constantes probantur in fide regis aeterni, qui mandata, quae legerint, etiam tormentis prohibentibus implere contendunt"[62]; the reason for such intransigence is that "hac brevi melior est lux illa perpetua, et dulciora sunt quae permanent quam quae pereunt bona."[63] Persistence in faith in the most extreme circumstances is the path to salvation – an element specific to hagiographic literature, whereby the steadfastness itself – even leading to temporal death – ensures eternal life for the martyr. The crucial aspect, which sets Pollio irrevocably on the road towards martyrdom, is the public recognition of being a Christian. That is, assuming publicly an identity which exceeds the boundaries of common expectation. What counts is not so much Pollio's fearlessness in front of death, but his adherence – both theoretical and practical – to the Christian moral code. His warning, "nec est prudentiae caducis postponere sempiterna"[64], calls for a rigorous observation of this code. Thus, the confession which triggers martyrdom is the public confirmation of an identity visibly molded by the faith in Christ. The commandments Pollio summarizes are not mere words read by him on occasion, but represent a veritable *forma vitae* to which he strives to keep regardless the consequences.[65] Pollio's martyrdom is the culmination of a perpetual witnessing of Christ which begins with believing in one true God, and becomes manifest in social behavior. Therein must be sought also the absence in the narration of the *imitatio Christi* vocabulary.[66] The martyr embodies in speech and deed the perfect Christian, and it is he who should be imitated by the audience.[67] Pollio is not a God-man, as Christ; he is an entirely human

---

62   *Pass. Poll.* 2.

63   *Pass. Poll.* 3.

64   *Pass. Poll.* 3.

65   Cf. *Pass. Poll.* 2: "devoti et constantes probantur in fide regis aeterni, qui mandata, quae legerint, etiam tormentis prohibentibus implere contendunt".

66   Again in contrast to the Passio Irenaei. See, for example, *Pass. Iren.* 2.3: "Gaudeo si feceris ut Domini mei passionibus particeps inveniar."

67   Cf. the redactor's words in the epilogue, "Qui eius venerabilem passionem sed et sancti episcopi eiusdem civitatis Eusebii … hodie cum gaudio celebrantes, deprecamur divinam potentiam, ut nos eorum [= Pollio and Eusebius] meritis participes esse concedere dignetur" (*Pass. Poll.* 3).

person, who successfully carried out Christ's commandments[68], representing a model which could be entirely appropriated by potential imitators, Christians contemporary with and posterior to the redactor (since they should not worry about, nor should they hide behind any difference of condition). Their witnessing consists in never letting the small things have priority over the eternal ones – with all the effects this priority has on their beliefs and their life. They are expected to reach the standards set by the martyr in his speech.

2.4.

By now, it is clear that Pollio's confession, with its strong apologetic dimension, is not a mere attempt to confer some degree of historical credibility to the martyr.[69] The quick passing over of the contents of faith, notwithstanding their responsibility for the martyr's death, and the long peroration that follows about how to be a good Christian denote a shift of focus in comparison to traditional apologetics.[70] It is equally clear that the text is not meant to be just a record of past events, but it appeals to the sensibilities and inner worlds of those who read it or heard it during liturgy. We must not forget that we are in the time of mass-conversions. Christianity is becoming the official religion of the empire; political careers and social welfare depend more and more on adherence to the imperial credo[71] – but that does not necessarily trigger a genuine conversion. Jerome, Ambrose, Augustine – just to name a few – constantly militated against the loosened moral standards of their fellow Christians. In parallel, paganism led one last great battle in the central dioceses of the Western Empire.[72] These phenomena clarify why Scriptural quotations and paraphrases play such a little role in Pollio's confession. In such circumstances, a revival of apologetic arguments,

---

68 This made him, of course, an imitator of Christ, and, although the text does not express it, he must have been perceived thus by its Late Antique hearers.

69 Vs. Simonetti, Sugli atti, 73.

70 In apologetic literature the emphasis was placed on demonstrating that pagan gods are mere wood and stone animated by demons. The societal aspects of Christian conduct served as additional advertisement, to emphasize the superiority of the faith in Christ and the blessings it brings for society at large. Here the accent is inversed.

71 For example, Gratian employed preferentially Christians to fulfill Roman magistratures.

72 In 385, Symmachus estimated the imperial climate safe enough to petition Valentinian II for the restoration of the Victoria altar. The petition attracted Ambrose' violent rebuke, starting with the very *Ep.* 17.

appealing by nature to the common sense of their addressees, carries out a missionary and propagandistic agenda, while advocating also the need to educate mass-converts, to initiate them in the Christian way of living. The Passio Pollionis becomes a manual of Christian orthopraxis which relies on the functional complex derived from its apologetic content: propaganda, catechesis, identity-constructor. Its message is that belief in one God and the renunciation of idols is not enough; that being a Christian in name, and acting like Probus, is not Christian at all; that, in fact, a follower of Christ wears his/her faith in his/her dealings with others.

3. The accusations Brought Against Pollio: The Issue of Virginity

3.1.

Upon hearing that Pollio is the chief of the readers, Probus asks, mockingly, if he speaks of those readers "qui leves mulierculas vetant, ne nubant, ac pervertere et ad vanam castitatem suadere dicuntur?"[73] Apologetic literature did not face such accusation[74], but it is not a stranger to the scriptural universe. We encounter it, for example, in the apocryphal acts of Peter.[75] It may be true that this text provided the model for the Passio's compiler; still, the tone of the accusation almost echoes the notorious involvement of Jerome in the development of asceticism among women belonging to Roman upper classes.[76] In answer to Probus' accusation, Pollio himself adopts a more positive attitude towards marriage, when he urges "virgines integritatis suae... obtinere fastigia, coniuges pudicam in creandis filiis conscientiam custodire."[77] The quoted replies might be dismissed as mere *topoi*, were it not for the debate surrounding the primacy of virginity over mar-

---

73   *Pass. Poll.* ms., f. 74v.

74   The apologists had, indeed, to explain the obvious phenomenon that Christianity first spread among women and slaves, the naïve strata par excellence. New here is the method by which Probus wants Christians to have attracted female converts: the preaching of a strict asceticism.

75   *Acts Pet.* 33–36.

76   On Jerome being blamed for instilling in several women an extreme asceticism, see John N. D. Kelly, *Jerome: His Life, Writings and Controversies* (New York: Harper and Row, 1975), 108.

77   *Pass. Poll.* ms., f. 74v.

riage, emerging in the period concerning us.[78] Pollio's more balanced
view sounds as a defense and a veiled advertisement at the same time:
it is not true that Christianity prohibits marriage and procreation; instead, it recommends a proper conduct no matter what a woman
should choose.

3.2.

The appropriate behavior of Christian women was certainly an important issue on the daily agenda. Another Sirmian Passio originating
around the same time, that of Serenus (BHL 7595–7596)[79], approaches
the topic in similar terms. The text narrates that Serenus, a wandering
monk, sought refuge in Sirmium after the outbreak of the Great Persecution, where he cultivated a garden. When an inappropriately dressed
woman entered Serenus' garden with seducing intentions, the monk
admonished her and refused her entrance ("increpavit eam, monens ut
egrederetur, et ut honesta matrona, disciplinate se haberet"). The
woman pleaded with her husband, a member of Maximian's (=
Galerius') entourage, who finally obtained Serenus' arrest from the
emperor. Interrogated, the monk confessed: "increpavi et dixi, quod
non recte versaretur mulier, quae illa hora egressa de domo viri sui
esset." Are we to conclude from here that there was a problem with the
morality of women? Or, rather, that the text reflects the growing
awareness of ascetic spirituality characteristic for the late 4th century?
The Passio Pollionis certainly does not react against it. Despite its
strong societal dimension, the confession does not censure it; nevertheless, we do not assist to a praising of asceticism and virginity over marriage. In the redactor's view, both are equally valuable choices[80]; he is
not interested in fostering either. What he demands from people en-

---

78 See, e.g. Elizabeth A. Clark, Theory and Practice in Late Ancient Asceticism, *Journal
    of Feminist Studies in Religion* 5/2 (1989), 25–46; David G. Hunter, The Virgin, the
    Bride and the Church: Reading Psalm 45 in Ambrose, Jerome, and Augustine, *ChH*
    69 (2000), 281–303.

79 Published from one manuscript by Iohannes Bollandus in ActaSS Februarii, vol. 3
    (Antwerp: Apud Iacobus Meursius, 1658), 365.

80 The pagan upholding of marriage and procreation had its role in this cautious dis-
    course. Pursuing the same apologetic goal, the redactor wants to show that Christi-
    anity defends also those ideals the pagans think are proper to their mentality (see the
    contrast which makes itself felt in Probus' quoted accusation). But it also brings a
    sharper – more befitting – ethical awareness to the business of marriage.

gaged in both conducts is constancy and a continent attitude – in accordance with the spirit of the times.

4. Conclusions

The entire Passio is constructed around the central theme of the confession. It leads in a climactic structure to the passage on Christian orthopraxis. As I hope to have proven, Pollio's passion is meant to shape the identity of an already well-established Christian community, faced, on one hand, with a mass of first or, at the most, second generation converts, who adopted Christianity rather by interest than by genuine attachment; and, on the other hand, with the social impact of the pagan revival and ascetic mentality. To such a community, the text provides the correction of their behavior, too imbibed perhaps with what one might call 'pagan' remnants, and the confirmation of their incipient ascetic calling. With Pollio's words, Christian precepts "corrigunt noxas et emendant."[81] Christian identity has, first and foremost, irrevocable consequences on the way a person – be that an emperor, an ascetic, or a common believer – acts and interacts in society. If, for the martyr, the moment when he seals his belonging to Christ is the public confession, for the post-edict Christian, who should imitate the martyr, this confession consists in leading a socially Christian life.

It is not the place here to assert or infirm the existence of a historical martyr Pollio. That a person named Pollio was martyred during the Great Persecution is very possible. That he was honored with a cult on the spot of his execution is probable. Relics were attached to his name. But the rest of his biography, including his trial and his bold confession is nothing more than the retrospective imagination of later piety. Pollio became what he was expected to be in the eyes of late 4th century Christians. Whoever composed his Passio lived in an age when celebrants of the cult of the martyr became interested in his life. What matters is that this Passio served to exhort, encourage and mold the world-view of generations of Christians who read it.

---

81   *Pass. Poll.* 2.

D. Crossing Borders

JOHAN LEEMANS

The Martyrdom of Sabas the Goth: History, Hagiography and Identity

1. Introduction

This contribution about the *Martyrdom of Sabas* (*Passio Sabae*) takes us to Eastern Europe in the first half of the 370's. At that time the Danube formed the northern frontier of the Roman Empire. Throughout the fourth century much of the trans-Danubian area between the Dnepr River (present day SW-Russia) in the East and the Carpathians (present day Romania) in the West was occupied by a single ethnic group and culture: "the Goths" (or "the Scythians" as they are called in many sources). Situated west of the Dniestr River and south of the Carpathian Mountains, the area where much of the action described in the *Passio Sabae* took place was part of this Gothic territory. Throughout the fourth century this area was occupied by the Tervingi, one of the major Gothic tribal confederations, a largely pagan ethnic group, with, it would seem, only a small minority of Christians[1]. In the course of the fourth century the Goths' relations with the Roman Empire were characterized by tensions, military operations and carefully balanced treaties. In the years 366–369 the Roman Emperor Valens had engaged three intensive military campaigns against the Gothic confederation led by Athanarich. The result was a complex treaty, negotiated on a boat in the middle of the Danube.[2]

---

1   Herwig Wolfram, *Geschichte der Goten von den Anfängen bis zur Mitte des sechsten Jahrhunderts: Entwurf einer historischen Ethnographie* (München: C.H. Beck, 1979), 123–131.

2   The best general survey of the Tervingi and their contacts with the Roman Empire still is Peter J. Heather, *Goths and Romans 332–489* (Oxford: Clarendon Press, 1991), 84–121.

Immediately after the end of his military confrontation with the Romans, Athanarich started persecutions against the Christians in his area. They lasted from 369 to 372 and seem to have been more than just coincidental local pogroms. We have quite a few sources that inform us about these persecutions. Jerome mentions it in his *Chronicon* for the year 369 and speaks about many martyrs and people who fled the persecutions.[3] Other, less detailed sources concur with Jerome in that quite a few Christians died a martyr's death during these persecutions (Epiphanius of Salamis, Ambrose, Socrates and Sozomenus).[4] Yet, the source par excellence is a contemporary narrative about events related to this persecution in a small township[5]: the *Martyrdom of Sabas*[6]. Most of the scholarship on this text is actually *drawing on* the text in view of reconstructing the history of the Goths[7]; quite understandably, since there are very few other texts which provide so much information

---

3   Jerome, *Chron.* ad a. 369, in *Hieronymi Chronicon*, hg. von Rudolf Helm, GCS Euse-
     bius VII (Berlin: Akademie-Verlag, 1984), 245.20–22.

4   Epiphanius, *Pan.* 70.15.4, in Epiphanius, *Panarion haer. 65–80; De fide*, hg. von Karl
     Holl, GCS Epiphanius III (Berlin: Akademie Verlag, 1985), 248.18–25; Ambrose, *Exp.
     Luc.* 2.37, in *Ambrosii Mediolanensis opera IV*, cura et studio M. Adriaen, CChr.SL 14
     (Turnhout: Brepols, 1957), 47.517–520; Augustinus, *Civ.* 18.52, in *Aurelii Augustini De
     civitate Dei libri XI–XXII*, curaverunt Bernardus Dombart et Alphonsus Kalb,
     CChr.SL 48 (Turnhout: Brepols, 1955), 651.56–652.61; Socrates, *Hist. eccl.* 4.33.7, in
     Socrates, *Kirchengeschichte*, hg. von Günther Christian Hansen, GCS N.F. 1 (Berlin:
     Akademie Verlag, 1995), 269.20–22; Sozomenus, *Hist. eccl.* 6.37.12, in Sozomenos,
     Historia ecclesiastica – Kirchengeschichte, übers. und eingel. von Günther Christian
     Hansen, vol. 3, FC 73/3 (Turnhout: Brepols, 2004), 820.13–19.

5   With regard to the reality of persecution in a small village, comparative material
     from Anatolia is provided by the *Passio Athenogenis*, in Pierre Maraval, ed., *La Passion
     inédite de S. Athénogène de Pédachthoé en Cappadoce (BHG 197b). Introduction, édition,
     traduction. Appendice: Passion épique de S. Athénogène de Pédachthoé. Edition et traduc-
     tion*, SHG 75 (Bruxelles: Société des Bollandistes, 1990), and the *Passio* of Theodore of
     Sykeon, cf. Stephen Mitchell, *Anatolia. Land, Men and Gods in Asia Minor. II. The Rise
     of the Church* (Oxford: Clarendon Press, 1993), 122–151.

6   First edition by Hippolyte Delehaye, Saints de Thrace et de Mésie, *AnBoll* 31 (1912),
     161–301, here 216–221; repr. in Gustav Krüger/Gerhard Ruhbach, eds., *Ausgewählte
     Märtyrerakten. Neubearbeitung der Knopfschen Ausgabe* (Tübingen: Mohr Siebeck,
     ⁴1965), 119–124. In what follows references (between round brackets in the main text
     and all the quotations in the footnotes) are to the Delehaye-edition. An English trans-
     lation, whence this article draws its quotations, is included in Peter Heather and
     John Matthews, *The Goths in the Fourth Century*, Translated Texts for Historians (Liv-
     erpool: Liverpool University Press, 1991), 104–110.

7   Edward A. Thompson, The *Passion of St. Saba* and Village Life, in Id., *The Visigoths in
     the Time of Ulfila* (Oxford: Clarendon Press, 1966), 64–77; Heather, *Goths and Romans*,
     103–107; Heather and Matthews, *The Goths*, 102–3; Wolfram, *Geschichte der Goten*,
     120–122.

about the organization of the Gothic confederation and its influence on events at the level of a township. Moreover, early medieval historians and specialists in hagiography alike agree that great historical value is to be attached to it. The validity of the already formulated scholarly analyses remains unchallenged: it is a fact that the *Passio Sabae* can be read as an historical source for the Gothic persecution and for the events about Sabas[8]. Yet the hermeneutical potential of this narrative is not reduced to a mere historical reading: it is the purpose of this paper to read the *Martyrdom of Sabas* as a piece of hagiography[9]. I will first present the content of the text. Then I will approach it as a hagiographical document which, finally, will lead to considerations about how this

---

8   In his critical appraisal, Hippolyte Delehaye, who was usually very circumspect with regard to the historical value of hagiographic documents, showed uncommon enthusiasm for the *Passio Sabae*. See Delehaye, Saints de Thrace, 289–291. In his view, the unconventional elements in the presentation of the persecution (the sympathy of the – largely pagan – population, the almost neutral attitude of the persecutors in the first phases, the series of 'curious' episodes, unparalleled in hagiographic literature) make this narrative "une des perles de l'hagiographie antique" (ibid. 291), "un enchaînement de faits presque tous vraisemblables, racontés avec l'inimitable accent de la sincerité" (ibid. 290), its reliability is in no way undermined by 'details' such as Sabas' vision or his resistance to torture, nor by the borrowings from the *Martyrdom of Polycarp* (for more details on these, see below). Cf. also Hippolyte Delehaye, *Les passions des martyrs et les genres littéraires* (Bruxelles: Société des Bollandistes, 1920), 146–150. Delehaye's conclusions are shared by Joseph-Marie Sauget, Saba, *BSS* 11 (1968), 532, who considers that, although the epistolary form parallels *Mart. Pol.*, "il corpo del testo si presenta degno di credito"; and Stefan C. Alexe, Saint Basile le Grand et le christianisme roumain au IVe siècle, in Elizabeth A. Livingstone, ed., *Papers Presented to the Eight International Conference on Patristic Studies Held in Oxford from 3 to 8 September 1979*, StudPatr 17/3 (Oxford: Pergamon, 1982), 1053. The best discussions of the text as such are to be found in Knut Schäferdiek, Märtyrerüberlieferungen aus der gotischen Kirche des vierten Jahrhunderts, in Hanns Christof Brennecke/Ernst Ludwig Grasmück/Christoph Markschies, eds., *Logos. Festschrift für Luise Abramowski*, BZNW 67 (Berlin and New York, 1993), 328–360; repr.: Knut Schäferdiek, *Schwellenzeit. Beiträge zur Geschichte des Christentums in Spätantike und Frühmittelalter*, Winrich A. Löhr/Hanns Christof Brennecke, eds., AKG 64 (Berlin/New York: Walter de Gruyter, 1996), 169–202, here 169–180. Schäferdiek, however, like all the interpreters of this text, doesn't focus on the hagiographic character of the *Passio Sabae*.

9   As in the case of most reliable martyr-acts, the two lectures, historical and hagiographical, do not exclude each other. The fact that the redactor wrote about events that had indeed happen did not prevent him in any way to use literary-rhetorical conventions, motifs, a certain taste in heroicizing the narrative and its protagonist, which, although they do not touch the sequence of events, transform the text's intentionality and reception. As I hope to prove in the following, Delehaye's conclusion that the *Passio Sabae* does not show any traces of conformity to some model (Saints de Thrace, 290) cannot be sustained; instead, it should be integrated in a literary network characteristic for any hagiographic text.

text may have contributed to the construction of a Christian identity within the different contexts in which it was received, handed over and, in the process, got new meanings attached to it.

2. The Content of the Text

The lion's share of the text is devoted to the narrative of Sabas' martyrdom (3–7). This quite long section is preceded by a prologue (1) and a generic description of the martyr's many qualities (2) and followed by an account of the recovery of his relics by Soranus, the *dux Scythiae*, and their transfer to Cappadocia (8). The text ends with an exhortation to Christians in the Roman Empire to celebrate the martyr's memory and spread his fame, followed by a brief concluding prayer and doxology.

The title is followed by a prologue (1) which sets the tone for the rest of the hagiographical narrative. This prologue opens as follows:

"Now, more than ever, is the saying of the blessed Peter proved true, that 'in every nation he that feared God and worked righteousness is acceptable to him' (Acts 10:35). This is confirmed now in the story of the blessed Saba, who is a witness of God and our Saviour Jesus Christ"[10].

Especially the words "in every nation" (ἐν παντὶ ἔθνει) are significant here. Sabas was a Goth by race[11] and living in Gothia. As Gothia was not known as Christian territory, the quotation of Acts 10:35 serves to introduce to the Christian audience in Cappadocia (and beyond), a Christian from across the borders of the Roman Empire as the hero of the story. By virtue of the way he lived, suffered, and died, Sabas "feared God and worked righteousness" and thus was, just like all other martyrs and saints, acceptable (δεκτός) to God. As a Goth living in Gothia, he

---

10   Heather and Matthews, *The Goths*, 104; *Pass. Sabae* 1 (216.25–29 Delehaye): Τὸ εἰρημένον τῷ μακαρίῳ Πέτρῳ καὶ νῦν κραταιῶς ἀποδέδεικται, ὅτι ἐν παντὶ ἔθνει ὁ φοβούμενος τὸν Θεὸν καὶ ἐργαζόμενος δικαιοσύνην δεκτὸς αὐτῷ ἐστιν· ἐπιστώθη γὰρ τοῦτο καὶ ἐν τοῖς κατὰ τὸν μακάριον Σάβαν, ὅς ἐστι μάρτυς Θεοῦ καὶ σωτῆρος ἡμῶν Ἰησοῦ Χριστοῦ.

11   Debate surrounds the *Passio*'s allegation that Sabas was indeed Goth by ethnicity. Already Joseph Mansion, Les origines du Christianisme chez les Goths, *AnBoll* 33 (1914), 12 formulated the theory that Sabas was considered a Goth because he was living in the land 'Gothia', and not because he was a native Goth. He draws his arguments on the *Passio*'s insistence in drawing a contrast between Sabas and the milieu where he lived, cf. *Passio Sabae* 2 (216.30 Delehaye). Heather and Matthews, *The Goths*, 104 note 18, allow for the possibility of a mixed, Romano-Gothic descent, as Sabas seems to have been a popular name in Asia Minor at that time.

"shone out like a light in the firmament, 'in the midst of a crooked and perverse generation' (Phil 2,15), imitating the saints and eminent in their company in upright actions according to Christ"[12].

Having thus discussed the topical elements of race and fatherland (γένος and πατρία), the author proceeds in the rest of the prologue with a stereotypical encomiastic characterization of its hero, which carries strong Scriptural overtones (borrowings from Ephesians and Philippians). Sabas is presented as a holy man. From his youth onwards he sought but εὐσέβεια to our Saviour and Lord Jesus Christ, and this perfect virtue (ἀρετὴν τελείαν) to Him amounted to an intimate knowledge (ἐπίγνωσιν) of the Son of God. From childhood onwards he fought against the Enemy, overcame the evils of this life and 'attained the prize of the high calling' (Phil 3:14). The prologue concludes:

"for the sake of his memory and the edification of the worshippers of God after his liberation in the Lord, he bade us not to be idle but write of his triumphs."[13]

The description of these achievements opens with an extensive panegyric of the martyr's human and religious qualities (2). The passage, to which we will come back later, is full of stereotypes and interlaced with a few borrowings from the New Testament. This description may contain one nugget of historical information. It is said that Sabas sang Psalms in the Church and did so with dedication (ψάλλων ἐν ἐκκλησίᾳ καὶ τοῦτο πάνυ ἐπιμελόμενος)[14]. The statement could simply refer to his participation in worship, but it seems that the qualification that he did so "with full dedication" may best be interpreted as an indication that he was a lector or cantor of his local church. This would explain why he was singled out: as a member of the lower clergy he certainly must have been much more likely to draw his persecutors' attention[15].

Then the narration of the events leading to the hero's martyrdom starts (3–7). From the text the following general narrative can be de-

---

12   Heather and Matthews, *The Goths*, 104; *Pass. Sabae* 1 (216.30–217,1 Delehaye): ἐν μέσῳ γενεᾶς σκολιᾶς καὶ διεστραμμένης ἐφάνη ὡς φωστὴρ ἐν κόσμῳ, μιμούμενος τοὺς ἁγίους καὶ μετ' αὐτῶν ἐν τοῖς κατὰ Χριστὸν κατορθώμασι διαπρέπων.

13   Heather and Matthews, *The Goths*, 104; *Pass. Sabae* 1 (217.9–11 Delehaye): μνήμης καὶ οἰκοδομῆς τῶν θεοσεβῶν χάριν μετὰ τὴν ἐν κυρίῳ ἀνάλυσιν αὐτοῦ οὐκ ἠρεμεῖν ἡμῖν ἐπέτρεψεν ἀλλὰ γράψαι τὰς ἀριστείας αὐτοῦ.

14   *Pass. Sabae* 2 (217.17–18 Delehaye).

15   Schäferdiek, Märtyrerüberlieferungen, 174; Heather and Matthews, *The Goths*, 105 note 21.

duced. Sabas was a man without land, money or family. In the village
where he lived, Christians were a minority, but well-integrated into the
social fabric. In the decisions concerning the village, the *synedrion*
played a key role. Apparently everybody, regardless of status or property, had the right to speak there[16]. The village was included within the
large tribal confederation of the Tervingi[17]. Its ruling class included the
"judge", who is the leader, and the group of the *megistanes*, some sort of
élite or nobility[18]. These *megistanes* took, according to the text, action
against the Christians in Sabas' village three times. With regard to their
third interference, the person of Atharidos is introduced, as the son of
the *basiliskos* Rothesteos. It remains unclear whether these *basiliskoi* did
belong to the *megistanes* or occupied a level in between, but the text
clearly shows that it was Atharidos who ensured the presence of the
central nobility at even the lowest local level.

As mentioned above, the text distinguishes three phases in the persecution of the Gothic Christians. At first (3) the *meganistes* put pressure
on the Christians in the village to eat meat that had been sacrificed to
idols. The villagers show great solidarity. It is decided that they will
furtively exchange the sacrificial meat by normal, non-sacrificial meat
which the Christians can eat publicly, in the presence of their persecutors, without having to compromise their faith. Sabas, however, refuses
the proposal, and declares that "if anyone eats of that meat, this man
cannot be a Christian"[19]; consequently, he is thrown out of the village
for some time.

The second phase does not present a motif for persecution, but it
can be inferred from the actions related to it that it consisted in an order
that Christians should bring a sacrifice to the *daemones*. Again the villagers try to evade difficulties: they plan to make a solemn oath to the
persecutors that there are no Christians at all in the village. Sabas, however, says loud and clear in the *synedrion* that he is a Christian and that

---

16   The data in the *Passio Sabae* that concern the local socio-political life have been ana-
      lyzed in great detail by Thompson, The *Passion of St. Saba*, 67–74.

17   On the organization of this confederation, see Heather, *Goths and Romans*, 97–105.

18   Heather and Matthews, *The Goths*, 105 note 22, rightly remark that earlier scholar-
      ship may have seen too easily in the megistanes an allusion to a very specific sort of
      élite, a very specific group in the organization of the Tervingi (they refer to Mk 6:21
      where the same word indicates the 'lords' of Herod the Great. Regardless how speci-
      fic a notion it is here, the fact remains that the megistanes clearly refer to a leading
      group on a supra-local level. Cf. *Pass. Sabae* 3 (217.26–27 Delehaye): οἱ κατὰ τὴν
      Γοθίαν μεγιστᾶνες.

19   Heather and Matthews, *The Goths*, 105–106; *Pass. Sabae*, 3 (217.34–35 Delehaye): Ἐάν
      τις φάγῃ ἐκ τῶν κρεῶν ἐκείνων, χριστιανὸς οὗτος εἶναι οὐ δύναται.

he does not want to adopt the solution proposed. Whereupon the villagers swear to the persecutors present that "there was no Christian in the village except one"[20] – that is, Sabas. The persecutor inquires whether Sabas is rich (and hence potentially dangerous). This is not the case and hence he is simply thrown out of the village again.

The third phase of the persecution (4) is announced as a "Great Persecution" (διωγμοῦ μεγάλου). Sabas travels to "another village" to celebrate Easter together with the priest Goútthikas, but eventually ends up with the priest Sansala, whom he presumably knew. During the third night after the feast, Atharidos comes with a gang of bandits to the village. They lift Sabas and Sansala from their mattresses and torture them during an entire day. When their torturers are asleep, a woman frees them. When Atharidos discovers this, he binds them and orders Sabas to be hanged on the main beam of the house (5). They are brought sacrificial meat that had been offered to idols, which both Sabas and Sansala refuse to eat. Instead they have a witty dialogue with Atharidos's men who had brought the meat. Enraged by the insults Sabas is making about his master, one of the men throws a javelin at him, but it miraculously fails to injure the martyr. This brings Sabas to a final sarcastic remark (6), whereupon Atharidos orders to kill him. The men take Sabas to the river Musaios – present day Buzău River – and after a final lively exchange with the men and a prayer to God he is drowned (7). At the end the text gives precise chronological indications: Sabas died on 12th of April 372. Names of consuls and emperors (Valentinian and Valens) are mentioned.

The final chapter (8) narrates what happened to the relics of the martyr after his murderers had dragged him out of the water. They left the corpse behind without burial but dogs or wild animals didn't touch it. The members of the local community (the ἀδελφοί) collected the remains, which were sent to Cappadocia through the intervention of Iunius Soranus, the *dux Scythiae* who brought them there (μετήνεγκεν).

The translation, which occurred with the approval of the *presbyterium* (presumably of Gothia), is also attested in Basil of Caesarea's *Letters 155, 164 and 165*. There we are informed that Basil was at the receiving end and that also Vetranio of Tomi played an intermediary role[21].

---

20 Heather and Matthews, *The Goths*, 106; *Pass. Sabae*, 3 (218.5–6 Delehaye): μὴ εἶναι ἐν τῇ κώμῃ αὐτῶν χριστιανὸν πλὴν ἑνός.

21 The precise analysis of these letters is fraught with difficulties which hinge around the identification of the addressees. We are not going into these details as they do not influence our analysis of the *Passio Sabae*. Essential is that the relics were brought to Cappadocia and that Basil received them and patronized the installation of a cult for them. Edition of the letters in: Saint Basile, *Lettres*, Texte établi et traduit par Yves

The relics' translation indicates, so the *Passio* says, only the first step in the spreading of Sabas' martyrdom and renown throughout the entire Catholic Church.

As interim conclusion I would, in line with the many scholars who have great confidence in the historical core of the narrative of this document[22], lend credence to the following basic elements. Sabas, a native Goth, was a Christian not belonging to the higher classes of his township. He died a martyr's death in the context of an anti-Christian persecution or persecutions, during which also quite a few other Christians died[23]. This persecution may have been triggered by the Roman anti-Gothic campaigns of the immediately preceding years, more than likely at the initiative of the (probably at that time still largely pagan) nobility of the Tervingi confederation. Furthermore, there is no particular reason to doubt the chronological indication of the *Passio* that Sabas died on 12th of April 372. The same applies to the indication that his relics have been translated to Cappadocia, probably Caesarea (because of Basil's involvement).

The rest of the story consists of hagiographical *topoi* and narrative elements, the historical value of which is hard to ascertain. In what follows I hope to show with some examples that much of the meaning of this text can be found exactly in these unhistorical elements of the narrative.

3. Literary Analysis: Patterns, Motifs, Intentions

From the presentation above it is clear that the *Passio Sabae* presents a gripping story. It must have been a good read and it is easy to understand that such stories about native saints must have been popular and widespread in the local community who must have been proud of "their" hero. Yet, the author's ambition went further than that. According to the prologue, he also wanted it to be edifying to readers beyond

---

Courtonne, vol. II, CUFr (Paris: Les Belles Lettres, 1961), 80–81 and 97–101. English translation in: Heather and Matthews, *The Goths*, 113–117. Secondary literature: Alexe, *Saint Basile*, 1049–1059; Robert Pouchet, *Basile le Grand et son univers d'amis d'après sa correspondance: une stratégie de communion*, SEAug 36 (Roma: Institutum Patristicum Augustinianum, 1992), 451–465; Constantin Zuckerman, *Cappadocian Fathers and the Goths*, TrMém 11 (1991), 473–486, here 473–479.
22   See n. 8 above.
23   See n. 3 and 4 above.

this local level[24]. This is hardly surprising: presenting the martyr as a source of inspiration and a model of imitation is a hallmark of hagiographical literature[25]. In the execution of his task as a hagiographer, the author of the *Passio* is employing many stereotypical strategies and his discourse shares many elements with other hagiographical texts. I will substantiate this claim by pointing to parallels with other martyr texts. In doing so it will also become apparent in what ways the author of the *Passio* is using these stereotypical elements to achieve his aim of edification.

A first striking feature, one that is recognized by the most vehement defenders of the *Passio*'s reliability, is the literary influence exercised by the *Martyrdom of Polycarp* on the *Passio Sabae*. Two textual parallels enclose the narrative in a circular frame reminiscent of the *Martyrium Polycarpi*, one in the title (1), the other at the end of the narrative (8). In his address, the author of the *Passio Sabae* writes:

"The church of God dwelling in Gothia, to the church of God dwelling in Cappadocia and all the other communities of the holy catholic church in

---

24 *Pass. Sabae* 1 (217.9–11 Delehaye); cf. *Passio Perpetuae et Felicitatis* 1 in Herbert Musurillo, ed., *The Acts of the Christian Martyrs*, (Oxford: Clarendon Press, 1972), 106–108; *Mart. Pionii* 1.2 (ibid. 136.9–11). Some examples from passages from Cappadocian panegyrics in which this imitation-theme is formulated *expressis verbis*: Basilius Caesariensis, *In XL martyres* 1 (PG 31, 508–509); *In Mamantem* 1 (PG 31, 589); *In Gordium* 1–2 (PG 31, 489–493); Gregorius Nyssenus, *De S. Theodoro*, ed. by Johannes P. Cavarnos, in: Guntherus Heil/Johannes P. Cavarnos/Otto Lendle, eds., *Gregorii Nysseni Sermones. Pars II*, GNO X 1/2 (Leiden: Brill, 1990), 62; 69; Id., *In XL martyres II* (ed. by Otto Lendle, GNO X 1/2, 159–160; quoted *infra*); Asterius Amasenus, *In sanctos martyres*, 2–3.1; 11.2, in: Asterius of Amasea, *Homilies I–XIV*. Text, Introduction and Notes by Cornelis Datema (Leiden: Brill, 1970), 135; 141; *In avaritiam* 1 (ibid. 27); *In Phocam* 1 (ibid. 115).

25 Cf. Peter Brown, The Saint as Exemplar in Late Antiquity, *Representations* 1 (1983), 1–21. For an overview of motifs and practices related to hagiographical literature, see Alison Goddard Elliott, *Roads to Paradise: Reading the Lives of the Early Saints* (Hanover/London: University Press of New England, 1987). The custom and the mentality behind hagiographical literature are aptly summarized by Elizabeth Key Fowden, *The Barbarian Plain: Saint Sergius between Rome and Iran*, The Transformation of the Classical Heritage 28 (Berkeley: University of California Press, 1999), 8, speaking of the *Passio Sergii et Bacchi*: "The Passio... should be seen within the framework of his [sc. the hagiographer's] purpose, which was to describe the crowning of a martyr. In such a work, accounts of historical events might be historically inaccurate, but it did not matter, as long as they fulfilled their purpose of setting the symbolic scene in which the current of God's redemptive grace could flow through the miracleworking saint to his followers".

any place; may the mercy, peace and love of God the Father and our Lord
Jesus Christ be multiplied"[26].

With exception of the place names, this is a literal quotation of the title
of *Martyrium Polycarpi*. Similarly, the exhortation to support and in-
crease the martyr's veneration echoes a similar sentence at the end of
the *Martyrdom of Polycarp*[27].

It is commonly assumed that the text accompanied the relics during
their transfer. One can easily imagine that the letter-form invited itself
as the narrative frame for the martyrdom and that this triggered the
author's idea to re-use the title of *Martyrium Polycarpi* as the title to his
own writing. From this it might be concluded, as some scholars have
done, that the title, and therefore the entire prologue and epilogue,
have been added slightly later to the originally composed body of the
text, which can be seen also as a stand-alone narration of Sabas' martyrdom[28]. The hypothesis is not implausible, but *ad contra* one could
argue that the text as we have it now can be read as a coherent whole
and that, as a subsidiary argument, the two manuscript witnesses of the
text do not bear traces of a redaction in several stages.

The references to the *Martyrium Polycarpi* are certainly not coincidental, and the meaning of their use exceeds the mere similarity of
cases as exposed above. *Martyrium Polycarpi*, a text dated in the middle
of the second century, had become by the middle of the fourth century
a text that was widely known, and had become, through its inclusion in
Eusebius' *Church History*, already part of Christian collective memory.
Reminiscences to *Martyrium Polycarpi* in martyrial literature are no
exception[29] and in that sense the title of the *Martyrdom of Sabas* is, in its

---

26   Heather and Matthews, *The Goths*, 104; *Pass. Sabae* 1 (216.21–24 Delehaye): Ἡ
     ἐκκλησία τοῦ Θεοῦ ἡ παροικοῦσα Γοθίᾳ τῇ ἐκκλησίᾳ τοῦ Θεοῦ τῇ παροικούσῃ
     Καππαδοκίᾳ καὶ πάσαις ταῖς κατὰ τόπον τῆς ἁγίας καθολικῆς ἐκκλησίας
     παροικίαις, ἔλεος, εἰρήνη, ἀγάπη Θεοῦ πατρὸς καὶ κυρίου ἡμῶν Ἰησοῦ Χριστοῦ
     πληθυνθείν.

27   Cf. *Pass. Sabae* 8 (221.21–23 Delehaye): καὶ τοῖς ἐπέκεινα ἀδελφοῖς σημάνατε, ἵνα
     ἐν πάσῃ καθολικῇ καὶ ἀποστολικῇ ἐκκλησίᾳ ἀγαλλιάσεις ἐπιτελῶσι, and Mart.
     Pol. 20.1 (16.30–32 Musurillo): μαθόντες οὖν ταῦτα καὶ τοῖς ἐπέκεινα ἀδελφοῖς
     τὴν ἐπιστολὴν διαπέμψασθε ἵνα καὶ ἐκεῖνοι δοξάζωσιν τὸν κύριον τὸν ἐκλογὰς
     ποιοῦντα ἀπὸ τῶν ἰδίων δούλων.

28   Delehaye, Saints de Thrace, 289–291; Schäferdiek, Märtyrerüberlieferungen, 173.

29   A ready example is the *Passio Theodori*, whereby Theodore's final prayer is strongly
     inspired by that of the Smyrnean martyr in *Mart. Pol.* 13–14. Cf. Hippolyte Delehaye,
     De S. Theodoro martyre: II. S. Theodori passio prima, *AASS Novembris IV* (Bruxelles:
     Apud Socios Bollandianos, 1925), 38 note 2.

conscious adaptation of *Martyrium Polycarpi*, not an isolated case[30]. By the intertextual link with *Martyrium Polycarpi*, Sabas and his *Martyrdom* are intentionally put in line with the tradition of a venerable predecessor.

After the prologue, before the narrative proper begins, a long passage describes in a general way Sabas' many qualities in a long enumeration. Knut Schäferdiek writes about this passage that it is "eine allgemeine Charakterisierung des Sabas, die im wesentlichen aus erbaulichen, mit neutestamentlichen Anführungen durchsetzten Leerformeln und Stereotypen besteht..."[31]. No doubt Schäferdiek's assessment is correct and no doubt the author included this passage because it belonged to the narratological script, and the reader would expect it there anyway[32]. Yet, this passage is very long and there might be more to it. I think that through all these stereotypes, it also paints an image of what the ideal, perfect Christian looks like, according to the author and the milieu in which the text originated. Some elements of Sabas' portrayal merit further discussion.

It is striking that the very first feature mentioned is that Sabas was orthodox in faith (ὀρθὸς τῇ πίστει). Here one may certainly suspect a deliberate link with his being a Goth by race. Due to Ulfilas' Arianism there was a general association between Goths and Arianising tendencies[33]. Given that the relics and the *Passio* were to be sent to Basil of Caesarea, the author of the *Passio* may have wanted to avoid every

---

30   For other parallel passages / borrowings, see Boudewijn Dehandschutter, *Martyrium Polycarpi: Een literair-kritische studie*, BEThL 52 (Leuven: Leuven University Press, 1979), 46–47; 165–167; 172–173; Gerd Buschmann, *Das Martyrium des Polykarp*, KAV 6 (Göttingen: Vandenhoeck & Ruprecht, 1998), 76; 356. Re-use of material from other texts deemed useful for his own purpose was part and parcel of the hagiographer's writing activity, characterized by the frequent use of stereotypical scenes, characters and narrative framework. David Woods, The Emperor Julian and the Passion of Sergius and Bacchus, *JECS* 5 (1997), 335–367, has showed that the *Passio Sergii et Bacchi* is a fictive narration based on an earlier document; other examples include the *Passio Typasii*, whose source of inspiration was the *Vita Martini* of Sulpicius Severus, or the fictitious *Passio* of Menas of Cotyaeum, based on Basil of Caesarea's *Homily in Praise of Gordius*. Cf. F. Scorza Barcellona, Per una lettura del Passio Typasii Veterani, *Aug.* 35 (1995), 797–814, and, respectively, P. Peeters, *Orient et Byzance. Le tréfonds oriental de l'hagiographie byzantine*, SHG 26 (Bruxelles: Société des Bollandistes, 1950), 38–41. In the Latin West, the *Passio Donati, Venusti et Hermogenis*, for example, relies on material from the Pannonian *Passio Pollionis* (for which see above, pp. 179–198).

31   Schäferdiek, Märtyrerüberlieferungen, 174.

32   Parallel examples: Basilius Caesariensis, In XL martyres 2 (PG 31, 508C–509C); Gregorius Nyssenus, *De S. Theodoro* (GNO X 1/2, 65); Gregorius Nyssenus, *In XL martyres Ib* (GNO X 1/2, 145); Asterius Amasenus, *In Phocam* 5 (119.6–18 Datema).

33   Heather and Matthews, *The Goths*, 104 n. 20.

shred of a doubt as to the martyr's orthodoxy (without giving more details about what "orthodox" exactly boiled down to!). Besides orthodox, Sabas was also devout (εὐλαβής) and speaking loud and clear to everybody on behalf of the truth (πρὸς πάντας εἰρηνικῶς ὑπὲρ ἀληθείας φθεγγόμενος). These elements underline Sabas' allegiance to the orthodox faith in word, deed and way of life.

Another striking element in Sabas' portrayal is that he is also exhibiting features of an ascetical lifestyle:

> "He took thought neither for money nor for possessions except the bare necessities. He was temperate, self-controlled in all things, uninitiated in woman [singular, n.a.], abstinent, observing all fasts."[34]

By the 370's this attention for moderation and continence in matters of sexuality, earthly possessions or food had become part and parcel of the image of a perfect Christian. The flourishing of *de virginitate*-literature in this period bears testimony to this but the frequent presence of ascetic elements in martyr stories is equally telling an indication for the widespread presence of ascetical ideals and the zeal with which church leaders promoted them[35].

With regard to the idolatry of paganism Sabas had, so the *Passio*, an equally balanced way of handling things: 'He bridled the idolaters not by acting as if superior to them but by going along with them, as befits humble persons'[36]. It is normal that the *Passio* contains one or more passages in which pagan cults are ridiculed. This is part of the hagiographical standard repertoire[37]. It is somewhat surprising, not to say ironic, though, to read that the martyr consistently criticized pagan-

---

34 Heather and Matthews, *The Goths*, 105; *Pass. Sabae* 2 (217.18–20 Delehaye): οὐ χρημάτων, οὐ κτημάτων πλὴν τῶν πρὸς τὴν χρείαν φροντίζων, νηφάλιος, ἐγκρατὴς ἐν πᾶσι, γυναικὸς ἀμύητος, ἀπεχόμενος, νηστεύων παρ' ἕκαστα.

35 Basil of Caesarea's *Homily in Praise of Gordius* is a case in point: in part of the sermon Gordius is portrayed as an *alter* Elia, seeking refuge in remote areas and living a simple life. Cf. Johan Leemans, Martyr, Monk and Victor of Paganism: an Analysis of Basil of Caesarea's Panegyrical Sermon on Gordius, in Id., ed., *More than a Memory. The Discourse of Martyrdom and the Construction of Christian Identity in the History of Christianity*, ANL 51 (Leuven: Peeters, 2005), 45–81.

36 My transl. *Pass. Sabae* 2 (217.15–16 Delehaye): ἐπιστομίζων τοὺς εἰδωλολάτρας καὶ οὐχ ὑπεραιρόμενος ἀλλ' ὡς πρέπον τοῖς ταπεινοῖς συναπαγόμενος. Cf. Heather and Matthews, *The Goths*, 104, "reproaching the idolaters and not 'exalted overmuch' [cf. 2Cor 12:7], but 'condescending to men of low estate' [Rom 12:16] as is fitting".

37 See, for example, *Mart. Cononis* 5.2 (190.5–9 Musurillo); *Acta Marcelli* 1.1 (ibid. 250.7–10); *Mart. Dasii* 1–4 (ibid. *The Acts*, 272–274); *Pass. Crispinae* 2.4; 3.1–2 (ibid. 304.28–306.3; 306.7; 306.15–6); *Pass. Sergii et Bacchi* 6, ed. by Cornelius Byeus, in: *ActaSS Octobris*, vol. *III* (Antwerp: Joannem Nicolaum vander Beken, 1770), 864; or Gregorius Nyssenus, *De S. Theodoro* (GNO X 1/2, 67.3–24; 68.9–15).

ism and did so in a constructive manner, by way of dialogue rather than by a unilateral condemnation. After all, the storyline of a *Passio* is built precisely on the logic of opposition between the characters representing paganism and Christianity and the *Passio Sabae* is no exception: in its narrative section one can hardly find a trace of such a constructive, humble attitude. It is clear that in this initial passage the author is portraying Sabas in a general, almost abstract way, as a model-Christian.

Indeed, like many other martyr texts, also the *Passio Sabae* owes much of its liveliness to its oppositional character: martyrdom is a combat between the martyr and his persecutors, between paganism and Christianity, between God and the devil. At times the opposition almost gets cosmological proportions[38]. The use of polemical language certainly contributes to its shaping. This is especially strongly so at key-passages in the story. The very beginning of the narrative proper places the main characters center-stage (3). About Sabas it is said that "not once but many times before his consummation did he display a pious deed in faith"[39]. The first of these occurred when "the chief men [*megistanes*, n.a.] in Gothia began to be moved against the Christians"[40]. The passive mode "began to be moved" suggests that they were acting as accomplices of the Devil who was the real instigator and source of their evil deeds. The same formulation occurs a bit later, when Sabas' second pious deed is introduced: "On another occasion, when a time of trial was moved in customary fashion by the Goths"[41]. The beginning of the third episode of persecutions (4) – the "Great persecution" – is introduced as follows: "Afterwards, when a great persecution was stirred by

---

38   The Devil as instigator of the persecutions and the martyr's chief opponent has a rich pedigree before the fourth century, as has been explored by Gérard J.M. Bartelink in several contributions: Μισόκαλος: epithète du diable, *VigChr* 12 (1958), 37–44; Id., A propos de deux termes abstraits désignant le diable, *VigChr* 13 (1959), 58–60; Id., Les démons comme brigands, *VigChr* 21 (1967), 12–24; Id., ΒΑΣΚΑΝΟΣ: désignation de Satan et des démons chez les auteurs chrétiens, *OCP* 49 (1983), 390–406; Id., ΑΝΤΙΚΕΙΜΕΝΟΣ (Widersacher) als Teufel- und Dämonenbezeichnung, *SE* 30 (1987-988), 205–224. But also the martyr homilies of the Cappadocian Fathers, roughly contemporary to the *Passio Sabae*, abound in this oppositional language whereby the Devil is the martyr's main opponent; cf. e.g. Gregorius Nyssenus, *De S. Theodoro* (GNO X 1/2, 65,6–9); *In XL martyres Ia* (GNO X 1/2, 141,18–19); *In XL martyres Ib* (GNO X 1/2, 147,16–148,10; 148,26–149,3; 149,10–12; 149,22–150,5; 150,23–26; 151,4–5; 154,11–14); *In XL martyres II* (GNO X, 1/2, 163,22–164,1; 164,11–14; 164,17–165,1); *In Stephanum I* (GNO X 1/2, 75,13–76,11; 79,12–80,8; 80,16–81,19; 94,8–14).

39   Heather and Matthews, *The Goths*, 105; *Pass. Sabae* 3 (217.25–26 Delehaye).

40   Heather and Matthews, *The Goths*, 105; *Pass. Sabae* 3 (217.26–27 Delehaye).

41   Heather and Matthews, *The Goths*, 106; *Pass. Sabae* 3 (218.3 Delehaye).

the infidels in Gothia against the church of God…"[42]. When the narrative episode shifts to the final stage, namely when Sabas is apprehended at Sansala's house, this is introduced as follows: "there came at the behest of the impious ones Atharidus… with a gang of lawless bandits"[43].

The way in which the main characters are presented – often almost in passing – contributes to the oppositional framework[44]. Sabas is frequently styled 'the blessed' (μακάριος)[45] or, at the end of the story, the saint (ἅγιος)[46]. He is fearless (ἄφοβος)[47]; both he and Sansala are "servants of God" (τῶν δούλων τοῦ θεοῦ)[48]. When he refuses to mislead the persecutors by eating non-sacrificial meat as if it were sacrificial meat, he "prevented them all from falling into the Devil's snare" (καὶ διεκώλυσε τοὺς πάντας μὴ ἐμπεσεῖν εἰς τὴν παγίδα τοῦ διαβόλου)[49]. In the second episode of persecution the martyr's opponent is styled "the persecutor" (ὁ διώκτης)[50], "the leader of the outrage" (ὁ ἄρχων τῆς ἀνομίας)[51] and the lawless (ὁ ἄνομος)[52]; in the last phase they are "his torturers" (οἱ δήμιοι)[53]. The servants of Atharidos who are to execute Sabas and Sansala are styled "servants of lawlessness (οἱ ὑπηρέται τῆς ἀνομίας) or simply "his murderers" (οἱ φονεῖς)[54].

Many of the stereotypical elements in the hagiographical narrative about Sabas function within this dichotomic framework and contribute to it. Firstly, there is the feature of παρρησία, freedom of speech, mentioned at the end of the panegyrical section, almost as a crown of the long list of Sabas' qualities:

---

42 Heather and Matthews, *The Goths*, 106; *Pass. Sabae* 4 (218.16–17 Delehaye).
43 Heather and Matthews, *The Goths*, 107; *Pass. Sabae* 4 (219.2–3 Delehaye).
44 See Delehaye, *Les passions*, 239–254.
45 *Pass. Sabae* 3 (217.32 Delehaye); *Pass. Sabae* 7 (ibid. 220.19; 220.33–34).
46 *Pass. Sabae* 6 (ibid. 220.7).
47 *Pass. Sabae* 5 (ibid. 219.26).
48 *Pass. Sabae* 4 (ibid. 219.10).
49 *Pass. Sabae* 3 (ibid. 217.35–36).
50 *Pass. Sabae* 3 (ibid. 218.5; 218.8)
51 *Pass. Sabae* 3 (ibid. 218.10).
52 *Pass. Sabae* 3 (ibid. 218.14).
53 *Pass. Sabae* 5 (ibid. 219.23); *Pass. Sabae* 6 (ibid. 220.10–11).
54 *Pass. Sabae* 7 (ibid. 220.17) and, respectively, *Pass. Sabae* 8 (ibid. 221.10).

"In sum he preserved an unblemished 'faith working through love' (Gal 5:6) never hesitating to speak out [παρρησιάζεσθαι, n.a.] on all occasions in the Lord."[55]

In fact, the entire story of Sabas' road to martyrdom can be read as an exemplary application of the virtue of παρρησία. This is most clear in the second episode of persecution. When the inhabitants of the village are planning to swear a solemn oath that there are no Christians in the village, Sabas comes forward in the *synedrion* and declares: "Let no man swear on my account, for I am a Christian"; as introduction of this (probably fictive) quotation of the martyr's words, Sabas is mentioned as, "again speaking out" (παρρησιασάμενος)[56]. παρρησία is a quality our Sabas has in common with the heroes of many other martyr stories. Used in the Scriptures to characterize freedom of speech in spite of every impediment (Acts 4:27–31; 4Macc. 10:5), παρρησία quickly became a *topos* in hagiographic literature, and a central virtue for a martyr[57]. The earliest Christian testimonies of the term occur in the *Martyrium Polycarpi* and in the *Martyrdom of Lyon and Vienne*, where it is applied to Blandina, to Alexander and to the entire group of martyrs[58]. Other martyr acts also offer examples of a martyr's παρρησία towards the judge, with or without explicitly using the term[59]. Also in the pane-

---

55 Heather and Matthews, *The Goths*, 105; *Pass. Sabae* 2 (217.23–24 Delehaye): καὶ τὸ ὅλον ἄμεμπτον πίστιν ἔχων δι' ἀγάπης ἐνεργουμένην, ὡς μηδὲν διστάζοντα αὐτὸν παρρησιάζεσθαι πάντοτε ἐν κυρίου.

56 *Pass. Sabae* 3 (218.6 Delehaye): Ὁ δὲ Σάβας παρρησιασάμενος πάλιν καὶ παρελθὼν ἐν μέσῳ τῷ συνεδρίῳ ἔλεγεν· «Ὑπὲρ ἐμοῦ μηδεὶς ὁμόσῃ· ἐγὼ γὰρ χριστιανός εἰμι.».

57 An overview of occurrences can be found in Gérard J.M. Bartelink, Quelques observations sur Parresia dans la littérature paléo-chrétienne, *Graecitas et latinitas christianorum primaeva. Supplementa* 3 (1970), 35–37.

58 *Mart. Pol.* 10.1 (10.3–4 Musurillo): μετὰ παρρησίας ἄκουε· Χριστιανός εἰμι; respectively, *Mart. Lugd.* 1.18 (ibid. 66.23–24): [fearing for Blandina] μὴ οὐδὲ τὴν ὁμολογίαν δυνήσεται παρρησιάσασθαι διὰ τὸ ἀσθενὲς τοῦ σώματος; *Mart. Lugd.* 1.49 (ibid. 76.28): [on Alexander] γνωστὸς σχεδὸν πᾶσι διὰ... παρρησίαν τοῦ λόγου; *Mart. Lugd.* 2.4 (ibid. 82.27–28): [on the entire group] πολλὴν παρρησίαν ἄγοντες πρὸς πάντα τὰ ἔθνη.

59 Especially interesting with regard to the meaning of the term παρρησία is the *Martyrdom of Tarachus, Probus and Andronicus*. During the interview the magistrate Maximus asserts that παρρησία can only exist between people of equal social rank. Tarachus admits he is not of equal rank but explains that his παρρησία is grounded not in social rank but in the power of God. See *Pass. Tarachi, Probi et Andronici* 7, in Daniel Ruiz-Bueno, ed., *Actas de los Mártires*, Biblioteca de los auctores cristianos 75 (Madrid: Biblioteca de auctores cristianos, 1951, repr. 1962), 1112–1113.

gyrics on martyrs delivered by the Cappadocian Fathers, this feature typical of martyr texts is present[60].

Sabas is focused on the interests of εὐσέβεια, of true religion and hence is not hindered by worldly concerns or by doubts what would be wise attitude. Instead he shows in his freedom of speech a stubborn determination and tunnel-vision combined with a good measure of wit. The message is clear: for a true Christian, there is no room or need for doubt. Hence, Sabas refuses the possible compromises offered by his fellow-inhabitants of the village. And when offered sacrificial meat, he has the following dialogue with the men who brought it:

> "Saba said: 'Who is it that gave these orders [= sent the meat, n.a.]?' They replied, 'Our lord Atharidus'. And Saba said, 'There is one Lord, God in the heavens; but Atharidus is a man, impious and accursed. And this food of perdition is impure and profane like Atharidus who sent it.'"[61]

Gregory of Nyssa's *Panegyric on Theodore the Recruit* offers a nice parallel of a witty dialogue from which the martyr emerges as winner. When his judges are holding back for a moment, one of them engages in the following dialogue with the martyr:

> "'Theodore, has your God a Son? Does he beget, just like man, with passion?' 'With passion', he said, 'my God did not beget but I do confess the Son and I call his begetting fitting for God. You, however, o pitiable man with the intellect of a child, don't you blush or hide due to your confession in a female god and your veneration for her, a mother of twelve children, a kind of very fertile demon who just like a hare or a sow effortlessly conceives and gives birth!'"[62]

Theodore and Sabas remain steadfast in the faith, not showing a shred of doubt when meeting opponents, whom they are, on the contrary, meeting with confidence. This determination is also reflected in the

---

60　E.g. Basilius Caesariensis, *In Gordium* 3 (PG 31, 497B68) ἐν περιφανεῖ τοῦ θεάτρου γενόμενος, ἀτρέπτῳ τῇ παρρησίᾳ ἐξεβόησε... Cf. also Gregorius Nyssenus, *De S. Theodoro* (GNO X 1/2, 66.4–15) – but without using the term παρρησία.

61　Heather and Matthews, *The Goths*, 108; *Pass. Sabae* 6 (220.1–5 Delehaye): Λέγει ὁ Σάβας· «Τίς ὁ ἀποστείλας ταῦτα;» Οἱ δὲ εἶπον· «Ὁ δεσπότης Ἀθάριδος.» Ὁ δὲ Σάβας εἶπεν· «Εἷς δεσπότης Θεὸς ἐν οὐρανοῖς ἐστιν· Ἀθάριδος δὲ ἄνθρωπος ἀσεβὴς καὶ ἐπικατάρατος· καὶ ταῦτα ἀκάθαρτά ἐστι καὶ βέβηλα τῆς ἀπωλείας τὰ βρώματα, ὡς καὶ ὁ ἀποστείλας αὐτὰ Ἀθάριδος.»

62　Gregorius Nyssenus, *De S. Theodoro* (GNO X 1/2, 66.18–67.3): Ἔστι γὰρ, ἔφη, υἱός, ὦ Θεόδωρε, τῷ σῷ θεῷ; καὶ γεννᾷ ἐκεῖνος ὡς ἄνθρωπος ἐμπαθῶς; — Ἐμπαθῶς μὲν, ἔφη, ὁ ἐμὸς Θεὸς οὐκ ἐγέννησεν, ἀλλὰ καὶ υἱὸν ὁμολογῶ καὶ θεοπρεπῆ λέγω τὴν γέννησιν. σὺ δέ, ὦ νηπιώδη τὸν λογισμὸν καὶ ἄθλιε, οὐκ ἐρυθριᾷς οὐδὲ ἐγκαλύπτῃ καὶ θήλειαν ὁμολογῶν θεόν, καὶ ὡς μητέρα δώδεκα παίδων τὴν αὐτὴν προσκυνῶν, πολυτόκον τινὰ δαίμονα κατὰ τοὺς λαγωοὺς ἢ τὰς ὗς εὐκόλως καὶ ἐγκυϊσκομένην καὶ ἀποτίκτουσαν.

way they deal with the frequent tortures they undergo[63]. After he had been beaten, burnt and made running behind a chariot, Sabas happily tells his torturers:

> "'Did you not drive and beat me across burned wastes, onto the sharp points of thorns, naked and without shoes? See, whether my feet are injured and whether I have wheals on my body from this, or from the beatings you inflicted upon me.'"[64]

Here too Gregory of Nyssa's Theodore the Recruit is offering a nice parallel. Having refused to apostatize, he tells his persecutors the following:

> "'In honouring deceiving demons with the name god you are wrong. To me Christ is God, the Only-begotten Son of God. Because of my faith in him and my confession of it, let he who is wounding me cut me; let he who is whipping me lacerate me; let he who is burning me bring the flame close; let he who is taking offence at these words of mine cut out my tongue, for each part of the body owes to its Creator an act of endurance'"[65].

Sabas is not broken by his tortures; on the contrary. He still has the energy and breath to ridicule his torturers because they are so ineffective. In sum, his ὑπομονή matches the cruelty of his torturers. Even more so, he not only answers them but the tortures literally left no trace on his body. The latter element is repeated three times very explicitly in the *Passio*[66]. At the end of the text it occurs a fourth time. Atharidos' men are not drowning Sabas with force and violence but, knowing he will cooperate, they use a wooden block so that he would be preserved immaculate (ἄχραντον), "a symbol of salvation" (τῆς σωτηρίας τὸ

---

63 The joyful acceptance of the prospect of being tortured, even the explicit request for it, is present in many of the classical acts of the martyrs as well as in the Cappadocian Fathers' martyrial homilies: cf. Basilius Caesariensis, *In Gordium* 5 (PG 31, 500C); *Mart. Cononis* 5 (190–191 Musurillo); *Pass. Iuli Veterani* 3.1 (ibid. 262–263); *Pass. Irenaei Sirmiensis* 2.2–3 and 4.9–12 (ibid. 294–295 and 298–299); *Pass. Crispinae* 3 (ibid. 306–307); Gregorius Nyssenus, *De S. Theodoro* (GNO X 1/2, 66.8–12).

64 Heather and Matthews, *The Goths*, 107; *Pass. Sabae* 5 (219.13–16 Delehaye): «Οὐχὶ διὰ χέρσων κεκαυμένων ἐπὶ τὰ ὀξέα τῶν σκολόπων τύπτοντες ἠλάσατέ με γυμνὸν καὶ ἀνυπόδετον; ἴδετε, εἰ ἐβλάβησαν οἱ πόδες μου καὶ εἰ ἐν τῷ σώματί μου ἔχω μώλωπας καὶ ἀπὸ τῶν πληγῶν ὧν ἐπηνέγκατέ μοι.»

65 Gregorius Nyssenus, *De S. Theodoro* (GNO X 1/2, 66.6–12): δαίμονας δὲ ὑμεῖς ἀπατεῶνας πλανᾶσθε τῇ τοῦ Θεοῦ τιμῶντες προσηγορίᾳ· ἐμοὶ δὲ θεὸς ὁ Χριστός, ὁ τοῦ θεοῦ μονογενὴς υἱός. ὑπὲρ τῆς εὐσεβείας τοίνυν καὶ τῆς ὁμολογίας τῆς εἰς ἐκεῖνον καὶ ὁ τιτρώσκων τεμνέτω καὶ ὁ μαστίζων ξαινέτω καὶ ὁ καίων προσαγέτω τὴν φλόγα καὶ ὁ ταῖς φωναῖς μου ταύταις ἀχθόμενος ἐξαιρέτω τὴν γλῶσσαν· καθ' ἕκαστον γὰρ μέλος τὸ σῶμα τῷ κτίσαντι χρεωστεῖ τὴν ὑπομονήν.

66 *Pass. Sabae* 5 (219.13–16 Delehaye); *Pass. Sabae* 6 (ibid. 220.14–15); *Pass. Sabae* 8 (ibid. 221.11–12).

σύμβολον) it is added[67]. The integrity of the martyr's body, also after tortures, is a recurring element in martyr texts. In the *Martyrdom of Polycarp* it is described how the fire of the pyre curves around the body like a vault, without touching or baking the flesh[68]. Something similar we read in Basil of Caesarea's *Homily in Praise of Julitta*: there it is said that the fire envelops the body while preserving its integrity so that it can serve as a worthy object of veneration[69].

A further literary element typical of hagiographical texts to be mentioned here are the visions and miracles. Beyond fulfilling the expectations of the audience and adding to the narrative flavour of the story, they also contributed to its meaning. There are two instances where the miraculous comes in, both occurring during the third phase of the persecution. The first instance occurs when, during the "Great Persecution" Sabas is underway to his friend the priest Goutthika to celebrate Easter with him. On his way he is confronted by a huge and shining appearance in the form of a person who orders him to turn around and to go to the priest Sansalas, apparently another of his friends. According to Sabas' knowledge this Sansalas was away because he fled for the persecution across the Danube to the Roman Empire. Not knowing that Sansalas had returned because of Easter, he answers the person in his vision that Sansala is not there and he indicates he wants to move on to Goutthika. Whereupon a second miraculous event happens: though it was a bright, sunny day with a cloudless air, suddenly so much snow fell that he could simply not continue his way. Understanding that it was God's will that he should go to Sansalas, he does so[70].

The vision and miracle explain how Sabas ends up at Sansala's house, and translate for the reader Sabas' providential election to become a martyr (it was God's will that Sabas should be seized by the persecutors, so that he might be rewarded with the crown of martyrdom). More importantly, though, they portray Sabas as somebody who does God's will and, reversely, as somebody with whom God is communicating through vision and miracle.

Later on divine support for the martyr is confirmed. When the men of Atharidos had taken him to the river to be drowned, they are deliberating among themselves to let him go. Sabas tells them to follow their orders and points out that, at the other end, angels are already awaiting him in glory to welcome him. The phenomenon of the *psychopompoi*, the

---

67   *Pass. Sabae* 7 (ibid. 221.5).

68   *Mart. Pol.* 15 (14–15 Musurillo).

69   Basilius Caesariensis, *In Iulittam* 2 (PG 31, 241A11–16).

70   *Pass. Sabae* 4 (218.16–33 Delehaye).

angels receiving the saint and leading him to the heavenly realm, is very common in late antique literature[71]. The point is that only Sabas could see the angels waiting for him; to his persecutors this glorious reality remained invisible. By the end of the fourth century the martyr's glorious reception in the otherworld had become a literary *topos* with which many images were associated[72]. The steadfastness in the Christian faith that Sabas had developed since his youth and, especially, had shown during the long period of persecution is rewarded by God's support through visions and miracles and, in the end, to the extension of his glory into this world.

A final element that deserves to be highlighted with regard to the *Passio Sabae* is that its 'theology of martyrdom' is in line with the 'kairological' idea of martyrdom present in many Christian texts. Martyrdom is not a shortcut to heaven which is to be sought eagerly, nor is voluntary martyrdom a desirable practice. On the contrary. Although he remains resolute in his strict observation of Christian precepts, Sabas does not trigger persecution upon himself, his παρρησία has nothing provocative, and he is let go twice before being actually arrested. Only when the final decision is brought and Sabas has uttered his final prayer, it is time for his martyrdom. Then it is his καιρός, and then Sabas can lawfully contradict his executioners' attempts to let him free. Whether the three episodes of the persecution are actually historical realities and denote a certain social conduct in the Gothic society or not, is not the place here to discern, nor is it the hagiographer's primary concern. On a narratological level, though, it is clear that these three episodes are invested with theological value: they are read in light of a grand soteriological scheme in which martyrdom, decided, sanctioned and set in motion by God's providence as a reward for the Christian conduct of the protagonist, becomes the sacrament of salvation. Of Sansala, who dies together with Sabas, it is even explicitly said that he fled across the border to the Roman Empire because of the persecutions. Only when he has returned and his καιρός has come it is time for him to die and then even Sabas' intervention is null and void[73].

---

71 Athanas Recheis, *Engel, Tod und Seelenreise: das Wirken der Geister beim Heimgang des Menschen in der Lehre der Alexandrinischen und Kappadokischen Väter*, TeT 4 (Roma: Storia e letteratura, 1958).

72 Cf. Jacqueline Amat, *Songes et visions: l'au-delà dans la littérature latine tardive*, Études Augustiniennes. Série Antiquité 109 (Paris: Études augustiniennes, 1985), 393–403.

73 *Pass. Sabae* 7 (220.16–31 Delehaye).

4. The *exemplum* of Sabas and Christian identity

In the prologue it was said that the *Passio* had an edifying purpose.
Using terminology more en vogue nowadays, one can say that this text
wanted to make a contribution to the development of the religious
identity of its hearers and readers. In what way could Sabas have been
an example, a model worthy of imitation to other Christians? I think we
have to distinguish here between several periods and audiences, both
in Gothia and in Cappadocia.

With regard to Christianity in Gothia the years 375/6 (or maybe
even earlier)[74] are a watershed. Then Athanaric was succeeded at the
head of the Tervingi confederation by Fritigern, who embraced Christianity. In the logic of the confederation this meant that – at least nomi-
nally – the majority followed the leader and converted to Christianity, a
state of facts which produced a rather different audience for the *Passio
Sabae* (an audience in need of foundational stories to legitimize this new
identity).

Under Athanaric, the *Passio* may have inspired the Christian minority with awe, fear and admiration, but also with courage and confidence in the assumption of their Christian identity. They could easily
'live' Sabas' story and step into the oppositional framework. They will
have enjoyed the martyr's παρρησία and wit, and have seen in the
story an adequate expression of the persecution they had experienced,
as well as a powerful support and encouragement: that steadfastness in
the faith in troubled times is praised and rewarded.

Once Christianity had become in ca. 376 the majority's religion
within the confederation, the *Passio Sabae* will have functioned differ-
ently. Firstly, it will have reminded the Gothic Christians of a not so
distant past where Christianity was a persecuted minority. Secondly,
the general value of Sabas as an ideal Christian, as somebody who lived
for God alone, may have been inspiring. Thirdly, it will have worked as
a powerful identity-marker for the 'veteran' Christians as opposed to
the 'new' converts: to them it might be a powerful part of their identity;
it was 'their' legacy, much more than that of those who became Christian en masse under Fritigern.

Because of our relative lack of knowledge of Late antique Christianity in Gothia, it is hard to substantiate the value that the *Passio Sabae*
might have had for the *extra fines* audience, and move beyond more or

---

74 Overviews in: Wolfram, *Geschichte der Goten*, 68–83; Heather, *Goths and Romans*, 122–
    142.

less educated guessing. The situation is different for the *Passio*'s reception in Cappadocia.

Firstly, the final chapter of the *Passio* itself narrates the translation of the martyr's relics to Cappadocia, accompanied by the text of the *Passio*. We also have the letter in which Basil of Caesarea gladly acknowledges receipt of the text and voices his enthusiasm about it in strong terms[75]. Secondly, the presence of the relics in Cappadocia, presumably in Caesarea, would ensure Sabas an annual feast-day during which the local Christian community would gather around his relics. It will have been a day in which, alongside more mundane matters, such as buying and selling at the market or pub crawling, also the martyr's memory was central – especially in the liturgy, of course[76]. The sermon would have been a panegyric on the saint, in which the homilist could re-enact, re-interpret and re-contextualize the martyr's story. Thus, stories of a sometimes distant past could breathe with new life and inspire an audience. Basil of Caesarea's panegyrical sermons *On Julitta* and *On Gordius* are beautiful examples of this process. It is easily conceivable that the Gothic martyr Sabas could become under Basil's pen and voice a model of steadfastness in the faith in difficult circumstances; an example of perseverance and true faith, a model-Christian also. In the *Passio* more than enough material was available to do so.

Thirdly, part of the the Cappadocian Church itself was going through difficult times in the first half of the 370's. The *Passio Sabae* itself contains an echo of this in that it says to its addressees that "we who have been persecuted, just like you". This was certainly language Basil will have understood. His letters dating from that period display quite a number of scattered references to instances in which the part of the Christians Basil reckoned himself to (Neo-nicenes) suffered violence, exile, maltreatment etc[77]. Some of his descriptions are clouded in

---

75   Basilius Caesariensis, *Ep.* 164 (97–99 Courtonne).

76   On the celebration of the annual panèguris and the combination of liturgical and more mundane activities, see Johan Leemans, Celebrating the Martyrs: Early Christian Liturgy and the Martyr Cult in Fourth Century Cappadocia and Pontus, *QuLi* 82 (2001), 247–261; Id./Wendy Mayer/Pauline Allen/Boudewijn Dehandschutter, eds., *'Let us die that we may live': Greek Homilies on Christian Martyrs from Asia Minor, Palestine, and Syria (c. AD 350–AD 450)* (London/New York: Routledge, 2003), 15–22; Vasiliki M. Limberis, *Architects of Piety: The Cappadocian Fathers and the Cult of the Martyrs* (Oxford: Oxford University Press, 2011), 13–26.

77   See, for example, the very *Ep.* 164 (97–99 Courtonne); *Ep.* 195 (ibid. 148); or *Ep.* 243 (ed. in Saint Basile, *Lettres*, texte établi et traduit par Yves Courtonne, vol. 3, CUFr [Paris: Les Belles Lettres, 1966], 68–73). A more complete survey is given by Benoît Gain, *L'Église de Cappadoce au IVe siècle d'après la correspondance de Basile de Césarée (330–379)*, OCA 225 (Rome: Pontificum Institutum Orientale, 1985), 374–384.

rhetoric, probably he may be exaggerating, but nevertheless one gets the impression of not all that smooth times. In quite a few of these descriptions Basil is employing the rhetoric of persecution, the oppositional logic also. One can imagine that this will have provided a context in which new martyr material will have been corn on his mill. Unfortunately no panegyric on Sabas is extant to pursue this line of inquiry further.

5. Conclusion

Sabas, a native Goth belonging to the confederation of the Tervingi, lived in a small township across the borders of the Roman Empire. He died a martyr's death in the context of an anti-Christian persecution or persecutions under Athanarich (369–372). This persecution, during which many other Christians also died, was probably instigated by the (at that time still largely pagan) nobility of the Tervingi confederation, as repercussions of the preceding military troubles with the Roman Empire (perceived as Christian Empire). Sabas most probably died a martyr's death on 12th of April 372, and not too long after that his relics have been translated to Caesarea in Cappadocia, where they were welcomed by Basil.

Beyond this historical layer, the *Passio Sabae* should, in the first place, be seen as a literary writing crafted along the lines of the art of hagiography. As the multiple references to Cappadocia show, it was composed in view of the imminent relic transfer, a fact which invested its author with a certain rhetorical and thematic disposition in accordance with the Cappadocian theology and rhetoric of martyrdom. The author's first aim was to present Sabas to his readers – Gothic and Cappadocian alike – as a source of inspiration and a model of imitation. Besides the basic tenets of the martyr's story, the text mainly consists of hagiographical *topoi* and traditional narrative elements, many of them echoing the contemporary practice in Asia Minor, but drawing also from the most intimate elements of hagiographic discourse in general. The parallels with other martyrs' stories listed in this article speak for themselves. In this sense, Delehaye was indeed right when assessing the *Passio Sabae* as "une des perles de l'hagiographie antique"[78].The text is a harmonious combination of history, hagiography and rhetorics, resulting in a versatile and flexible masterpiece, from whose manifold hermeneutical layers different audiences could, in different contexts,

---

78   Delehaye, Saints de Thrace, 291. Cf. note 8.

actualize the ones closest to their expectations and needs. This hypothetically applies to the Gothic audiences of Late Antiquity; it certainly applies to the Cappadocian audience, and even to the modern scholarly audience, if we are to judge from historical evaluations.

Dmitrij F. Bumazhnov

Der Tod des Einsiedlers für einen Verbrecher beim heiligen Isaak von Ninive und im *Liber Graduum*

Ein neues Zeugnis für die „Märtyrer der Liebe"?

1. Das Problem

Im 65. Traktat des ersten Bandes der auf Syrisch überlieferten Texte des Isaak von Ninive[1] findet sich eine weitgehend selbstständige Abhandlung, die die Barmherzigkeit zu ihrem Thema hat.[2] Ihre von mir besorgte deutsche Übersetzung lautet wie folgt[3].

1. Ich ermahne dich auch, o mein Bruder, zum Folgenden: dass in deiner ganzen <monastischen> Lebensweise das Gewicht der Barmherzigkeit das Übergewicht haben möge. **2.** Durch sie, <nämlich> durch diese Barmherzigkeit, wirst du wahrnehmen, dass es Gott über dem Weltall gibt.

3. Unsere eigenen <Umstände> werden für uns zum Spiegel, um darin den wahren Prototyp zu sehen, <nämlich> in denjenigen <Dingen, zu denen> die <göttliche> Substanz wesenhaft gehört. **4.** Durch diese und <durch die> ihnen ähnlichen <Dinge> erleuchten sie uns, so dass <wir> auf Gott hin bewegt werden im reinen Intellekt. **5.** Ein ruchloses Herz wird nie rein.

6. Ein barmherziger Mensch ist sein eigener Arzt: den Nebel der Finsternis vertreibt er wie mit einem starken Wind aus seinem Inneren. **7.** Sie (d.h. die Barmherzigkeit) hat eine gute Belohnung bei Gott gemäß dem Wort (S.

---

1   Das einzige gesicherte Datum aus dem Lebens des heiligen Isaak ist die Zeitspanne zwischen 676 und 680, als er – allerdings für eine sehr kurze Zeit – zum Bischof von Ninive geweiht wurde. Zur Biographie des Isaak vgl. Sabino Chialà, *Dall'ascesi eremitica alla misericordia infinita. Ricerche su Isacco di Ninive e la sua fortuna*, Biblioteca della Rivista di Storia e Letteratura Religiosa, Studi 14 (Firenze: Olschki, 2002), 53–63.

2   Syrischer Text: Paul Bedjan, ed., Mar Isaacus Ninivita, *De perfectione religiosa*, (Paris 1909), 455,13–458,1; englische Übersetzung: Arent Jan Wensinck, trans., *Mystic Treatises by Isaac of Nineveh translated from Bedjan's Syriac Text with an Introduction and Registers*, Verhandelingen der Koninklijke Akademie van Wetenschappen te Amsterdam. Afdeeling Letterkunde, Nieuwe Reeks, Deel XXIII № 1, (Amsterdam: De Akademie, 1923), 305–307.

3   Die Verseinteilung stammt von mir.

456) des Evangeliums des Lebens: „Selig ist der Barmherzige, denn ihm wird Erbarmen zuteil",[4] nicht nur jenseits, sondern auch geheimnisvoll hier. **8.** Welches Erbarmen ist größer, als wenn jemand, durch das Erbarmen zu seinem Mitmenschen bewegt, zum Teilhabenden an seinem Leiden geworden ist? **9.** Denn unser Herr befreit seine Seele aus dem Dunkel der Finsternis, welche die intelligible Gehenna ist, und bringt sie zum Licht des Lebens für ihr Behagen. **10.** Und schön sagte der selige Evagrius: „Der ebene[5] Weg entsteht aus Barmherzigkeit."

11. Deswegen lass, wie ich <schon> gesagt habe, das erbarmungsvolle Herz in deiner ganzen <monastischen> Lebensweise Vorrang haben, und du wirst Frieden mit Gott finden. **12.** Gib Acht, dass nie durch dich etwas Böses einem <anderen> Menschen zustößt, auch nicht einem bösen. **13.** Und wenn es in deiner Macht liegt, einen ungerechten <Menschen> vor dem Bösen zu bewahren, vernachlässige <es> nicht. **14.** Wenn der Fall <des anderen Menschen> fern von dir ist, gehe nicht hin und setze dich nicht ein für eine Angelegenheit wie diese, denn es ist nicht deine Aufgabe.

15. Wenn aber der Fall in deine Hand gegeben ist, und du darüber verfügst, <weil> er dir als Versuchung völlig unerwartet zugefallen war, und Gott, indem Er <dies> zulässt, dich auf die Probe stellt, nimm dich in Acht, dass du nicht des Blutes des Ungerechten mitschuldig seiest dadurch, dass du dir wegen seiner Erlösung keine Mühe gäbest. **16.** Versuche dagegen mit deiner ganzen Seele ihn zu retten, auch wenn <du> für ihn sterben <solltest>.

17. Dann bist du wahrhaftig ein Märtyrer und wie einer, der um der Sünder willen den Kreuzestod auf sich nimmt. **18.** Und bitte Gott, dass dies[6] nicht von dir gefällt werden möge, sondern, wenn er Böses verdient hat, möge er (S. 457) das Urteil für seine Tat durch die Hände der anderen entgegennehmen. **19.** Nicht deine Sache ist es zu schauen, was seine Taten verdienen. **20.** Durch deine Hände soll ihm <nur> Gutes zuteil werden.

21. Denke an Den, der alles[7] trägt, während die Taten aller Menschen vor Seinen Augen sind; sie leuchten vor Ihm klarer als die Sonne. **22.** Und Er ist in der Lage, wenn Er will, alle Menschen mit dem Atem Seines Mundes zu vernichten. **23.** Du bist nicht dazu befugt, ein Urteil über die Taten und diejenigen, die sie begehen, zu fällen, sondern <nur> dazu, dass du Erbarmen für die Welt erbittest, für die Erlösung aller wachst und am Leiden aller Menschen – Gerechter und Sünder – teilhast.

---

4   Mt 5,7.

5   šapyā, das gleiche Wort wie in *„reiner* Intellekt", „ein ruchloses Herz wird nie *rein"* oben.

6   Nämlich das Todesurteil.

7   Bzw. das All.

24. Und du weißt, wenn jemand <es>[8] verdient, egal, wer er sei, er wird nicht lange darauf zu warten haben, dass die Justiz ihn mit den Händen von anderen fesselt, die sich dafür eignen. **25.** Du aber beschäftigst dich mit der Erlösung deiner Seele und bist zum lebendigen Märtyrer geworden. **26.** Gleichfalls gebührt es nicht, dass du <etwas für diesen Menschen> wünschst und anstrebst außer zu bitten, <dass> die Barmherzigkeit Gottes auf ihn <herabkommen möge>, so dass er sich ändere, gemäß dem Willen Gottes werde und in Gerechtigkeit aus dem Leben scheide, nicht zur[9] Vergeltung der Ungerechtigkeit.

27. Sei statt Rächer – Befreier, statt Streitsüchtiger – Friedensstifter, statt jemand, der <einen anderen> ausliefert, – Märtyrer, statt Kläger – Verteidiger, statt Ankläger – Anwalt[10]. **28.** Tritt für[11] die Sünder ein, dass sie Erbarmen finden, und bete für die Gerechten, dass sie <so> erhalten bleiben. **29.** Die Bösen bekämpfe mit der Sanftmut und die Eifernden setze mit deiner Güte in Verwunderung. **30.** Die, die das Gerechte lieben, beschäme mit deiner Barmherzigkeit. **31.** Mit den Bedrängten sei bedrängt in deinem Verstand. **32.** Liebe jeden und sei fern von jedem. **33.** Gedenke (S. 458) des Todes und bereite dich auf deinen Einzug in ihn vor.

Der Verfasser, selbst ein Einsiedler, richtet seine Worte an einen Mitbruder, der ebenfalls als Mönch alleine lebt bzw. leben soll.[12] Neben allgemein gehaltenen Ermahnungen zur barmherzigen Gesinnung[13] wird von Isaak auch ein konkreter Fall behandelt: was soll ein Eremit tun, wenn er durch einen Zufall dazu kommt, über Leben und Tod eines Verbrechers Recht sprechen zu müssen?[14]

Wie ungewöhnlich diese Fragestellung schon an sich ist, noch unerwarteter erscheint eine als möglich angesehene Folge der beschriebenen Situation. Nach Isaak muss der Mönch als Richter den Angeklagten auf jeden Fall freisprechen, auch wenn er schuldig ist.[15] Dies kann jedoch dazu führen, dass der Richter selbst zum Opfer, ja zu einem Märtyrer wird und sein Leben verliert:

---

8   Die (Todes-)Strafe.

9   Wörtlich „in".

10   sənī'grā < συνήγορος.

11   Wortspiel: „für" (ḥəlāp̄) ist das gleiche Wort wie „statt". Die syrische Entsprechung für „statt Kläger – Verteidiger, statt Ankläger – Anwalt" ist bei Wensinck nicht übersetzt.

12   Vgl. V. 32: „Liebe jeden und sei fern von jedem." Zu Isaak als Einsiedler und Lehrer der Einsiedler siehe z.B. Patrik Hagman, *The Asceticism of Isaac of Nineveh*, Oxford Early Christian Studies (Oxford: Oxford University Press, 2010), 139–147.

13   V. 1–10.

14   Vgl. V. 12–16.

15   V. 13.15–16.18–20.23–24.

16. Versuche dagegen mit deiner ganzen Seele ihn zu retten, auch wenn <du> für ihn *sterben* <solltest>. **17.** Dann bist du wahrhaftig ein *Märtyrer* und wie einer, der um der Sünder willen den Kreuzestod auf sich nimmt. <...> **27.** Sei statt Rächer – Befreier <...>, statt jemand, der <einen anderen> ausliefert, – *Märtyrer* <...>

Diese Ausführungen bieten Anlass für Fragen. Was für eine Lebenssituation – etwa ein weltliches, kirchliches oder möglicherweise ein freies Gericht – wird von Isaak vorausgesetzt? Wie kann ein Einsiedler über Leben und Tod eines Verbrechers entscheiden? Warum droht ihm selber der Tod, wenn er einen Schuldigen freispricht?

Ohne eine allseitig zufriedenstellende Erklärung formulieren zu können, möchte ich im Folgenden eine Parallele zur zitierten Passage anführen, die m.E. ihren Kontext einigermaßen erhellt.

2. Die Parallele

Als oben angesprochene Parallele kommt, wie es scheint, der 30. Traktat des syrischen Stufenbuches, bekannt als *Liber Graduum*,[16] in Frage, wo ein Konflikt zwischen den sogenannten Märtyrern (bzw. Jüngern) der Liebe und den sogenannten Märtyrern (bzw. Jüngern) des Glaubens dargestellt wird. Peter Nagel untersuchte diese Kollision in einem Artikel, in dem er auch die deutsche Übersetzung der relevanten Textstücke des 30. Traktates des LG bietet.[17]

Nagel bringt die im 30. Traktat des LG beschriebene Spannung zwischen den „Märtyrern der Liebe"[18] und den „Märtyrern des Glau-

---

16 Im Folgenden LG. Der LG wird in das Ende des 4. Jahrhunderts datiert, als Entstehungsort wird Adiabene im heutigen Nordirak angenommen. Zu allgemeinen Informationen über den LG und seine Forschungsgeschichte siehe Pablo Argárate, Ktābā dmasqātā oder Liber Graduum. Ein Überblick über den Forschungsstand, in: Dmitrij Bumazhnov, Emmanouela Grypeou, Timothy B. Sailors und Alexander Toepel, eds., *Bibel, Byzanz und Christlicher Orient. Festschrift für Stephen Gerö zum 65. Geburtstag*, OLA 187 (Leuven u.a.: Peeters Pub, 2011), 239–258. Eine ausführliche Bibliographie zum LG findet man bei Grigory Kessel, Karl Pinggéra, *A Bibliography of Syriac Ascetic and Mystical Literature*, Eastern Christian Studies 11 (Leuven u.a.: David Brown Book Company, 2011), 53–60.

17 Peter Nagel, Die „Märtyrer des Glaubens" und die „Märtyrer der Liebe" im syrischen Liber Graduum, in: Bärbel Köhler, ed., *Religion und Wahrheit. Religionsgeschichtliche Studien. Festschrift für Gernot Wießner zum 65. Geburtstag* (Wiesbaden: Harrassowitz, 1998), 127–142. Zu nennen wäre auch die Studie von Shafiq Abouzayd, *Violence and Killing in the Liber Graduum*, Aram Periodical 11/12 (1999-2000), 451–465.

18 Syrisch sāhdē dəḥūbbā, z.B. in LG 30,4 (PS I,3, 869,18–19 Kmosko), ihre andere Bezeichnung im 30. Traktat des LG ist talmīḏay ḥūbbā (bzw. talmīḏē dəḥūbbā), „Jünger der Liebe", siehe z.B. LG 30,4 (PS I,3, 869,11 Kmosko).

bens"[19] in Verbindung mit der sonst für den ganzen LG typischen Gegenüberstellung von den gerechten und vollkommenen Christen.[20] Für die Gerechten des LG gilt die Erfüllung der „kleinen Gebote", die „in der Goldenen Regel und im Dekalog zusammengefaßt sind".[21] Die „großen Gebote" sind vornehmlich in der Bergpredigt formuliert und haben nach der Lehre des LG die Vollkommenen im Blick. Ein anderer Name dieser zweiten Gruppe lautet auf Syrisch īḥīḏāyē,[22] eine Bezeichnung, „die sich einer eindimensionalen Übersetzung widerstrebt" und im LG „am ehesten als ‚alleinig' oder ‚einzigartig' interpretierbar" ist.[23] Es muss hervorgehoben werden, dass das gleiche Wort in den Texten Isaaks „die Einsiedler" bedeutet.

Die „Märtyrer des Glaubens" werden von den „Sekten"[24] und von den „Heiden"[25] verfolgt und getötet.[26] Ihrerseits „erheben sich die Jünger des Glaubens wider die Jünger der Liebe und verfolgen sie aus Unwissenheit, während die Jünger der Liebe erdulden, wie geschrieben steht: ‚Die Liebe erduldet alles und hält alles aus.'" (1Kor 13,7).[27] An einer anderen Stelle heißt es ausdrücklich, dass diese Verfolgungen für die „Märtyrer der Liebe" durchaus blutige Konsequenzen haben können: „Die Märtyrer der Liebe aber werden von den ‚Hausgenossen des Glaubens' verfolgt und getötet."[28] Der Autor des LG qualifiziert dieses Vorgehen eindeutig: „Die also, die töten, sind nicht Jünger des Glau-

---

19   Syrisch sāhdē dǝhaymānūṯā, z.B. in LG 30,4 (PS I,3, 869,18–19 Kmosko), andere Bezeichnung ist talmīḏē dǝhaymānūṯā, „Jünger des Glaubens", siehe z.B. LG 30,4 (PS I,3, 869,10 Kmosko).

20   Nagel, Die „Märtyrer des Glaubens", 129–130. LG 30 unterscheidet zwischen den „Vollkommenen" und den „Jüngern (bzw. Märtyrer) der Liebe", die eine unmittelbare Vorstufe der Vollkommenheit darstellen. In der folgenden Analyse von LG 30 werden die „Vollkommenen" in ihrer Unterschiedenheit von den „Jüngern (bzw. Märtyrer) der Liebe" nicht berücksichtigt.

21   Nagel, Die „Märtyrer des Glaubens", 129.

22   Eine Ableitung von ḥāḏ, eins.

23   Nagel, Die „Märtyrer des Glaubens", 129–130.

24   deḥlāṯā, LG 30,4 (PS I,3, 869,21 Kmosko).

25   ḥanpē LG 30,4 (PS I,3, 869,21 Kmosko).

26   Nagel, Die „Märtyrer des Glaubens", 131, denkt dabei „am ehesten an die Christenverfolgungen unter Schapur II. seit dem Jahre 339", lässt aber letztlich die Frage „völlig offen".

27   Übersetzung: Nagel, Die „Märtyrer des Glaubens", 134, syrischer Text: LG 30,4 (PS I,3, 869,10–14 Kmosko).

28   Übersetzung: Nagel, Die „Märtyrer des Glaubens", 135, syrischer Text: LG 30,4 (PS I,3, 872,15–17 Kmosko). Nach Nagel, Die „Märtyrer des Glaubens", 135 (n. 38) handelt es sich bei den „Hausgenossen des Glaubens" (= Jünger des Glaubens, = Märtyrer des Glaubens; syrisch: bnay bayta dǝhaymānūṯā, LG 30,4 (PS I,3, 872,17 Kmosko)) um einen negativ besetzten Ausdruck, der auf Gal 6,10 basiert.

bens, sondern Jünger des Satans."[29] LG benennt auch unmissverständlich den Grund der Verfolgung:

> Die Hausgenossen des Glaubens aber, da sie sich durch den Glauben im Besitz der ganzen Wahrheit dünken, entrüsten sich wider ihn, sobald ein Mann der Liebe nur ein Wörtlein sagt, das ihnen verborgen ist, und töten ihn: „Zu welchem Zwecke", heißt es, „lehrt ihr etwas, was nicht in der ganzen Kirchengemeinschaft gepredigt wird?" Dabei erkennen sie nicht, dass niemand die ganze Wahrheit erlangt, so er nicht liebt wie der Herr und seine Apostel, und „er bläst sich nichtig auf in seinem fleischlichen Sinn", sagt Paulus (Kol 2,18).[30]

Der Kern des Konfliktes zwischen den beiden Gruppen ist also die von den Jüngern der Liebe verbreitete Lehre, die die andere Partei als von dem allgemeinen Glaubensgut abweichend auffasst und nicht verstehen kann. Der Inhalt dieser Lehre ist in den Worten „Dabei erkennen sie nicht, dass niemand die ganze Wahrheit erlangt, so er nicht liebt wie der Herr und seine Apostel" angedeutet. Die Erkenntnis der „ganzen Wahrheit" wird somit vom Erlangen der vollkommenen Liebe abhängig gemacht, die den Aposteln und dem Herrn selbst eigen war.

Das mit dem Begriff „Liebe" zusammenhängende Konfliktfeld hat eine theoretische und eine praktische Dimension und äußert sich in unterschiedlichen Auffassungen der christlichen Mission bzw. der Predigt innerhalb der Gemeinde, die die Jünger des Glaubens und die Jünger der Liebe auf den Tag legen. Die zwei Gruppen, die im 30. Traktat des LG als Missions- bzw. Predigtobjekt auftreten, sind die oben bereits angesprochenen „Sekten" bzw. „Heiden", sowie die „Bösen" und Sünder.[31] Durch die gleiche Brille betrachtet der LG auch das wechselseitige Verhältnis der Jünger des Glaubens und der Jünger der Liebe.

Das Verhältnis der *Jünger der Liebe* zu den drei Gruppen wird im LG 30 wie folgt charakterisiert:

---

29 Übersetzung: Nagel, Die „Märtyrer des Glaubens", 135, syrischer Text: LG 30,4 (PS I,3, 873,12–13 Kmosko).

30 Übersetzung: Nagel, Die „Märtyrer des Glaubens", 135, syrischer Text: LG 30,4 (PS I,3, 872,19–873,4 Kmosko).

31 Nach LG 30,1 zählen dazu die „dreisten, aufrührerischen und schamlosen Menschen", sowie „Huren, Ehebrecher und Habgierigen", Übersetzung: Nagel, Die „Märtyrer des Glaubens", 132.

1) Die Sekten und Heiden:

„Von den ‚Sekten' nämlich werden sie (d.h. die Jünger der Liebe) nicht getötet, sondern sie haben Freude an ihnen, da sie diese in Demut lehren."[32]

2) Die „Bösen" und Sünder

„Der Jünger der Liebe <...> wiewohl er die Bösen, die Hochmütigen, die Überheblichen, die Ruhmsüchtigen und die Sünder kennt, mehr als jeder andere, dessen Liebe lässt gleichwohl nicht zu, sie auszugrenzen und ihnen zu sagen: „Mit euch will ich nichts zu tun haben, mit euch rede ich nicht", sondern er weist <sie> zurecht und vermahnt <sie>. Mögen sie ihn auch schmähen, schlagen, verfolgen und umbringen – er bringt es nicht über sich, wo er Frevel und Aufruhr sieht, nicht zurechtzuweisen, zu ermahnen, zu tadeln, zu lehren und geduldig anzuspornen. Nachdem er aber gelehrt und zurechtgewiesen hat, macht er sich klein an der Seele und arm an Geist und hält die, die geringer sind als er, für größer als sich selbst, erweist ihnen Ehre und wird reich in der Demut des Herrn."[33]

3) Die Jünger des Glaubens

Die „Jünger der Liebe" beten für ihre Verfolger (d.h. für die „Jünger des Glaubens") und lieben sie, während sie von ihnen getötet werden. Dabei folgen sie dem Beispiel des Herrn und der Apostel.[34] An einer anderen Stelle heißt es, dass die „Jünger der Liebe" auch für die „Bösen" beten.[35]

Die „Jünger der Liebe" predigen also sowohl den bereits oberflächlich christianisierten „Bösen" als auch den Andersgläubigen („Sekten" und Heiden) und ebenso den „Jüngern des Glaubens".[36] Die Heiden- und Sektenmission verläuft friedlicher als der Umgang mit den „Bösen", da diese die „Jünger der Liebe" zuweilen „schmähen, schlagen, verfolgen und umbringen". Außerhalb der Unterweisung verhalten sich die „Jünger der Liebe" den „Bösen" und Sündern gegenüber demütig und halten sich für geringer als jene. In Bezug auf ihre Verfolger und Mörder – damit sind sowohl die „Bösen" als auch die „Jünger des Glaubens" gemeint – gilt für die „Märtyrer der Liebe" das Liebesgebot.

---

32 Wir übernehmen hier die Übersetzung von Nagel, Die „Märtyrer des Glaubens", 135, syrischer Text: LG 30,4 (PS I,3, 872,17–19 Kmosko). Nagel übersetzt *ad sensum*, die vorliegende Konstruktion scheint nicht stimmig.

33 Übersetzung mit kleinen Veränderungen nach: Nagel, Die „Märtyrer des Glaubens", 137, syrischer Text: LG 30,8 (PS I,3, 881,6–20 Kmosko).

34 Vgl. LG 30,5 (PS I,3, 876,10–15 Kmosko).

35 LG 30,8 (PS I,3, 881,24–884,2 Kmosko).

36 Bezüglich der Predigt an die „Jünger des Glaubens" siehe oben das Zitat aus LG 30,4 (PS I,3, 872,19–873,4 Kmosko).

Wenden wir uns jetzt den Beziehungen der *Jünger des Glaubens* zu den drei Gruppen zu.

1) Die Sekten und Heiden:

„Auch die Jünger des Glaubens, auch sie erdulden von Seiten der Irrenden und werden von den Sekten verfolgt, weil sie deren Gegner sind, werden getötet und werden zu Märtyrern.[37] <...> Wegen dieses löblichen Eifers werden sie (d.h. die Jünger des Glaubens von den Sekten und Heiden) umgebracht, währenddessen sie ihre Mörder und Verfolger nicht lieben, sondern schmähen[38] <...> Unter ihnen (d.h. den Jüngern des Glaubens) gibt es solche, die ihre Mörder und Verfolger hassen, und solche, die sie nicht hassen, aber auch nicht lieben."[39]

2) Die „Bösen" und Sünder

„Deshalb hält der Glaube seine Jünger von jedem Bruder fern, der wie auch immer einen schlechten Wandel führt oder in dem eine gewisse Unreinheit steckt <...>.[40] Der Jünger des Glaubens <...> spricht also: ‚Was zwingt mich, die Leute (d.h. die Sekten und Heiden) zu lehren und beschimpft zu werden?'[41] <...> Die Jünger des Glaubens aber sondern die Bösen aus der Mitte der Guten aus und werfen sie hinaus mit den Worten: ‚Schert euch weg aus dem Weizen, ihr Unkraut und Übeltäter! Es sei ferne, dass wir <...> mit euch beten <...>'."[42]

3) Die Jünger der Liebe

Wie schon oben dargelegt, werden die „Jünger der Liebe" von den „Jüngern des Glaubens" verfolgt und getötet.[43]

Die Unterschiede zwischen den „Jüngern des Glaubens" und den „Jüngern der Liebe" betreffen also das Verhältnis zu den Sündern und „Bösen" einerseits und den Sekten und Heiden andererseits. Während die „Jünger der Liebe" diesen beiden Gruppen predigen und mit ihnen Umgang pflegen, werden die „Bösen" und Sünder von den „Jüngern

---

37 Übersetzung: Nagel, Die „Märtyrer des Glaubens", 134, syrischer Text: LG 30,4 (PS I,3, 869,14–18 Kmosko).

38 Übersetzung: Nagel, ebd., 135, syrischer Text: LG 30,4 (PS I,3, 872,3–5 Kmosko).

39 Übersetzung mit kleinen Veränderungen nach: Nagel, ebd., 136, syrischer Text: LG 30,6 (PS I,3, 876,17–20 Kmosko).

40 Übersetzung: Nagel, ebd., 132, syrischer Text: LG 30,1 (PS I,3, 861,9–12 Kmosko).

41 Übersetzung: Nagel, ebd., 137–138, syrischer Text: LG 30,8 (PS I,3, 881,20–24 Kmosko).

42 Übersetzung: Nagel, ebd., 138, syrischer Text: LG 30,9 (PS I,3, 884,21–26 Kmosko).

43 Vgl. LG 30,4 (PS I,3, 869,10–14 Kmosko) und LG 30,4 (PS I,3, 872,15–17 Kmosko).

des Glaubens" gemieden und verpönt, während sie selbst von den Heiden und Sekten blutigen Verfolgungen ausgesetzt sind.

Eine abweichende Haltung besteht auch in Bezug auf das Verhältnis der „Jünger der Liebe" und der „Jünger des Glaubens" zu ihren jeweils unterschiedlichen Verfolgern: Während die „Jünger der Liebe" ihre Feinde lieben und für sie beten, vermögen die „Jünger des Glaubens" ihre Verfolger höchstens nicht zu hassen, die Liebe zu ihnen kommt für sie nicht in Frage. In beiden Fällen ist es die mangelnde Liebe der „Jünger des Glaubens", die den abweichenden Praktiken und Einstellungen zugrunde liegt.

Es scheint berechtigt zu vermuten, dass die Liebe zu den „Bösen" und Sündern sowie die Liebe zu den eigenen Mördern und Verfolgern Themen der Lehre sind, die den „Jüngern des Glaubens" von den „Jüngern der Liebe" vor Augen geführt wurde und jene so ärgerte, dass sie sich daran machten, die „Märtyrer der Liebe" zu töten.[44]

3. Die Applikation

Was hat nun der oben skizzierte Konflikt mit dem Text des Isaak von Ninive zu tun? Er lässt sich, wie mir scheint, besser verstehen, wenn man annimmt, dass die Rolle des Einsiedlers der von den „Märtyrern der Liebe" in Bezug auf die „Bösen" und die „Jünger des Glaubens" gleicht.

Tatsächlich wird der Adressat von Isaak ermahnt, sich immer von der mərahmānūṭā, der Barmherzigkeit, auch gegenüber „einem Bösen"[45] leiten zu lassen. Das gleiche Wort verwendet auch der LG für seine Bösen. Umgekehrt verwendet der LG für „lieben" neben ḥabb[46] auch

---

44 Nagel, Die „Märtyrer des Glaubens", 130, nimmt an, dass der Grund der im LG erwähnten innerkirchlichen Verfolgungen die Vorstellung der „Vollkommenen" von einer geistigen Kirche ist, deren Abbild die irdische Kirche ausmacht. Im LG 30,6 heißt es nun tatsächlich, dass auch die „Vollkommenen" Opfer der Verfolgung (durch die „Jünger des Glaubens"?) sein können, ansonsten sind es die „Jünger der Liebe", die den Verfolgungen der „Jünger des Glaubens" ausgesetzt sind. Die spezielle Untersuchung von Peter Nagel, Die sichtbare und die unsichtbare Kirche im syrischen „Buch der Stufen" (Liber Graduum), in: Hermann Goltz, ed., *Stimme der Orthodoxie 3. Festschrift für Konrad Onasch* (Berlin-Karlshorst: Verlag der Berliner Diözese der Russisch-Orthodoxen Kirche [Moskauer Patriarchat], 1996), 40–42, hinterlässt den Eindruck, dass die „Vollkommenen" die Lehre von der unsichtbaren Kirche äußerst vorsichtig vertraten, ohne die Gefühle der sichtbaren Kirche sichtlich zu verletzen. Die Frage bedarf einer weiteren Klärung.

45 bīšā, vgl. V. 12, syrischer Text: Isaak von Ninive I,65 (456,11 Bedjan).

46 Vgl. sāhdē dəḥūbbā, „Märtyrer der Liebe".

rḥem, ein Wort, das die gleiche Wurzel wie die Barmherzigkeit bei Isaak hat.[47] Generell ist die Rolle der Barmherzigkeit bei Isaak analog der von der Liebe im LG 30.

Indem der Einsiedler von Isaak einem Verbrecher barmherzig begegnet und ihn zu rechtfertigen sucht, macht er also annähernd das Gleiche, was die „Jünger der Liebe" gegenüber den „Bösen" im LG praktizierten, und zwar in den Augen der bei Isaak nicht genannten aber wohl vorauszusetzenden christlichen Gruppe, die den „Jüngern des Glaubens" entsprechen soll. Diese Ungenannten sind über das milde Urteil des Einsiedlers empört, weil sie den Verbrecher für des Todes würdig halten, und bringen den Richter um, weshalb er nach der Aussage Isaaks zum „Märtyrer" wird.[48] Auch in diesem Fall liegt eine mit dem LG vergleichbare Terminologie vor.[49] Gemeinsam den beiden Texten ist auch das Gebet für die „Bösen".[50]

Eine interessante Abweichung vom LG stellt der Vers 26, der dem Einsiedler verbietet, für den Verbrecher etwas zu tun, was – abgesehen von dem Freispruch vor Gericht – über das Gebet hinaus geht. Dem liegt möglicherweise die Befürchtung zugrunde, dass sich der Einsiedler mit den „Bösen" zu stark einlässt und sich unnötig den Vorwürfen der „Eiferer"[51] aussetzt. Der LG berichtet dagegen, dass die „Jünger der Liebe" den „Bösen" predigen und mit ihnen Umgang pflegen.[52] Möglicherweise ist diese Vorsicht eine Frucht der bitteren Erfahrung mit den „Eiferern".

---

47   Vgl. z.B. die Ableitungen von rḥem in LG 30,4 (PS I,3, 873,7–8 Kmosko) und məraḥmānūṯā in Isaak von Ninive I,65 (455,14 Bedjan).

48   Vgl. V. 17.

49   Vgl. die mehrfach angesprochene „Märtyrer der Liebe". Eine weitere terminologische Parallele liegt im gleichen Namen īḥīḏāyā für den Einsiedler bei Isaak (in unserem Stück ist das Wort zwar nicht belegt, aber sonst ist es in den Schriften Isaaks allgemein verbreitet) und dem Anfang von LG 30,1: „Wer ein īḥīḏāyā werden und ganz den Geboten der Liebe folgen will <...>", Übersetzung: Nagel, Die „Märtyrer des Glaubens", 132, syrischer Text: LG 30,1 (PS I,3, 860,4–5 Kmosko). Dem Kontext lässt sich nicht eindeutig entnehmen, ob der Autor an die Vollkommenen und die „Jünger der Liebe" zusammen oder an eine der beiden Gruppen denkt.

50   Vgl. V. 26 und LG 30,8 (PS I,3, 881,24–884,2 Kmosko).

51   Vgl. V. 29, die Eiferer könnten eine Parallelerscheinung zu den „Jüngern des Glaubens" sein. Sehr charakteristisch ist V. 30 „Die, die das Gerechte lieben, beschäme mit deiner Barmherzigkeit", in dem die Barmherzigkeit über das gerechte Handeln gestellt wird.

52   Das Thema wurde bereits angesprochen, vgl. die Übersetzung von LG 30,8 (PS I,3, 881,6–20 Kmosko) oben.

Dem LG fehlt auch völlig die für unseren Text zentrale Vorstellung vom Gericht und die damit zusammenhängende Terminologie.[53]

Besonders ist der V. 25 „Du aber beschäftigst dich mit der Erlösung deiner Seele und bist zum lebendigen Märtyrer geworden" zu erwähnen, der ebenfalls ein dem LG unbekanntes Phänomen anspricht. Die Bezeichnung „lebendiger Märtyrer" fußt nämlich auf der bei Isaak beliebten Auffassung der Askese, die in ihr ein freiwilliges Martyrium sieht.[54]

4. Fazit

Der 30. Traktat des LG zeugt davon, dass das in dem syrischen Stufenbuch mit aller Schärfe durchgezogene Modell einer doppelten Ethik (Gerechte/Vollkommene bzw. „Jünger des Glaubens"/„Jünger der Liebe") durchaus seine Probleme hatte, die die ostsyrischen christlichen Gemeinden im späten 4. und frühen 5. Jahrhundert zerrissen. Die auf der unteren Stufe stehenden Gemeindeglieder nahmen am meisten Anstoß daran, dass die Fortgeschrittenen ihre Lebensweise als zu wenig christlich einschätzten und ihnen ihre eigenen Ideale predigten. Diese Spannung entlud sich in Überfällen auf die „Vollkommenen", welche offensichtlich nicht selten fatal für sie endeten. Aus dieser Situation heraus entstand der Name „Märtyrer der Liebe", den man den getöteten „Vollkommenen" gab.

---

53 Vgl. z.B. V. 27 sənī'grā < συνήγορος. Man tut sich auch schwer daran, eine passende Mönchsgeschichte zu finden, die die von Isaak vorausgesetzte Situation illustrieren würde. Das 10. Apophthegma des heiligen Ammonas (4.–5. Jahrhundert, Ägypten) berichtet davon, wie Ammonas verhindert, dass ein unwürdiger Mönch aus der Mönchsgemeinschaft vertrieben wird. Indes liegt weder eine Gerichtssituation vor, noch ist Ammonas zu dieser Zeit Einsiedler, sondern bereits Bischof. Keineswegs droht ihm auch der Tod. In der *Historia Monastica* 9ff. des Thomas von Marga (9. Jahrhundert) wird Mar Jaqub der Brüderschaft von Berg Izla verwiesen, weil er die laxe Haltung einiger Mönche nicht angezeigt hat (der Hinweis von Dr. Nestor Kavvadas). Die entfernte Ähnlichkeit dieses syrischen Beispiels zu Isaak von Ninive I,65 besteht darin, dass Mar Jaqub die Sünder nicht beim kirchlichen Gericht denunziert. Eine Todesstrafe wird in seinem Fall nicht im Entferntesten erwogen.

54 Vgl. z.B. Isaak von Ninive II,3,2,62–63 (der syrische Text ist nicht ediert), italienische Übersetzung: Paolo Bettiolo, trans., *Isacco di Ninive, Discorsi spirituali. Capitoli sulla conoscenza, Preghiere, Contemplazione sull'argomento della gehenna, Altri opuscoli*, Collana Padri orientali (Magnano: Edizioni Qiqajon, 1985), 102–103 und Isaak von Ninive, III,12,37–51; italienische Übersetzung: Sabino Chialà, transl., *Isacco di Ninive, Discorsi ascetici. Terza collezione*, Collana Padri orientali (Magnano: Edizioni Qiqajon, 2004), 176–181.

Im späten 7. und frühen 8. Jahrhundert scheint diese Situation insofern eine Fortsetzung gefunden zu haben, als einige Einsiedler die Konflikte der Weltchristen, die an sich vor das weltliche Gericht gehörten, nach dem Maßstab des Gebotes der Feindesliebe entschieden. Dass sich die benachteiligte Seite dabei an dem Schiedsrichter vergehen konnte, geht aus dem Märtyrertitel hervor, den Isaak von Ninive in diesem Zusammenhang gebraucht. Theologisch wertet er diesen Fall als Nachfolge Christi durch den bewusst auf sich genommenen Tod für den freigesprochenen Verbrecher.[55]

---

55   Vgl. V. 17.

List of Contributors

Timothy D. Barnes, D. Phil., Professor emeritus of Classics and Honorary Fellow at the University of Edinburgh.

Theofried Baumeister, Dr. theol., Professor emeritus of Church History and Patrology at the University of Mainz.

Dmitrij F. Bumazhnov, Dr. phil., Heisenberg scholar at the University of Göttingen.

James Corke-Webster, Doctoral Student at the University of Manchester.

Anthony Dupont, Ph.D., Post-Doctoral Researcher at the University of Leuven.

Peter Gemeinhardt, Dr. theol., Professor of Church History at the University of Göttingen.

Peter Kuhlmann, Dr. phil., Professor of Latin Studies at the University of Göttingen.

Johan Leemans, Ph.D., Research Professor of Christianity in Late Antiquity at the University of Leuven.

Ekkehard Mühlenberg, Dr. theol., Professor emeritus of Church History at the University of Göttingen.

Hajnalka Tamas, Doctoral Student at the University of Leuven.

Index

Biblical Writings

Ancient Writers

Modern Authors